EDUCATING GIFTED AND TALENTED LEARNERS

Donald F. Sellin, Ed.D.
Professor, Special Education
Western Michigan University
Kalamazoo, Michigan

and

Jack W. Birch, Ph.D.
Professor, Special Education and
Educational Psychology
University of Pittsburgh
Pittsburgh, Pennsylvania

AN ASPEN PUBLICATION®
Aspen Systems Corporation
Rockville, Maryland
London
1980

Library of Congress Cataloging in Publication Data

Sellin, Donald F. 1934-
Educating gifted and talented learners.

Bibliography: p. 335
Includes index.

1. Gifted children—Education—Curricula.
2. Talented students—Education—Curricula.
3. Individualized instruction. I. Birch, Jack W.,
joint author. II. Title.
LC3993.2.S44   371.95'3   80-19565
ISBN: 0-89443-295-8

Library of Congress Catalog Card Number: 80-19565
ISBN: 0-89443-295-8

Printed in the United States of America

1 2 3 4 5

To our wives,

Lucy Sellin and *Jane Birch*.

The first author would also like
to pay tribute to another
Lucy in his life,

Lucille Neff Clay,

a gifted teacher.

Table of Contents

Unit I:

Overview

Curriculum and methods of instruction for gifted and talented students comprise the major contents of this book. The first chapter recounts recent and earlier events, then projects future prospects. It sets the stage for the application of curricular and methodological individualization for gifted and talented pupils by teachers, principals, and other educators.

The rest of the book is divided into four units.

The first unit is devoted to the Life Cycles of Education from early childhood through adulthood. It acquaints the reader with the educational priorities derived from the understanding of human development. This unit is particularly pertinent to the selection of curricular goals and instructional practices for able learners.

The next unit treats of a Common Curriculum Core for gifted and talented learners. It offers a means for educators to examine the existing curriculum in their own schools. It highlights the four most frequently encountered curriculum components—the basic skills, environmental awareness, career education, and talent development. This unit should prove helpful to subject matter specialists while also building bridges of understanding between and among educators from different specializations.

The third unit, on Tactics of Individualized Education, presents broad alternatives for individualization of education. The rapid rate of development of gifted and talented students encourages accelerating the pace of learning. For some pupils, it is especially appropriate to expand and enrich the curriculum beyond the task commitment and interests of their chronological age peers. Obviously, it is reasonable to suppose that most able learners would experience both acceleration and expansion of the curriculum. Suggestions are made for educational prescriptions as well as for appropriate tactics.

This unit also offers two other instructional approaches: one calls for teacher initiative to motivate and inspire pupil learning, the other involves taking

1

advantage of pupil initiative and motivation that is present already. Tactics for each option are presented.

The last unit considers Confluent Education. Affective outcomes are given equal priority with academic and skill outcomes. This chapter is particularly relevant for leadership development. The confluence of affect and cognition puts the spotlight on education as a helping relationship. This chapter, too, provides concrete insights into the processes of mentoring, so highly prized in gifted education.

FORMAT

Each unit has a similar format. The Unit Synopsis and Key Ideas segment serves as advance organizer to orient the reader. The Prototype example or model illustrates the relevance of content. Chapters are organized around topic headings. Each unit culminates with Enrichment Activities that serve to summarize and to stimulate applications and transformations of the material. The overriding purpose of these activities is to offer guidance for teachers and principals and to keep a dual focus on individual fulfillment and social contribution.

Chapter 1

Background: Perspectives and Prospects

SYNOPSIS AND KEY IDEAS

Only a few gifted and talented children and youth receive a satisfactory education. The number whose elementary, secondary, and higher education is excellent is even smaller. That state of affairs is undesirable and unnecessary.

This chapter establishes a context for understanding the nature of appropriate education for gifted and talented learners. The Prototype section supplies an example of good quality programming that can be conducted in almost any contemporary school system. The prototype of Yourtowne is characterized by careful advanced preparation; willingness to specify outcomes and operations; and full teacher, parent, and pupil involvement.

The section on *The Historical Context* traces the evolution of interest in gifted and talented young people. It points to a tradition of service based on respect for the uniqueness of each person. It illustrates the practical validity of research about the gifted and talented.

The section on *The Current Context* illustrates the current American balance between individual and social needs and among policies, services, and resources. The evolution of leadership by the states and by the U.S. Department of Education has been an inspiration. Gains are being consolidated and it now is possible to identify preferred practices.

The section on *Maintaining and Expanding Opportunities* looks to immediate future tasks. Informed understanding is in a growth phase both within and without the education community. The label "gifted and talented" is not a golden passport to proper education. Misconceptions are identified and confronted in the section on *Persisting Misconceptions.* A sound future can be built only if we respect the key role of teachers and the essential support role of administrators and parents in the pursuit of improved quality of instruction and services for gifted and talented children and youth along with heightened quality education for all other pupils, too.

YOURTOWNE: A PROTOTYPE

Prototype: Something that illustrates typical qualities; a model or an example that may be followed or adapted.

What are *typical* qualities that should be present for any school system to assert that it has an acceptable program for gifted and talented pupils? Here are six fundamental characteristics to look for. The acceptable program is:

1. *comprehensive,* covering preschool through higher education;
2. *continuous,* being available for the pupil's entire school career;
3. *balanced,* including equal opportunity to work in all curricular and extracurricular areas;
4. *participatory,* involving regular and special teachers, pupils, parents, and community resources in both decision making and instruction;
5. *flexible,* being adaptable to changes in school and pupil conditions; and
6. *individualized,* encouraging instruction based on close matches between pupil characteristics and what is taught and how it is taught.

The description of Yourtowne that follows illustrates these six key themes of programming. Yourtowne's scheme passes the "Cocobapaflin (COmprehensive COntinuous BAlance PArticipatory FLexible INdividualized) Test."

However, this prototype deliberately leaves out several very relevant details. It does not enumerate the various inservice activities that helped prepare the town's teachers and administrators for their special roles. It does not tell how individualized pupil plans were drafted and approved. It omits other essential elements, such as a means of evaluating the outcomes of the operation. The prototype is a structural outline on which a program can be built. Assess its merits with that in mind.

Education Program Components

The Yourtowne design for the education of gifted and talented pupils has a major component and four supplementary components.

The Major Program Component: Basic Scholars

The main component, the *Basic Scholars Program,* includes the four others. It is open to all pupils who earn a high enough achievement test score and subject grades to qualify. It also may include all pupils with high enough intelligence quotients even though their school grades may not qualify them. The latter pupils must indicate that they wish to improve their grades and their teachers must agree that those pupils are making sincere efforts. Pupils become part of the Basic Scholars Program with the approval of the program coordinator upon nomination by their teachers, parents, and school principal. The program is open to everyone, kindergarten through 12th grade, who meets the requirements. It is not compulsory, though. Students who qualify are not required to be part of the program.

The Basic Scholars Program focuses on skill and understanding in reading, language, and mathematics at every grade level from kindergarten through 12th. Admission calls for attaining at least one of these criteria:

1. standardized achievement test scores in mathematics, reading, and language averaging at least 25 percent above the norm for the pupil's grade
2. report card grades in the top 10 percent of the class in mathematics, reading, and language
3. individual test intelligence quotients (IQs) of 125 or more

The objectives are (a) to encourage students to increase their reading, writing, and mathematics understanding and skills, (b) to motivate students to qualify for the Basic Scholars Program, and (c) to guide students who already are basic scholars into one or more of the four other components of the activities for gifted and talented pupils in Yourtowne's schools.

Four Supplemental Program Components

The four other program components are Special Interest, Advancement, Talent Development, and Human Service. Basic scholars may add one or more of these four or simply may stay with only the Basic Scholars Program component. It is possible to move into or out of the four supplemental components during the school year with approval of the teachers, parent, principal, and program coordinator. If a pupil falls below and remains below the Basic Scholars Program standards for two consecutive report periods, however, removal from the supplementary components will follow unless the teachers, coordinator, and parents agree there are extenuating circumstances. The pupil's continuation in the Basic Scholars Program also will be reviewed with teachers and parents.

The *Special Interest Component* gives opportunities for pupils at all grade levels to pursue learning beyond the range of usual class activities. Elementary pupils in the regular curriculum, for instance, ordinarily study the denominations of the United States money system's coins and bills and learn to make change. A Special Interest study, however, could take a basic scholar elementary pupil into the history of money or into the functions of banks or into the fluctuations of the dollar on international exchanges. Similar potentialities for

Special Interest study are plentiful in both elementary and secondary schools and in all aspects of the curriculum.

Special Interest work is encouraged under certain conditions, such as when:

1. the basic scholar has completed all regular assignments satisfactorily
2. the time taken by the Special Interest study does not interfere with completion of continuing regular class work (although it may call for being away from the regular class group occasionally)
3. professional guidance and monitoring of the pupil's Special Interest study is available from a teacher or other school staff member as needed
4. the quality of the Special Interest work is evaluated and reported to the pupil and to parents

Each local elementary and secondary school makes available a number of publications for teachers, pupils, and parents that give suggestions about Special Interest projects in mathematics, history, writing, science, literature, psychology, government, communications media, and other curricular fields, as well as in extracurricular fields. This component also deals with career implications of student projects, as do all the other components.

The *Advancement Component* has two parts—age-grade advancement, and advanced standing in subject matter. For the first of these, there always will be some children who ought to have the opportunity to attend some or all of their classes with older pupils. Basic scholars have their work reviewed at least once each year by the school principal, their teachers, and a school psychologist to determine whether it would be advantageous to arrange a partial or complete age-grade acceleration schedule. Parental approval is necessary for any such move. The pupil's own feelings are considered, too.

For advanced standing, arrangements are made through regional colleges and universities to implement already existing procedures such as those monitored by the College Entrance Examination Board. Each basic scholar's work and achievement records are reviewed at least annually by the teachers and the school's counselor to determine whether to recommend an advanced standing course or courses. As in all other program plans, parental approval and the four conditions for Special Interest work are required for age-grade advancement or advanced standing.

The *Talent Development Component* offers opportunities for discovering and fostering talent potential among pupils. Some talents begin to show themselves at an early age. Many great musicians were performing at age 8, 9, or 10 and were composing significant works while in their teens. Some talents that involve extraordinary motor skills and stamina (swimming, acrobatics, figure skating) reach their peaks in the teen years. Great performers in the dance, in the theater, and in painting usually begin early. Other talents such as creative writing tend to take longer to mature, but their early foundations are of great importance.

The Yourtowne approach (a) offers encouragement to pupils with known talents and (b) includes in-school activities that actively seek to identify new talent. The encouragement phase operates as follows:

- Art, music, physical education, and writing teachers are asked twice each year by principals to supply the names of children in all grades who show outstanding promise or very high present capability in the performing and creative arts.

- Parents are asked to indicate which of their children are studying privately in the creative and performing arts.

- Principals and counselors work with each case to ascertain that the schools' facilities are being used to their fullest to encourage these children.

- Principals and counselors compile information banks of resources that give scholarships in the performing and other creative arts, and share their findings with parents, pupils, and teachers.

The augmentation phase of this component operates in every school and in kindergarten through 12th grade. Each pupil who shows signs of talent is encouraged to develop it. The child is put into contact with someone from the school or the community who will devote time to furthering those special skills, abilities, and understandings, be they in sports, music, writing, sculpture, dance, or other talent areas.

The Talent Development Component is monitored in regular meetings of a task force of teachers representing the entire school system, augmented by parents and by performing and creative arts teachers from the community and nearby colleges and universities. The program coordinator convenes the task force and works with it.

The *Human Service Component* gives basic scholars experiences in helping others. It is an in-school operation in which basic scholars learn new and advanced skills of social and vocational importance while they work as volunteer assistants to members of the school system's faculty and staff. Basic scholars must meet the same four conditions to take part in this component as they must to participate in the Special Interest and Talent Development Components.

The program coordinator determines in conferences with pupils, principals, and teachers the nature and scope of service assignments in each elementary and secondary school. It is not "free labor" to be used indiscriminately. An essential part of each such assignment is that it has:

- educational objectives of value that match the needs of the basic scholar assigned
- clearly defined and challenging responsibilities
- a definite beginning and ending time
- professional guidance from a school faculty or staff member
- an evaluation that is shared with pupil and parents

Some such activities are being carried on successfully in every Yourtowne elementary and secondary school. For instance, secondary and elementary. students serve as teachers' assistants in class work and tutoring. Others prepare bibliographies in the library. Still others help to plan improvements in courses. This Service Component capitalizes on what needs to be done anyway, adds other important service opportunities, and assures that scholars have practical experiences in applying what they know.

Pupil Activities

Yourtowne's five-part program is designed to maintain gifted and talented pupils in their regular classes while they receive regular education plus whatever special education their abilities require. It is not a "pullout" program in the sense that groups of gifted and talented pupils are withdrawn from regular classes at specified times to be with a special teacher for certain periods each week.

The program also does not call for transporting highly able pupils to centers for certain activities. Instead, the activities are carried out with the children in their own schools, mostly in their own classes.

Of course, some basic scholars leave their regular classes from time to time, but always with the teacher's approval and with the conditions under each of the components being met in advance.

There are groups of gifted and talented pupils who meet and work together, too. These are informal groups of basic scholars, however, and their meetings arise out of some mutual instructional need or other program purpose. Thus, the groups are expected to form, change, reform, and disband when the need no longer exists.

Staff and Responsibilities

It is the responsibility of the principals to establish and maintain the components of this program in the schools over which they have authority. They make use of the program coordinator's office to assure that each school's program, while to some extent unique, also is consistent with school system-wide guidelines.

Teachers and Librarians

In each school one teacher and one librarian are identified to give joint overall instructional leadership for gifted and talented pupils. The librarian serves as a continuing resource person for basic scholars and their teachers. Special attention is given by the library to the location and dissemination of instructional materials for these basic scholars. Depending upon the size of the school, the two leaders are allocated one or more periods per day for their continuing work, as noted above, and as consultants to other teachers and as teachers of minicourses for inservice continuing education for other teachers.

Program Coordinator and Assistant Coordinator

These are staff positions. Their purpose is to assure consistent and continuous development of gifted and talented education systemwide. They provide guidance and offer consultation to the operating staff. They also have responsibility for maintaining smooth interactions between this program and all the rest of the school system's operations.

These two positions are essential to program success from the very beginning. They organize and operate a systematic and continuous inservice education effort in all the schools. They collect data on all gifted and talented pupils. To a very large extent principals use the coordinator and assistant as resource persons for the details of the program as it gets under way. Liaison with other educational and business and community agencies also falls under their office. In short, full staffing of these positions from the outset has a most significant bearing on the achievement of program stability and effectiveness.

Yourtowne's Board of Education believes that a sound and workable design for the education of gifted and talented children and youth is in place in the community's elementary and secondary schools. The board and the superintendent say it is not a "fancy" program, but one that is solid, with all of the essentials that such pupils need for appropriate education.

The program and its related components did not arrive full blown. Its sense of direction emerged from the efforts of many persons. Their open and thorough activities resulted in wide acceptance. The seven major steps in program implementation were to:

1. obtain board of education approval and orient principals and teachers
2. appoint program coordinator and staff and identify teacher/librarian instructional leaders at schools
3. identify basic scholars and prepare an Individualized Education Plan (IEP) for them
4. establish Community Advisory Group(s)
5. plan and conduct inservice for teacher/librarian leaders
6. introduce four other components formally
7. set up evaluation schedule for basic scholars and report regularly to board of education and community

Persons associated with special education for gifted and talented students recognize that it flourishes best when viewed as a part of the whole educational system, not as apart from it. They know that all pupils, not just those who are gifted and talented, profit from individualized and specialized work. They realize, too, that the interest and participation of regular class teachers, specialists, principals, and all parents and pupils are needed to do any educational job well. And they know full well that a program for gifted students cannot remain a good one if the school system does not keep elevating its sights for all of the pupils in all of the schools.

THE HISTORICAL CONTEXT

Gowan (1977) traced the historical origins of interest in gifted and talented persons. In his view, the interest is prompted by: (1) regard for the dignity of the individual person, (2) curiosity about the unfolding of human development, and (3) concern for the nurture of the unusual or unique. His analysis identified three distinct epochs: Pre-Terman, The Terman Era, and Post-Terman.

The Pre-Terman Era

The origins of the gifted child movement in America seem rooted in the late 19th and early 20th century work of psychologists Granville Stanley Hall, John Dewey, J. M. Cattell, and Louis Madison Terman. Their orientation was toward the individual. Each person was, to them, a unique mind and soul, worthy and precious, and capable of positive development. Thus all exceptional persons are valued, including the gifted and talented. Carl Rogers, Leta Hollingsworth, and E. Paul Torrance are examples of more recent influences stemming from those earlier humanistic roots.

The next step—the measurement of individual differences—led to a union between mathematics and psychology. Frederick Kuhlmann, Edward and Robert Thorndike, J. P. Guilford, Cyril Burt, and Alfred Binet were pioneers in the discovery and measurement of every kind of human capacity. Measurement, in turn, led to the exploration of development, or the unfolding of abilities. Jean Piaget and Erik Erikson can be taken as early leaders with a view of development as a unity made up of affective, cognitive, and psychomotor domains.

The contributions of this era are: (1) a picture of human development as the continuing expanding of new skills; (2) a view that human nature *can* be understood, balanced against a modest affirmation that much remains to be understood; (3) concern for the unusual as a basis for understanding the usual; and (4) esteem for the dignity of the person. This epoch created the context for Terman's contributions.

The Terman Period

Terman's work was made possible by Binet and Simon, who invented the first feasible method of measuring human intelligence. Their 1908 version of a mental scale won worldwide acclaim.

The heart of their brilliant work was the concept of mental age. Like others, they had observed that as children grew older they could reason better, remember better, and perform better such other mental functions as paying attention, counting, and understanding and solving everyday problems.

Binet and Simon hit on the idea of putting together a series of increasingly difficult tasks such as tying shoes, naming parts of the body, working puzzles, defining words—tasks that called on thinking, remembering, learning, and problem-solving activities. They then asked children of different ages to perform the tasks. The two investigators established, for example, that 9-year-olds, on the average, were able to do certain of the problems. They found that typical 10-year-olds could do all the ones that 9-year-olds could do, plus some that those 9-year-olds could not. Going in the other direction, they found average 8-year-olds able to reason, remember, and the like, but less well than the 9-year-olds. Building on their discovery of a consistent relationship between age and ability, Binet and Simon put together a sequence of approximately 40 different tasks or tests to try with a child, each taking little more than two or three minutes and each calibrated against a large array of Parisian children to determine at what age they typically were able to respond correctly.

Armed with that sequence of progressively more difficult tasks, one could interview a new child, administer the tests (starting with easy ones and going up to a point where the child missed enough in a row to show there was little point in going on), and end with an indication of the child's mental age. That was determined by the point at which the child no longer passed the tests. For instance, if an 8-year-old passed all the tests up to and including the 8-year level, the child was said to have a mental age of 8 years. If, instead, the child passed all the tests up to and including 11 years, the child's mental age would be 11, in contrast to an actual life age, or chronological age, of 8.

The genesis of the mental age scale in France stimulated mental measurement activities worldwide. A few years later a German, Stern, invented the intelligence quotient (IQ). Stern recognized that the mental age gave a useful indication of a child's present mental status or amount or stage of intellectual development. He conceived of an added dimension of mental measurement, however, that would be derived by dividing a child's mental age at a given time by the child's chronological age at the same time. The resulting quotient (MA/CA=IQ), if stable over time, would give information as to the *rate* of the child's mental development, too. These indicators of *stage* of mental development (MA) and of *rate* of mental development (IQ) triggered a burst of mental measurement activity.

The method Binet and Simon used to create the mental age concept, which in turn led to the intelligence quotient concept, ultimately proved to be of great importance, too. Their procedure—the calibration of increases in age with increases in thinking and learning capacity—opened the door to standardized testing of school achievement. Before that time school attainment tests were essentially localized. Each teacher in a local school made tests as needed and each test covered just what that teacher had taught. There was little comparability from school to school. But by making tests from sample material from the arithmetic or history textbooks of the various grades, for instance, and administering the tests to all the pupils in a number of schools, it became possible to determine what scores were earned by the average fourth grader, the average fifth grader, and so on.

Thus the method pioneered by Binet and Simon to build a tool to assess mental development was adapted to construct and standardize school achievement tests, too. These standardized tests (called norm referenced) could supplement the teacher's own personally designed tests (called criterion referenced). As a result, teachers then could answer two significant questions:

(1) How well do pupils learn the specific material I am teaching? (Determined from results of teacher-made criterion referenced tests.)
(2) How do these pupils' achievements compare with the achievements normally reached by similar pupils elsewhere? (Determined by comparing the scores local pupils earn with the averages, or norms, for all pupils in similar grades and subjects on the standardized tests.)

Thus the Binet and Simon method, plus the mental age and intelligence quotient concepts credited respectively to them and to Stern, laid the foundation for scientific individual pupil appraisal. For the first time it seemed to be possible to look objectively at a pupil's achievement status in relation to that same individual's level of mental development and also to assess with equal objectivity the level of school achievement and the level and rate of mental development of any student in relation to one or more others.

It was Terman who perceived possibilities such as a method of measurement applicable to all children including the gifted, verifying stages of human development, and the initiation of long-range studies.

Lewis Terman was born in 1877 into a farming family in Indiana. He began college in 1892 and, graduating in 1898, gained a teacher's certificate while serving assignments as a rural teacher. Three years later he entered Indiana University and was graduated in 1903 with an M.A. degree. The following fall Terman entered Clark University, from which he received a Ph.D. in 1905. He studied under G. Stanley Hall, and his fellow students included Kuhlmann and Gesell. He became a high school principal in California until he joined the faculty of Stanford University in 1910. There he pursued the adaptation, revision, and extension of the Binet procedures that culminated in the publication of the Stanford revision and extension of the Binet-Simon Scale. It was standardized on 905 children, 5 to 14 years of age. It called for a trained administrator and could be used with only one child at a time, hence the expression: individual test. It has been long-lived and popular.

In 1921 Terman undertook a new and equally monumental project that would have established his place in history even if he had not authored the most popular individual intelligence test in America. It was a series of longitudinal studies of 1,528 gifted children, age 3 to 19. The first report was published in 1925. The studies, following the same individuals, continued after Terman's death in 1956, with the most recent in 1977, and are destined to continue into the 21st century. They are financed largely by royalties from the Stanford-Binet.

The 1914 publication in England of *Hereditary Genius*, a major study of British men of eminence (as cited in Gowan, 1977), probably influenced the thinking of Terman and others in the United States, but it is difficult to be certain. Inferential evidence comes from the fact that Terman himself published in 1916 a work under the title *The Intelligence Quotient of Francis Galton in Childhood.*

Terman's long-range studies provide reason to reject the stereotype of the gifted as puny, introverted, otherworldly, narrow-focus, emotionally unstable persons. Instead, the valid image turned out to be one of healthy, well-rounded, committed, responsible, and likable persons. And he showed that gifted and talented children tended to maintain those qualities throughout life.

While there are some failures and problem people among gifted persons, they are proportionately fewer than among persons in the average intellectual range.

Terman's studies are descriptive. They do not attempt to explain the origins and the development of giftedness and talent. Also, the children came from a very predominantly Anglo, middle class area. While the term "genetic" appears in the title of the series of investigations, no serious effort is made to tie giftedness to general or specific genetic theory. Gowan reminds us that these limitations in Terman's pioneer effort ought to be viewed as guidelines for subsequent research.

It seems plain that Terman's background as a teacher and principal surfaced in this preeminent psychologist even while he was being lauded for accomplishments in methodology and measurement. Terman used also "talented" and "gifted" interchangeably, with the conviction that high cognitive ability was a common property of all forms of extraordinary and highly valued accomplishment.

The Post-Terman Period

Following Terman's initial probes, other able investigators joined in the study of gifted and talented individuals. *Great Musicians as Children* was the title of a biographical exploration by Schwrimmer (1930). Leta Hollingsworth (1926) reported her work with children with IQs above 180. Paul Witty (1930) began his longitudinal look at 100 gifted children. *The Intelligence of Scottish Children* (1933) illustrated the worldwide interest.

Some educators and scientists at the time thought that proper training could make any child a prodigy. Others believed gifted children to be social misfits, physically delicate, and vulnerable to mental illness. A 1922 report by Terman found evidence contrary to those suppositions. He also pointed out that children with gifts and talents are found in minority cultures and in poverty-stricken homes and neighborhoods. Maria Montessori in Italy reached the same conclusion. Not until much later, though, did these children receive the sustained serious study and help they deserved.

The benchmark studies of the post-Terman period include at least the following:

- Guilford's proposed Structure of Intellect theory encouraged movement from a general factor (G) explanation of intelligence to one of intelligence in terms of multiple factors that could be related to identification, curriculum adaptations, and teaching procedures.

- Pegnato and Birch (1959) established the utility of *effectiveness* and *efficiency* as research constructs. These constructs enable comparison of identification procedures.

- The work of Getzels and Jackson (1960) as well as Torrance expanded the understanding of creativity.

- The investigations of Gallagher and Aschner and of Meeker (1969) applied and tested the utility of the Structure of Intellect concept as a guide to curriculum design.

- Passow's and Goldberg's work with underachievement among gifted and talented pupils showed the importance of a focus on basic skills as well as the pupil's need for identification with a supportive teacher.

- Pressey and Stanley vividly reemphasized the naturalness and appropriateness of acceleration in terms of age, of curriculum, or of both, for most talented students, plus the important role of the mentor and an atmosphere of furtherance.

HISTORY'S LESSONS

Today's information and understanding regarding gifted and talented children, youth, and adults derives from a variety of broad principles and theories of development. It is not strange, then, that variations in perspective exist and compete for attention and approval. It is a necessity to compare and contrast divergent views to form an outlook on the nature and nurture of gifted and talented learners. Table 1-1 may help in that process. It combines ideas from Gowan (1977) and ourselves.

A fundamental lesson from history of the gifted child movement points out that the attitudes of society toward the gifted and talented child, adolescent, and adult definitely affect the form and quality of special educational provisions. It also is historically accurate that the development of athletic talent has preferred status today. One consequence is that boys and girls with superior athletic aptitude are sought out and given opportunities to practice intensively. The special and extra training usually is viewed as a necessary condition to stimulate the participants' existing talents to an ultimate potential. Special facilities and equipment also are seen as necessities for that potential to be displayed and viewed. Moreover, the coach (teacher) is especially honored and rewarded for production of participants who win subsequent honors. We join with Gowan (1977) and others in recognizing and applauding, not disparaging, this reality. It is to be hoped that other talents and gifts will receive similar rewards and status.

Table 1-1 Surface vs. Basic Concepts Regarding Human Potential

Surface Symptom	Basic Concept	Helpful Consequences
Gifted child	Creative individual	Giftedness is an estimate of potential, not an IQ score. Creativity is its means for expression.
Growth	Development	Development is stepwise, epigenetic, discontinuous. Recognizes that while sequence is universal, the individual has a personal timetable.
Acceleration and Enrichment	Inducing creativity Appropriate developmental tasks: quality in curriculum stimulation	Curriculum expertise, subject matter competence, and support for the person are invoked. Goal separated from strategy or tactic.
Intelligence	Structure of intelligence	The many dimensions of power, quickness, accuracy, and resourcefulness in physical, social, and emotional behavior are prized.

Adapted from concepts of the authors and "Background and History of the Gifted Child Movement" by J. C. Gowan in *The Gifted and Creative*, J. C. Stanley, W. C. George, and C. H. Solano (eds), The Johns Hopkins University Press, 1977.

An additional lesson from history is that education does not homogenize pupils. Rather, education increases individual differences. That happens within each pupil (intraindividual differences) and from pupil to pupil (interindividual differences). The record of the past, too, shows that the same education for all is not the appropriate education for all. That becomes more and more evident as pupils progress upward through the grades.

Advocacy on behalf of the gifted and talented person is a part of advocacy for all those with marked individual differences. Advocates recognize that placing a high value on ability and talent is neither elitist nor restrictive. Instead, it is part of a movement for the liberation of the gifts and talents of all persons. A high quality, free, and public education for highly able students of all ages cannot develop fully or survive long unless it rests on a foundation of high quality, free, and public education for everyone.

Yet even the most well-intentioned advocates of upgraded education for gifted and talented persons base some of their arguments on shaky premises that may not do much good. Witness this editorial:

The Genius Gap

In recent years, the federal government has taken a series of belated steps to identify, encourage and nurture extremely bright children. In 1972 Congress set up the Federal Office for the Gifted and Talented, which has received $2.5 million a year since 1976. Another $5 million is channelled to gifted-pupil programs through other federal agencies. But measured against other educational appropriations, those sums are far from overwhelming.

There are many explanations for the half-hearted approach to helping gifted children. For one thing, young geniuses and their parents don't form a sizeable constituency. For another, efforts to identify gifted children conjure up dark visions of totalitarian "brain-farming." And, finally, egalitarian-minded Americans in and out of Congress are often simply uncomfortable with the fact that nature deals some children a dramatically better hand than others.

Fortunately, there are signs that such attitudes may be on the wane. A House-Senate conference committee in Washington has proposed increasing appropriations for gifted-child programs by more than 500 percent. That legislative change of course ought to be accompanied by a realization on the part of educators that the compassionate ends of "special" and "adaptive" education apply to the gifted as well as the deprived.

When catalogues of oppressed minorities are compiled—and their compilation is now something of a cottage industry—geniuses tend to be overlooked. Yet according to a persuasive article in Newsweek magazine this week, geniuses—especially child geniuses—are the victims of an invidious non-discrimination.

While huge sums are rightly appropriated for the education and welfare of children with learning disabilities, there has been no similarly serious commitment to alleviating the special problems of youngsters with IQs in the statistical stratosphere. The assumption seems to be that a 12-year-old capable of teaching himself calculus shouldn't need special help from the educational bureaucracy or from government.

But that assumption is misinformed and even cruel. Gifted children whose superior intelligence is not recognized can become discouraged with schoolwork altogether and, paradoxically, fall behind in their studies. And even those children who do manage to manifest their talent may find themselves promoted academically but stifled socially. Intellectual precocity and social immaturity can make for an obnoxious combination, and it is common for child geniuses to become pariahs whether they are placed according to their chronological age or according to their mental age. The cliche that a thin line separates genius and madness too often becomes a reality. (Reprinted from the *Pittsburgh Post-Gazette*, Saturday, October 21, 1978, p. 4, by permission of John C. Craig, Jr., Editor, ©1978.)

On the one hand, the editorial expresses its advocacy for its target on very solid ground—namely, that gifted and talented individuals deserve attention on the same premise that all other pupils with marked individual differences do. Then the final sentence reinforces a serious misconception about genius and madness. It perpetuates an inaccuracy that has been a source of great worry and anguish to parents and children alike. Educators and parents must encourage the views of such editorial writers in general, while providing information that helps them to do an informed job next time.

THE CURRENT CONTEXT

Evidence of Progress

The Karmes and Collins (1977) national survey of teacher certification requirement in force in the states found that at least 20 institutions of higher education offered degree programs and that six states had formal certification requirements to teach gifted and talented pupils. This suggests that teacher education institutions are exerting efforts that can lead to the adoption of certification by more states. The content of the courses required for certification or offered by colleges was not specified. Karmes and Collins urged that identification of needed competencies should be undertaken. We strongly endorse that position. We also encourage colleges to design their own preparation programs, in cooperation with teacher groups and with school systems. Colleges that do so now issue their own certifications of competence to teachers in the absence of state certification.

Bruce-Mitchell and Erickson (1978) surveyed existing school practices regarding the education of gifted and talented children. They were able to compare their results with those from the 1971-1972 school year, thus providing an estimate of progress. In general, they found advances during the six years. More students were being identified and more were being served. More states had statutes, regulations, and policy statements, more money was being allocated, and more personnel were being assigned. More training was available.

The actual extent of the gains, though, was not encouraging. In 1977 there was a potential of 1,352,915 persons of school age in need as compared to 437,618 actually estimated as served. Only 18 states reported an official plan. Twenty-seven states employed at least one full-time state specialist, while 14 had part-time assignments. Eight states accounted for 91 percent of total state funds allocated. The states specifically budgeted $47 million compared to the approximately $3 million specifically allocated by the federal government.

The final generalization by Bruce-Mitchell and Erickson (1978) was that their survey could be a source of challenge or evidence of national neglect. They chose to infer that actual commitment to equal educational opportunity was emerging.

The 1970s were certainly the decade in which the elements of a national policy were forged. A 1978 report by Karmes and Collins provides insight into the status of terminology. With replies from 45 states, they found 28 that used essentially the same definition of a gifted and talented pupil. That signaled a major national trend toward consistency in professional terminology.

Examination of these definitions revealed an image of the gifted and talented as persons who (1) were superior in measured cognitive, motoric, and personal/social attributes; (2) possessed potential for superior performance of a variety of worthy kinds; and (3) were perceived to require differentiated educational programs. Behavior manifestations such as leadership were referred to, for example, even though assessment of such behavior was not as well refined as was assessment of intelligence or school achievement. These Karmes and Collins findings do illustrate a strong influence of federal leadership upon state policy regarding definitions.

A Balance of Individual and Social Priorities

The spurt of Soviet technology in the 1950s that produced Sputnik also spawned a "Child Buyer" mentality (see Chapter 16) that threatened to exploit human ability into narrow channels. Since then a balance has grown between the individual needs of able persons and society's need for their contributions. The American educational community has moved from unintentional neglect* through natural and social selection to exploitation and finally to genuine regard for nurture. Figure 1-1 expresses the balance that has emerged.

---

* It sometimes is argued that there never was widespread actual neglect of gifted and talented persons in the United States. Instead, it is pointed out that publicly supported secondary education and now publicly supported college, graduate school, and professional education really is equivalent to special attention to the gifted and talented, for they are the ones most likely to profit. What are the pros and cons of this argument?

Figure 1-1 Individual and Social Outcomes of Educational Priorities

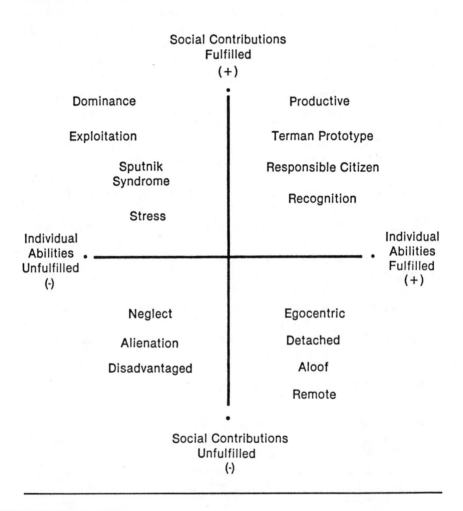

The upper-right quadrant portrays the positive and balanced consequences of the Yourtowne School District program. The upper-left portion represents exploitation. In the lower right is a pattern that encourages a distorted stereotype of able persons. The lower left reflects the tragedy and waste of neglect. We see evidence that the upper-right quadrant is gaining ground for children of both sexes and from all backgrounds.

Evidence of Permanence

In 1978, Congress passed and President Carter signed major legislation to provide continuing support to the states for special education for gifted and talented children. It was incorporated into the Elementary and Secondary Act (Title IX, Part A, P.L. 95-561) as if to reaffirm that such special education should be a part of what goes on in the regular schools. Proposals for such legislation were introduced in the Senate by Jacob K. Javits, Republican of New York and Robert T. Stafford, Republican of Vermont. The following selected remarks by Senator Stafford provide a sense of the legislative intent.

What distinguishes the bill I am introducing is that it would acknowledge and reinforce existing professional and administrative interaction between the special education of gifted and talented children and the special education of handicapped children. The advantages of doing so are:

Historically, special educators and administrators have perceived themselves as belonging to a profession committed to the education of all exceptional children, handicapped, and gifted.

Already 26 of the States take the combined (exceptional child) direction in their statutory and/or administrative approaches.

Such an approach avoids both the duplication of many existing delivery systems and the impossible task of creating wholly new delivery systems nationwide.

The U.S. Office for Gifted and Talented already is housed within and is under the jurisdiction of the U.S. Bureau for Education of the Handicapped.

There is substantial support throughout the Nation for maintaining and reinforcing in this session of the Congress the "combined systems" or "exceptional child" administrative approach.

The following organizations [he listed 13 national groups plus associations representing 19 states] have endorsed an expansion of the Federal role which would reinforce the linking of special education delivery systems across the spectrum of exceptionality. This list includes both groups which are primarily advocates for the gifted.

It is important that the future of those programs be as successful as possible. The bill I am introducing clearly indicates to the Commissioner of Education [now the Secretary of Education] the need for further strengthening of and attention to the gifted and talented component within the Bureau of Education for the Handicapped. It provides for expanded Federal support, with funding authorization independent from that provided for handicapped programs.

It should be recalled that the first special education component within the U.S. Office of Education was the section on exceptional children and youth, established in 1931. The basic strength of this bill is that it builds upon this historic action and keeps all special education programs together administratively. This bill would maintain and expand the successful existing delivery systems. (*Congressional Record,* April 5, 1978, p. S 4185.)

Declarations of Commitment and Federal Policy

Congress through Title IX, Part A, of P.L. 95-561 declared its assumptions about education for the gifted and talented. We summarize them in these three points:

1. The nation's greatest resource for solving critical problems is its gifted and talented children. The nation's potential for solving problems may be lost unless the special abilities of the gifted and talented are developed during the elementary and secondary school years.
2. Gifted and talented children from economically disadvantaged families and geographical areas are not often well served due to inappropriate services. Needed services include planning, development, operation, and improvement to meet and fulfill the potential of all highly able children.
3. A variety of resources must be brought to bear on this issue, resources that include state and local educational agencies, state and private institutions of higher education, volunteer organizations, and private schools.

Definition

The act further affirmed earlier definitions by saying that the gifted and talented were:

children, and where applicable, youth, who are identified at the preschool, elementary, or secondary level as possessing demonstrated or potential abilities that give evidence of high performance capability in areas such as intellectual, creative, specific academic, or leadership ability, or in the performing and visual arts, and who by reason thereof require services or activities not ordinarily provided by the school.

This legislated definition is widely respected. Most states use it or one very similar (Karmes & Collins, 1978). Yourtowne's way of identifying gifted and talented pupils is consistent with it. We believe, though, that the P.L. 95-561 definition will not remain static. It already is being modified by social need influences (Newland, 1976) and by the application of the three trait cluster concept of Renzulli (1978). In essence, Newland reminds us that social forces change, and when they do so do the nation's (or the world's) requirements for aviators, artists, attorneys, actors, advocates, athletes, and auto mechanics. Thus, social need helps determine who is considered gifted and talented and how many are required.

Renzulli presses another point, namely, that what we call giftedness and talent is made up of a combination of three trait clusters: above-average general abilities, task commitment, and creativity. He argues that educational efforts in behalf of gifted and talented pupils can be improved by definitions that give equivalent weight to all three clusters. We, too, hold that much more conscious attention needs be given to a research-based definition that capitalizes on Renzulli's ideas. We expect that the 1980s will see strong moves in that direction. The curriculum adaptations and teaching methodology preferred in succeeding chapters make use of Renzulli's notions.

Priority Intentions—Educational Agencies

P.L. 95-561 gave priority to the states to move on these urgent Congressional concerns: identify the educational needs of gifted and talented children; supply programs of sufficient scope, size, and quality, with appropriate consideration to the educational needs of the disadvantaged; and assure statewide planning and technical consultation to local school districts. Federal funds were to be only a share of costs, to be pooled with local and state resources. Thus the higher significance of state leadership and local initiative does emerge in this legislation.

The measure calls for a partnership among schools, colleges, and other agencies and organizations to pursue quality education for the gifted. The intention of Congress is to ensure that (1) programs are initiated and (2) implications and verifications from operations are shared widely.

The U.S. Department of Education

In 1972 an Office of the Gifted and Talented was established at the federal level in what was then the U.S. Office of Education. There had been sporadic efforts in that direction during the three decades before 1972, but none had been able to find a solid foothold. There now is a clear conception of the importance of special education for highly able students in the U.S. Department of Education. It is voiced firmly and unequivocally by leadership in the Office of the Gifted and Talented. It shows in the statements and activities of the personnel of the Bureau for Education of the Handicapped, where that office is located.

The role of the Department of Education emphasizes leadership and technical assistance to states and local districts on behalf of the gifted and talented. It appears that commitment will endure.

Practices—Preferred and Otherwise

Reynolds and Birch (1977) outlined emerging standards of education and service for gifted and talented pupils. They speak of preferred practices as those that represent high quality programming. They contrast preferred practices with prevailing practices that are more common and are of lesser quality. Their presentation summarizes lessons learned from research and from the experience of practitioners. Their list of 12 preferred practices contains four main themes: individualized planning, individualized programming, participation, and coordination:

1. *Individualized planning* starts with identification very early in the child's school experience or even in the home before school begins. At a minimum, there should be provisions for kindergarten review. Ideally, school districts establish linkages for referral from existing preschool programs and solicit parental nominations. Identification data supplies the foundation for planning. It should include a range of assessment procedures that encompasses cognitive, motor, social, emotional, and creative behavior, using appropriate forms of measurement. The outcome should be a written plan with provision for at least an annual review by participants.

2. *Design of an individualized instructional program* is the primary goal of planning. Two key elements are necessary. First, school policies should be amenable to early admission to and early exiting from school. There is nothing magic about age 5 or age 17 as criteria. Early admission to kindergarten or first grade and advanced placement in higher education are well-proved helpful adaptations for many gifted and talented young people. These learners also benefit from flexible scheduling. In the second key element, the pupils are helped to select classes or content not usually scheduled for their age peers. For example, a gifted fifth grader may elect advanced math and attend a high school class for it, but remain with peers for most other curriculum experiences. The preferred setting for most education, however adapted, would be the pupil's regular local school and class rather than special classes or special schools. Regular classes with special provisions and supportive services brought to the gifted student proves the most appropriate location for a variety of sound educational reasons.

3. *Participation* highlights the involvement of all who have a stake in the particular pupil's education. This central concept is that shared tasks are tied to shared responsibilities. Parents, teachers, and the learner are partners. The team of parents, learner, and educators should have support services and consultation available from other teachers expert in subject matter, in consultation, and in materials and methods. There also are obvious needs for administrative support. While the participants may vary according to the educational agency, any given program needs assistance from more than the teacher and the learner alone.

4. *Coordination* is a complex, demanding, and essential task. We have never seen smoothly operating education for gifted and talented pupils that did not have a coordinator. The management of pupil identification, pupil records, program elements (policies, resources, services), and program standards must have attention. Other typical tasks are recruitment and orientation of volunteers to serve as a talent bank for the program and of professional educators in the school system for program support.

Program literature points also to the need to coordinate inservice training, consultation, and evaluation. Participants, administrators, parents, and resource persons require orientation and opportunities for further development through inservice programs. Consultation is needed and sought by participants; it can be as routine as advice or as complex as problem solving. Evaluation of the summative type compares results against stated objectives. The formative type examines the program process, step by step, to see if what was supposed to occur did occur in actual practice. Evaluation's purpose is improvement, not simply fault finding.

In our view, coordination of education for gifted and talented pupils includes advocacy. Advocacy can mean speaking for or defending others. Consequently, coordination implies representing the best interests of learners, parents, and participants.

Smidchens and Sellin (1976) surveyed 116 graduate students in general education to tap some of their feelings about gifted young people. The graduate students were very willing to teach them, but gave significantly lower priority to gifted children's need for special educational services. The Smidchens and Sellin study updated and extended the 1963 Weiner and O'Shea report. In general, involvement with good quality programs produced the most favored reactions toward the necessity for special education of the gifted and talented. Supervisors of general education were the most supportive.

A follow-up study by Weiner (1968) of 406 school psychologists demonstrated a similar relationship between experience with a high quality program and positive support. Our observations, too, point first to the great significance of supportive adults in fostering the full development of gifted and talented children, and second to the fact that professional training is advantageous in helping teachers and other educators to understand and to react responsively to the special educational needs of such children. Yourtowne's design is intended to fulfill the preferred practice standards.

MAINTAINING AND EXPANDING OPPORTUNITIES

Parker (1976) observed that analytic studies of lives of eminent persons revealed that they were reared in encouraging environmental conditions that helped them as young gifted and talented persons to develop their unique abilities both within and outside of the formal educational system. That argues for the potential beneficial effects of superior environments for all pupils. Parker commented:

> Educators have treated the most able only as educational curiosities, as if nothing were to be learned from their extraordinary performances. . . . To continue the current attitude toward brilliance—that it is only a curiosity haphazardly bestowed—robs us of the lessons that could be learned from brilliant youngsters. (p. 240).

The attitudes of significant adults in the lives of gifted and talented children certainly are controlling influences in the quality of their environment. Teachers, principals, supervisors, and other professionals engaged in educational settings establish the tone of those environmental settings.

For example, Cornish (1968) found that teacher perceptions did influence their nomination of pupils for enrollment in educational programs for the highly able. Perceptions of gifted children that are tied to memory, recitation, and research skills alone narrowed the ability to identify more versatile pupils. R. L. Johnson (1976) presented similar results with respect to creativity. He reported on the development of a 50-item self-report scale, *Something About Myself.* The procedures uncovered discrepancies between teacher and pupil perceptions. Teachers favored artistic performance and intellectual attributes and tended to ignore self-confidence, individuality, and initiative. Jacobs (1972) compared the academic expectations held by trained teachers of the gifted and talented and practicing teachers in regular grades. As might be expected, trained teachers were more positive about the benefits of programs, potential future achievement, and estimates of expectations for school performance. Moreover, Jacobs reported no difference between the general educators and a sample of representatives of the general public.

We conclude that increases in understanding and in professional competence among educators parallel increases in concern and zeal for high quality educational opportunities for talented children and youth. Investments in professional preparation ought to be accompanied by heightened and expanded educational provisions.

PERSISTING MISCONCEPTIONS

Ignorance, tradition, and prejudice keep alive misconceptions that interfere with the growth of special education for the gifted and talented. The dissemination of accurate information can dispel these false notions:

False notion: "Gifted children get along very well in spite of their schooling." Certainly an occasional one does. But the fact remains that about half of the nation's gifted and talented children and youth drop out of school before completing college. That can scarcely be called "getting along well."

False notion: "Enrichment simply by the regular teacher is the best plan for educating the gifted." When compared with education integrated by a team of regular and specialist teachers, enrichment by regular teachers alone runs a poor second.

False notion: "Special education produces a snobbish, elite group." Follow-ups of gifted students who have received special education disproves that, in study after study. In fact, special education for the gifted produces more thoughtful, sensitive, and socially conscious children and adults.

False notion: "Special education separates gifted children from other children, and that is bad because it removes the challenging minds from the rest of the group." Actually, in today's comprehensive elementary, middle, and secondary schools, no more separation is required for special education for the gifted than for any other group. And research evidence supports flexible instructional grouping for both gifted and talented and for other children.

False notion: "It is bad when gifted children become the responsibility of special education along with all the other exceptional children." That point of view is rarely seen in print, but it does intrude into conversation. At worst, it is plain bigotry. At best, it is ignorance of the role of the special educator as an expert in individualizing curriculum and teaching methods to accommodate extreme individual differences.

False notion: "You can't really tell who most of the gifted children are until they are quite far along in school, and many are late bloomers who don't show up until the college years." To be sure, there are some youngsters who blossom in their teens or later. But the vast majority can be readily identified quite early. Four out of five can be found by age 3 or 4. And very, very few gifted and talented children can escape detection by ages 6 to 8 if the best available means are applied to seeking them out. With rare exceptions, talented children can be found in the early years, the time when planning for their special education should begin.

False notion: "You want to push these children, and you will rob them of a normal, happy childhood and turn them into nervous wrecks." In the tense hustle of today no doubt some children are being forced beyond their capacities. No one wants pressure cooker education for any child—gifted, talented, or otherwise. The best assurance of normal and happy development for a highly able child is special education planned and paced to suit the youngster's emerging gifts and talents, through wise and well-trained teachers and counselors available for guidance both for child and parents. Under such a program, gifted children flourish.

These seven misconceptions are only a few of the more serious ones. You may know of others that you would add to the list. Strong emotions tend to be engendered by exceptional children. We must be wary of the pitfalls of emotionalism as we move toward the rational goal of maximum opportunity for self-fulfillment on the part of the gifted and talented and the maximum benefit of all society which should follow.

Reynolds and Birch (1977) as well as Hallahan and Kaufman (1978) note that misconceptions can have a spillover effect as well. Misconceptions worry parents. They produce lingering uncertainties in the gifted and talented individuals themselves. They leave a negative image with the public.

Frequently encountered misconceptions appear in brief form in Table 1-2. Try them on your friends as true-false statements. Actually all 25 are false. Either they are denied emphatically by research evidence or they are exceptions rather than the rule.

Informed persons who are willing to confront and correct misinformation are needed to advance the educational interests of able pupils. Moreover, able persons themselves and their parents also may require informed guidance in such matters.

Table 1-2 Persisting Myths About Gifted and Talented Persons

1. Parents of average or retarded children cannot have gifted children.
2. Gifted and talented people are physically weak.
3. Gifted and talented people are morally lax.
4. Gifted and talented people tend to be mentally unstable.
5. Gifted and talented people are socially inept and narrow in interests.
6. Most eminent men and women were indifferent scholars as children.
7. Most gifted and talented children are flash in the pan performers.
8. Gifted and talented people have a single talent.
9. Gifted and talented people tend to be odd.
10. Gifted and talented people tend to feel superior to other people.
11. Grade skipping, or acceleration, harms gifted and talented children.
12. Gifted and talented children require a different curriculum.
13. Teachers are poor identifiers of gifted and talented children.
14. Special classes are to be preferred to inclusion in regular grades.
15. Identification of gifted and talented children should be delayed until grade 3.
16. Enrichment of the regular curriculum is not effective.
17. Parents of gifted and talented children are conceited.
18. An IQ test is the only identifier of giftedness and talent.
19. Gifted and talented persons require no undue educational provisions.
20. Society has little need of its gifted and talented citizens.
21. College graduates are brighter than noncollege graduates.
22. Special education of the gifted and talented causes elitism among students.
23. Gifted and talented students dominate other students in regular grades.
24. Memory is the best index of human intelligence.
25. Interest in educating gifted and talented persons is of importance only since the 1960s.

Adapted from "Giftedness and Talent: High Rate of Cognitive Development" by M. Reynolds and J. W. Birch, in *Teaching Exceptional Children in All America's Schools,* Council for Exceptional Children, 1977; and from *Exceptional Children* by O. P. Hallahan and J. M. Kauffman, Prentice-Hall, 1978.

The Key Role of Teachers

Teacher and pupil make up the axis around which services are delivered and organized. Specialists with advanced training in the education of the gifted and talented must work as genuine colleague-consultants to teachers, in our view. Passow (1978), too, pays tribute to teachers, assigning them the central function in programming. He observes that it is the teacher's competence that dictates the use or misuse of alternatives.

A report by Tshudin (1978) also testifies to the crucial role of teachers. Her sample consisted of 420 educators, 309 of whom were identified as superior teachers. Personal qualities, classroom behavior, and other professional behavior of superior teachers were distinctive characteristics:

Personal qualities: These teachers (1) were humorous and enthusiastic, (2) were more involved in activities outside the classroom, (3) viewed "hard work" as necessary for success, and (4) were more willing to accept advice and consultation from a variety of sources.

Classroom behaviors: These teachers (1) based discipline on incentives rather than upon punishment, (2) used more variety in teaching methods, (3) used more variety and student-centered appeal in pupil/class activities, (4) assigned less homework, (5) supplemented tests with checklists, folders, and projects for assessment, and (6) showed more evidence of teacher-pupil planning.

Other professional behaviors: These teachers (1) pursued goals related to student confidence, (2) were willing to prepare lesson plans in detail, (3) were more willing to depart from prepared lesson plans, (4) were better in organizing classroom space and materials, and (5) worked harder at individualization of instruction.

The teacher of the regular class is the central professional in the educational enterprise for the learner and the family. For us, regular class teachers are the frontline of educational opportunity for able learners and all other pupils. Research and experience confirm this position.

Teachers perform vital roles in the identification of all able pupils and especially those for whom traditional procedures have been inadequate, such as children from minority groups. Teachers guide and nurture both pupils and parents. Teachers form alliances with other citizens in advocacy of programs of high quality and substance. Teachers' instructional skills widen pupil interests and increase pupil competence. Finally, teachers individualize education in order to adapt existing curricula to match the needs and the accelerated rates of development of able pupils.

Commitment to Quality

It is easy to confuse a program or a service with an educational principle. For example, it may be natural to believe that gifted and talented children need special classes, that curricula should be different, that special programming requires different standards, and the like. To a limited extent that may be accurate, but it is a superficial view of education for exceptional children and youth. The principle, rather, is that able learners ought to learn more rapidly, acquire more information and understanding, and learn to learn on their own at increasingly complex levels. Discussions that start with special classes, curriculum, and tactics bypass the central teacher competency needed for fruitful intervention—namely, individualization of instruction and guidance. Listings of standards for program operation do represent distillations of experience and research. However, such lists are useless if they ignore the guiding principle of individualization.

The prototype of Yourtowne School District reflects an organization of educational and community resources designed to implement an Individualized Education Plan for gifted and talented pupils. In Yourtowne they are dubbed basic scholars. Other communities may organize in different ways to educate such pupils. It is not too extreme to say that *quality originates with the principle of individualization.* For example, the staff position of coordinator of the Basic Scholars Program does not ensure a high standard of quality for Yourtowne. It is the completion of individual pupil activities designed to accomplish predetermined outcomes matched to those specific pupils' needs that is the hallmark of quality. The position of coordinator is simply one very important means to help fulfill the principle of individualization.

Virtually all of today's leaders in the education of gifted pupils suggest that there are several vital dimensions of quality. Many suggest a checklist of priorities for consideration. For example, identification is a prime element in that pupils are, indeed, located. A related standard is the ability, or capability, to generate outcomes or expectations from the inventory of identification procedures. Evidence of continuity of planning and program implementation among faculty at all levels requires attention. Evaluation and monitoring of pupil progress has received emphasis and attention. Participation of parents and specialists with teachers also has become a significant element. These dimensions possess the common objective of matching a person's individualized educational profile to those tasks that need to be learned to assure increasing maturity and mastery.

It is one thing to recite standards of quality; it is another to be internally committed to them. The development and endurance of services for the gifted and talented will depend upon the commitment of educators and parents to pursue the objective of high quality of instruction and services.

SUMMARY

1. Education on behalf of gifted and talented learners must develop as an open program, which means that enrollment is not restricted by narrow criteria. It also must be available to pupils regardless of grade level.

2. A comprehensive model has at least five component services oriented toward general and specific pupil needs: (1) A Basic Scholars component emphasizes essential skills. (2) A Special Interest Component encourages pursuit of curriculum in depth. (3) An Advancement Component is directed

toward acceleration of either the pupil or of content areas. (4) A Talent Development Component focuses on performance dimensions. (5) A Human Service Component is oriented toward opportunities to help others while learning. All five components are supported by allocation of resources available to the school district.

3. History's lessons confirm that (a) environment, especially helpful adults, shapes the nature and direction of human potential; (b) genetic explanations do not fully account for the incidence of giftedness and talent; (c) human ability cannot be described by a single test score; (d) theory is a fundamental tool to guide practice; (e) misunderstanding, prejudice, and stereotypes hamper progress, and (f) a body of reliable knowledge about gifted and talented persons exists.

4. The 1970s were a period of significant educational progress. The decade closed with legislation that contributed a multidimensional definition of gifted and talented, one that has gained wide acceptance. The start of the 1980s decade witnessed expansion of the leadership role of the U.S. Department of Education.

5. Individualized planning and instruction, participation, and coordination are minimal essentials for high quality education for highly able pupils. Preferred practices are known and are attributes that have been proved. These are the considerations around which policies, services, and resources can be assembled most effectively. The Yourtowne example gives further meaning to the term "needs." The aspiration of Yourtowne's professional staff is to identify each child's capability for increased competence in scholarship, for enlargement of interest, for advancing at an individual pace, for extending present abilities and developing new ones, and for being of service to others while learning. Quality in any community's educational program is the evidence that practices, policies, services, and resources are directed toward these needs.

UNIT ENRICHMENT

1. Review documents. Consult the state plan for the gifted and talented and/or the plan of your local school district. How would/could you rewrite the prototype of Yourtowne? What elements would be added. What elements would be missing?

2. Reflect on your experiences. Recall three episodes in your experience as a student, regardless of level, that describe your favorite teacher. Recall three episodes in which a teacher was not so favorably remembered. Compare the episodes. What attributes of effective teaching can you identify? Does the comparison account, in any way, for your selecting

teaching as a career? Does the comparison enable you to identify any influences on your behavior in educational/instructional settings?

3. Can you imagine if Alfred Binet were alive today? How do you suppose he might view the use of his scale? What would be his reaction to Terman's work? Can you visualize Binet presenting testimony to Congress in support of or opposed to P.L. 95-561? What might be an outline of his testimony?

4. Read the novel, *The Child Buyer,* by John Hersey. List the characters in the book who either testified or were important to the potential "specimen." In two brief sentences describe why each one was willing to "sell" the child. How does Hersey's book provoke your thinking about gifted children, educational goals, and the prudent use of human ability?

5. Review media coverage of gifted persons in your own local community (TV, radio, newspapers, newsletters, and the like are appropriate). What aspects appear to draw the most attention? Are presentations favorable and accurate? What would you recommend for coverage?

6. Interview ten teachers to identify their perceptions of high quality services. Request the teachers to free-associate to terms such as: (1) meeting the needs of children, (2) quality education, (3) teaching as a career, (4) gifted child, and (5) individualized education. Write down the responses. What educational priorities seem to emerge? What attributes of gifted persons emerge? Could your results be a basis for inservice?

The Life Cycles of Education

SYNOPSIS

Knowledge of life cycles, or human growth and development as a sequence of tasks, helps teachers and principals in several ways. First, they understand that each child proceeds on a personal timetable of learning skills and understanding necessary to cope with life in the context of individual expectations and social reactions from peers and adults. Second, they understand that their professional knowledge is to be applied to an individual gifted or talented person whose rate of development is both rapid and individually unique. They understand that "truths" about the exceptional child are to be applied very selectively to any particular person within the group. Third, they recognize accelerated development as natural for these learners and they adapt to and enhance individual patterns of development.

This unit also reminds educators that there is no separate psychology, sociology, or education for the gifted and talented, but there is knowledge about how psychology and education apply to such persons and knowledge about the social context in which their education takes place. Further, human development is seen to begin early and to continue throughout a lifetime; it is not confined to ages 5 to 18. The unit also builds on the three most pertinent facts about gifted and talented persons from which educational implications flow:

1. The most significant characteristics about gifted students are their accelerated rates of learning and the extensiveness of their learning, which combine to bring them into contact with content and ideas much earlier than most of their chronological age peers.
2. The persisting mythology and mystique about superior human ability tends to create psychosocial distance between gifted and talented persons and their families, teachers, and peers. *That need not happen.* Un-

less combated, though, they separate highly able persons from adults and peers who could be helpful.

3. Educational programs of high quality do make a difference. There really is sufficient knowledge for positive guidance.

This unit is organized into four chapters. They correspond roughly to the way public schools are organized, the content of teacher preparation, and major epochs of development. The unit is predicated on the assumption that the family is a natural ally of the school. This view respects the family as the child's first teacher and as the pupil's natural advocate and mentor. In this sense, the family and the school are bound in a common alliance and confederacy.

The year 1979 was celebrated as the year of Dr. Albert Einstein. It also was the first International Year of the Child (IYC). Although it was a worldwide undertaking, there was no standardized, unified program with multination agreements to conduct cooperative projects. Rather, the deliberate intention was to encourage individualized celebrations. The central theme of the IYC was to encourage and promote actions on behalf of the needs and rights of children as expressed in the United Nations Declaration of Children's Rights. The UN statement, as quoted by Jahnsmann (1979), affirms that all children are entitled to protection and nurture, including specifically "free education and recreation and equal opportunity to develop their individual abilities." That has special relevance for children with potential gifts and talents, for individualization of education is the only way to bring that kind of potential to full flower.

KEY IDEAS

It is recognized now that early childhood (e.g., birth to approximately 8 years) is a crucial time for nurture. These are, educationally, life's most valuable years. Preschool education can be home based or in day care or other group settings. It is the substance, the content, and the quality of relationships, rather than the setting, that counts most. Losses sustained in the earliest years cannot be made up fully later.

Later childhood (e.g., ages 9 to 12) represents a period of negotiation. The child will be moving from protection to permission. The complexities of formal operations encourage pupils to test the limits of protection and open wide possibilities for identification with adults and their values.

Adolescence is a time of promising prospects, of exciting and varied options. It also is a time of reflection about one's values, goals, and options. It can be the best of times for parents and teachers. The young gifted and talented person's movement (sometimes zigzag) from intelligence to wisdom can be rewarding to watch for both adolescent and consultant. But adults cannot impose wisdom. The best they can do is share it, without strings attached.

Adulthood has its own distinct epochs and its own distinct tasks. These cover the pursuit of personal life satisfaction in the context of making social contributions. Learning is lifelong and monitoring the development of the young is a primary adult life theme. Of course, monitoring and mentoring can happen at any age. The processes are not restricted to adult-to-child or to adolescent or young adult relationships. Monitoring and mentoring implies willingness by both parties to share and to take prudent risks.

Most factors that promote growth and development in highly able persons no longer are mysterious. The factors can, to a large extent, be controlled by individual actions of professional educators and the family through existing individualized modes of education; different education seldom is necessary.

A PROTOTYPE

This selection shows that productive adulthood does not burn out, but continues to reflect rich contributions of talent to ordinary life. It illustrates the dynamics of mentoring and, perhaps most of all, it shows the boundless strength of the human spirit. Wilhelm's (1979) title is apt.

A Singular Man

Five years ago, a frail, tousled English physicist steered his electric wheelchair to the front of a lecture room at Oxford's Rutherford Laboratory to deliver a paper entitled "Black Hole Explosions?" For months he had sat on his findings, refusing to believe his own calculations. Finally, his old tutor had persuaded him to overcome his reticence and go public. The paper caused a sensation throughout the world of physics. Its author was Stephen Hawking—a most singular man.

Then 32, Hawking already was being rated by many as the intellectual heir to that *magister ludi* of science Albert Einstein, whose visions of gravity and space-time remain the most monumental descriptions of reality yet conceived by man. Nevertheless, Stephen Hawking was uncharacteristically nervous about his Rutherford presentation. "That question mark (in the title) reflected my own uncertainty," he recalls.

Lights in the lecture room were dimmed in order that slides of Hawking's key equations might be viewed. Slides were necessary because few could understand Hawking's distorted speech, one side effect of his severe, wasting neuromuscular disease. Yet at this historic event it seemed that his audience, made up largely of skeptical particle physicists, had more trouble with Hawking's reasoning than with his speech. At the conclusion, the moderator, John Taylor, best known for his popular books on black holes and speculative investigations into psychic phenomena, declared, "Oh, this is rubbish!"

Today, many judge those same conclusions to be the first step in an attempt to merge Einstein's theory of general relativity, which describes reality on the cosmic scale, with quantum mechanics, which describes reality on the nuclear scale. A linkup between these two cornerstones of understanding has long been thought the Holy Grail of physics. Einstein himself spent his last 30 years in frustrated search for this linkup.

But Hawking's life has not always been history-making and fireworks. Born to an intellectual Oxford family on January 8, 1942, the young Hawking decided to become a scientist before his 10th birthday. "I was always interested in how things worked, always taking things apart." He pauses to let a broad, infectious smile cross his face. "But I wasn't so keen on putting them back."

During his early years, Hawking's innate brilliance was camouflaged by laziness. From the age of 11 he received a full scholarship at the private St. Albans School north of London. Yet a year later he was still required to write copybook exercises in futile attempts to cure his untidiness. His father, a well-known research scientist in tropical diseases and a professor at University College, Oxford, where Hawking entered early, even was concerned that his son might not pass the entrance exam.

Hawking's blithe undergraduate attitude became notorious. He never took notes during lectures, fell asleep in tutorials, and in at least one class ripped up a lengthy paper after it had been delivered and rebelliously lobbed it into the wastebasket. Long of hair and fingernail, and generally unkempt, Hawking definitely was more hippie than *Homo literarium*. Above all, he was popular, passing the most crucial test of any Oxford undergrad—that is, even the head porter liked him.

The last term before final exams, Dr. Robert Berman, Hawking's tutor, remembers his astonishment at being told, "Do you know? Stephen actually is working two hours a day."

"I think it was partly a fault of the Oxford system that I could get away with it," confesses Hawking, reflecting on his squandered undergraduate days. "Lecturers were not at all relevant to the actual courses, and the lectures were rather badly given, so I often didn't bother to go. All the work I did was for my tutors, who were very good. It is only through them that I learned anything at all."

With graduation upon him, and uncertain about his future career, Hawking applied for a job with the British Ministry of Works, then forgot to go in for the exam. "Had I passed," Hawking adds with a grin, "I probably would have ended up taking care of monuments."

He came close.

In order to win a necessary scholarship to graduate school, Hawking needed to achieve a first (equivalent to a magna cum laude) in his final examinations, but he fell short. The dons, in a relatively unusual move, extended Hawking a second chance through a 20-minute long "viva" (oral) test. Professor Berman remembers this crucial occasion: "The examiners were intelligent enough to realize that they were talking to someone more intelligent than they were."

"Now, Mr. Hawking, what are you going to do next?" one of the examiners queried.

Undaunted, he replied: "If I get a first, I'm going to Cambridge. If a second, I will stay here. So I expect you will give me a first.

They did.

The brash young man hoped to study under famed astronomer Fred Hoyle, founder of Cambridge's Institute of Astrophysics, but was assigned instead to Dennis Sciama, who, much to his credit, quickly recognized Hawking's thus far wasted talents. "From the beginning, Stephen virtually always said 'But . . .' to any statement of mine," recalls Sciama. "He always had such a cogent feeling of what we were discussing. It might happen after a couple years with a bright student—but not after one month." Finally challenged, Hawking blossomed quickly, finishing with a thesis any of whose four separate sections would have qualified him for his doctorate, and which formed the basis for his rapid ascendancy to world-class physics.

After a post-Oxford summer trip to the Middle East, where some speculate he may have been infected by a rare virus, Hawking had begun to stumble in his walk, to have difficulty tying his shoes, and to slur his speech—all symptoms of a degenerative neurological illness called amyotrophic lateral sclerosis, commonly known as "Lou Gehrig's disease."

"Initially, I was very depressed," says Hawking. "I thought there wasn't any point to working because I wouldn't live long enough to get my Ph.D. But then I met Jane at a party, and got engaged, so things seemed not so black. Then I realized that if we were to get married, I would have to get a job. That was when I started working, and it was about the time when I began to make professional progress. It was a turning point."

Asked if he worked unusual hours, all-night hours, like Nobel physicist Julian Schwinger, for example, Hawking quickly responds, "Is he a family man?"

Stephen works hard at fatherhood, playing chess with Robert, who has begun to beat his illustrious opponent, and admiring "Lucy-lu's" dancing. "I never work at home," says Hawking, ". . . well, hardly ever. But if I have off moments when I'm not engaged in something else, or playing with the children, then I do think about my work."

How does one remain sane dealing with such alien concepts so far removed from common sense?

"It's entirely a matter of what you've gotten used to," replies the physicist. "One can get used to the most incredible things. Someone from 200 years ago might think that everything we have today is counterintuitive, but we accept it as natural because we've grown up with it. Since I've spent quite a while thinking about these things, they appear to be quite natural."

Compare this with what Albert Einstein said in a 1933 Oxford lecture: "To him who is a discoverer in this field, the products of his imagination appear so necessary and natural that he regards them, and would like to have them regarded by others, not as creations of thought but as given realities."

Like Einstein, Hawking's achievements rely on his unique and stubborn instinct to ask the right questions, make the proper assumptions, then see all the way through the problem before it has been worked out. Caltech's Thorne, a close friend for many years, says that "in terms of inspiring insights, a 10-minute conversation with Stephen is worth a 10-day meeting with the average scientist." Yale astrophysicist Douglas Eardley once gave a seminar knowing that he had avoided preparing a long and difficult calculation central to his talk. "I just did not know how to go about solving it. At the end, Stephen quickly pointed out a few elegant methods to get the result. He has a fine geometrical mind, and is really good at mathematical jujitsu. His power of pure concentration can come up with the answer before the calculations are done. It is the essence of the creative process."

"There is a perfection about Stephen's work, a purity that is like Mozart's," adds Werner Israel. "There is a pattern in every single paper he has written, a translucency in all that he does. It's as if he composes entire symphonies in his head."

Because he cannot casually walk to a blackboard and chalk up equations as they occur to him, or even jot them on a notepad, Hawking is forced to hold the complex pages of mathematical Sanskrit in his head. As a consequence, he has developed an awesome sense of mathematical efficiency in creating innovative shortcuts. Post-doctoral fellows are assigned to him to do much of the handwork on intricate calculations, yet it is Hawking who dictates the final papers.

Polly Grandmontagne, a secretary at Caltech, vividly recalls Hawking's visit there a few years back. He would dictate to her in labored phrases, slowly spelling words she could not understand, occasionally dropping his head to one side as he tired from the strain of talking. The day after one particularly grueling session, recounts Mrs. Grandmontagne, "Stephen came back in and said that he had made a mistake on a certain page, that the equation should run thus-and-so." He had remembered the entire 40-page paper, and in reviewing it in his mind that evening had caught his error.

Says Hawking, "My goal is obvious: complete understanding of the universe. But I think it would be very presumptuous to say that I expect to get the complete solution."

"One goal of my work has been to understand whether the universe has a meaning, and what our role is in it. I've always wanted to know why the universe exists at all, and what was there before the beginning."

"There may be ultimate answers, but if there are, I would be sorry if we were to find them. For my *own* sake I would like very much to find them, but their discovery would leave nothing for those coming after me to seek. Each generation builds on the advances of the previous generation, and this is as it should be. As human beings, we need the quest."

Reprinted from "A Most Singular Man" by John L. Wilhelm by permission of *Quest/79, 3,* 33-36, 39-40, © 1979.

SUMMARY

This unit presents the gifted and talented person in the perspective of educational development. It is organized sequentially from early childhood through adulthood. Focus is on the continuous, rapid, and rich growth that should be expected when the interface between the gifted and talented individual and the education agency is kept at an optimum level. The teacher is seen as the key person who, with the help of other educators and of parents, guides and monitors the necessary individualized education.

Chapter 2

Early Childhood: A Good Start in Life

TIME CAPSULE

Developmentally, childhood ranges from the sensorimotor stage through concrete operations and from the preconventional to the conventional stage of moral development. Educationally, it is conventional to divide the period into three parts. One is from birth to age 2 or 3. The home, the day care center, or both combine to form the main locations where children receive education, if they receive any. We do not know how many potentially gifted and talented children are lost during this time from lack of stimulation. Most children are at the mercy of chance, so far as educational stimulation is concerned in this period, and certainly for some infants and toddlers these years are empty. All children, and especially precocious ones, need and profit from loving encouragement of development in very early childhood.

Then 3- and 4-year-olds are in what is called the nursery school period. A small minority do attend nursery schools, but the home and the day care center remain the principal locales for whatever education is received. Nursery schools, where they exist, tend to be private, supported by fees and tuition paid by parents. The next big step in free public education in this country may well be in the direction of the nursery school, for its social and educational values are recognized increasingly.

The next period spans kindergarten and the first three grades. Even though kindergarten is an integral element of the public schools in many states, it is not always as well known for its encouragement of gifted and talented pupils as it should be.

For every child, exceptional or not, this three-phase period is potentially explosive in terms of acquisition of skills, information, and attitudes. The main task of educators and parents is to unleash that potential. Furthermore, the younger the child, the more rapid the rate of cognitive development.

Approximately 50 percent of raw intellectual power develops by about age 4. And, as we have said, it generally grows unattended in any formal sense.

The sensorimotor period is preparation for the foundations of language and socialization. The nursery school period, itself, is a form of preparation for initial school learnings for which the child has two years. And the K-3 grades, themselves, are rather a "crash" course in the basic skills upon which much of the subsequent instruction and personal inquiry are founded. A striking fact is that children have relatively little time to prepare for their school careers.

These early years, so profoundly important for all children, carry a special meaning for those who are gifted and talented. They are the years in which originality is best awakened and rewarded. They are the years in which human symbol systems are best learned. And they are the years during which the foundations of sound mental health are best laid—the mental health qualities that will allow exceptional individuals to live comfortably with the inevitable loneliness to which their extraordinary cognitive, affective, and motoric exploits lead. Systematic educational intervention in the early years, then, is imperative if a truly appropriate education is to be provided gifted and talented pupils in any nation.

The educational growth of these children in early childhood consists of psychomotor, cognitive, and moral development. It can move at a swift rate. Wyne and O'Connor (1977) summarized what has been written regarding the status of gifted and talented children in terms of Piagetian understandings and concluded:

> Gifted children appear to skip some sub-stages in the cognitive development sequence ... Gifted development is characterized by a broader and deeper conceptual grasp at each stage of cognitive development ... The gifted child will develop, at a younger age, the ability to deal with issues in the affective domain, especially moral ethical matters and sensitivity to the feelings of others. (pp. 206-208).

YOURTOWNE'S RESPONSES

Yourtowne's special education for gifted and talented children starts formally in kindergarten but it actually begins much earlier. Volunteer activities, planned and conducted mainly by high school basic scholars and their teachers, reach into homes and day care centers to touch and guide infants, toddlers, and nursery age youngsters and their parents.

Four purposes motivate the volunteers. The initial objective is to stimulate and maintain optimum conditions of educational development for all preschoolers of the Yourtowne community—gifted, talented, handicapped, and all others. The second is to locate exceptional children as early as possible in order to assess their individual learning characteristics. Third, it is part of the informal design for preschoolers that individualized parent-child educational plans be made and implemented whenever the parents wish in the years before formal schooling starts. The fourth objective is to gather the information necessary for Yourtowne's elementary schools to be ready for the gifted and talented preschool children when they arrive for the first day of kindergarten or first grade.

It should be noted that the last objective amplifies the older idea that children should show readiness for school. Certainly they should. They ought to have learned to leave their parents, for example, without undue stress, and to spend the day away from home with teachers and peers. But readiness should not be entirely one-sided, according to Yourtowne's philosophy. Kindergarten, first grade, and other grades should be flexible, able to match the aptitudes of children who are markedly advanced, children who need prolonged help, and children who have other special needs.

Yourtowne's attention to preschool gifted children is coordinated by three members of the high school staff—a librarian, a home economics teacher, and the social studies teacher who is responsible for the elective high school course in psychology. These three jointly guide a number of activities, most of which are carried out by a high school student service club. The cadre of the club is basic scholars, but any high school student is welcome to join and work in one or more of the club's activities.

Several years ago club members wrote and published an attractive booklet called *Bringing Out Your Baby's Gifts and Talents.* The booklet is presented by the club to the parents of each newborn in Yourtowne. A student committee checks newspapers, hospital records, and courthouse records, compiling weekly lists of births. Booklets are sent or delivered to parents within about two weeks of each birth announcement. The publication, which is revised and updated periodically, contains information about:

- constructive, stimulating parenting practices

- singing, talking, and listening activities that build a base for language

- the advantages of learning to speak two languages while very young

- a motor development curriculum for infants that covers the first 18 months

- acquainting the infant with music and rhythm

- building concepts of quantity, including numbers
- similarities and differences in colors, shapes, forms, and textures
- engaging in pretending and other styles of play
- the availability of the toy lending library
- early school admission policies and practices
- telephone numbers parents may call for information on the early education of gifted children

Another committee of the student service club is responsible for a column in the Yourtowne paper under the title: "Brightening Your Baby's Future." The column's theme is that education really starts at birth, and the quality of very early childhood experiences makes a lasting impression. The column addresses all children—typical, handicapped, and gifted and talented. The emphasis is on practical things parents and older siblings can do to foster imagination, reasoning, coordination, language development, and a wide range of interests for each child, while encouraging every evidence of independent development. Many of the columns are written cooperatively by students, with helpful monitoring from the high school English teacher who also is faculty sponsor of the student newspaper. The assistant editor of the Yourtowne paper, Selma Jenkins, also has taken an interest in the student-prepared column that runs regularly in her publication. She responded warmly to the opportunity to take a mentor role with several of the students when it was suggested by the coordinator of the Basic Scholars Program.

The initial uncertainty and bewilderment of several parents of highly gifted toddlers in Yourtowne was allayed when they talked with experienced teachers, other parents of exceptional children, and older such students themselves. Speaking in full sentences by 1 year of age, learning to recognize printed words and numbers by age 2, reading, drawing, picking out tunes on the piano by age 3 to 4—to say nothing of asking penetrating questions—these and similar behaviors can alarm as much as please parents. The student service club keeps a roster of parents of highly able children who are willing to share experience with others who are not yet sure of themselves in caring for their precocious infant or toddler. Such contacts often ripen into close family friendships. Thus, application of the mentoring principle can have enriching fringe benefits.

CURRICULUM ADAPTATIONS

Preschool

To citizens in general and even to some educators it may be startling and even awkward to speak of curriculum for the very young child. It would seem more natural to speak of curriculum for the primary grades or perhaps the nursery period. By curriculum we mean what is deliberately taught, under professional supervision, and with societal and individual parental approval.

Jordan (1973) summarized research that confirms the efficacy of deliberate instruction of infants. B.L. White (1975) extended Jordan's review, emphasizing respect for the great importance of learning in the first three years of life.

Robinson, Robinson, Darling, and Holm (1979) specify the roles of educators and of parents of gifted and talented preschoolers, declaring that they must harmonize their knowledge of the child and of developmental benchmarks with their knowledge of helpful interventions, thus reaching agreement on what should make up the very early childhood curriculum. For each child, individualization should be the rule.

Individualization does not necessarily call for one-on-one teaching, though. Frequently several children need and are ready for the same activity at the same time. Then one adult or older sibling can work with the group, achieving individualization for each. Deliberately teaching language, motor skills, and social development provide opportunities to engage very young children together. Chronological norms should be understood. They give limited guidance, though, since the gifted child's pace ought to exceed normal expectations.

One of the least complicated ways to estimate how much ahead of normal cognitive development talented preschoolers might range works this way. First, obtain the child's intelligence quotient from the Binet, Wechsler, or equivalent individual test administered by a qualified school psychologist. Then multiply the child's actual current age in months (for $2\frac{1}{2}$-year-old, 30 months) by the IQ converted to a decimal fraction (IQ 140=1.4, for instance). The result is 42 months, or $3\frac{1}{2}$ years. Thus it can be predicted that it is natural and appropriate for a $2\frac{1}{2}$-year-old of IQ 140 to have acquired cognitive development resembling that of an average child of $3\frac{1}{2}$ years. Used by professional persons who exercise reasonable caution, this approach to prediction of potential can be of help in setting individual pupil goals. The formula has a number of variations and limitations. Like other attempts to reduce human characteristics to formulas, it has a margin for error. It should be thought of as one way to help in planning and as subject to correction if more direct information about the child's behavior contradicts the prediction by exceeding it.

The Role of Early Childhood Curricula

Educators need to familiarize themselves with the scope and sequence of early childhood curricula so as to be alert to what to present next when very young gifted and talented children show readiness for more complex tasks. Scott (1975) recommends focus on four curricular areas: language (understanding/receptive and oral expression), memory (visual and auditory), visual motor (large and small muscle as well as eye-hand coordination), and concepts. This last category covers concepts of color, size, number, classification by similarities and differences, and positions in space such as near, far, beside, up, and down. Jordan (1973) reminds educators and families that preschool objectives ought to recognize that: (1) it is not uncommon for 3- and 4-year-olds to be closer to actual reading than is supposed; (2) gifted children often are distinguished by high attainments in language very early in life; (3) the pattern of full-time motherhood is changing due to economic circumstances, necessitating supervised day care; and (4) there are benefits to society as well as to the family for the availability of organized preschooling programming at home and in day care settings.

Jordan also points to the numerous options for precocious children in the age span 2 through 4. In some communities, it is literally necessary to enroll one's infant at birth to have a space in a nursery or kindergarten when the child will be 3 or 4. In other areas, early schooling is freely available.

Philosophies about the education of young children vary, too. The most common "task" focuses on the child's readiness for school tasks. Within the same philosophy, both emphasis and methods vary. Some specialists believe in high structure with strong focus on academic and conceptual factors. Other specialists favor socialization—learning to share the attention of an adult, to leave the home, to generalize learnings to the home, and to be accepted within a group. There is no overwhelming evidence to "prove" any particular approach better than another. The evidence does suggest that preschool experience is most helpful when matched to the child's needs and when there is follow-through to take advantage of the child's assets.

B.L. White (1975) recognizes that both parents and educators now are justifiably wary of "educational" toys. The most significant consideration for toys is safety. Beyond that, toys should be open ended to allow varied uses. That is to say, the central element in enhancing child development is how toys and related materials are used, rather than their color, shape, or other intrinsic characteristics.

Curriculum Content and Quality

The actual content of the curriculum for very able young children ties closely to the *quality* of the relationship between the child and the adult figure. That is plain in the writing of Briggs (1970). Her thesis for parents is that motivation, intellectual growth, and creativity intertwine. Self-esteem is a key variable. Everyday situations provide opportunities for adult and child to establish the quality of most relationships. For example, a child's wagon may become stuck on a rock. The parent resists the temptation to lift the wagon off. The child persists in tugging it forward. The parent mildly informs the child that the wagon is stuck and inquires if there isn't another way. The youngster "hunkers" down, inspects the situation, and dashes off to fetch a shovel. The rock is dug out. The parent is surprised and enchanted, having thought that pushing the wagon backward would have been "easier."

Another example: a mother is preparing a salad that contains spinach and oranges. Her son watches her peel the skins and discard the seeds. He wonders why oranges and spinach would be good. The mother resists the acid remark that she would delight in serving bad-tasting food. She recognizes the intelligence that lies behind the questions. The combination is new to the child. His most frequent earlier association with orange is orange juice. She allows him to examine the skin and seeds to comprehend why they aren't eaten. The result is a connection between seeds and trees and oranges. Some important conceptual building blocks are in place.

In both examples parents shared a learning experience and supported the child's curiosity. Both parents, according to Briggs, also utilized the principles of enriched language environments to facilitate cognitive progress. Children, within the limits of physical safety, very much need that kind of freedom to explore and interact.

The examples adapted from Briggs typify the behavior of preschool educators. To a casual observer, preschool may seem "merely" play until recognition dawns that play is the work of young children in exploration and manipulation. The educator chooses content for the curriculum—content that leads the child to label experiences, to facilitate problem solving, to create opportunities for learning, and to encourage social opportunities. The juice and cookies are more than refreshments; they serve to bring pupils together for sharing. Story time serves similar purposes. The educators may have pictures on the wall that relate to the story. There may be frequent interruptions by the teacher to "check" comprehension, to allow children to dramatize, to anticipate coming events.

Physical education and physical fitness should have a valued place in the preschool curriculum for the gifted and talented child. Eason, Smith, and Fagot-Steen (1979) organized information about physical activities for preschool gifted children in a report that serves as a positive example and supplies helpful guidance. Its overall theme is that activities should match what an assessment shows are needs of the individual child. They stress these motor skills: (1) balance, (2) agility, (3) coordination, (4) speed, and (5) sport skills of catching and throwing. The physical fitness component includes (1) strength, (2) endurance, and (3) flexibility. The perceptual motor component covers (1) kinesthetic, (2) visual, (3) auditory, and (4) tactile. Their program is rooted in developmental theory as the basis for assessment and selection of activities. The completeness of the report is an attractive feature.

Eason et al. also report on the conflict between an old stereotype and a new stereotype. Terman's studies wiped out the old stereotype of gifted and talented pupils as weak, undersized, and puny. The difficulty is that a new group stereotype now pictures the exceptional person as above average in almost all physical attributes. This new group stereotype can result in neglect of physical activities, according to Eason et al. They observed that one effect had been neglect of gifted children with awkward and unsynchronized movement skills and children with sensorimotor and associated verbal learning difficulties. In the course of five years they counted 500 children who met the criteria of gifted and talented and who evidenced neglect of either coordination or perceptual motor skills.

Eason et al. recommend several instructional considerations. First, take advantage of the child's conceptual strengths. Encourage the child to confront difficulties and use insights to master them. There may be a high initial reluctance by the child, so the educator will need to alert the individual to his/her steady rate of challenge. Second is the factor of challenge. Charting enables each child to view its progress and sets the stage for self-competition. Third, a child often will display a plateau, that is, stay at one level of competence until an insight will seem to "suddenly" remove the obstacle. The teacher's role is flexibility, a readiness to change task level and teaching procedure at almost a moment's notice, as the child's needs change.

The Primary Grades

Jordan (1973) sees the curriculum of the primary grades as possessing the theme of opportunity for the child. It is opportunity for access to learning and opportunity to demonstrate mastery. This theme should be especially evident for highly able pupils upon entering kindergarten or first grade.

Subsequent chapters will present the idea that most curricular content for exceptional pupils should be referenced to the standard curriculum and adapted to the individual child's rate and style of learning. The regular teacher, as curriculum implementer, should have sufficient authority and responsibility to maintain a favored position for educational management.

Birch and McWilliams (1955) list several ways in which teachers can be effective in the application of professional knowledge about curriculum with the focus on specific pupils. These ways could be separated into general and particular.

The first general consideration involves help and guidance in making rapid progress without being held back unduly to a typical pace. Teachers need to anticipate that less time will be required by gifted and talented pupils for basic skills acquisition and that there is little danger of pressing students for achievement beyond their capabilities. Children are resilient and are quick to show if they are being pushed excessively. On the other hand, gifted pupils also are quick to learn to just get by if they sense the teacher doesn't want them to work up to their capabilities. Teachers, pupils, and parents all are most satisfied when each pupil feels that there is encouragement from all quarters to move ahead in skills and to broaden content and concept learning at the child's own pace, rather than being held to the average rate of progress of the class. There is, of course, considerable heterogeneity among talented children in primary grades. (To be sure, all ages are heterogeneous. However, the younger the person, the more immediately apparent is the effect, for older individuals often have learned to adapt, to become one of the crowd.) Consequently, general approaches will need continuing modification. Individuality is precious; it should be fostered.

The second general task is to take full advantage of the child's early mastery of skills. A number of gifted children, for instance, enter kindergarten knowing how to read, and that number is increasing. Consequently, a heightened curriculum pace can be initiated for reading early in the school experience. The same is true for mathematics for a number of these children. In turn, this means that identification already is well along and individualized planning should begin early. These factors help teachers to project reasonable expectations about achievement goals and objectives for pupils who are mature beyond their years. Early advancement in reading, arithmetic—or both—unlocks the doors to broader and more independent study in the arts, sciences, and humanities at a young age, too.

One specific tactic that should be available in every school district is early admission to kindergarten and first grade. Every preschool gifted and talented youngster ought to receive thoughtful consideration for early admission. Indicators of high priority for early admission are: (1) two years advanced mentally, (2) interested in and motivated for school, and (3) able to leave the home for a full day without trauma.

Early admission can have a wide range of benefits to the child. This should be a home and school decision. The district should have contact mechanism to receive recommendations from preschool education providers as well as from parents. Moreover, all teachers should be alerted as to their roles in referral.

A second specific tactic is use of the parent consultant. Though writing for parents, Mantz (1979) provides teachers with insights into parent concerns and needs for consultation. Her discussion suggested the following questions:

1. Is my child gifted?
2. Why are there programs for gifted children?
3. Who decides if a child is gifted?
4. What are schools for the gifted and what can they do?
5. How can I nurture giftedness?
6. How can I work with the schools and teachers?

EDUCATIONAL PRIORITIES

Key Features

Robinson, Roedell, and Jackson (1979) highlighted two key features about preschool programming for gifted and talented children. These features emerge as "universals" regardless of one's philosophy about preschool education. One is the principle of variance and the other is the principle of individualization.

Variance between children is obvious. There is no typical gifted preschool child. Exceptional children are a mixed lot, at least as heterogeneous as any other group that has one or two common qualities. Use of a "giftedness syndrome" falsely forces widely different persons into a group mold.

A correlate is that each talented child reflects much personal variance. Robinson et al. cited the example of a 3-year-old child who had the attention of a 5-year-old, the reading proficiency of a 10-year-old, and the small motor skills of a 3-year-old. This child is "typical" only in the sense of the range of intraindividual variance.

If the principle of variance is accepted, then the principle of individualization follows as a reasonable implication. Robinson et al. refer to educational individualization as attaining the proper match between child and task as described in Chapter 1. They cite the example of a 3-year-old to illustrate their beliefs about matching. They acknowledge that the youngster could be treated appropriately neither simply as a fifth grader nor solely as a preschooler. Instead of such simplistic extremes, they advocate selection of content relevant to the child's strengths and to adapt materials at the individual's level of attention and motor skills. The adaptation is made at child's level, not at what is considered average for 3-year-olds. Robinson et al. are most force-ful in their advocacy of direction of efforts toward sources of strength and adapting to other areas. They observe that, in their experience, language and conceptual skill usually move ahead at a faster pace than does small muscle motor development. They avoid the teach-to-strengths vs. teach-to-weakness dispute. Their advocacy is for all pertinent areas to be considered and matched.

We recommend along with these writers that besides "intellectual" empha-sis, preschool programs ought to stress group discussions, social activities, and motor development. Group discussions enable children to test out ideas and share in such conversations, a forum not ordinarily available in the home. Social activities are designed to facilitate the give-and-take in sharing and respecting the needs of others. Motor activities emphasize small motor and eye-hand coordination. These skills are stressed so that very able children, at their individually different paces, can acquire the skills sufficient to approxi-mate the match between their reading competencies and related writing inter-ests and requirements. In this connection, access to typewriters often allows young gifted children to produce legible and well-organized prose before they would be able to do so in their own handwriting. That can minimize the frustration connected with knowing how to do something and being physical-ly incapable of putting that knowledge into action. Teachers who invent ways to close that gap for talented pupils, using such technological aids as type-writers and tape recorders, or other devices such as simulations, are contrib-uting to both the substantive education and the mental health of these chil-dren.

Appropriate early education of precocious children is consistent with the doctrines of early education in general. That is to say, early education is the education of both parents and children. Teachers at this level have to be competent as educators of both the young and the parents.

Robinson et al. (1979) identify priorities for programming for early child-hood education based upon their analysis of the literature and their experi-ence in the operation of a university-based intervention program for gifted and talented preschool children. Both of these identified sources confirm that early childhood programs are undertaken to serve children *and* their parents. Robinson et al. identify the following as helpful for parents:

1. creating a sense of urgency and support for early intervention programs
2. devising an effective and efficient system of identification
3. establishing helping relationships with parents to provide practical guid-ance in parenting skills that are particularly important for families with gifted and talented youngsters

4. designing and delivering educational services aimed at the optimal match between learner capacity and curriculum expectations

In turn, according to Robinson et al., these general priorities have three subset priorities: identification, parent relationships, and educational programming. All planning and implementation must prize the heterogeneity of the very able children identified at this period of life. This recognition is the essential common thread that intertwines all through these priorities.

Emphasis

If one were to hoist banners to display the points of emphasis necessary for excellent early childhood education for gifted and talented learners, a series of essays collected by B. Johnson (1977) would generate provocative ideas. The banners might proclaim:

- The Early Years—Don't Waste Them
- The Next Steps
- Anticipations and Expectations
- Myths and Sooths

To bolster the position that the early years are very important for talented children as well as all others, Abrahams (1977) cites data to show that 50 percent of development is completed by age 4, with an additional 30 percent by age 8, and the remaining 20 percent by ages 17 to 18. He counters the reservations of those who oppose preschool education because they believe it deprives children of family-based warmth and security. He observes that children can profit from enriched environments provided by both a school-based educational program and stimulation in the home. Preschool education expands, extends, and adds to the child's fund of experiences. Abrahams refers to 227 published sources that, taken together, inspire an emphatic "yes" that preschool programs provide positive results.

A central force in any helpful preschool program is the staff of competent paraprofessionals and professionals who (1) understand the needs and development of the young learner (2) work closely with the parents, and (3) prepare a suitable stimulating environment. Helping parents means to encourage them to listen, to talk, and to provide affectionate, consistent support for the child. These are some of the first steps a parent can take. Another step for the parent is to ascertain that the preschool environment is of truly high quality.

One characteristic of a sound preschool environment is that it be free of myths about gifted preschoolers. H.B. Robinson (1977) identified three myths (syndrome, difference, and education) that can impair otherwise helpful programs. It is not sufficient merely to avoid these myths; there must be philosophical alternatives as well.

The myth of the "giftedness syndrome," says H.B. Robinson, is a stereotype that frightens a number of parents and otherwise competent teachers. The "early ripe—early rot" misconception may still persist, though Terman's contributions exploded that false image of gifted persons long ago.

Terman's work, on the other hand, has been misinterpreted to create a new mythology about IQ. H.B. Robinson did not assail IQ testing per se, but did attack its uses. He observed that the IQ is used as a global passport to opportunity to a greater extent than it merits. He notes that even widely used multiple batteries too often simply parallel the general factor of IQ. His plea is to acknowledge the IQ's real values and also to recognize the many additional ways that talents, or even a single talent, can be manifest. His view parallels that of J.C. Stanley (1979). Stanley deplores the practice of admitting students to special programs of mathematics based on an IQ criterion even along with evidence of superior mathematical performance. It is as though the IQ alone were the sole and sufficient rite of passage into individualized instruction. Actually, superior academic performance is what the IQ is expected to predict, and if the superior performance is, itself, already directly observable, what is the need to predict it?

The second myth holds that gifted and talented children are so quantitatively and qualitatively different from the rest that they require an almost completely different curriculum from that for other children. H.B. Robinson (1977) reminds adults that precocity is essentially an accelerated rate of normal development, not development *different* from that of the rest of humanity.

True, gifted and talented children and youth ought to acquire extraordinary depth and range of knowledge. They also ought to attain extremely complex conceptual heights. Moreover, they should do so both earlier in life than do other pupils and to a more remarkable degree. Those expected achievements, though, are not so much substantively different from what others reach as they are extensions, extrapolations, and advanced syntheses. Thus, it may be useful to speak of curriculum for gifted and talented students as differential (Ward, 1962) in the sense that they need opportunities to deal with the same domains of knowledge as do others, but with more deliberate emphasis on higher mental processes (i.e., analysis and reintegration) and in more involved combinations. But that does not mean different in the sense of a different kind of content. Exceptional pupils' needs certainly are well served by the study of literature, economics, biology, languages, mathematics, music, history, and the other components of curriculum ordinarily associated with formal schooling, when the content is adapted to their abilities.

Another common error in observations of gifted children is failure to realize that what is labeled "different" is behavior normally associated with an older child being displayed by a younger one. An 8-year-old using formal operations appears "different;" in reality, the behavior is appropriate but early. The child has made the transition sooner; that is the essential point. For example, for a 2-year-old to learn multiplication and division and toilet training is remarkable by age rather than by behavior. The implication is not to dismiss early achievement; the implication is for preschool educators to respond to it with competence.

That educational facilities for gifted and talented children are essentially absent in today's schools is another myth that requires correction, according to H.B. Robinson (1977). His experiences in delivering educational services to gifted preschoolers complements the Search for Mathematically Precocious Youth project. What is going on as a normal part of the curriculum in one part of the school (physics laboratory experiments or the production of a play in the high school) may be just what is needed by a gifted or talented pupil who is locked, by age and tradition, into the elementary or middle school segment of the school system's structure.

> The problem is matching existing needs (of students) to existing programs and getting around the ordinary rules of eligibility ... What we seem to need are good educational brokers—who understand the needs of individual children, and know how to gain access to the programs. (p. 10).

These experiences also reflect the weaknesses and limitations of separating gifted children into isolated units.

The experiences of Berkovitz (1977) complement Robinson's insights about what constitutes a suitable educational environment for gifted and talented preschoolers. Berkovitz provides the perspective of a psychiatrist with a decade of experience in active consultation with public schools. He urges teachers and parents not to be misled by "narrow" displays of talent that might obscure attention to the complete development of the child. Verbal fluency, for example, is so highly prized and rewarded that adults may reason that the child can talk; ergo, early language means early success. Adult-like conversations become exercises in charm. The quality and the content of thought are ignored. Information gaps increase and may even be ignored deliberately on the ground that basics are boring. The child learns that approbation can be gained with minimal effort by the exercise of verbal fluency.

And so expectations are raised until some ultimate confrontation with reality that leaves parents defeated, teachers frustrated, and the child anxious.

The alternative is attention to the child as a complex person. It means that curriculum must be rich in varied opportunities. Emphasis upon verbalization must be balanced and early experience in sustained effort to master basics should be encouraged.

PARENT EDUCATION

The Components

Robinson, Roedell, and Jackson (1979), based upon their experiences in the operation of a university-affiliated program for young gifted children, observed that successful programs are directed toward parents as much as toward the children themselves. The programs allow parents a forum for discussions about their concerns. Robinson et al. note that mothers and fathers generally reflect mixed reactions about their roles as parents of a gifted child. For example, they are proud of their child's abilities. They also are concerned about their abilities to provide challenge and stimulation. Sometimes they are uncomfortable about unwelcomed public attention, as when their 3-year-old reads the menu in a restaurant and draws remarks from the patrons and employees. Some parents are accused by friends and relatives as being "pushy," which creates unnecessary guilt. Many reflect dread about the capacity of the public school to receive their child.

The response of good preschools to these parental mixed feelings takes several directions. First, parents need reassurance and confirmation of their child's abilities. They need to understand that their child's unusual learning ability is a natural occurrence for some children. Second, parents of younger children can be put into contact with more experienced parents who can provide sound guidance. It appears that the stereotype that most affects parents is the totally false notion that genius is closely and causally linked to insanity. Third, documentation of abilities can inspire parents to plan for the future and future services. Fourth, individualization of instruction provides parents with ideas for use in the home.

Addressing Parent Concerns

Given that very early identification and nurture of able children has a high priority, Kaufmann (1976) reminds educators that parents require nurture as well. However, it is very evident that little in anyone's formal education prepares them for parenting and for understanding giftedness and talent.

Kaufmann's concepts have merit. They could be the basis of organizing the content of inservice for educators and for parent forums. The format could include: (1) knowing a gifted child, (2) the home as a learning center, (3) conditions of nurture, and (4) parent power.

Knowing a gifted child would emphasize the parent as observer. Functional signs of accelerated development could be reviewed. These include advanced behavior with respect to: (1) vocabulary, (2) memory, (3) attention span, (4) probing questions, (5) independent action and initiative, (6) judgment, (7) general information, and (8) comprehension. No one attribute has higher status; it is the general pattern and rapidity of learning that provides the clues.

Recognition of gifted and talented behavior is only the first step; follow-through is next. Parents ought to be encouraged to *act.* Kaufmann recommends that they be encouraged to maintain records of their child. She found that schools usually requested that parents supply data related to gifted and talented child identification. Parents should be helped to anticipate this need for documentation so they are not placed in awkward positions about recollections long after the fact.

The Parent-Teacher Association in Yourtowne for a number of years has sponsored a "Baby Book" project as part of its community service work. Birth announcements alert committee members and trigger a series of events. First, a committee member contacts the new parents to offer congratulations. Then a baby book is delivered or sent as a gift. It is explained that the PTA encourages parents to keep developmental records because it is fun and because accurate records can have both medical and educational value in the preschool years and at the time of school entry. The baby book is thorough and is attractively and sturdily bound. Several pages list the businesses, industries, associations, and individuals whose sponsorship make the gift possible.

Parents may feel reluctant to insist upon what they consider special attention. That reticence may cause them to ignore their child's advanced behaviors. Parents may find themselves under heavy and unexpected cultural pressures for equality, or pressures to refrain from anything that might be taken for a boast. Such mothers and fathers need emotional support to risk these pressures. Yourtowne's very early childhood intervention strategies, mentioned above and earlier, are designed to help parents to be constructively assertive on behalf of their children.

The home as learning center refers mainly to relationships. The good home as a learning center provides safety (physical and psychological) and well-mentored opportunities for relating to people. While toys, books, and the like are helpful, as are tactics of stimulation, the quality of parent-child and child-child relationships is the focus. Materials and tactics are means of encouraging questioning, exploration, and speculation. The best relationship, like the best educational toy, is one that is open ended and has multiple possibilities for use. This encourages the flexibility, fluency, originality, and elaboration so highly prized as components of creativity.

Special conditions of nurture further extend the theme of relationships. These conditions assume high urgency as the parent considers enrollment of the precocious child in day care, in preschool, or in kindergarten. The parent is a major source of self-esteem for the child and as a teacher of values. Here the values may range across religions (i.e., Amish, Muslim), ethnicity (i.e., Germanic, Latin), race (i.e., Indian, black), and many other dimensions of human difference that can be reflected in life style preferences. These are very significant roles, especially if the values of the home conflict even in the least degree with the values of the educational agency. The school has the responsibility to adapt to legitimate value differences and to teach and model respect for such divergence.

Conflict also can arise as the child receives feedback from the outside world regarding its abilities. In turn, learning difficulties and lack of achievement may emerge as tasks for remediation for the family to negotiate with the school.

Parent power encourages parents to forge alliances among themselves and with others. The central mission is to organize and mobilize community (including the school's) resources. Kaufmann (1976) listed examples of effectiveness in state associations. The examples had a common theme: informing parents of sound educational policy as the basis of presenting well-organized, articulate special education plans to policymakers for adoption. She also credited parents as valuable sources of consultation for other parents and for educators. Kaufmann found these to be the kinds of questions parents raised frequently:

1. What and how did you tell your child about being gifted?
2. How have you handled situations in which you felt your child's grades were not a reflection of its abilities?
3. How have you provided for your child's many interests and what have you done when you couldn't provide for these interests?
4. How have you handled an unsympathetic teacher?
5. How has the presence of an acknowledged gifted and talented child affected other children in the family and how do you enhance such a child's abilities in the home?
6. What advice would you have for other parents?

When such questions are discussed among parents, many varied and helpful responses surface. The successful experiences of parents of gifted pupils furnish an excellent content base for guidance through consultation.

Enriching Parent/Child Interactions

The SCAMPER model (Eberle, 1971) enables parents to transform ordinary, everyday objects or events into opportunities for wonder and speculation. Kaufmann commends it, too. An illustration is the shoebox. Examples could include:

1. Substituting—if you needed a shoebox, what else could you use?
2. Combining—what could you make with two shoeboxes and six toothpicks?
3. Adapting—how would you change a shoebox for a spider?
4. Modifying (larger/smaller)—what would Paul Bunyan use for a shoebox?
5. Putting to other uses—how else could shoeboxes be used?
6. Eliminating—what would happen if shoeboxes had no lids?
7. Revising/rearranging—what would happen to shoes if feet were round?

An attractive feature of SCAMPER is its open-ended nature. No parent or educator should feel compulsion to complete every item. The intent is to create an invitation to conversation. It provides the teacher or consultant with a tactic of more structure than do the general guidelines provided by Briggs (1970) that were described earlier. This structure may prove more helpful for the parent who feels an initial uncertainty about how to start.

Simulation

It is relatively less difficult to simulate many aspects of the human condition than it is to devise actual experiences to generate empathy toward highly able learners. We have found two simulation activities particularly helpful for parents and teachers. The group and the context may alter the outcomes, of course.

One activity is a variation on a party game. The learner announces: "I'm going to take a trip to the moon. If you bring the right thing, you can come." Participants, one by one, volunteer items. The following items may emerge: space suit, fuel, books, pencil, power pack, food, soup, and a flag. The "correct" responses of food and books are rewarded. In the next round, responses of spoon, hook, brook, goose, helmet, radio, pad, and ray gun are offered. The first four are rewarded as correct. By the fourth round, all items volunteered are double o words.

Perceptions vary. Some persons will center upon the social consequences of being "right" in the game and upon the reactions of the group. Some are very pleased to have achieved by deduction the common element from relevant examples. Some are attracted by the necessity of working out the varieties of double o words. All enjoy telling how they "caught on" to what would be accepted.

A second simulation activity involves an index card with the following information:

Which one is different?

(1) dog (2) cat (3) horse (4) car

Which one is different?

(1) 36 (2) 144 (3) 27 (4) 24

The leader asks the group to volunteer answers, one item at a time. Typically, there will be differences of opinion; for each difference there will be a reasonable logic. For example, in item one, horse may stand out as a five-letter word, or car as the only inanimate object. In item two, 144 as "a three-digit number" may stand out, or 27 as an uneven number, although someone will observe that 27 is the only one that cannot be divided evenly by 12.

Subsequent discussions usually will focus on the variety of perceptions. There usually is recognition that one-answer questioning has its limits. An increased sensitivity toward respecting process surfaces.

SUMMARY

Education for gifted and talented children cannot begin too early. Schools should reach out to parents to help them nurture gifts and talents in their children before formal schooling starts. Once in school, adaptations in the regular curriculum ought to begin immediately, for children are developing at an extremely rapid pace in these early years. The Yourtowne model offers a practical design that can be adapted.

Chapter 3

Later Childhood: The Transitional Years

TIME CAPSULE

This period in chronological age terms starts at about 10 years and goes to about 12, though some would take it to 14. In educational terms, later childhood ranges from fourth grade through sixth, although some districts would include seventh or eighth grade. The theme is transition. The move is from childlike to adultlike feelings, values, reasoning, and logic. Moreover, this also is the period of transformation from the physique of childhood to the adult body.

This can be a stirring time for both parents and teachers. There is an engaging excitement about the child's increasing competence to approximate adult thought and language. One is increasingly impressed by the child's ability to be sensitive to the needs of others. Language becomes a highly significant medium for managing relationships. The breadth and depth of topics grow, challenge, and stimulate.

Another attractive feature of this period is the child's identification with adult models, real or fictitious, live or dead. Not content with mere imitation, the gifted and talented child seeks to understand the values and beliefs of adult models. Consequently, teachers may be judged by different standards. For example, Brophy and Everton (1976) discovered that primary grade pupils react toward their teachers differently from the way upper elementary pupils do.

Primary grade children view their teacher without much critical assessment. Their teacher is nice because the teacher *is* the teacher. Later, elementary pupils apply tighter standards. The teacher has to "prove" competence to the students. Personal attributes of empathy, sensitivity, clarity, and reasonableness become more significant. The teacher's value as a consultant can become an important influence, especially as regards gifted pupils' perspectives on effort, career development, and independent action. The teacher's role, as perceived by the child, changes from authority to adviser.

Another key feature of this period, for learners in general, is the speed of transition. The September crop of fifth graders seems like babies to teachers and by the end of the year appears highly independent. Teachers need to be alert to shifts and to anticipate the child's readiness to take advantage of genuine partnership relationships. Intellectual development, identification with adult values, and accelerated pace of change create the challenge of this period.

For most children, fourth grade is a significant *educational* transition akin to the transition between later childhood and secondary school, between secondary school and college, and between college and graduate school. Over one summer, the school's focus shifts sharply toward applications of content. Homework and deferred assignments became paramount. For the child who has been accustomed to lessons to be completed within the class period, the more elaborate and extended assignments required adaptation (in the Piagetian sense) to one's new world.

Another transitional task for the child is the nature of content organization (Jarvis & Rice, 1972). Later childhood instruction features integrated and correlated content. Social studies, science, language arts, and mathematics, for example, are less likely to be compartmentalized. Children are expected to apply and generalize knowledge consciously and deliberately. The question/answer type of teacher and pupil interactions give way to more and more complex demands simply by the content and structure of textbooks and materials.

These transitions should not be viewed as excessive or inappropriate. Teachers need to recognize that pupils reflect varying degrees of readiness for transition, and teachers ought to vary their pace and structure accordingly.

Programming for later childhood is a time of transition for school districts, too, according to Jarvis and Rice. For a variety of reasons (e.g., economic, psychological, instructional), the organization of grades four through nine is in a continuing state of flux. Typically, the junior high school is organized around grades seven through nine while the middle school is organized around sixth through eighth grades. School districts move back and forth between the two arrangements. Teachers often are uncertain as to their roles, functions, and requisite competencies. Teacher certification for secondary and elementary levels frequently overlaps for grades seven and eight. Public and private education are not altogether firm in their sense of direction for later childhood. One trend suggests that ninth grade should be recognized formally as the beginning of secondary schooling. Another trend is the recognition of sixth grade as a transitional point in the psychological and physical world of the child.

EDUCATIONAL PRIORITIES

Teachers of gifted and talented learners find three clusters of concepts helpful in planning and in instruction. One cluster centers on understanding the general purposes of education for later childhood, the second relates to the special needs of exceptional pupils, and the third deals with understanding the educational implications.

Understanding the Educational Purposes of Later Childhood

Jarvis and Rice identify four purposes of education for later childhood (e.g., up to ninth grade).* One is to provide a bridge linking elementary school to high school. One example is the move from self-contained classes to a "departmentalized" system.† Expectations regarding independent assignments will be evident, as in homework assignment notebooks. Due dates will be extended with less teacher intervention. Sometimes, this preparation for high school becomes too zealous. It should be remembered that removal of structure should be at the child's pace and accomplished in consultation with alert parents.

A second purpose is guidance regarding preadolescence and adolescence. Teachers and consultants can help pupils comprehend their physiological maturity and new responsibilities. This need not be a time of trauma, but rather a time of anticipation.

A third purpose is to create opportunities for exploration and self-appraisal. Jarvis and Rice (1972) recommend career development as an especially helpful option. They advocate instruction to provide time for opportunities for students to sample a rich scope of information and skill opportunities related to careers. Sometimes this period is viewed as the "crash course" for high school. A more helpful view would be to emphasize demands to facilitate competence. However, the child needs the safety and security to test out, to elect, and to sample unfamiliar areas. Spanish, for example, might be viewed better as an opportunity for self-appraisal for aptitude than as a drill for tenth grade.

---

* Be aware that these are process objectives voiced by educators. They are not the same as the child's objectives, or the parents'. For both the latter, objectives tend to be more content oriented and more personal.

† The increase in open space elementary school building configurations and the advances in team teaching of the 1970s is sharply altering the concepts of "self-contained" and "departmentalized" in many school systems.

A fourth purpose is the continuation of general education. It is the hope of Jarvis and Rice that later childhood not be viewed as a "miniature" high school, with its overtones of fierce interscholastic competitions. The central theme should be facilitation of talent and abilities on an individualized basis. Group activities are appropriate to the extent that children are not rushed into standards of unrealistic perfection.

Understanding Educational Needs of the Gifted and Talented

Birch and McWilliams (1955) identify at least three ways in which teachers can be helpful. First, teachers can help able students to apply themselves to difficult and routine tasks. Such pupils may find attention to mechanics and detail annoying because the tasks slow them down. Second, attention should be given to higher order processes and operation in the language arts and mathematics. Superficial flashing through should be discouraged. The third consideration is to maintain touch with reality in the content being taught.

> For example, forego conducting pseudo-learned discussions about the current international crisis in favor of practical and meaningful discussions on how to maintain the local park, or provide equipment for the new playground (Birch & McWilliams, 1955, p. 23).

Their observation should not be interpreted to mean that all discussions about international and national events must be postponed. The key idea is that there is value for immediate outlets for applications.

Understanding the Implications

Teachers can derive and think about two implications. One consideration deals with opportunities for maximizing the transition from stages of intellectual development to readiness and mastery of more complex behaviors. This consideration could be labeled as enabling the child to *learn how to learn* by conscious attention to the tactics of problem finding and solution. This means, also, that the child learns how to learn thoroughly. A second consideration is that both child and teacher take advantage of established and accepted sources for acquiring and refining a personal value system and respect for other and larger value systems.

In the literature on the education of gifted and talented children and youth there is one persisting theme: "programming" and "parenting" for highly able persons. This theme tends to emphasize *time*. It is not uncommon for concerned adults to break out into a rash if an able child is idle. There seems to be a compulsion to organize and structure time in a relentless fashion to fill all voids. The sources that have been cited, however, really stress the need for time for the able student to reflect and speculate. There needs to be time for the quality of relationships described earlier. This need is illuminated by a conversation with Mike, an able pupil of 11, who informed his listener that,

M. "I figured it out! It's a relief!"

L. "I bet you can tell me more."

M. "Well, you lived during World War Two and your parents lived through the Depression, right?"

L. "Yes, that's true."

M. "Well, I thought everything turned out O.K. Right?"

L. "More or less. Mostly, people get through. It took a lot of effort. I wonder why 11-year-olds are thinking about the war and the Depression."

M. "Well, I was watching the TV news and listening to you and Mom talk about inflation and how tough it is to keep up. And I get worried because every year things are more expensive. And I get to wondering how I could afford a house and have enough food."

L. "Things seem to be out of hand for lots of people. And you're wondering if things will work out for you."

M. "That's right, but I figured it out."

L. "And?"

M. "Well, people got through the war and the Depression O.K., and those were bad times. So I guess we'll get through these times."

L. "You really have a sound hunch. I suppose people need to believe that things *can* work out. It means a lot of work, though, to make good things happen."

M. "Well, I understand, but I wondered if it even could happen, and I remembered about those other times."

L. "Yes, you did. I hope when you're worried, you would talk it over with us" (e.g., either parent).

M. "Well, O.K. But it's fun to figure things for yourself."

MAXIMIZING THE TRANSITION

This section is devoted to ways to facilitate transition from concrete operation into formal operation, if one wishes to use the concepts of Piaget. The intent could be rephrased as facilitation of higher order operations.

Instruction for able learners is referenced to content and to skills to which "mental operations" are applicable. Each pupil's performance should be studied to give leads for individualized attention to the underlying processes or concepts in which they may need help. Another purpose of this section is to identify instructional resources for teachers.

Teaching Learners about Learning

Pupils should be taught to understand how human learning, and particularly their own learning, takes place. Teachers also ought to help pupils comprehend their instructional tactics. Whimbey (1977) suggests procedures that enable teachers and pupils to engage in a mutually helpful dialogue about teaching tactics and sees the dialogue as applicable to a wide range of content.

Whimbey advances the following analysis, beginning with a question:

What day follows the day before yesterday if two days from now will be Sunday? (p. 225).

The solution to the problem (e.g., Thursday) does not require abstractions or creative dynamics. The solution is derived from the conscious use of systematic and sequential thought. This use is characterized by breaking a problem into clear, sequential steps. Teachers are familiar with the process. This approach helps students learn to do it for themselves.

According to Whimbey, students can be categorized as one-shot thinkers vs. more methodical thinkers on the basis of their behavior, not necessarily their IQ. For example, consider this problem:

Ten full crates of walnuts weigh 410 pounds while an empty crate weighs 10 pounds. How much do the walnuts, themselves, weigh, 400, 390, 310, 510, or 420 pounds? (p. 255).

The one-shot thinker leaps to 400 pounds. The more systematic or orderly thinker views the weight as made up of two parts—the crates and the walnuts. There are varied ways to do this that do not require elegant mathematics to achieve a reasonable answer of 310 pounds.

The difficulty in teaching thinking is that the usual way to teach a skill is to: (1) have the teacher demonstrate/explain the skill and (2) have the student practice the skill. Needless to say, it is difficult to observe someone "think." Whimbey advocates that both student and teacher think aloud while they work through ideas, as in the following example:

If the word *sentence* contains fewer than nine letters and more than three vowels, circle the first vowel. Otherwise circle the consonant that is farthest to the right in the word. (p. 257).

Teachers report that they encourage pupils to verbalize all their steps. Students can be encouraged also to draw illustrations. Teachers give prompts or cues to remind pupils to read the entire problem and to attend to all information.

In the above example, the student would read the entire problem aloud. The student would discover two conditions: nine letters and three vowels. A first step could be to count the letters to identify that *sentence* has fewer than nine letters. The next step would be to count the vowels, to identify that there are not more than three. So the student decides not to circle the first vowel but to circle the *c.*

Whimbey (1977) observes that these activities can be conducted in small groups. He notes also that these exercises can be adapted from existing comprehension questions found in textbooks and workbooks. He described how an elementary level Spanish class was enlivened by using these tactics applied to problems presented in Spanish, with students answering in that language. Students from economically disadvantaged backgrounds received A and B grades while their counterparts in a more traditional approach, not using these tactics, received Cs and Ds. This suggests the desirability of studying further the application of the Whimbey procedure both for identifying and teaching gifted and talented pupils.

The point to be made is that students seem to profit from the opportunity to experience a systematic process that can be applied to content. Replacement of content by process exercises is not advocated by Whimbey. Rather, if a student becomes bogged down by subject matter, verbalization allows for a fresh and direct intervention into the process underlying reasoning. Because it makes the pupil's thought process public, the tactic enables the teacher to monitor the student in a helpful manner.

Teachers so often are urged to teach "higher order" skills that the above procedure may be perceived as mundane and routine. Renzulli and Callahan (1977), though, recommend informing learners about both learning and attention to the scope of processes. Figure 3-1 displays a view of the overlapping dimensions of the most frequently encountered models in the literature of the education of the gifted and talented, those of Bloom, Guilford, and Piaget. Renzulli and Callahan remind teachers that pupils too often may be rushed into higher order processes prematurely. A more fruitful approach is to help pupils establish a foundation of learning how to approach tasks systematically and methodically and to do so in a fashion that allows them and their teachers to monitor their step-by-step attack on problems.

Figure 3-1 Overlapping Dimensions of Cognitive Processes In School-Age Learners

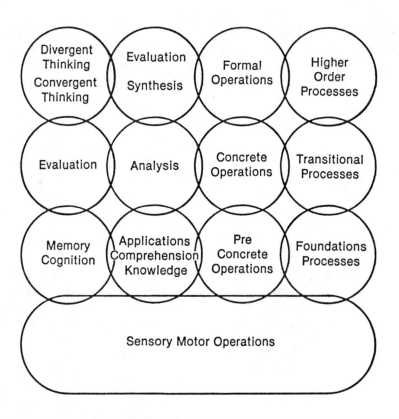

Learning to Manage One's Learning

Fern (1976) observes that gifted and talented pupils not only need instruction in managing their learning but also need to manage the chaos that unbridled curiosity may generate. Helping students develop systematic approaches can be helpful. Bartlett (1978) recommends stimulation through the use of structured activities. He also emphasizes the use of a dialogue to focus pupil attention on explicit behaviors.

The learning how to learn has a dimension of when. Much of the literature is focused upon *prior* and *during*. *After* has its role. A time-dimension-oriented dialogue can be used to encourage self-evaluation.

Self-evaluation of products is another strategy for helping pupils. Wooster (1979) advocates mutual negotiation between teacher and pupil. Her three-step process enables both parties to establish criteria, a rating scale, and use of the rating scale. Step 1 defines the criteria the student will use. These include questions such as: How will you know? What are some of the qualities? How will arguments be carried out? Step 2 helps students develop understandable descriptors for each criterion. Step 3 encompasses the use of the criteria and rating procedures by the student.

Wooster's procedure for self-evaluation also implies a fourth step. The student and the teacher compare their own separate ratings and their reasons for differences of opinion. Students will value the process, according to Wooster, to the extent that they perceive that their opinions are valued. One additional component of the fourth step is to evaluate the helpfulness of the criteria and descriptors. Suggestions for revision then can be identified. Wooster also observes that the process can be applied to group discussion, to oral presentations, and to products. Her process provides an alternative as well as complement to the tactic of self-looping.

Understanding Opportunities for Learning

The SCAMPER procedure described in Chapter 2 and that of Whimbey (1977) are two illustrations, among others cited, of existing opportunities for gifted and talented pupil-teacher helpful interactions. Furths and Wachs (1974) identify similar opportunities for teachers in the context of transition from concrete operations to formal operations. A key feature of their advice to teachers is their interpretation of Piaget regarding thinking. They press the point that intelligence and thinking are both constructive and creative. They entertain grave reservations about the common practice of separating critical and creative thinking. They propose, instead, that human development involves both the construction and creation of ideas, classifications, and other processes.

Under the general term of "logical thinking," Furths and Wachs identify opportunities for teachers to maximize thinking skills. They advocated that these opportunities take place, as the preferred option, within the structure of the standard curriculum. They take special note of classification, ordering, permutations, and probability. Their suggestion is to help children discover "rules" that are generated by their experiences, not parrot the rules laid down by the teacher.

Few activities can be shown to "train the faculties of the mind." It is more reasonable to engage in educational activities that can be demonstrated to serve specific and overtly useful purposes.

First, such activities provide the teacher with functional opportunities for observation of either present skills or of transfer skills. Second, these activities can teach the language of skills such as "prediction" or "similar." Third, they can liberate the child from the "one right answer" mentality to demonstrate flexibility in approach to problem solving. Fourth, these activities can be used to transfer skills to relevant content skills and to relevant out-of-school situations.

Activities, in isolation, may relieve a certain tedium; however, there should be some useful context for their application. We are concerned that some programs for the gifted and talented run the risk of being seduced by "games/puzzles" and function without substance. By contrast, the program that endures recognizes the context of useful purposes and the individualization of instruction as the basis for selection of experiences and activities.

Kennedy and Newman (1976), too, urge caution about the exclusive use of games for program content for gifted and talented learners. They recommend that teachers maintain a content-centered reference.

Helpful Examples

Classification is required by many school tasks. Furths and Wachs (1974) say this skill involves grouping, or sorting, by using a rule or principle. Within large groupings, there can be subclasses. Biology, for example, has its particular system of classification. Phonics is built upon rules organized around certain properties of words. The most basic skill in classification involves recognizing similarities and differences. An attribute of the formal thinker is the use of labels while the concrete thinker attends more to physical attributes. One helpful scheme for teaching sequence could be: (1) single property, (2) class discovery, (3) overlapping attributes, and (4) generation of classes. Examples of these activities are presented in Table 3-1.

Ordering is as common as classification in the life of a learner. Ordering can involve time (e.g., first, second, etc.) as well as attributes of size. A teacher might cut the panels of a comic strip into its component parts. The child's task would be to arrange them into a logical pattern. A chalkboard variation would be for the teacher to print XXOX and invite completion of the sequence. The attractive feature of this activity is that more than one solution is possible, such as (1) XXOXXXOX or (2) XXOXXOXX. Another approach to ordering would involve size. A teacher could use sticks or disks of different sizes. Children would be asked to arrange ten objects in any order. A child would be encouraged to order the objects by their size relationships. A somewhat more difficult task would be to place four or five objects in a series, with the remainder in the appropriate relationships.

Table 3-1 Examples of Classification Activities

Descriptor	Outcome	Example Activities
Single Property	To teach the pupil to respond to the term "different."	Objects which are mutually exclusive (e.g., triangles of same size but 50% red and 50% blue) are presented. Child sorts the red ones and discards the "different" ones.
Class Discovery	To discover that an object can be sorted into more than one obvious attribute. To learn to respond to the term "similar."	Objects which are similar by virtue of two dimensions but differ on one attribute (e.g., 3 triangles, 3 squares, and 3 circles; one blue, one yellow, and one red). Child is encouraged to group however seems appropriate. Child discovers at least two possible methods (e.g., by same shape or same color).
Overlapping Attributes	To discover that an object can belong to two or more classes at the same time.	Objects which have an additional dimension such as size (e.g., small, middle size, and large). Student will discover multiple groupings of size x color x shape which can be recombined. Child is encouraged to continually refine categories.
Generation of Classes	To discover flexibility in dimensions and switching dimensions.	Teacher holds an object/picture (e.g., pen) and encourages the child to describe its use as writing, tapping, to break, to turn, etc. The idea is to practice multiple uses.

Adapted from Furths and Wachs (1974).

Permutations refer to a person's ability to attend to the various ways fixed items can be reversed and recombined. For example, the series 1, 2, 3 can be written as a multiplication expression without changing the product as: 123, 321, or 213 for a total of six possible combinations. The expression 1, 2, 3, 4 can have 24 possible combinations. The difference between the more concretely oriented child and the more logical or formal style child is the systematic way the latter will approach solving the combinations. Another example would be to label four sides of a table red, yellow, blue and white. The teacher then could arrange four children around the table and direct them to discover how many different seating combinations they can make. They would be encouraged to initial each colored sheet to keep track. A variation could be for the teacher to write KNOX on a chalkboard. Children could take turns devising the various combinations to make 24 (e.g., $1 \times 2 \times 3 \times 4 = 24$).

Probability, or prediction, is another common skill. It also is the basis for inference from common events. Probability or prediction calls for judgments of greater or lesser likelihood, possibilities, or odds. The more concrete child is inclined to the view that events are either random luck or that there are fixed possibilities such as yes, no, or maybe. The more logical or formal child is inclined to view circumstances as altering instances and cases.

Activities should expose children to predictions beyond 50/50 chances. For example, a dish contains eight yellow marbles and four blue marbles. One child may be blindfolded and asked to pick a marble. The child would be asked to predict (to teach the language) the color of the marble. Given 12 marbles, the odds would be 8/12, or 2/3, for yellow as against 4/12, or 1/3, for blue. The observer children can comprehend the process. Another variation would be to not replace the marble to observe how the odds change. Colored spinner charts also can be used in which 75 percent of the spaces are black and 25 percent white. Another variation is to have two spinner charts with one 75 percent black/25 percent white and the other 66 percent blue/33 percent red. Before each spin, children are asked to predict the likelihood of the spinner's pointing to certain colors. When two charts with similar colors but of different proportions are used, the complexity of prediction is heightened.

Furths and Wachs (1974) advocate transfer from artificial games to actual situations to help children learn the connection between school and real life. Probability, for example, could be applied to: (1) how many trucks will pass by the window in the next 20 vehicles, the next 20, and so on; (2) which grade should a 9-year-old be in; could there be 7- or 8-year-olds; (3) how many peas in a pod; and (4) in sentences on a random page what are the odds that the first word will be The?

MAXIMIZING THE MODELS

The Nature of the Process

Obvious learning is not confined to cognitive structures, to formal materials, and the like. Every child learns from contact with the environment. In American society, television, for instance, is a significant source of learning for children. An added important source in later childhood is the influence of other personalities. In technical terms, these are sources of social learnings by which the learner forms a values system. The formation of a values system involves the dual process of identification and modeling. In everyday situations, identification and modeling would be synonyms. In technical terms, identification is the process of seeking out model sources, while modeling describes the behavioral consequences of emulating the models.

Unit V is concerned with the issues and strategies of values education. This chapter focuses on two models available to teachers of gifted and talented learners.

Teachers and parents do not lose influence on pupils in later childhood. Rather, children are asserting independence. This assertion is a positive step toward learning to acquire a mentor as well as a first step toward an examination of pertinent issues. Teachers and parents will be more effective if they learn to manage the process rather than resist it.

Inferences about Influence

Schauer (1976) attaches great importance to social learning for gifted and talented pupils during later childhood. Appropriate role models, he believes, are very important for guidance. Moreover, role models serve the child as outlets for expressing curiosity and for exploratory behavior. Modeling can affect gifted learners' selection of reading materials. The major difference between gifted and talented pupils and the nongifted and nontalented that Wolf (1976) found is that the exceptional are more inclined to be influenced by combined adults and peers. The other pupils were more inclined to follow adult leads. Bandura (1971), too, concluded that highly able students are more selective in their sources of influence. They thoughtfully appraised external sources balanced against internal values.

Inferences about identification with another person can be drawn from investigations such as Mauer's (1979). Identification is perception of similarity between oneself and another based on common and valued traits. Her interest was reader identification with a character in a children's story about two boys. In one version neither was disabled and in the other version one boy was disabled. Inferences about identification were based upon responses to the following questions: (1) If you were feeling bad, which boy would know how you feel? (2) If you were feeling frightened, which boy would know how you feel? (3) Which boy is a better friend? and (4) Which boy is most like you?

Bandura directed attention to the process by which an individual seeks to model personal behavior upon that of another. The process starts by observation of a person's behavior to verify that some specific behavior is absent. Then that specific behavior is displayed by another for the person's attention. If the displayed behavior is then copied or approximated, the inference is made that modeling has taken place.

All people, gifted and talented or otherwise, use at least two major processes to acquire the behaviors of a model. Both methods involve observation. The *associational* method involves observation of events that appear to produce a result. The person learns that certain behaviors are rewarded and otherwise encouraged. The person, consequently is inspired to imitate the behaviors of individuals who are associated with encouragement and reward. The *organizational* method can be understood as a higher order cognitive process. The method is characterized by the person's possession of component elements involved in a behavior. The person, through observation, practice, or motivation, learns to transform components into a new and preferred pattern of behavior.

Encouragement and reward are necessary conditions that influence modeling, especially in the person's early stages of imitation. Bandura cited Piagetian constructs to reinforce the importance of encouragement as a supportive condition for adaptation.

Models: Living or Dead?

Positive consequences of modeling in a school situation were described by Elam (1978). His review of how one junior school was transformed met Bandura's (1971) criteria. Elam paid tribute to a principal's leadership and to cooperative efforts of the faculty to maximize student aspirations. The outcomes were of benefit to all pupils, including those who would be considered as culturally disadvantaged gifted (Frasier, 1977).

Lincoln Junior High School was caught in a bind of tension and conflict among its students (Elam, 1978). The senior high school was free of student turmoil since disruptive students tended to drop out before reaching that level. The elementary grades were not so class conscious. At the junior high level, though, resentment, frustration, and elitism surfaced. Teachers were made to feel like law enforcement officials rather than educators. Parents were fearful for the physical safety of their children. Enrollment in the local private school soared as a result. The physical condition of the Lincoln building was deplorable and created the image of a loser. Vandalism and apathy outpaced and defeated restoration.

Within two years, this junior high school changed to an attractive building with an image of pride. New paint is everywhere. Students are engaged in cleaning, decorating, and are otherwise responsible for the change and up-keep. The library now is heavily used and well supplied. Its improved furnishings and decorations were supplied, in part, by students. In fact, the costs of improvement have been largely financed by student fund-raising projects. Parents report that their children are eager for school. Curriculum reflects futuristic courses. Essay contests are possible now. Students also have pulled together to raise funds for a classmate. It does not require a research degree to infer that "something" happened. Also, it is obvious that the "something" captured the attention, retention, motor involvement, and motivation of the participants.

That "something", according to Elam, was an unorthodox approach triggered and led by the building principal. Students were viewed as consumers of education, not activists against it. Schools, therefore, need to be physically attractive, to encourage learning, and to enable students to participate in their own growth. Parent involvement and communication about the school's aspirations is essential for its pupils. The principal appeared committed to "selling" education to students as fully as a fast-food chain is committed to selling its products to students.

The principal's first step was built on the hypothesis that students need positive role models who are living. Historical figures can appear remote and their achievements seem abstract. A living figure can provide a concrete example that can be seen and observed. The principal selected a sports figure to represent his criterion—a concrete example. The athlete chosen was Steve Garvey, star first baseman of the Los Angeles Dodgers. The second step was to assess the students' favorite teams and players. The third step was to contact the team and obtain the player's willingness to lend his name to the school. The fourth step was to obtain school board approval. This was forthcoming despite community reactions that the whole project was a promotional stunt. What followed was a domino effect.

Students were inspired by the name change to Steven Garvey Junior High School and even more inspired by the willingness of Garvey and his wife, Cynthia, to travel to their campus for the dedication ceremony. Project ABC—A Beautiful Campus—was launched. Students worked together for A Beautiful Campus, including raising $1,200 for remodeling. Doors, beams, floorboards were painted Dodger Blue. The Tom Lasorda Library (after the Dodger manager) was refurbished as was the Cyndy Garvey Lounge (she formerly was a school counselor). The students wanted their "new" school to match their pride. The students visited Dodger Stadium. For many, it was their first trip out of their county. They had the feelings of winners, confident in the external changes they had wrought.

The visit by the Garveys, according to Elam, was a capstone for students. Garvey's remarks stressed respect and love for parents, having faith in something larger than self, and finding a person to admire and being a friend to that individual. Elam reflected admiration for Garvey's understanding of adolescents. (Garvey was once an education major.)

Elam recognized that naming a junior high school after a sports figure is unconventional. However, he observed that because of Steve Garvey Junior High School, students are gaining the basic skills by which to understand and know Lincoln, primarily through its transforming the atmosphere of a school into a suitable learning environment appropriate for all pupils. One is struck by the principal's creative concept and by its application. Moreover, one is impressed by Steve Garvey's willingness to lend his name and support as a mentor figure for an entire school.

An additional discussion of relevance in this kind of situation can be found in an article by Frasier (1979) regarding culturally disadvantaged gifted (her term) learners. She cited the need for values education (such as the Simon procedures in Unit V) and the need to organize appropriate role models.

An Adult's Guide to TV

Television is a reality that has its advocates and detractors. Advocates cite the rise in reading readiness scores after Public Broadcasting Service (PBS) programming became available. Other supporters observe that TV enables children to sublimate inner feelings. Still others point to the values of docudrama to inform young people of historical events. In 1978, the production of "Holocaust" enabled persons under age 20 to comprehend this human tragedy in the same manner served by the production "Roots" and "Roots II." Detractors decry the exploitation of commercials, the mindless violence, and the discouragement of conversation among family members. The key idea is that TV can be an opportunity for helpful adult intervention, and parents as well as teachers should understand the basics of managing it appropriately.

An approach to appropriate and effective use of TV viewing by children is advanced by Adler (1978). The key feature of his recommendations is that teachers should share ideas with parents since most TV viewing is done in the home. He proposes that TV viewing be thought of as potential opportunities for parents to: (1) communicate values, (2) help children develop critical thinking skills, and (3) build family relationships.

TV viewing is not confined to Saturday and Sunday mornings and to PBS stations. Together, this accounts for only 13 percent of the average child's viewing time. The average 6- to 11-year-old spends 33 percent of its viewing time between 8 and 11 p.m., Monday through Saturday, and between 7 and 11 p.m. on Sunday (when school is in session). TV viewed by later elementary school age children is actually adult programming.

Adler advised parents to: (1) pay attention to what TV programs children are watching, (2) make sure that children do not misinterpret what they see or hear, and (3) check out what feelings or questions a program has left with a child. Adler identifies organizations that are open to parent affiliation and that seek to improve children's TV. He also identifies four common areas of TV viewing that he believes need parent guidance: (1) fantasy and reality, (2) TV characters, (3) violence, and (4) advertising. These could be pertinent discussion topics for parents of gifted and talented children.

Adler offers several guidelines about fantasy and reality. He starts from the position that children do not have adult standards. Parents need to reinforce the child's impression that: (1) characters are actors, not teachers, law enforcement officers, physicians, etc.; (2) docudramas are not actual truth; (3) science fiction is only a fictional view of the future; and (4) superstrength is a special effect, not real. Parents can help their children by: (1) reviewing the story after viewing to assess understanding, (2) having family members make up different endings, (3) taking the child to see a high school play to comprehend that TV is only a play, and (4) turning off the sound to focus attention upon production and special effects aspects.

Characterization of people on TV can have the positive effects of exposing gifted and talented children to persons and elements of life which would otherwise be unavailable to them. Unfortunately, the portrayals have fit TV schedules. For example, solutions to complex problems must be found within 30- to 60-minute segments. Sometimes portrayals of family life and life styles become stereotyped. Positive portrayals, though, can encourage *communication* and *shared* activities by parents and children. Parents could encourage these two positives through discussions of: (1) what things have we done as a family which would make an interesting TV script, (2) what actors would we get to play our family, (3) do TV families have the same problems as our families, (4) how much is our family like the TV families, and (5) if TV watching is so popular, why don't TV families watch a lot of TV? Families could conduct a stereotype hunt to call attention to sex role, handicappism, etc. A fertile source of stereotyping would be the portrayals of gifted and talented persons.

Violence is a continuing problem. The most serious aspect of violence is that it is often presented as a "just" solution to problems. Aside from physical violence, verbal abuse often is tolerated as comic relief. Parents do have the right to restrict TV viewing. Violence also can be found in the news. Adler advised parents to consider the following discussion points: (1) how do you feel when you see violence, (2) is violence ever justified, and (3) were there any alternatives to the violence in the show we just saw?

Commercials seem inescapable. Adler cited evidence that young children do not distinguish between commercials and programs. Parents can assess this by asking their child to tell them which is which. Children, including highly able ones, also need to understand that commercials are for the sponsor's benefit, not for the child's. Parents can help children understand "tricky" techniques. The most common techniques include use of special effects (e.g., close-ups/lights) to make products appear bigger, faster, more elegant, etc.; using a famous person or TV character to endorse a product; using excitement to sell a product as fun through music, animation, and many very brief shots (many angles). Parents would be well advised to point these out and encourage children to do likewise. Gifted and talented children at all age levels find this kind of detective work stimulating and challenging. They also enjoy being responsible for their self-development of personalized rules for TV viewing.

SUMMARY

The move from the end of childhood to the beginning of adulthood must be paralleled, for gifted and talented pupils, by educational offerings that match and complement the fastpaced personal changes taking place. For most, that means much more independence than teachers and parents ordinarily are ready to allow. Cognitively and affectively the highly able pupil of this age sheds the trappings of childhood and surges forward toward adultlike understandings and value systems so rapidly that the monitoring of the student's self-understanding needs to have a very high priority with professionals and family alike. Adult models take on great significance.

Chapter 4

Adolescence: Promising Prospects

TIME CAPSULE

Adolescence has no universally agreed upon beginning and ending. Its age bounds are approximate, starting in the early teens and running into the early twenties. It is a time of career start-up for many gifted and talented youth. This time span, educationally, normally ranges from eighth grade through the first two years of college, depending upon the school district, but it is more advanced for highly able young people.

Just as many districts now incorporate kindergarten as an integral part of the schools, some districts consider the community college as making up public school's 13th and 14th grades. Enrollment provides low-cost, good quality education, as well as a culturally acceptable holding pen for many youth during an important transitional period. For some students, the transition may be toward transfer to a four-year degree-granting institution. Some community colleges also sponsor one- to two-year specialized, technical preparation for transition to work roles. The community college also can be a resource to school districts for advanced placements for younger gifted and talented students.

The more conventionally recognized period for secondary schooling is ninth through 12th grades. This is a period of prospects and choices. Adolescents are encouraged to keep their options open and flexible, especially with respect to career choices.

A highly significant point for parents and teachers is that gifted and talented children frequently are precocious in all aspects of adolescence, particularly emotional and intellectual. In short, it is normal for many 9-, 10-, or 11-year-old gifted children to be intellectually and emotionally well into adolescence, even though socially and physically they apparently are not. By the same token, many exceptional youngsters of 16 or 17 can be past the latter adolescent stages that still preoccupy their other age peers.

81

There is a mythology about this period that hampers adolescents, teachers, and parents. This mythology conditions the ways in which relationships are conducted. One myth is the rebellion of teenagers that conditions an adversary relationship. The difficulty is that teenagers have been conditioned by the media to believe that they *should* be in rebellion. Otherwise, they could be accused of reflecting behavior unbecoming a teenager. The increasing maturity associated with continuing development of formal operations can be a source of delight to adults. Mentally, the teenager does have the structures and intellect of an adult. What the adolescent may lack is the wisdom of historical perspective. The tactics of consultation (Unit V) can aid in building helpful relationships.

A second myth is that adolescents are all alike. "Teen" after a number does not convey automatic membership in a gang. Unevenness of development persists throughout this period. This fact helps account for adult misperceptions of teenagers as unstable. The physical changes do create a focus on one's body and a certain self-centeredness would be expected. If one were to paint a picture of teenagers as a group, an image of decency and enjoyment would be the most accurate. Interviews with teachers of gifted and talented teenagers generate these impressions. These students themselves also leave these impressions. Their readiness to test the limits of childhood and to seek out the boundaries of responsibility can be a source of satisfaction for adults. Participation in this process offers professional and personal rewards to teachers and to parents. This readiness for adulthood engenders, particularly in the exceptional adolescent, a willingness to press for increasing responsibility. This pressing can be done with style and grace, which also can characterize the response. When opinions differ, disputes (not necessarily armed conflict) will arise. These should be opportunities for negotiations, not power struggles.

A third myth arises from a paradox in the expectations held by adults for gifted and talented teenagers. There seems to be a mixed message. On the one hand, there is the message of the hope of the future and the leaders of tomorrow. On the other hand, there are regulations and limitations, arbitrarily enforced. These mixed messages are created when giftedness is acknowledged in the abstract and when adults really respond only to the person's birthdate. The best corrective step is individualized educational planning and implementation.

Jordan (1973) advises secondary level educators to be aware that adolescence is a period of changing psychological processes. The challenge for parents, principals, and teachers is to be flexible enough to adapt. Positive steps include: (1) encouragement of increased student control and responsibility in school life, (2) assistance to students in realizing the wide range of available roles, (3) instruction in family life and parenting, (4) emphasis upon personal responsibility for public affairs, (5) exposure to Life Cycles Research both for anticipatory guidance and to prevent intergenerational conflict, (6) consideration of values and their influence upon behavior, and (7) use of vocational guidance in subject matter content.

Jordan urged that educational efforts with adolescents recognize the varying rates with which individuals move into periods of uncertainty and identity seeking. The teenager should be neither rushed nor restrained.

The positive aspects of adolescent behavior and their immediate tasks are listed by Jordan as intellectualism, style, reflection, altruism, and idealism. These five elements should define the characteristics of secondary schools that include gifted and talented students.

Intellectualism means a willingness to examine ideas and to pursue the goals of inquiry. Jordan observes that secondary schools can create favorable attitudes toward inquiry so that bright students do not have to feel compelled to conceal their abilities. Tactics include electives, flexibility in accelerating the path of instruction, and "success" experiences for all students. Style refers to open recognition and tolerance for the impromptu nature of student taste in clothes, slang, or music. It is not uncommon for adults to view exploratory adolescent preferences as deliberate attacks upon adult standards. Reflection means that adolescents need time to think and to take inventory of events. It also means that adolescents (like adults) will have lapses into immaturity. Teenagers need reminders, not panic. Altruism stems from the motives to do good and make a contribution. This quality can generate highly satisfying points of contact between adults and adolescents. There should be defined policies to allow teenagers to be of service. Some policies in school may need to be built into collective bargaining contracts with teachers and other employees. Idealism deals with the sense of the right and just. Teenagers should not be ridiculed for their drive for perfection. Rather, their idealism should be encouraged and appropriate internships should be found in which it can be expressed in action.

As a final point about this period, one cannot help being attracted to Barry's (1976) discussion of education as prospects for change. She speaks of education as preparation for Einstein's world and views change as relative on both individual and social bases. Emphasizing the need for a values system to prize quality in education, she observes that informed citizens will press for quality in all aspects of life. She urges joint partnerships within and without the educational community to press for high quality change. Barry's sense of quality is affirmed by Plowman's (1978) view of education for gifted and talented learners. His conviction is that education should not flinch from the efforts necessary to liberate the mental and physical energy of such students.

The quest for quality, according to Rockman (1979), is not confined to what schools do to and for adolescents. He advises teenagers to seek the

Exhibit 4-1 Teenagers Preparing for the Future

Paul Zindel, playwright and author, "The Effect of Gamma Rays on Man-In-The-Moon Marigolds;" "Pigman;" Beverly Hills, Calif.— The key word is INSIST.

They must: Insist that schools have relative curriculums or complain. Insist upon asking questions. Insist upon understanding the need for guilt in this world so we don't harm each other.

Insist they are not duped by moronic, ruthless moguls, greedily siphoning their big bucks whether by rock, disco, movies, television, or whatever.

Insist parents show their love. Insist they be open to receive it. Insist they develop their physical bodies as well as their minds. Insist their voices be heard in the politics of the world to save our dying planet.

They must refuse to be bombarded by pedagogy. They must lose the sense of shame connected with archaic morality, but must not do anything to hurt another human being.

They must keep the banner stiff in the wind that H. L. Mencken hoisted for them: "Youth though it may lack experience is not devoid of intelligence. They can see through sham with sharp and penetrating eye."

Rev. Jesse L. Jackson, National President, Operation Push, Chicago—An educated mind and sound character are the major carriers of our youth into a better tomorrow.

Our young people must do with their intellects what so many people are adept at doing with their bodies: bring the skills of the gymnasium and playing field into the study hall. Their cognitive skills must become equal to their motor skills.

This requires commitment to long-term goals at the expense of short-term pleasures, while avoiding distractions like drugs, alcohol, promiscuous sex and violence. With 39 percent of our youth unemployed, being better prepared will not solve the total problem but it will certainly give them a better shot at it.

There's no other way to go. Our young people must push for excellence against the odds—doing less than one's best is a sin— knowing effort will exceed opportunity for a long while to come. There's nothing wrong with their genes but there may be something wrong with their agenda.

Arthur Daigon, Ed.D., professor of secondary education, University of Connecticut, Storrs, Conn.—Teen-agers should be taught personal autonomy (self-determination); the essential meaning of wealth and poverty; what a family of their own is all about; about other people, races and groups; how to be alone and in a group; how to gain a sense of identity and self; what it is to be male or female in our society; what it means to grow older, and, of course, a skill or vocation which will enable them to earn an income.

(Television has emphasized the importance of money in our society. Now the poor youngster clearly sees what others have.)

With the possible exception of vocational skills, our schools are woefully inadequate in responding to these needs. As schools shrink back into the safety of basics, they are putting the emphasis on commas, periods, spelling, etc.—the form rather than the idea.

Those things that educators can measure are prized, the things that can't be are ignored. Yet it's ideas—the substance, not the form—that will lead our youth to fulfilling futures.

Reprinted from the *Pittsburgh Press* by M. Rockman, April 14, 1979, p. c3, by permission of the publisher, © 1979.

counsel of adults on assuming responsibility for their own preparation. The replies of three "mentors" are presented in Exhibit 4-1.

EDUCATIONAL PRIORITIES

Helpful Understandings

Secondary programming for highly able pupils has its own priorities based largely upon speed and thoroughness of learning. According to Keating (1979), highly able secondary students require 50 to 75 percent less time to learn material than do average students. Keating further observed that the period from 1958 to 1978 generated understandings that require high priority considerations, namely:

1. The attitudes held by administrators, teachers, gifted and talented pupils, and the general student body are influential. Negative attitudes can and will dampen the gifted pupil's willingness to participate in programs.
2. A renewed interest is seen in adjusting curriculum to match learning rate. Tactics of acceleration of either subject matter and skills, or the student, or both, now reach high levels of sophistication and are valued alternatives to simple horizontal enrichment.

3. Parents, boards of education, school administrators, and teachers recognize the essential nature of coordination of program elements and coordination for individual pupils. Coordination involves policies and practices as well as practical guidance for pupils.

Keating (1979) commends two general directives for educators in behalf of gifted and talented pupils. One presses for the concentrated effort necessary to create a variety of educational opportunities. The second asks for the creation of a system of counseling and coordination to bring student and opportunity together.

A review of the options commonly used by secondary schools has been provided by Keating. Special schools and separate, self-contained classes or sections based upon an IQ track or academic achievement or other criteria of giftedness and talent are not as popular as they once were.* One senses that these arrangements are being replaced by considerations and options chiefly related to individualization of education.

Yourtowne's counselors serve all children and youth. The coordinator of the Basic Scholars Program, though, does three things that help implement Keating's directives. Each year there is a half-day inservice seminar for the counselors that concentrates on counseling adapted to the needs of gifted and talented pupils. The content of the seminar responds to needs assessments that are drawn from counselors, parents, and the basic scholars themselves. Second, the coordinator helps counselors keep current on the education of very able students by circulating to them, throughout the year, such significant journals as *Exceptional Children* and *Journal for the Education of the Gifted.* Third, the coordinator distributes regularly to counselors an updated list of community individuals who have proved to be effective mentors, along with the areas in which they have shown willingness and skill at informal counseling. School counselors sometimes join forces with mentors to respond to the particular needs of basic scholars.

The adapting and matching of needs of gifted and talented pupils to curriculum, according to Keating, can be referenced in large part to the nature of content as closed vs. open. For example, mathematics and science are viewed as closed content in the sense that life experience is not altogether a condition for success. The humanities were perceived as more open to sensitivities provided by life experience. The elective selection of courses is much more com-

---

* Unit III notes that magnet schools may be an exception. In strict terms, however, magnet schools are not based upon an IQ criterion. The magnet school serves highly motivated pupils around a theme of interests and performance. Furthermore, magnet schools do not always require full time (five days a week, 180 days a year) enrollment. A magnet school can feature released time from one's school for part-time enrollment in a particular program.

mon now in secondary schools. That facilitates taking advantage of the so-called open/closed content of curriculum. Honors sections of a subject with defined enrollment criteria have become popular. Minicourses, as either course replacements or as electives, have been a means of catering to the special abilities and interests of gifted and talented students.

A major difficulty with the providing of such altered course structures can be that the course is assumed to be the program. Counselors, teachers, and principals may assume that having honors sections and exotic electives constitutes a curriculum for the gifted and talented. Such an assumption violates the "adapt and match" principle and it does not meet either the criterion of comprehensiveness or the criterion of flexibility. Keating advocated attention to teacher qualifications, content and methodology, and guidance of students in selection of courses. He observed that teachers have been willing to develop minicourses in spheres of their interest and competence. The curriculum that becomes fixed loses touch with individual student needs.

Robinson et al. (1979) used the analogy of the broker to illustrate the role of coordination. Keating (1979) used the analogy of the cafeteria, with a counselor assisting the highly able student to balance pacing with expansion as well as to balance selections.

The delivery of services to gifted and talented pupils at secondary levels will be influenced by decisions about issues and selection of options. Both influences operate within the context of constraints, understandings, and directives. Decisions were identified by Keating as choices about: (1) acceleration and enrichment, (2) accommodation of wide ranges of ability, and (3) attitudes toward gifted students. Choices were described as alternatives for grouping (e.g., special needs, special classes, etc.) and alternatives for coordinating program elements.

Dimensions of Decisions

Decisions about services involve the weighing of available evidence, available resources, attributes of students, and the resources necessary for balance. Typically, acceleration vs. enrichment is raised as though it were a serious issue. We agree with Keating that negative attitudes against either tactic probably originate from experiences of educators with obsolete and poorly designed programs. Arguments about acceleration vs. enrichment miss key features of individualization of instruction: (1) either provision enriches and advances the student, (2) either provision is subject to administrative convenience, (3) either provision is a decision about how a student will spend time and about what the student will be doing. Novelty, relevance, and challenge are criteria for appropriateness for the how and what. Keating appears to be in sympathy with Stanley's (1979) opinions about quality and pacing. Certainly educators ought not reject the principle of acceleration out of hand for reasons of either misunderstanding or outdated information, or because it is too complex to manage.

As an example of highly successful acceleration, witness Martha Jane Cameron, who walked across the State University College stage to accept a B.S. degree in liberal arts. What made it unusual was the time sequence; one month later she was graduated as valedictorian of her high school senior class in Yourtowne.

Going on 17, Martha Jane was among the youngest college graduates in her state. But she belonged to an even more select group: 23 youngsters from the state that year who won college degrees though they had never attended college classes.

The State University system operates an External Degree Program. While going to high school in Yourtowne, Martha Jane amassed 130 college credits, 10 more than the graduation requirement (she couldn't resist electives and directed independent study in economics and political science). The work was done at home. Her high school teachers and librarian helped both by answering questions and offering suggestions and by administering the course exams that came from the office of the State Chancellor of Higher Education. The B.S. degree cost less than $400, plus books.

While Martha Jane was the only graduating high school senior in Yourtowne who already had a college degree, she was not the only college student in the 12th grade class that year. With three others, and four students in the junior class, she enjoyed informal seminars and social activities. They called themselves the High School Plus Gang.

The New York Regents External Degree Program, the Thomas A. Edison College in Trenton, N.J., and the Board for State Academic Awards in Hartford, Connecticut, are three examples of higher education agencies that recognize college level work completed in other settings. All lead to associate's or bachelor's degrees and hold to high academic standards. The American Council on Education (1 Dupont Circle, Washington, D.C., 20036) publishes a guide to approximately 150 accredited institutions where external students may earn some or all of required academic credits off-campus.

Accommodation to a wide range of student abilities is not entirely new either to secondary schools or to education of the gifted and talented. What is new is a trend toward using advanced placement tests, teacher recommendations, and student performances for eligibility or standards for acceleration and enrichment. The global IQ is being supplanted rather than supplemented. There appears to be a shift toward recognition of specific talents and abilities. The Terman concept of general intellectual aptitude is not rejected. What is rejected is the practice of using IQ as a condition for enrollment in advanced science or mathematics, for instance, for a student who already has demonstrated capacity but who does not meet the traditional criterion of IQ. This practice may create more work for administration but it has the advantage of creating flexibility for students, of widening the scope of opportunity for identification and individualization of instruction, and of nurturing abilities.

Terman's work did change thinking about the gifted from a perception of them as narrow eggheads to a more accurate reflection as well-rounded persons. It may be a sign of the times that there is sufficient security now to recognize and restore a balance. One is struck by the content-centered literature with its Terman general ability perception. One is struck also by the emphasis on the special talent perception in developmental level literature. These impressions leave one with increased certainty about the validity of the Individualized Education Program with its emphasis upon the person and its outcomes of matching.

Teachers are a powerful influence on attitudes toward programs and gifted and talented pupils. There should be, in the school system, sufficient support and guidance for their efforts.

Encouraging Maturity

Responsibility and maturity are learned behaviors, usually copied from models. To learn constructs such as "responsible" and "mature," children require adults as examples, adults who are willing to *be* responsible for their own behavior and who *are* mature and resourceful in the face of adversity. Ginott (1972) invokes the term *mensch* to describe the product of human models for teenagers. He sees the qualities of such a person as compassion and courage. Mensch also refers to a person whose life is guided by an inner core of strength and a code of fairness and justice.

Ginott equates responsibility and maturity as his way to identify guidelines for responsible adults committed to impart responsibility to teenagers. He advises adults that their responsibilities are to set standards and demonstrate values and to inform teenagers of what one expects and respects. He observes that teenagers will oppose and test; the responsible adult recognizes that no one can mature by slavishly following orders. Opposition is to be anticipated.

A key feature of Ginott's advice is for adults to discriminate between restrictions and limits. Restrictions ignore feelings, usually uttered in anger, and are couched in the You-message (see Unit V). Limits attempt to preserve self-respect, anchored in values, and reflect the I-message. Restrictions belittle aspirations while limits redirect energies. Limits prize a certain permissiveness about feelings but are firm as to behavior. The responsible adult has sufficient strength to endure temporary animosity when limits are perceived as restrictions. Ginott's views offer added endorsement that the tactics of nurture apply to this period.

Encouraging Prospects

The encouragement of prospects requires the encouragement of students to pursue excellence. Tannenbaum (1962) tells of a survey of adolescent attitudes toward brilliance. He sampled 615 students split approximately evenly between honors students and average students. He learned that teenagers find the label "brilliant" to be neither especially attractive nor repelling. Students are neither accepted nor rejected on the basis of either high achievement or high IQ. Popularity, per se, is a function of behaviors that seem to have little to do with giftedness itself. A pertinent finding was that moderation in scholastic efforts is valued while effort in athletics is preferred. Consequently, schools do need to create a climate of intellectualism, as Jordan (1973) advocated.

The Robert Sterling Clark Foundation (1977) compiled essays by gifted students on the prospects of educational opportunities. Their recommendations for educators are for: (1) opportunities for mentors, (2) opportunities for independent study, (3) introduction to career education, and (4) participation in student government. These recommendations were advanced on the basis of self-reports of gifted and talented students about personal experiences they found statisfying and valid. Boston's (1976) report on mentoring, too, deserves attention for its advocacy of the procedure as well as for its emphasis upon matching student to mentor. These sources concur with Treffinger's (1978) recommendations for self-directed learning such as independent study. He endorses the concept of self-looping, but his major emphasis is upon the student's learning to identify and distill problems. To encourage that is one indication of a school's prizing intellectual effort and of its readiness for independent action. It also is an indication of the school's commitment to teaching responsible autonomy.

WIDENING THE PROSPECTS

Independent Study and Research as Induction

One means of widening a gifted and talented adolescent's prospects is to encourage individual initiative for learning through one's own investigations. Varied tactics of independent study and personal research to expand and enrich the standard curriculum will be mentioned later (see Unit III).

The teacher or mentor at the secondary level needs to think about at least two primary objectives. One objective is to help gifted and talented students refine their skills and methods of conducting research and investigations as well as their skills in communicating the results and implications of their findings. The second objective is to build and strengthen in these students a personal commitment to becoming better at managing their own learning. This objective includes making clear to exceptional adolescents that in doing research they first act upon their own curiosity and then learn how to manage that curiosity. The mastery of these makes one a problem finder. The key feature is to induct the able adolescent into the role of problem finder as well as problem solver. Many can solve problems. Only a few can define and delineate them so they can be solved.

Learning to Find Problems

According to Drew (1976), the initial barrier to investigation for both the student and the teacher or mentor is the development of a *problem statement*. The student needs to understand that the technicalities of methodology and the mechanics are the means, not the end product. The teacher will assist the pupil to comprehend that the problem statement is the context in which all other elements of investigation are placed. Ideally, the student will comprehend that finding a problem is a natural connection between the individual's own curiosity and fulfilling that curosity. The creation of a problem statement can be presented not so much as a technicality but as a process for managing curiosity constructively.

The development of a clear problem statement is not unrelated to personal/professional considerations. Teachers may be tempted to present students with fixed lists of problems within the teacher's own competence. It also takes time to negotiate topics of mutual interest. Teachers may feel reluctance to share responsibilities with a second or third party for fear of being perceived as uninformed. Drew, however, encouraged teachers and mentors to pursue the process of encouraging student-centered problem statements. He cited the following as possible outcomes: (1) the student will be able to apply the tactics of formulating problem statements to other situations, (2) the student will gain confidence, and (3) the student will produce a product of personal satisfaction and technical soundness. Moreover, learning to find problems and learning to state manageable problems can be the clearest evidence to adolescents of their increasing maturity as evidenced by their ability to manage their own learning.

Problem finding, according to Drew, first describes the ways in which a teacher or mentor removes the obstacles that might block transforming an idea or an initial curiosity into a reasonable statement for inquiry and enable students to identify their command of information regarding the topic. The second step orients students to existing sources of information, both expert opinion as well as the literature of earlier investigations. The third step requires dialogue among the student, the teacher or mentor, and information sources. In the dialogue, if not before, students become aware of the role of theory as a way to account for existing information and as a means to predict events. Students will learn that one test of theory is its predictive validity, its ability to forecast events. Moreover, students will recognize that theory provides the context into which their own curiosity must be meshed. The teacher or mentor encourages the protege to discover that self-learning originates with a gap in knowledge and culminates with the narrowing of the gap.

Learning to Distill a Problem

This distillation of a problem consists of the movement from finding an interest to the production of a problem statement that can be investigated objectively. It requires narrowing down to a specific topic that identifies: (1) the variable of interest, (2) operational definitions, and (3) statements of hypotheses or questions. Typically, the topic centers on the effects of some condition on the matter at interest. The student's search of the literature and interviews will identify suspected sources of influence. Drew writes of this identification as the isolation of the experimental variable (the independent variable).

Many factors, or variables, influence phenomena. The teacher's task is to communicate the fact that phenomena may be dependent upon many sources and that the investigator's task is to control or manage many variables so that the impact of the experimental variable can be determined.

An operational definition recognizes the limitations of dictionary definitions. The operational definition describes the ways in which variables are used, measured, and/or inferred.

The hypothesis or question, according to Drew, can serve one or more of three purposes. One purpose is the development of theory. The hypothesis can serve to organize an If/Then speculation, as if certain events are observed then certain results will happen. A second purpose is to determine the thoroughness and accuracy of the hypothesis when employed for prediction. This purpose moves from speculation to action. The third purpose is to aid teaching. This use enables the teacher to focus pupil attention on consideration of relevance. In fact, this third use is the common tactic of debate (e.g., be it resolved that. . .) and the tactic of the lawyer's brief.

Wider Applications

Drew's (1976) work refers not to the behavioral sciences alone; it is widely applicable. For example, a pupil could examine the Battle of Gettysburg to test hypotheses or resolve questions regarding the significance of the Union occupation of the Roundtops. The Sasquatch Bigfoot phenomenon affords an opportunity to mesh student interest and construct questions or build hypotheses to supply an induction to mindstretching investigations. Students can engage profitably in experiments involving nutrition, especially balanced nutrition as a life habitat. Parapsychology, a high interest topic for students and parents, opens another aspect of research.

Research often is misperceived as proving one thing over another. Actually, that kind of horserace research is not the most commn. Rather, outcomes may demonstrate the validity of a procedure or a method of measurement or a technique that contributes to knowledge about the tactics of research. Another equally significant outcome can be to document that some phenomenon does, in reality, exist.

Recognition of these purposes and outcomes can help the pupil and teacher or mentor to negotiate the product or outcome. Some pupils find their reward in research that leads to the production of a position paper, a theoretical or analytical proposing of the If/Then consequences. Other students prefer to test the utility of procedures useful to inquiry. Still others prefer the organization of ideas into a debate format, or prefer the testing out of effects. These preferences can be viewed as different pupil aptitudes or styles against which to match treatments of problem finding and identification. Informing students of these options and these preferences represents a helpful preface before launching into technicalities.

Drew (1976) reminded teachers and mentors that they should respect safeguards concerning the protection of human and animal subjects. School districts need to be informed of these policies. Moreover, parents should be made aware and be willing to give their consent.

PACING THE PROSPECTS

A Prospect of Promise

A promising prospect for teenagers, educators, and their families has been the increasing cooperation between schools and institutions of higher education. This cooperation introduces added and helpful flexibility into the educational lives of able persons. Educators at all levels recognize that new times challenge them to find different ways to adapt to the accelerated pace of information buildup and to the accelerated capabilities of able students. Public schools and institutions of higher education have found a variety of ways to screen eligible pupils, to link them to appropriate resources, and to provide appropriate follow-up.

The same care and precision required for pacing within the elementary and high schools also is needed when using higher education as a resource. The prudent institution of higher education consults with public schools to take advantage of their general expertise regarding able learners and their specific expertise as to each individual learner.

Anderson (1976) conducted a survey of bright, prospective college students. Out of 28 potential variables in attracting student interest in attending a particular college, four were the most potent; (1) tuition cost, (2) credentials of the faculty, (3) research/scholarship orientation of the institution, and (4) fiscal strength/resources of the institution. He found that early contact orients a student of high potential toward future enrollment.

An account of recognition is provided in Exhibit 4-2. One is struck by the pace students can maintain as well as the responsiveness of schools and universities to provide recognition to these students who may be unaware of their abilities.

Exhibit 4-2 Just Call Them Mathematically Precocious

Surprise! That was Nathan Franzen's and Rebecca Young's initial reaction when these middle school students heard they were mathematically precocious youth.

That's the description given to hundreds of seventh and eighth graders who were found to have a high aptitude for mathematical reasoning, according to a Johns Hopkins study here and elsewhere across Pennsylvania and adjoining states.

The 12- and 13-year olds took the college entrance Scholastic Aptitude Test and many, like Nathan and Rebecca, scored higher than the average 12th grader on the grueling math section. And they have not had a full year of algebra yet.

Nathan scored a 600, Rebecca a 510 on the test which has a maximum of 800 points. The average 12th grade college-bound male scores 494; the average female makes a 440, according to Julian Stanley, a professor of psychology who heads the continuing study of mathematically precocious youth.

Stanley, whose studies have tested more than 10,000 mathematically talented students since 1972, said many have no idea of their vast potential for abstract reasoning.

He believes it's important to identify these students as soon as possible. Otherwise, they have a tendency to become bored with math class, because it's too easy.

Stanley sent Rebecca, Nathan, and the others who participated in his talent search several recommendations encouraging them to absorb as much math as quickly as possible.

This would include taking two math courses in one year; going to a nearby high school or college to take advanced math, physics, or computer science courses; skipping grade levels; taking the SATs every year; and entering a university early.

Nathan already plans to learn algebra I on his own this summer and take algebra II or geometry next school year.

Stanley and his colleagues sponsor a concentrated advanced math course for these youngsters during the summer at Hopkins.

In 40 hours, the students, depending on their abilities, could zip through algebra I, II, and III, trigonometry, analytical geometry, and pre calculus.

For the average student, it would take 500 hours to learn these subjects, Stanley said.

All 33 students who attended last summer's five-hour-a-week session learned at least two full years of math. Stanley expects about 144 students for this summer's intensive course.

The professor figures that a mathematically precocious youth is able to pick up algebra I in only three to 15 hours, if given a good mentor. The youngsters are given standardized tests throughout the summer to ensure they actually have mastered the various math levels.

Each year Stanley sends letters to every public, parochial, and private school which has seventh and eighth graders in Pennsylvania, Delaware, West Virginia, Virginia, Washington, D.C., and Maryland. He suggests that the students who have shown a flair for math take the SAT test when it is administered in January to all college-bound students.

"We are looking for students who show a potential for abstract reasoning; they don't necessarily have to know a lot," he explained.

Some 3,600 students took the SAT this year for Stanley's study. More than 25 percent scored above the average college-bound senior on at least one of the three sections: math, verbal, or written English.

Ten students scored 700 or better in math. The highest was a nearly perfect 790, Stanley said.

The students also are invited to a ceremony, which was held recently at Hopkins where they are awarded books and scholarships for taking a college class, depending on their scores. Rebecca and the others who attended also received certificates.

These youngsters probably will enroll in college before they reach 12th grade, receive doctorates and become mathematicians, physical scientists, electrical engineers, computer scientists, statisticians or economists, Stanley predicted.

Reprinted from the *Pittsburgh Press* by C. Marcus, May 13, 1979, J1, by permission of the publisher, © 1979.

Schools and institutions can cooperate in a variety of ways to offer students options of advanced college standing while in high school. In very general terms, these can be reduced to broad clusters, according to Radcliffe and Hatch (1961). The early publication data of their work should reinforce awareness that advanced standing options are not a new fad, soon to fade away. One option is early admission to college, prior to normal high school graduation. The second option has the student remaining in high school but accumulating college credits to achieve advanced standing. The Radcliffe and Hatch report cited: (1) improved communications between colleges and high schools, (2) improved planning to accommodate individual student needs and achievement, (3) opportunities for students to elect courses in their college curriculum that otherwise would have been unavailable, and (4) financial savings to students. Advanced standing also serves to motivate superior students by the recognition afforded by their performance as well as by the challenge of pacing of which they are capable.

Olivas (1975) and J. F. White (1975) noted the inclination of community colleges to offer adaptations for highly able pupils. This is indeed a promising prospect, given the prevalence of such institutions. The most common provisions include: honors sections of courses, independent study, honor societies, and financial aid based upon achievement. White affirmed the prevalent use of independent study as well as of advanced standing on a case-by-case basis. There is a trend to formalize programming through the designation of an administrator/coordinator.

A further example of the cooperation between high schools and institutions of higher education is presented in Exhibit 4-3. This option is called STEP, or Secondary Talented Education Program. The student remains in high school, but achieves advanced standing. Another attractive feature enables teachers to extend educational opportunities to their gifted and talented students and also to expand their own knowledge. Finally, the STEP option is founded upon joint planning that involves the student, the school district, the institution, and the family.

Exhibit 4-3 An Example of Cooperative Programming

Program Description

• The Secondary Talented Education Program—University of Pittsburgh (STEP-UP) is a program to help schools design individualized educational programs for gifted and talented students. STEP-UP, a form of accelerated academic study, can be used to supplement the more comprehensive programs developed by school districts. It is particularly appropriate when limited resources might otherwise prohibit the development of a program of advanced study for students.

• Through STEP-UP, gifted high school students may pursue rigorous college-level work or actual college courses, without leaving the high school setting. The program makes available college-level materials well-suited for the gifted high school junior or senior. The materials have been developed specifically for independent study by distinguished University of Pittsburgh faculty. These materials may be used as the basis of advanced high school courses or in conjunction with the University as introductory college courses.

• The eight courses of study are both a logical extension of the high school curriculum and a "step-up" into the college curriculum. They have been selected from over 100 courses developed for independent study by the University's External Studies Program. The courses, which are described in detail ..., are: (1) Economics 780—Introductory Economics, (2) Economics 748-Consumerism, (3) Fine Arts 785—Masterpieces of Western Painting from the Renaissance to the Present, (4) German Literature 780—German Contributions to World Literature (in English), (5) History 840—Colonial America, (6) Music 781—The Symphony, (7) Psychology 780—Introduction to Psychology, and (8) SGS 757—Energy: A Technological, Economic, or Moral Crisis?

Program Alternatives

Using the Materials as the Basis of a High School Course

School districts (or intermediate units) may purchase the curricular materials and related administrative materials from the University and assign a faculty member from the school district to supervise the student's individualized educational program. (The cost of each set of curricular materials is shown [in the] brochure. Related administrative materials will cost $20-40.) School districts using this option are invited to enroll the faculty member in a one-day intensive seminar offered by the Pitt faculty developer of the materials. The cost for each faculty member will be $50.

Enrolling the Student in College-Level Courses

Students may be enrolled in STEP-UP courses at the University by the school district or by parents through the school district. Students will be required to have parental permission and the approval of their high school.

A Pitt faculty member will assume responsibility for supervising and evaluating the student; contact hours will be established for the student to reach this faculty member by phone. In addition, the school district may appoint a local high school faculty member to work with the student; such a mentor, while not responsible for the student's progress in the course, will provide valuable encouragement and a link between the course and the student's total high school program.

The student will study independently during designated study halls in school and in the evenings at home. During the term he/she will attend three Saturday workshops at the University. Exams will be forwarded to a selected school official (normally the librarian) who will supervise their administration and forward them in pre-addressed envelopes to the University faculty member. Upon the successful completion of the course, the student will be awarded three college credits. In the vast majority of cases, these credits will be transferable to any institution of higher education that the student might later attend.

The cost under this option will be tuition and student fees ($157) plus the cost of curricular materials. For the first course taken by a student, there will also be an application fee of $15.

Program Elements

• The courses have been specially developed for independent study. Each term a subset of these courses will be offered for gifted students participating in the STEP-UP program.

• All course materials are available to students, school districts, and intermediate units. The approximate cost of each set of course materials is listed after each course description. (Prices are subject to change.) These study materials, which are often coordinated with a textbook, include:

- overviews, introductions, or rationales to orient the student;
- specific instructional objectives for the student to achieve;
- comments, notes, and elaborations on important points;
- study questions, sample tests and projects, and answer keys to formatively direct student learning.
- When a school district decides to purchase the materials for use in a high school independent study project, the high school faculty member will also receive related administrative materials, including:
  - a special faculty-to-faculty introduction to the course;
  - recommendations for topics to be covered in meetings with the student;
  - a complete set of any formal evaluation instruments used at the University;
  - a guide for independent study course management.

Reprinted from STEP-UP brochure by permission of Michael B. Spring, Associate Director, External Studies—STEP-UP, University of Pittsburgh, Pittsburgh, PA 15260.

Some educators reject advanced placement out of hand because an able student might not be able to drive or not congregate and socialize in the student pub. It is unfortunate that students are not consulted as to their preferences. There are any number of regular students, for example, who cannot drive because of impairment. There are any number of students who don't drink because of personal temperament or because of religious belief. Appropriate counseling and the resourcefulness of able students and their families can indeed provide genuine enjoyment and social growth outside the pattern espoused by *most* students.

Encouraging Career/Vocational Prospects

Ellis (1976) concludes that communication between specialists in career education and specialists in education of the gifted and talented is increasing. However, the notion of career education tends to be rooted in academics and the arts. While increasing communication is reported, it has taken place because of informal contacts. Sanborn (1976) urges educators of the gifted and talented to be assertive in creating interest among the wider educational community in career preparation.

The literature of career preparation, for example, vocational education, reflects the need for planning and identification of able students. Milne (1976) views the school counselor as . . . . a logical person to arrange for the identification of gifted and talented students and of community/school resources. He also reminds educators that the concept of the career ladder applies to the gifted and talented student. The essence of this concept is the recognition of several distinctive aspects of careers. Some careers are characterized by upward mobility. For example, a person may become a school bus driver and proceed to a teacher's aide. And finally, the person may progress to the status of a teacher with appropriate training. A common preparation in vocational education is for the person to have work experience in a craft/ trade first and then seek out a career in education. A second aspect is the combination of trades and crafts. For example, employment can be conditioned by seasons. A pupil may be attracted by carpentry, but also elect tool and diemaking to take up the slack. A third aspect is stepping out/starting out. This means that students may prolong a preparation period for economic or personal reasons. The counselor can be a helpful source of guidance for helping students to manage the various ranges of the process.

Milne (1976) also affirms the usefulness of individualized planning for career preparation. His model emphasizes the appropriateness of career education principles for gifted and talented learners.

Vocational agriculture illustrates one branch of education that attempts to promote its attractiveness to superior students. Both Diehl (1976) and Lee (1976) stress the need for able students to pursue careers in the diversity of opportunities available in agriculture. Both think of agriculture as a life style and as a form of social contribution. Both also advocate that the education of gifted and talented students include vocational agriculture. Lee recognizes that vocational agriculture needs to shed its image of a track exclusively for preventing high school dropouts. Diehl emphasizes the need for vocational agriculture to promote the contributions of American agriculture in domestic economics as well as its contributions to world stability.

Encouraging Responsibility

Reference was made earlier to Ginott's (1971) guidelines for adult/teenager relationships. Wilde and Sommers' (1978) as well as C. Johnson's (1978) emphasis is upon the relationship between school policies and responsible student behavior. Wilde and Sommers concentrate on the teacher's role and relationships with students.

C. Johnson prefaced his observations by sharing a classroom episode. He recounted a high school social studies class he was teaching in which the activity was reading a newspaper article about world events. The group was indifferent. He decided to divide the class into two groups. One group had a "dictator" to get things done. The dictator could shout, order, etc. The "democrat" had to involve others and share responsibilities, and could assign grades on the basis of effort. The expectations were that: (1) the leaders would experience the same difficulties as their teacher; (2) the different styles of leadership would produce different results; and (3) the different styles could be translated into comparisons of different governments. C. Johnson perceived the experiment as a failure. Both groups were equally cooperative, purposeful, and quiet. It was a "dream" class. C. Johnson was led to the conclusion that his 16-year-old students had responded to being responsible for their own behavior.

C. Johnson observes that schools and their policies overregulate student behavior to the point that the message to the pupils is that adults are taking over. While adolescents grope for responsible behavior, secondary schools entrench themselves into caretaking systems. For example, students are held responsible for their behavior in going from one class to another during school hours. They are held accountable for the hall pass. The paper becomes the relevant item. Rules are written for the exception rather than based upon a positive presumption. The principle of positive presumption applied to adolescents is the message of believing that they can live up to assigned responsibilities.

The failing grade is called by C. Johnson a significant obstacle to student responsibility. He observes that the F becomes a permanent stigma. Teachers thereafter may cajole and eventually may compromise by "passing" the student even though the pupil has not attained passing achievement. Rather than a permanent F, the student should receive "no credit" for the course. In this way, the student and school can renegotiate and correct what went wrong. To lose credit toward graduation is a sufficient consequence; to carry a permanent F is excessive. However, schools find it difficult to tolerate a temporary lapse. The important issue is how to help students learn from their mistakes without permanent penalty. The difficulty, for schools, is to separate evaluation from punishment.

C. Johnson (1978) recommends that school policies concentrate on the quality of discipline rather than the degree. He describes discipline as guidelines for present and future behavior and punishment as a concentration on past failures. Discipline is not laissez faire; discipline ties consequences to behavior. Discipline is based upon the decency of the majority of teenagers. For example, if a student abuses an open campus, then restrict that student rather than all students. C. Johnson shares an observation about his high school in that it is subject to all pressures of such schools—but has only a modest incidence of disruptive problems. This he attributes to the fact the school maintains fewer "rules." The policies of the school center on: (1) helping students to focus attention on how they can succeed in the future, (2) explaining the reasons for expectations of performance, and (3) encouraging students to be responsible for their learning as well as for their behavior.

Student responsibility for learning is a key feature of C. Johnson's discussion about encouraging pupil progress to maturity. He advocates tactics of inquiry learnings and independent study. He does not suggest that teachers stand back and watch students flounder. The teacher's role should be guide and mentor. The task for secondary education is to create policies that free teachers to help pupils succeed.

The discussion by Wilde and Sommers (1978) relates to classroom practices. Their recommendations distinguish and discriminate between teachers who conduct teaching as a contest between "me vs. them" and those who conduct teaching as a team effort. Aside from this distinction, they advance their recommendations in the context of prevention. These tactics are pertinent to secondary level schooling:

1. Students benefit from a rationale for subject matter. Students are open to appeals to present and future relevance.
2. Students benefit from being informed about the goals and objectives of a course at the beginning and being informed as individuals. One teacher was cited for her practice of using both a syllabus and a weekly memo individually tailored to each student.
3. Students benefit from choice and from participating in learning. The teacher can provide the broad guidelines/framework and the student can make decisions about implementations. This procedure encourages the teacher as mentor to collaborate with students in the finding and distillation of topics for inquiry.
4. Students benefit from participation in forming options for class rules and informing standards of evaluation. The teacher may need to help students form positive consequences if they have been conditioned to only negative ones. The purpose/outcome is to help students link their behavior to consequences. Teacher-imposed consequences "teach" the student that the adult is responsible for the student's behavior. Participation reverses the trend.

Discipline is a legitimate concern of educators. Able students require guidance about linkage of behavior to outcomes. One senses that sufficient information exists to enable educators to be responsible in their relationships.

SUMMARY

Counseling parallels instruction in importance for gifted and talented young people in the adolescent years. Encouragement, advancement, and career initiation take priority. It is wasteful to debate acceleration or enrichment. With few exceptions, every appropriate form of individualized education for highly able students is accelerative in nature. Quality is the key condition, whether in academic studies or in the learning of proper personal and social behavior.

Chapter 5

Adulthood as Generativity

TIME CAPSULE

Adulthood is now considered to possess its own distinctive tasks that appear at roughly similar ages in most adults. Sheehy (1976) found, though, that recognized high achievers usually experienced adult developmental tasks sooner, spent less time in acquisition, and were more resourceful in coping with life's shocks.

One significant obstacle to productive adulthood is the mythology about able and competent persons. Sheehy found that belief in scientific burnout after age 30 could be so deeply ingrained that otherwise intelligent persons believed and behaved as if it were true. Solano (1976) followed a sample of precocious children through adulthood, however, and essentially confirmed the early work of Terman. However, the myth of early ripe, early rot dies hard. Consequently, preparation for adulthood and engaging in adulthood requires dealing with the myths that indoctrinate persons to believe that life is over at age 30, 40, 50, or 65. Available research strongly contradicts that life is ever over until actual death. Instead, life is a series of opportunities for continuing growth and development. This is especially true for gifted and talented persons. Their earlier accomplishments often have brought them the admiration of their fellow citizens, young and old. Thus they have status that continues, status they earned and that persuades others to listen to them. Of course, there have been instances of abuse of that confidence. But many more times the wisdom of experience plus the constant trait of creativity combine to make adulthood, including its later years, a period of unflagging productivity.

Shining through the breadth and depth of adulthood, a central theme emerges: generativity. Generativity is the scientific construct to describe productive adulthood. Generativity, as will be seen, is the continuing of personal development, the refinement of one's career, and the sense of obligation to

103

serve others. These are complementary goals, and productive adulthood strives for them in reasonable balance.

GENERATIVITY AS PRODUCTIVE ADULTHOOD

Generativity has the key ideas of generation, of production, of contribution, of continuing creativity. It is a prime concern of Life Cycles Research, a branch of developmental psychology. Sheehy popularized this construct of generativity. Her work provides a helpful frame of reference for understanding generativity as a positive and natural aspect of adulthood. The term describes a process of continuing personal growth and development and of continuing service and contributions to others. The Peace Corps, VISTA, etc., are examples of this process.

Generativity as Commitment

Sheehy (1976) credits the psychologist Erik Erikson with identifying generativity as a key issue in adulthood. The adult is characterized by a voluntary commitment to guide new generations and to mentor younger associates. The generative adult does not seek to dominate others and does not seek worship for approval. The motive is for service without thought to tangible reward. Erikson, according to Sheehy, viewed generativity as a release of creativity and productivity. It can be expressed as becoming involved in a cause, consulting to or for a group, and teaching others.

Generativity as a Life Choice

Generativity is a choice for the adult. Typically, the effect of maturity is to recognize that one is responsible for one's own actions. This belief frees the individual to take charge of life and career. The person believes that the locus of control is internal, that one can shape events rather than be hammered and twisted by them. The alternative to generativity is passive resignation and self-centered despair. In one sense, generativity is a creative response to the alternative of stagnation in midlife.

Generativity has numerous outlets for gifted and talented persons. One is cultivation of talents through career changes. This process is not frantic, but a genuine liberation. A typical pattern is for the person to persist in a career and to direct personal energies toward improvement of skills to benefit others, not merely career advancement. For example, a stockbroker may share skills with a nonprofit organization to improve its financial base without fee. A teacher may agree to serve as a master or supervising teacher to share skills with preservice teachers.

Generativity has its risks. Sheehy observed that there is the possibility that one's new pursuits may fail. The more distinct possibility, however, is that one's peers may respond with envy and even polite hostility. When one's peers have accepted a placid state and are content to endure 10 to 20 years prior to retirement, the generative adult can be perceived as a threat. Even younger persons may view the generative oldster as an "overage" eager beaver who should make way. Sheehy observes that generativity is defeated more by peer reactions or work situation. The mythology is the stereotype of mid-life burnout. The belief in loss of abilities in the late 30s and early 40s is so extensive that even otherwise highly intelligent people believe it. Actually, gifted and talented persons find their abilities growing and maturing, not diminishing, in adulthood.

It is regrettable that adulthood as generativity is little taught at any level of education. People—and especially the most able people—usually are turned loose and allowed to fend as best as they can. The mythology is that adult life is a period of materialism and decline. Educators and many other professionals more often are found to be self-actualizing persons who find continuing challenge and productivity. Their experience and strategies for renewal are indeed wisdom that should be imparted to highly able students to expand this knowledge among the profession as well as among the wider public. It is obvious that gifted and talented learners will be sources of generativity—and anticipatory guidance for them would seem helpful.

UNDERSTANDING THE QUALITIES OF MENTOR

The Meanings of Mentoring

Mentor has at least three meanings. One derives from classical tradition, a second from the literature of the education of the gifted and talented, and a third from the field of developmental psychology.

Any standard encyclopedia will identify the classical origins of Mentor as a protector and adviser to the young son of Ulysses. During the 20 years of his adventures in the Trojan War and subsequent return voyage, Mentor, the faithful guardian, tutored the son and helped him attain adulthood. Today, the memory of Mentor is retained as meaning advise/counsel based upon some presumption of friendship.

The literature of education for the gifted and talented makes use of mentoring as a means to further experiences and opportunities for able learners. This usually refers to a person of competence who volunteers to instruct a student in areas of mutual interest. This book includes numerous instances of the ways in which mentoring has been used effectively as in internships and the example of the Junior Achievement movement.

The field of developmental psychology has described mentoring as a natural evolution of adult behavior. Life Cycles Research both extends the study of adult development and emphasizes the significance of mentoring. This significance relates to both the mentor and the protege. Sheehy has drawn a scattered literature together with relevant case history material that serves to illuminate the mentor/protege relationship. From the perspective of Life Cycles Research, mentoring describes a helping relationship between a mature person of competence and a younger person. Typically, the mentor is around age 40 and the protege is in the 20s. The typical relationship usually involves a career/occupational focus but also can include wider concerns. Mentoring is found in all occupational fields and is not restricted within similar occupations.

There is the recognition that educators (at all levels) serve as mentors to students and their parents. Mentoring also is not restricted to the 40/20 age span. A frequently encountered example can be found in scouting, as in the relationship between Cub Scouts (ages 8 to 10), and their Den Chief, a member of the Boy Scouts of America who serves as adviser and tutor. The socialization of handicapped children and adolescents has benefited from the organized efforts of YOUTH-ARCs (affiliates of local chapters of the National Association for Retarded Citizens) and of the Student Council for Exceptional Children (a university/college affiliate of the Council for Exceptional Children). These two organizations differ from usual volunteer efforts in that their young members provide practical guidance and a measure of protection of rights for exceptional children, youth, and adults. Both organizations provide more than companionship (not that companionship is to be downgraded), offering also a level of competence to assist the gifted person to learn and to practice increasingly higher level skills of social adaptation.

The literature of Life Cycles Research can be a helpful source of guidance about the relationship between mentor and protege. This literature can be instructive for educators since the role of mentor may present itself in the teacher/student relationship. It also can be helpful to educators in their matching, managing, and maintaining of the mentor-to-protege relationship. Finally, it can be helpful for adults to understand their pursuit of productive adulthood.

Positive Examples and Dimensions

Mentoring is a concrete example of generativity. Transactional Analysis affords another source of documentation of mentoring in adulthood. Young gifted and talented students quickly grasp its concepts and apply them. Berne (1964) identified positive forms of games that illustrate dimensions of mentoring as well as account for its origins. One example Berne cited was labeled

"Busman's Holiday." This activity describes a person's willingness to share one's competence outside of one's sphere of employment. Examples might include Peace Corps and VISTA, or the educator who teaches a religious nurture class or who advises a scouting program. "Homey Sage" is a second example. This is a person who is willing to share experience with others. This person is also characterized as a good listener. The sage is not offended if advice is not followed. The person does not have needs to dominate another. "Happy to Help" is a third example documented by Berne. This person is ready to provide help and to assist people in need. The person is not motivated to collect IOUs; satisfaction is in the ability to be helpful.

Berne documented and identified "They'll Be Glad They Knew Me" (TBGTKM), which accounts in part for the origins of a person's need to mentor. A common life script would be that a person has directly experienced the benefits of another individual in a formative period. The person recognizes that the benefactor has given freely of prestige and advice, and has created opportunities. There is the realization that a person's present status is due in a measure to one's own efforts and to the intervention of the benefactor/mentor. There usually are little means to "repay" the mentor except through thanks, which seems somewhat inadequate. The repayment comes about by serving as a benefactor and mentor to another person in similar circumstances. The life histories of persons cited in this text offer ample testimony to helpful early intervention and subsequent assistance to others. There is the continuing pursuit of development coupled with the development of others. The striving for personal success is based upon a motive to repay as well. It is a reflection to the helper that one's efforts were rewarded. One does not seek to be a carbon copy or a career clone. Rather one seeks to acknowledge the benefits of a helpful life experience.

Berne's account is highly consistent with Sheehy's (1976) review of biographical interviews. She found that adults characterized by generativity in midlife were further characterized by benefitting from the experience of a mentor at an earlier age. In fact, Sheehy reported that lack of a mentor in one's life could be a disadvantage. Selection of a career in the helping professions can be traced to a positive influence. However, Sheehy acknowledged and reminded her readers that mentoring could be found in all occupations.

Understanding the Mentor/Protege Relationship

Sheehy's biographical accounts and research validations provide helpful and anticipatory guidance to educators who would attempt to bring about the match between a potential mentor and a protege. The key features of matching would be that: (1) there are helpful outcomes for both participants, and (2) there are stages in the relationship.

In Life Cycle Research, the bulk of data has centered on the relationship between persons in their 20s and those in their 40s. The central task of the period of the 20s is establishing a career, with its associated excitement and its uncertainties. The personal issues can be: How do I get started? How do I put my aspirations to work? and Who can help me? The person who finds a mentor will be able to prepare for a lifetime career without losing one's own identity. Out of the relationship comes the confidence in one's own ability to succeed by one's own efforts. The mentor also serves as a buffer to protect the protege from unnecessary shocks from others who are threatened by less able people.

Sheehy observed that persons who have worked under mentors usually progress through career hurdles sooner, are better able to bounce back from career shocks sooner, and have firmer career goals.

For the mentor, the relationship provides an outlet for generativity. The mentor regards the person as a younger adult, not as a boy or girl or child. The mentor views the person as an individual of capacity and potential. The mentor views the role as supporting the younger person's dreams as well as the efforts necessary to put them into effect in the real world. The mentor serves as a nonparental, career role model.

There are no fixed time limits for the relationship. There appear to be somewhat observable stages in that there is one that might be labeled a *seeking*. At this level, the protege is seeking an alternative (not replacement) for parental guidance. The relationship has initial overtones of piggybacking upon a Stronger One. The protege's inexperience is the source. There also is the stage of *guiding*, in which the relationship and the protege mature. It is entirely possible that the protege will develop greater competence than the mentor. This may be more of a shock to the protege than to the mentor. The mentor has created the opportunities and the protege must develop them. The *phasing out* stage need not be awkward. The mentor may be reluctant to let go and the protege may feel insecure about abandoning a certain security. Most frequently, it is the mentor who certifies for the protege that the latter is "ready" for either colleagueship and/or independent action. The protege pursues a period of independence until ready to engage in mentoring.

AN ORGANIZED FRAMEWORK

Collective Advocacy

Mentoring has its natural, developmental aspects. Previous citations pointed up its validity as a tactic of genuine merit for gifted and talented learners.

For mentoring to flourish, commitment to the process may well require personal renewal as a key step in structuring a permanent framework. A first step would be the development of sound quality programs for exceptional learners.

Frasier (1977) has proposed "change agentry" on behalf of gifted and talented pupils as a key role for educators. These tactics were mentioned earlier; however, Frasier's comments reaffirmed the need and sense of urgency for initiative. An article in *Time* (1979) provides a concrete example of urgency regarding the need for a permanent framework of educational quality. This article reported on a lawsuit brought against a school district charging educational malpractice and neglect of a gifted student. It was reported, for example, that the child's behavior was diagnosed as that of a learning disabled pupil. It was only through determined advocacy that this error was reversed.

Nathan (1979) paid tribute to parents of gifted pupils who move beyond their home and their child in order to work for the collective good of all talented learners. Typically, such parents focus on curriculum and academic excellence, which many parents might consider the province of professionals. Indifference and negligence are the main enemies. For this reason, parents of the gifted and talented were advised by Nathan to examine the total curriculum of the school, since the child functions in a total environment. She urged parents and educators to work together and endorsed parents' involvement in advisory committees, study groups, and the like. She also advised parents to retain their own organizational identity.

Organized Advocacy

A safe prediction about the 1980s and beyond will be the emergence of parents' organized advocacy on behalf of gifted and talented learners. Ginsberg and Harrison (1977) on behalf of the Gifted Child Society (GCS) prepared a handbook for parents on how to mobilize, implement, and monitor educational programs for their talented children. Their handbook strongly urges an alliance between parents and their child's teacher. The alliance would take the form of establishing a local Gifted Child Society. Membership would be inclusive, not exclusive. It is the structure of the proposed society that provides continuing effort. The local society proposed by Ginsberg and Harrison arose out of their experiences at local, state, and national levels. The handbook is instructive for its insight into parent priorities and for anticipating the promising prospect of reasoned, but determined, parent assertiveness. The text is refreshing for its positive presumption that the educational community will respond to external initiative.

Purposes and Functions

The Gifted Child Society could perform direct services in the form of adult education regarding parenting skills and in the form of Saturday workshops and summer programming for gifted pupils. Some parents, gifted and talented themselves, quickly grasp the value of stimulating their children in intellectual and artistic activities. Many, though, are just as able but are discouraged from attempting to heighten their children's curiosity and increase their knowledge because they have read or otherwise been told that they shouldn't "push." The idea that human abilities will just naturally unfold and flower if left undisturbed is a pretty notion, but it just is not true for a great many of today's preschool and schoolage boys and girls. Moreover, correctly administered stimulation is good, not bad, for the young. Parents who share experiences and understandings in the camaraderie of association seem more likely to come to such sound conclusions and to learn to be more effective in putting them into practice.

An advocacy service would seek public school recognition and provision for gifted learners. The history of organizations for other exceptional children and youth suggests that parents and interested citizens (including professionals) initially will organize to establish identity and will emphasize direct services. This initial effort will evolve into public education attempts to obtain public sponsorship of programs for children and youth. Eventually, the organization will maintain an active advisory role to programs and will enlarge its scope on behalf of other persons.

These two purposes can be fulfilled through the use of standing committees. The recommended list provides insight as to the nature of the proposed organization. A maximum list would include:

Community Action	Library	Publicity
Curriculum	Membership	Research
Hospitality	Participation	Scholarship
Information	Newsletter	Ways and Means
Clearinghouse	Planning and Finance	Saturday Morning
Legislative Action	Program	Workshops

Leadership Roles

The executive directorship of the society would be a paid position. The director would be appointed by the board of trustees. The duties would involve (1) acting as the administrative assistant to the president, (2) facilitating and organizing the work of committees, (3) preparation of publications,

(4) representing the GCS before community groups, and (5) organizing GCS meetings. The executive director also would monitor activities and actions to be sure of conformity to the group's constitution. (A sample constitution was included in the handbook.)

The Orton Society offers a parallel example. Its mission is similar to the GCS in that it engages in direct service and organized advocacy only on behalf of children with specific learning disabilities. Typically, the Orton Society employs a salaried director who manages an individualized tutoring service. The director trains paid volunteers for tutoring. The president may assume the responsibilities of an executive director. The board of directors usually will include parents, citizens, and professionals who will provide and suggest informed policy. Financing is derived from fees, dues, fund raising, and grants from private sources. Consequently, the ways and means can vary according to local circumstances. Advocacy services can be a vital role on behalf of public education and school innovation.

Gifted pupils should not be overlooked as fund raisers. The present writers are familiar with a group that raised funds and learned economics. The students decided to market illuminary candles for the Christmas season. The students determined the cost of materials. To cover this cost, the pupils simulated a corporation and sold stock to raise money, with the promise of repayment, in this case without dividends. (In some instances buyers preferred to view their stock as a donation.) The students organized a production line and assembly process and recruited a sales force from among the class and friends. A modest commission for sales was set. Pricing was competitive consistent with prevailing prices so as to not offend merchants in the community. In certain instances, banks and gift shops agreed to sell the candles. These late elementary pupils were able to clear approximately $500 after expenses for donation to a Childrens' Hospital.

Parents as Philosophy Builders

One truly valuable service of an organization of parents and friends of gifted and talented children and youth can be to help the local teachers' association and the board of education regarding such students. Involvement of the PTA in the writing of a statement of philosophy can help win even broader support for it.

Philosophies of education usually are general expressions of belief and intention. They tend to be designed to link smoothly with the overall philosophy of the school system—the belief and value structure that affects all pupils. That is what happened in Yourtowne. Below is the philosophy statement put together by a representative group of parents, students, teachers, administrators, and school board members.

We believe in equal opportunity for education, according to individual ability and need so that all students may achieve to the full limits of their potential.

We believe this is necessary both for the individual's good and the good of society. While we recognize the importance of educating all students for their own sake, we look for a growing awareness of responsibility to society as an outcome of education.

We believe in the appropriateness of developing differential programs to provide for different abilities and needs, taking into consideration the social and emotional characteristics of the individual.

We believe these experiences should be challenging and also demanding of excellence in terms of integrity, self-discipline, and achievement.

In addition, we believe that for the gifted and talented program this includes providing a variety of programs that will both broaden and deepen the educational experience through the full length of schooling, and beginning as early in life as unusual abilities can be detected and nurtured.

We believe this can be accomplished only through the cooperation of the school district and the community.

We are convinced of the importance of having a clearly-worded and detailed Gifted and Talented Education Plan that recognizes individual differences among children and attempts to educate all highly able children in terms of their own strengths, interests, and potentialities. It is believed, too, that provision within the school district for the gifted and talented should benefit all students by providing a variety of opportunities through which students can explore their own abilities. It is felt that gifted and talented students are best served when provisions for special needs are made within the mainstream of the school system. However, special groupings within the mainstream may be appropriate, when learning advantages of the special groupings outweigh known or expected disadvantages.

SUMMARY

The gifted and talented adult is neglected by educators and is not well understood. Yet educators must recognize that they have responsibilities to maintain their roles as continuing educators during the generative period, too. Early burnout is not necessary; its inevitability for able persons is a myth. Mentor roles are rewarding. Organized parents, too, have important roles to play as citizens in addition to the direct care of their exceptional children. An important contribution can be toward establishing an agreed-upon philosophical base for special education for gifted and talented pupils.

UNIT ENRICHMENT

1. Determine if your community engaged in any particular celebration of the 1979 Year of the Child. Can you find any coverage in the media? Describe the ways in which the rights and needs of children were affirmed. In what ways could the schools reaffirm the United Nations Declaration? What common themes are encountered? In this and the following 16 other points, share your opinions or findings on every item.

Early Childhood

2. Prepare a letter of inquiry to a local service organization requesting how it might be able to help either educators or parents of gifted and talented pupils. Also ask about membership.

3. Interview professionals who operate day care, nursery schools, and/or kindergartens. Identify their key ideas about program content and parent involvement.

4. Consult with the principals of elementary grades in your school district. Determine what policies and practices exist for early admission. Prepare an improved policy statement that could be a model for all school systems.

Later Childhood

5. Organize a model for negotiation for teacher/pupil learnings and projects. Conduct a survey of students regarding their opinions about evaluation standards. Include opinions about the relative weight of teacher, learner, and class evaluations.

6. Develop a detailed outline for a position paper to advocate either the middle school or the junior high school as the "best" place to accommodate to the needs of gifted and talented learners. Interview faculty to obtain their opinions. If a school district has made such a change, obtain their reasons.

7. Conduct a poll of admired persons among your students. Identify the traits that account for the admiration. Poll your pupils as to the most admired students. What common features do you observe?

8. Consider this proposition: Teachers should watch TV on Saturday mornings to be aware of the values being portrayed for their students.

Adolescence

9. Conduct a survey to identify perceptions and opinions about adolescence. First, survey principals and teachers for their observations about the attributes of the senior classes over a four-year period. What ten qualities emerge? Second, conduct a survey of teenagers to identify the ten most common attributes of helpful adults. Compare the two lists to identify priorities and perceptions.

10. Interview and otherwise investigate the ways in which secondary schools in your geographical area take advantage of the positive attributes of teenagers as cited by Jordan (1973). Survey a sample of teenagers to identify the in-school and out-of-school interests that reflect these attributes. Perhaps a chart, or graphic display could be prepared. Also contact community agencies and churches to assess how teenagers are helpful.

11. Consult at least five published articles dealing with research or evaluation of school programs for gifted/talented learners. Determine and otherwise identify the means by which the authors established the context for their methodology, results, and discussion. Determine how their strategies could be applied to your own curiosities about education of the gifted. In what ways does experiencing this process enable you to advise others about personal inquiry?

12. Examine career preparation in your school district. Are the tactics of acceleration as evident in the vocational/technical curriculum as in the college preparatory curriculum? Is it possible for students to pursue a dual "track" (e.g., technical and academic) in your district?

13. Conduct a survey of school and teacher policies about educating exceptional pupils. Consult the Wilde and Sommers (1978) discussion about class and course practices. List examples of how your survey participants implement their suggestions. What conclusions do you draw about these practices in helping students learn responsible behavior?

Adulthood

14. Consider the topic of teacher generativity. Select educators you most admire. What qualities about them as persons and as practitioners are descriptive and distinctive?

15. If you were going to place an advertisement of 75 to 100 words to obtain a mentor, what key features would you emphasize? And reversing the process, what kind of advertisement from a protege draws your attention to be a mentor? For example, compose an ad from a protege. Com-

pare the two products. What elements of the mentor/protege relationship emerge?

16. Consider the Prototype for Unit II. What elements of both generativity and mentoring do you observe? How could these elements be formalized into educational practice?

17. Determine if there are any organizations and individuals in your community promoting the cause of gifted and talented children and youth. Summarize the activities.

Understanding and Teaching a Common Curriculum Core

SYNOPSIS

This unit and the next center on what to teach and on how best to teach it to highly able learners. The two units also pay particular attention to the coordination and correlation of content and to assuring continuity among levels of education.

Teacher preparation usually emphasizes one level of education (i.e., elementary, secondary, or middle school). Content preparation, too, is increasingly specialized. Yet, teachers who would work successfully with gifted and talented pupils must take a more comprehensive view, one that both *spans* and *specializes*. Consequently, this unit illustrates curriculum content while Unit IV emphasizes tactics involving individualization of education.

After analyzing a common curriculum core, the discussion falls into four content-oriented chapters. They sound major themes that are well-established points of contact among teachers with different specialties and at different school levels. These points of contact cluster around: the tool subjects and basic skills (e.g., language arts and mathematics), environmental awareness (social studies and sciences), career education (development and preparation), and talent education.

KEY IDEAS

1. Gifted and talented pupils profit from integrated and correlated instruction that facilitates and demonstrates the interdependence of knowledge and skills.

2. Individualized instruction has many forms that are applicable to a wide range of curriculum content and over a great age range.

117

3. Accelerating the pace of expectations and of content is a natural and reasonable response to a gifted and talented pupil's aptitude for rapid, thorough, and genuine learning.

4. Specially designed curriculum packages (e.g., designed cooperatively by subject matter specialists in a discipline and by professional educators) to challenge the most able students are best used at the pupil's own pace. If their use is founded upon a rigid schedule of 180 days and one period per day, and without regard for pupil aptitude, their best use is defeated.

5. Objectives of instruction for pupils become key determinants of curriculum. Key determinants derived from objectives can be used to generate criteria for the selection of materials and equipment.

6. Mentoring emerges as a proved strategy for both career education and talent education.

7. Tactics of differential pace and expanding curriculum are appropriate for career education, also.

A PROTOTYPE

Career education for gifted and talented pupils starts with career preparation that maximizes their wide interests and great potential abilities. A distinguishing quality of gifted persons, aside from breadth and depth, is the early emergence of competency. The following selection illustrates that precocity. It also spotlights the thoughtful concern for all human welfare that can characterize the motivation of gifted and talented persons.

School Children Make History

In Yourtowne the remodeling of a long established junior high school produced a well-equipped, handsome and readily accessible middle school building with grassy lawns and generous outdoor and indoor study, sports, and recreation spaces. While the structural changes were under way, classes had to be relocated and organized chaos often was the order of the day. In the midst of all the dislocations and alternatives four basic scholars/students and their librarian-mentor generated an idea: the collection and publication of an oral history of the old and soon-to-be defunct Stanton Hill Junior High School. They reasoned that if they could interview former and present teachers and principals and seek out long-since-graduated students still in the community they could piece together the story of the school from its opening in 1928 to the time of its conversion into a modern middle school.

Andy Cameron, Megan Washburn, Eric Moscowitz, and Annette Pulaski, sixth and seventh graders, formed a task force to get the job done. They enlisted a history teacher who helped design the project. Interview protocols were designed and field tested. Pilot investigations were run and critiqued. Tape recorders were borrowed and skill in their use was acquired. One of the school system's curriculum coordinators, Ms. Hawkins, held several brief seminars with the students and their teacher-partners, at their request. The purpose was to establish linkage between the English and Social Studies curricula and their work. The product, a local piece of oral history, was thus slated for a place in the future in Yourtowne's regular curricular offerings.

The process of collecting historical information by recording the spoken word encouraged these students to refine and to further expand verbal skills, questioning approaches, and interpersonal relationship qualities. A time-line and plan of activities made for real life experiences in estimating work planning, in gauging output, and in keeping to a predetermined schedule. The sorting out of nostalgic reminiscences from verifiable historical data sharpened decision making and clarifying competencies. The search for people to interview led to the learning of classic investigative procedures akin to those employed by detectives and other seekers of missing persons. Ownership of records, privacy and confidentiality of statements, permissions and copyrights, too, were substantive subjects of study.

Close to six months after it started the project culminated in two major events. First was the distribution of a booklet that summarized the project, a booklet authored by the four students. It was placed in all schools and public libraries in the Yourtowne region. The tapes, subject indexed and edited, were briefly described in the booklet, as was their availability for loan or copy from the Yourtowne Curriculum Library. The other major outcome was the presentation for all interested students and teachers of a workshop on "Planning and Conducting An Oral History Project." The workshop was held at the new Stanton Hill Middle School and, of course, Andy, Annette, Eric, and Megan were highlighted on the program.

Chapter 6

Understanding a Common
Curriculum Core

Teachers and school administrators feel strong pressure to "do something" for gifted and talented learners. It is difficult to resist the temptation to pile on more work (more of the same) or to add on special attractions (yoga, speed reading, model rocket building) without regard to individual pupil needs and interests, just to be able to show that "something" is being done.

Teachers and administrators who opt for a rational and orderly reaction to the mounting pressure to "do something" should find that they can respond in ways that both the general public and specific advocacy groups will respect. One element of the response should be an Individualized Education Program (IEP) type of approach that starts where the gifted and talented pupil is and builds from there. The second element should be a set of goals and objectives for each highly able pupil that are grounded firmly in the school's existing curriculum but that expand and extend it to suit individual needs and interests.

PROBABLE POINTS OF CONTACT

The Common Core

There is more agreement about curriculum content in the United States than one might suppose, given that 54 state and territorial school systems exist independently. This can be translated to mean that there will be more rather than fewer points of common contact among regular class teachers and specialists. A 1955 review by Birch and McWilliams and a 1976 one by Gallagher identify aspects of curriculum that receive common emphasis. Both sources reflected agreements that language arts, mathematics, social studies, and science are priority considerations for regular class teachers. Talent education requires collaboration among the regular class teacher, the

121

specialist in areas such as the arts and physical education, and a consultant in education of gifted and talented children and youth. A 1979 report edited by Passow confirmed these curriculum dimensions and introduced career education as a major additional curriculum emphasis. Consequently, the regular class teacher can expect to be involved in individualized educational planning, part of which is setting individual pupil long-range goals and short-term objectives in these common curriculum areas. These curricular clusters are consistent with those highlighted in the Yourtowne School District. They represent a common core of practice for all teachers regardless of level of education taught. It follows, then, that every educator who participates in the advancement of gifted and talented pupils needs to be informed about the nature of instruction in the tool subjects (language arts and mathematics), the sciences, and social studies as keys to awareness of their environment and the nurturing of careers and talents.

Outcomes of the Common Core

Teaching either content or skills to exceptional learners requires educators to examine their own understanding about the contribution of the content or skills to the pupils. Renzulli and Smith (1979) speak of payoff for highly able pupils in three forms: performance, product, and processes. Performance is commonly measured by scores from objective tests. Products are the tangible results of student effort such as displays, sculptures, poems, paintings, competitions won, or awards. Processes are the behaviors or operations necessary to create products and to achieve performances. All are important. The payoff forms called product and process, though, attract more interest from educators who are committed to individualized education of gifted learners. All three dimensions have their functions. Performance (e.g., knowledge, comprehension, application) lays the foundation for product and process. All three kinds of outcomes should be assessed in program evaluation.

Gallagher (1976) advocates that the tool subjects should stress higher order operations and the world of ideas. He believes that talent education should emphasize the solving of problems related to perfecting talents.

Table 6-1 is presented as an advanced organizer for the subsequent review of the key features of a common curriculum core for gifted and talented learners. Educators can be perplexed by the vast array of packaged instructional materials as well as by "teaching tips" in journals. The Key Features section of this table is designed to suggest possible criteria for selection of products and procedures.

Table 6-1 Key Features of a Common Curriculum Core for Gifted and Talented Learners

Curriculum Content	*Key Features*
Language Arts	Communication Skills
	Developing Values
	Functional Identification
	Self-Esteem
	Insight
Mathematics	Career Education
	Problem Solving
	Productive Thinking
	Intellectual Curiosity
	Functional Identification
Social Studies	Scholarship
	Human Relationships
	Filling in the Gap between Mental and Chronological Age
	Leisure and Recreation
Science Education	Imitation of the Processes of Scientists
	Active Participation
	Developing Values
	Satisfaction from Organized Study
Career Education	Personal Relevance for Subject Matter
	Career Development to Select and Establish Life Roles
	Career Preparation Necessary to Perform Life Roles
Talent Education	Learning the Skills of Problem Seeking
	Lesson of the Values of Teamwork
	Reinforcement for Persistent Efforts and for Self-Pride
	Possible Career Opportunities
	Leisure and Recreation Pursuits
	Physical Fitness Habits that Persist for a Lifetime
	Relevance to Subject Matter
	Learning and Practicing the Skills of Creative and Critical Thinking

KEY FEATURES OF THE TOOL SUBJECTS AND BASIC SKILLS

Language Arts

The language arts include reading, writing, listening, speaking, and perceiving. Perceiving (Gallagher, 1976) takes in awareness of: (1) oneself as an individual person, (2) the motivations in advertisements and other forms of influence, and (3) the connotations of language.

Birch and McWilliams (1955) took the role of language arts in a helpful direction by showing that the functional identification of gifted and talented individuals has long been closely linked to early and extraordinarily rich achievement in reading, writing, and speaking. During reading instruction sensitive teachers observe a particular primary age child's very rapid rate of skill acquisition in comparision with the majority of pupils in the class. They note also the child's more mature responsiveness to ideas and to the subtle meanings of words, especially humor and empathy. These signals are powerful indicators of advanced development.

The Gallagher notion of perceiving seems quite similar to what Birch and McWilliams speak of as critical reading skills. This describes the person's ability to grasp concepts and to act constructively after gaining comprehension. An example would be to relate relevant information to the regulation of one's behavior for personal and social purposes of merit and worth. Another would be to switch from an open to a questioning intake set when one recognizes that a news article goes beyond the facts and begins to editorialize. A follow-up constructive act might be to write a protest letter to the publisher.

Mathematics

Society values mathematics as a branch of human knowledge for its theoretical and practical virtues as well as for its mental discipline. Mathematics is a body of knowledge in its own right. It is essential to all sciences and its applicability is increasingly apparent in the arts and humanities.

It is the gifted and talented who will invent new and startlingly more productive theories and applications of mathematics. The day is long past, too, when gifted girls may be taught the potentially crippling and false notion that mathematics is a "boy's subject." A solid grounding and advanced skill in mathematics is as fundamental for all gifted and talented pupils, as is high competence in the language arts.

One Key Feature of mathematics is its opportunities to foster career education. In the midst of the press for mastery, able pupils must be made acquainted also with what a mathematician is or does and about the relevance of mathematics to most high-level occupations. Gallagher (1976) portrays mathematics as filled with excitement about new discoveries.

A second Key Feature of mathematics is its applications to problem solving. It provides students with opportunities to learn how to use data to arrive at decisions. For instance, how can local population trends help to determine whether to build a new school? What dislocations will result from the next steps toward a decimal system nationwide? How can they be minimized?

Why are Roman numerals not used more widely? Would Roman numerals make any difference to a computer? If a flipped coin comes up heads four times straight, what does that say about the result of the next flip?

The potential of mathematics to develop the Guilford form of productive thinking has been noted, too (Gallagher). Examples might be (1) How would our number system be different if human beings had six fingers on one hand and five on the other hand? (2) How many ways can 63 be expressed? (3) What would be the consequences if numbers had never been invented? and (4) What would be the consequences if the decimal system were applied to time measures, from seconds through weeks?

Birch and McWilliams (1955) point to the satisfaction of gifted and talented pupil's intellectual curiosity as another Key Feature of mathematics. Mathematics involves the what as well as the why and how of processes. They also remind teachers that mathematics provides another opportunity for functional identification of very able pupils through opportunities to observe the learner's pace, accuracy, and understanding in calculations as well as reasoning problems.

KEY FEATURES OF SOCIAL STUDIES AND SCIENCE AS ENVIRONMENTAL AWARENESS

Social studies and science introduce gifted and talented pupils to bodies of knowledge that are significant in their own right as academic disciplines. Each, too, has a history and a present that makes up part of every young citizen's cultural heritage. And each has a future in which pupils will take some part.

One perspective about the role, or place, of social studies and science in the general curriculum is the value of informing students about the world in which they live. "World" as used here really means the many worlds of one's culture, one's community, one's social institutions, and the other influences of one's environment.

Social studies inform future adults of their responsibilities as citizens and of the human consequences of technology. Science informs future adults about the prudent uses of resources, of technology, and of methods of inquiry for solving certain kinds of problems. While specialization of knowledge expands, there also is the pursuit of integration of knowledge among seemingly diverse professionals. For example, M. Wexler (1976), points to the integration of knowledge about psychology and sociology in the education of physicians. Consequently, the future physician will apply information about the psychological reactions of people to illness as well as the sociology involved in the delivery of medical care.

Social Studies

Among the potential benefits of social studies for gifted and talented pupils, one is to introduce the young child to the problems of the real world. Social studies are not entirely rooted in the past; there are immediate applications for the present as well as for anticipation of the future.

This curricular area also facilitates an appreciation of scholarship as sustained effort and learning to engage in balanced judgments. Another outcome can be the learning of principles that undergird the skills of human relationships and that go beyond the superficiality and narrowness of: (1) supply and demand explanations of economics, (2) sex drive explanations of motivation, (3) frustration explanations of aggression, and (4) unhappy adulthood explained by unhappy childhood.

Gallagher lauds discussions and simulation as helpful ways to engage gifted and talented pupils while broadening standard social studies content. He observes that social studies should encourage investigative activities similar to those developed by Renzulli (1977). Both Gallagher (1976) and Birch and McWilliams (1955) agree that social studies can assist gifted and talented pupils to close the gap between abstract intellectual maturity and real life experience. Deliberate education about values contributes to that same objective. The latter also credits social studies with aiding pupils to learn how to make prudent use of leisure and recreation. While this overlaps with the domain of physical education and talent development, there are significant opportunities through the social studies curriculum to acquire understanding of the importance of community and personal resources for recreation and leisure.

Science

Science instruction for gifted and talented pupils should encourage them to imitate the processes of the scientist. Teaching children about the products of science is important. But for gifted pupils especially, science should be taught as the continuing search for truth rather than through exclusive emphasis on close-ended, predetermined solutions to "science problems." Science also affords opportunities for active student participation in learning. Instruction ought not be confined to textbooks. Science education for exceptional pupils can scarcely avoid involvement with values, too. Scientists are concerned about the economic and political uses of technology. The 1970s were characterized by questioning of the premise that every scientific advance automatically was "good" or of worth. The supersonic airplane had few places to land. The controversies about DNA applications and the biological technologies of the clone received vivid illustration in the novel, *The Boys from Brazil.* National policy and ordinary life style are affected by decisions on alternative sources of energy.

Science education also can help pupils derive satisfaction from organized activity. This means, for instance, that the pursuit of interests can be directed to experiencing the rigor of the scientific method while satisfying curiosity.

KEY FEATURES OF CAREER AND TALENT EDUCATION

Interest in career education for gifted and talented pupils grew during the 1970s. Concern mounted that valid occupational information, vocational preparation, and career guidance be part of what such students learn in school.

The nurturing of talent is a traditional emphasis of the schools through sponsorship of art, music, drama, and physical and athletic competitions. It is recognized now that talent development for some pupils is the central thrust of schooling, not merely an avocational hobby or release of tension. Talents have career dimensions that require nurturing, monitoring, and management. Consequently career and talent development have more in common than formerly supposed. Career education is not restricted to the professions and disciplines or skilled trades and occupations. For some gifted pupils the academic disciplines and skills fill in the background of education, with studies such as the dance, sculpture, gymnastics, competitive sports, theater arts, or musical composition and performance taking the foreground.

Career Education

Career education has varied meanings. According to McCurdy (1975), it sometimes is easier to describe what it is not rather than what it is. Gardner and Warren (1978) wrestle with the definition problem in the context of gifted and nongifted handicapped students. Words and concepts such as career, vocation, occupation, job, and work dot the literature. Some specialists use these terms as roughly equivalent synonyms. Others make careful distinctions. For example, the concepts of work and job may refer to what one does to be economically self-sufficient or to provide for the material needs of others. Occupation, a more general descriptor, covers skills necessary to fulfill the demands of jobs and working. Thus, there can be a variety of jobs that fall under the occupational category of printing trades. Vocational connotes the psychological aspects of an occupation that involve interest, aptitude, and competencies. Career embraces the match in one's life among personal life goals, social expectations, vocational attributes, and occupational demands.

The majority of career educators believe that schooling ought to aim at assisting each pupil prepare for an independent life, one that is self-fulfilling and regarded as valuable by society.

Well-designed education for career competency and fulfillment rests on the programming principle of continuity throughout the entire school experience. Career preparation is less than adequate if it is deferred until the senior high school years. Career information can be blended into all content areas without impairment of content. As a matter of fact, career concepts and information sensibly melded with other content enliven subject matter by showing their personal relevance.

McCurdy speaks of career education as the means of applying career development to a school's existing structure of career preparation. Career development is the school's way of helping pupils to acquire the attitudes, knowledge, and skills necessary for them to plan, explore, and establish life roles. Career development's key feature is a firm foundation that integrates self-awareness information about aptitudes and interests with information necessary for career decisions, planning, and placement. Career preparation is the means by which schools develop the attitudes, knowledge, and skills necessary for performing life roles. This dimension requires a blend of academic education with vocational and technical education.

Table 6-2 presents a matrix based upon the McCurdy (1975) discussion. This matrix is intended to summarize the key features of career education. This matrix is helpful for both able pupils and for their teachers to help plan independent studies and projects to mesh the vocational (career development) and the occupational (career preparation). Anyone may use it to make an inventory of school and community resources. It also is a helpful planning chart to structure internships as described in Unit Three.

Career education emphasizes attitudes about self and about one's perceptions as worker, family member, and citizen. Personal job success, satisfaction, and tenure correlates more with affective factors than with level of either education or job skills. Human relationships are significant factors. An example of the interdependence of life roles of career, family member, and individual identity is illustrated by a report from the Institute for Social Research (1979) (Exhibit 6-1).

Understanding a Common Curriculum Core 129

Table 6-2 A Career Education Matrix

Career Development	Academic Education	Career Preparation Vocational Education	Technical Education
Self-Awareness and Assessment			
Career Awareness and Exploration			
Career Decision Making			
Career Planning and Placement			

Adapted from *Career Education in Michigan* by J.K. McCurdy, Michigan Department of Education, © 1975.

Exhibit 6-1 Young People Look at Changing Sex Roles

Attitudes about changing sex roles in our society have raised many questions about the structure of future marriages and families. Will the traditional family in which the husband is the principal breadwinner be replaced by new options such as both spouses working half-time or the wife supporting a non-working husband? Will women continue to be expected to perform most of the housework and child care?

Survey Research Center (SRC) scientists A. Regula Herzog, Jerald G. Bachman, and Lloyd D. Johnston recently looked at the attitudes of 1977 high school seniors for a glimpse of what might be in store. They asked the seniors to rate a variety of family/work arrangements as either "desirable," "acceptable," "somewhat acceptable," or "not at all acceptable." The data were collected as part of SRC's nationwide Monitoring the Future program.

"High school seniors of 1977 appear quite open to sharing family responsibilities between the partners," Herzog, Bachman, and Johnston found. Most thought wives should be able to work and husbands should help with child care and housework. But the researchers point out that there were still many seniors who felt that a wife should work only half-time or not at all. In addition, the wife was clearly preferred as the partner who would be expected to drop out of the labor force to care for preschool children.

When preschool children are not involved, according to the seniors, the wife should work. The arrangement of husband working full time and wife working half-time was least controversial for the seniors. Only about 4 percent said this option was "not at all acceptable." By comparison, both partners working full time was opposed by more males (25 percent) than females (14 percent), while the traditional employed husband with unemployed wife was unacceptable to more female seniors (38 percent) than males (13 percent).

Role reversal—with the wife working full time and the husband employed half-time or not at all—was very unpopular with the seniors. The Institute for Social Research (ISR) researchers report that about 85 percent of both males and females declared that alternative unacceptable. Seniors were slightly more tolerant of the alternative in which both spouses work half-time; about half said they could accept that arrangement.

The presence of preschool children in the family dramatically affects seniors' attitudes toward the wife's working arrangements, the researchers note. For a family with preschool children, the seniors clearly preferred that the husband work full time and the wife not hold paid employment. Forty-one percent thought this was the most desirable arrangement, while only 7 percent said it was totally unacceptable. Although most seniors favored the "unemployed" mother, a great many said it was acceptable for her to work half-time.

"Within this general pattern of preference for a nonworking mother, female seniors more often favor wives working half-time, while males more often favor wives not working at all," the researchers comment. The seniors were more egalitarian in their attitudes toward child care and household duties. When both parents work, the large majority of seniors said an equal division of child care would be desirable; 5 percent or less opted for any of the unequal alternatives. Even for a couple in which only the husband is employed, the seniors most often approved of equal sharing of child care (only 8 percent were opposed). Child care by only the mother was considered less acceptable (30 percent disapproved).

High school seniors also thought a working couple should share housework. That belief was not as strongly held as shared child care, however, and females favored it more strongly than males. The researchers suggest that "seniors may perceive the equal contribution of both parents as less critical for the outcome of housework than for the outcome of child care."

Reprinted from *ISR Newsletter,* Spring 1979, *7,* 3, 5, by permission of Institute for Social Research, University of Michigan, © 1979.

Talent Education

There are two major routes to talent* education, each quite different. Each is valid. Each is· necessary. Both should be present in an acceptable program for gifted and talented pupils.

Educational nurture or talent can center on the products of performance such as those in art, music, sports, drama, architecture, writing, design, and dance. Talent education also can focus on the processes associated with talented performance, commonly labeled creativity, productive thinking, and task commitment.

Gallagher (1976) highlights problem seeking as a Key Feature of talent education. Problem seekers are persons: (1) with self-confidence, (2) well-informed about fundamental knowledges, (3) able to analyze episodes of experience as to accurate recall, (4) able to determine the relevant from the irrelevant conditions for the·statement of problems, and (5) good at the application of valid strategies.

The Key Features of talent do not relate only to individual invention or to solo performance. Birch and McWilliams (1955) call attention to the need to develop teamwork skills in the sense of merging of individual identities necessary for a group performance, such as in a school band. Moreover, nurture of talent can foster pride in one's accomplishments and the sense of accomplishment in sustained effort either for the individual or the group. Birch and McWilliams observe, too, that physical education has its obvious outcomes related to career education as well as its outcomes for recreation and leisure. Maintaining physical fitness is a continuing task for all persons of all ages. Habits of physical fitness (including nutrition) begun during the school years are more beneficial than a "crash" program begun at age 30.

In a subsequent section, the attributes of the problem finder will be analyzed further. It will be seen that the varied ways humans deal with problems create major variances in treatments and emphases in the education of gifted and talented pupils.

---

* There have been other, broader uses of the word talent. Fleigler and Bish, as cited by Gallagher (1976), employed it to include high order abilities in mathematics, mechanics, science, expressing arts, creative writing, music, social leadership, and any other unique creative ability to deal with one's environment. Today the scope of the term talent remains an issue. Our preference is to use it to refer to a somewhat more conventionally recognized group of activities.

SUMMARY

All aspects of curriculum are important for talented and gifted students, and progress in all should be fostered. This chapter has recognized language arts, mathematics, social studies, and science as common components of curriculum identifiable in the nation's schools from kindergarten through secondary levels. Instead of stopping there, however, two other components have been added—namely, career education and talent education. The last two also have been given equal weight in our view of what is needed for appropriate education.

Chapter 7

Teaching the Tool Subjects and Basic Skills

The teacher of literacy skills to gifted and talented learners has three main responsibilities: (1) to maximize the key features of language arts and mathematics, (2) to help pupils understand language and mathematics as forms of communication, and (3) to assist students to integrate literacy skills into the content dimensions of school and life experiences. The purposes of this chapter are to: (1) help teachers see how their subject matter specialties can be made more applicable to gifted and talented learners, (2) provide communication among specialists in the tool subjects and other subjects, and (3) cite helpful examples.

LANGUAGE ARTS

General Structure

The language arts elements of curriculum for gifted and talented pupils should be designed and undertaken as a program of substance, not as an "add on." To establish that substance is present one should:

1. define the purpose and scope of the language arts as a subject area
2. establish expectations that are appropriate and individually matched to the needs of pupils
3. adopt a rational (e.g., philosophical or theoretical) basis or frame of reference that describes the content, skills, and expected products and achievements consistent with purpose and expectations

Kaplan (1979) thinks of language arts instruction for the gifted and talented as composed of exposure, analysis, and expression. *Exposure* refers to spelling out what is expected and how learnings are relevant. *Analysis* is the

133

study of the uses of language. *Expression* is the doing and producing aspects of language arts.

> Neither the introduction of content beyond the regular curriculum nor the extension of the curriculum beyond the age-grade curriculum will automatically designate these modifications as appropriate for the gifted. The relevance of curricular experiences for the gifted is contingent upon more than newness, uniqueness, or difficulty. (Kaplan, 1979, p. 157).

Simply put, the reading of high school or college level science fiction books by an elementary age gifted and talented pupil is not in and of itself acceptance as a *bona fide* adaptation for individualized programming. However, to rewrite *From Earth to Moon* or *War of the Worlds* in light of explorations of the moon and Mars can require both teacher and pupil to use exposure, analysis, and expression, a level of rigor that would fully qualify, if it were a learning activity matched in difficulty and relevance to the pupil's background and the school's curriculum, and if the teaching procedures used corresponded to the pupil's cognitive needs and learning style.

Writing

Language arts should be integrated and correlated with other content areas. Writing must be given attention in *all* instances in which it is used. "Creative writing," valuable as it is, cannot be accepted as *the* curriculum in writing.

Kaplan urged teachers to consider the purposes of writing and to apply high standards of quality under all circumstances. She observed that writing was undertaken for purposes of responsiveness, description, technical or operational reasons, and recording reflections. *Responsive* writing includes the forms of speech, letter, editorial, and poetry. *Descriptive* writing follows the forms of the news or journalistic account, advertisements, and lyrics. *Technical* writing focuses upon methodologies, operation, and procedures consistent with the standards of a profession or discipline. *Reflective* writings encompass the journal, memoir, and monologue. No one *purpose* is more creative than any other.

It would be appropriate to encourage the reflective writing of *My Life as a Million* for a mathematics class. Learning to write effective editorials teaches relevant skills for scientists. An example of correlation of language arts in a learning center with other school experiences is presented in Exhibit 7-1. The context was a school that participated in one's city campaign to attract a national convention. Two members of the site selection committee had visited

Exhibit 7·1 Lessons Learned

Whittier School
10th & Gilmore
Kansas City, Kansas

January 24, 1979

Dear Republican Site Selection Committee Members
Attn: Messrs. Ody J. Fish & Robert Carter

I hope you remember us kids. You came to Whittier School in Kansas to thank us for our letters and drawings. I hope you still have them. We never had anyone as important as you guys visit us. It made us feel good. We were honored very much to have you.

Even though you didn't choose our City for your convention we want you to know there are no hard feelings. Our class and I hope you have a nice time in Detroit, and have a successful convention and elect a Republican.

If you ever need any more drawings just let us know cause we will be happy to do them for you.

Thank you

RODNEY SHEWELL

Reprinted from *First Monday* Magazine, February 9, 1979, p. 11, by permission of the Republican National Committee, © 1979.

---

the school. The children learned lessons and it is obvious that adults learned from these children.

Reading

Instruction in reading requires teaching word attack skills, comprehension skills, and application skills. These are a necessary foundation.

But phonics, sight words, context clues, and structural analysis, despite their importance, are not the whole reading program. And this dimension of reading is likely to be the least difficult for gifted and talented pupils.

For exceptional students, even the earliest reading instruction ought to emphasize comprehension of an author's purpose (analysis) and acting upon the content (expression) in light of the context for reading (exposure). Writing, speaking, and listening should be stimulated by reading. In turn, these outcomes require attention to developing vocabulary, identifying main ideas, and using precise language to communicate ideas and interpretations. Kaplan recommends a correlated approach. Examples could include:

- Given a story or article, the student rewrites it to accommodate to different audiences.

- Given an oral report, the student changes ideas of minimal emphasis into maximum emphasis.

- Given either written or oral selections, the student converts the main idea into an equation, formula, or recipe.

- Given a selection, the student reworks vocabulary so that: (a) the meaning, or main idea, remains unchanged although different words are used; (b) the emphasis is on a new idea through different words, and (c) the reverse of the main idea is given prominence.

Kaplan's exposition provides a sense of confidence that the work of Bloom, Hastings, and Madaus (1971) is indeed applicable. The impression is left that comprehension and applications can be referenced to the cognitive domain. At the basic levels of comprehension the reader, for instance, is expected to accurately decode the content of an author. The Bloom et al. (1971) taxonomy suggests parallel activities that encourage the reader to make an elaborate analysis of author intentions. Readers are required to assess their own reactions and the author's intentions to make an evaluation that would suggest improvements.

There is much to be said for the use of learning centers, particularly if they engage students in language arts activities calling for application. Learning center activities, too, open opportunities to correlate reading with content areas. Learning centers may have the further advantage of built-in self-charting forms of monitoring pupil progress.

Speaking and Listening

Unit IV develops the idea that pupils must learn how to organize themselves to get the most out of discussions. Discussion involvement formats range from speaking as communication to active listening and the application of dissemination skills.

Kaplan's (1979) notion of purposes (responding, reflective, descriptive, and technical) for written communication applies also to speaking and listening. The student and teacher together can set objectives and exercises that lead to skill in altering tactics in light of their purpose and the audience.

An Integrated View

Figure 7-1 illustrates schematically an integrated view for the teaching of language arts for gifted and talented pupils. It discloses the teacher's role of exposure, analysis, and expression in relation to the nature of the content (mechanics, comprehension, and applications) to fulfill one or more purposes (responsive, reflective, descriptive, technical).

For example, suppose a pupil conducts an experiment on the paired-associates learning of nonsense syllables (e.g., ZIX—DWA) vs. meaningful syllables (e.g., TEX—MEX). The student, as part of the contract for the project, is to present the findings in a manner consistent with acceptable professional standards. The teacher could inform and direct (exposure) the pupil to consult the *Publications Manual* of the American Psychological Association Publications and Communications Board for guidance as to the format and conventions (mechanics) of preparation of articles for submission to journals in the behavioral and social sciences and professions (technical). (See Melton (1974) for a further consideration of the APA manual).

Figure 7-1 An Integrated Model for Language Arts

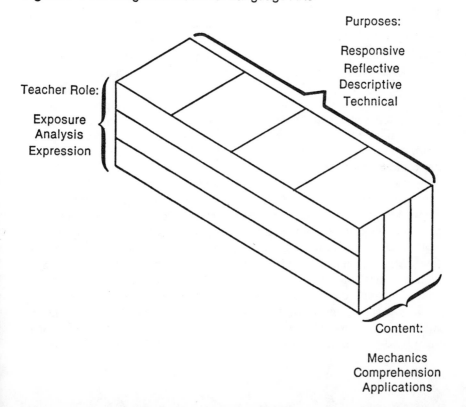

Purposes:

Responsive
Reflective
Descriptive
Technical

Teacher Role:

Exposure
Analysis
Expression

Content:

Mechanics
Comprehension
Applications

Integrative language arts instruction deliberately uses language arts skills in combination with other subjects and skills. Language arts is not separated artificially from the communications specific to a particular field. In practical terms, language and communication skills are given many and varied opportunities for practice.

An example of this style of teaching is illustrated by McRoberts (1979) titled, *What's in a Name?* In the "Name as Game," students write their first, middle, and last names. They then make as many words as possible from the letters.

In another activity, pupils rename the animals in the world according to one dominant trait (e.g., rename an ant using one adjective).

Names also have historical origins that children might wish to understand. Pupils might be interested in the historical origins of their own names as well as family history behind them. For example, Donald is a Scottish name that means Sky Prince.

Exploring opinions about names can be helpful. For example, suppose you could change your name, what would you choose? Would there be advantages to having Social Security numbers for names? Pick a verb and an adverb for a name. List inspirational persons of the same first names. "Who Knows My Name?" games are those in which significant facts are given about famous persons in any field.

Another operational illustration was shared by Soverly, Soverly, Giannini, and Matusik (1975). They recommended the newspaper as a teaching tool that has almost endless possibilities. The comics and sports can snare reluctant readers. The organization of the paper directs attention to the variety of purposes for writing. The content of articles affords opportunities for studying literature, art, music, social studies, and science. Comparing different papers' stories about the same event provides lessons on inference. Composing headlines illustrates how opinions and perceptions condition interpretations. Advertisements highlight the tactics for influence. Many more possibilities could be generated.

A final example (Ellington, 1979) illuminates criteria used in translations and interpretations. Too often the move from foreign languages to English is a mechanical, completely predictable input-output exercise. Students, and particularly the gifted, should be exposed to different translations of the same work to comprehend the options available. Ellington observed that translations require the person to think in two language systems since the languages do not always correspond precisely. Translators can choose to be literal or elect to attempt to convey context and purpose more freely.

The translator, according to Ellington, has the obligation to inform the reader of the option(s) employed. *Cyrano de Bergerac* has been translated literally as well as freely; the preface to one translation warns students of

French to beware since the intent was to convey the drama and conflict rather than assist pupils in a third-year course.

Motion pictures and television programs of actual events provide students with opportunities to exercise skills of translation and interpretation.

Ellington offers three criteria to apply to one's own translations and interpretations as well as to those of others.

1. Readability and comprehension: this attribute, knowledge of and sensitivity about both the language and the audience, leads to fulfillment of communication for the reader. For example, "hardness of heart" may not be as effective as "deeply disturbed by their indifference."
2. Context and sources: this means that the use of the translations or interpretations cannot transcend the quality of their sources. This criterion implies the exercise of scholarship for balanced judgment. It also implies objectivity about points of view.
3. Accuracy: this quality is as crucial as sources. For example, an anachronism may be fatal in one context, but not in another. Shakespeare placed clocks in *Julius Caesar*, which has never proved a serious flaw. Accuracy, however, becomes a potent issue when decisions about behavior are involved. For example, one contribution of the Wright Brothers was their correction of tables of stress factors of flight. Previous errors of calculations had thwarted earlier inventors who had not thought to challenge the givens.

MATHEMATICS

The Many Faces of Mathematics

Mathematics, according to Laycock and Watson (1971), is a fabric of interwoven threads. The nature of mathematics lies in its patterns of relationships. Mathematics goes beyond rote arithmetic, too, in that mathematics communicates ideas and reasoning processes. Arithmetic, or calculation, is an important skill, but not a sufficient skill.

One thread of mathematics deals with numbers as such. A second deals with counting or numeration and other uses of numbers. A third, sets and logic, conveys concepts and communicates ways of organizing thought. Measurement, the fourth thread, includes particular applications of mathematics. The final thread, geometry, is the language and concepts of space, volume, and distance. This way of thinking about mathematics invites consideration of its content as a symbol system in which individuals think and interact with others rather than as a routine, passive activity.

Aside from a subject matter and/or a career field, mathematics fascinates young and old with its properties as a hobby of continuing challenge. An account by Baker (1978) describes a person who can calculate the value of Pi to more than 9,000 decimal places. One may question the "practicality" of this feat. However, it does remain a remarkable achievement. At any rate, it would be hoped that all able students could find in mathematics both high excitement and challenge.

Salient Features of Programming

The comprehension of mathematical concepts and processes is tied less closely to life experience than are literature or social studies, for instance. Pace of instruction, therefore, can be set at whatever rate of speed a pupil is capable of, rather than being limited by noncognitive considerations. This feature, based on extensive research, led J. C. Stanley (1979) to conclude that *pace* of instruction is the top priority consideration with gifted and talented pupils. He lauds the intent of "special" curricula designed by mathematicians and educators to upgrade content and challenge higher order reasoning processes. However, Stanley argues that these adapted curriculum content and divergent thinking instructional tactics per se do not constitute optimum mathematics programming for superior students. His emphasis, rather, is upon accelerated pace. His priority, for the teacher, is first to locate able students and then to help them move ahead at their own individual rates of readiness and with competence.

Stanley acknowledged that acceleration of either curriculum or of pupil requires the kind of aggressive but thoughtful management that will be noted in Unit IV. It was his impression, though, that most educators resist providing this type of adjustment for gifted and talented pupils even though its academic and personal effectiveness are well established. Stanley urged educators to consider pace. For him, curriculum packages designed by mathematicians and teachers represent genuine improvements and advantages only if accompanied by teacher management sensitive to pupil pace. For example, academic and professional organizations of high status may prepare a valid mathematics curriculum. However, if each pupil is forced to spend 180 30-minute class periods on it because the materials contain 180 lessons, the central premise of pacing is defeated. If a student can demonstrate mastery within 30 days, or on the first day, that student's time should not be wasted.

The best use of mathematics curriculum packaged for able learners, according to Stanley, would be determined by the teacher's judgment and by pupil motivation to accelerate the pace. He speculates that subjects such as chemistry, physics, and computer science lend themselves similarly to variable pacing since their content is dependent substantially more upon verbal reasoning than life experiences.

Despite the evidence that mathematics achievement can be essentially independent of other knowledge, it is relevant to a variety of subject matter fields. However, this must be pointed out to pupils or they may miss it. For example, a student with both high motivation to serve people and superior mathematical ability probably will not *automatically* recognize that a career in statistics can fulfill both interests. Stanley called attention to the need for both the nurture of career components and the management of pacing, being careful to suggest linkages of the two for gifted pupils.

The work of Stanley and others spotlights the fact that high IQ (e.g., 130 or above) does not necessarily predict advanced mathematical reasoning. He expresses grave concern about identification and enrollment procedures based solely upon IQ criteria. Grouping mathematics students of the same age by the IQs *alone* actually produces very wide variance because the global intelligence test score is a summation of abilities, of which mathematical and verbal reasoning are only certain aspects. He advocates assessment geared to both aptitude and performance for identification and for individualized educational planning. Most important, if a pupil already is demonstrating precocity in mathematics (or other school work) it does not take a high intelligence test score to say that the pupil should be encouraged.

Priorities for Programming

Stanley (1979) struck several variations on the acceleration theme of programming for mathematically able pupils. The central idea is to help the pupil to get along better and faster in mathematics while also managing well the other aspects of the student's personal and social development. This perspective derives from his directorship of a project for the Study of Mathematically Precocious Youth (SMPY). The project was begun at the Johns Hopkins University in 1971 and has expanded into a nationwide network potentially available to public schools.

Among the most frequent school adjustment options encountered in the SMPY are the following: (1) fast paced classes, (2) grade skipping, (3) early part-time college study, (4) credit by examination, (5) early college admission, (6) college graduation in less than four years, and (7) bypassing the bachelor's degree. *Fast paced classes* may be Saturday morning sessions staffed by public school teachers jointly with university or college personnel and for which the student can receive school or college credit. *Grade skipping* is planned and individualized promotion that usually leads to early admission to high school. *Credit by examination* involves the use of such procedures as the Advanced Placement Program and the College Level Examination Program. The SMPY project can serve as a resource to alert students and schools as to how to maximize the impact of these options. A variety of such opportunities should be in place in school districts, available when concrete evidence of need is found by a high quality guidance program.

Early college entrance is turning out to be one of the more easily arranged agreements among the parents and pupil, the school district, and an institution of higher education. In one option, the student remains in his school district. The other option enables the student to receive on-campus instruction. (Recall Unit I for a fuller discussion.) These adaptations apply to the whole range of school age learners (e.g., 5 to 17) and are well within the capacities of modern school staffs.

Early college admission and *early college graduation* can be arranged by use of advanced standings earned prior to admission, or by taking a larger than standard number of courses each semester, or by attending summer sessions. Some students, according to Stanley, *shun the baccalaureate degree.* These students use their "pure" math studies as passports to career-relevant fields.

Stanley does not downgrade the status of the regular class teacher. Instead, his resume of SMPY experience provides clear guidance to teachers and to other school staff members in the helpful roles they can take in facilitating the entry of able students into situations where they are encouraged to progress at their individual rates.

Integrated Teaching

Stanley's (1979) contention that mathematics is relevant to other content areas is illustrated by suggestions advanced by Birch and McWilliams (1955). Their suggestions have the additional advantage of providing functional opportunities for arousing and holding pupil interest. Further, they can be adapted for pupils of varying ages. The students can:

1. collect and budget funds to feed class pets
2. collect records of class heights and weights
3. measure rainfall and snowfall
4. report on the history of money
5. analyze the school building in terms of metric methods of measurement
6. develop reports on the careers of mathematicians and their contributions to ordinary life
7. establish a time line regarding the history and the impact of numbers
8. analyze the impact of certain numbers in literature and culture such as the unique status of 3, 7, 11, and 13
9. estimate the costs involved in crafts projects
10. raise funds and budget for a class trip

11. consider the use of other number bases such as base 12 in which the system would be 0, 1, 2, 3, 4, 5, 6, 7, 8, 9, t, e, and 10; make up new names for t, e, and 10; reason out the process for calculations
12. develop drawings using geometric shapes
13. study probabilities involved in predicting the weather, batting averages, and traffic accidents
14. conduct statistical surveys of opinions, attendance, and effects of projects; use both reactive and nonreactive techniques
15. develop a career roster to show how mathematics is used and necessary for sports and games, cooking, clothing design, building construction, farming, budgeting, geometry, art, music, and other occupations and activities
16. develop and participate in a plan to coach a student in mathematics as such or in the mathematical aspects of another subject (i.e., longitude, latitude, map projections, and precession of the equinoxes in geography or astronomy)

SUMMARY

Some of the six points under this heading were made in other connections earlier. They are grouped here for emphasis, and they apply to all teachers.

One key role is the identification, facilitation, and management of gifts and talent, especially with regard to individualized pacing of instruction. A second role enhances the relevance of mathematics and language arts through integration of the tool subjects with other content areas. A third role guarantees that parents are fully informed as to the personal, social, and educational implications of their child's abilities. A fourth keeps teachers busy locating satisfying outlets (running interference) for gifted and talented learners to make use of abilities, including tutoring under supervision.

Dawkins (1979) points to a fifth possible role, as does Stanley (1979). It is understandable that either a high IQ or an unusual proficiency in verbal and conceptual aspects of the tool subjects can seduce parents, teachers, and the pupil into neglecting the fundamentals. To avoid that, teachers must monitor not only reasoning and inference skills but also such basic processes as word attack skills and calculations. "Poor in language and able in mathematics" need not be accepted. The well-rounded student requires well-rounded instruction. It is appropriate instruction for exceptional pupils to build on their strengths while, at the same time, strengthening areas in which they are relatively or actually low. The Dawkins report also declares that instruction in comprehension or interpretation should not be reserved for the elementary level, but should be applied any time or place it is needed.

The sixth key role for all teachers concerns career development and career preparation. Two major ideas are linked in this point. First, teachers and other educators ought to take every opportunity to illustrate the relevance of the tool subjects and basic skills to occupations in which highly able pupils evidence interest. Second, flexibility about vocations should be encouraged. Gifted and talented adults have more opportunities than most to shift jobs, and they need to be open to the possibilities in today's occupations as well as occupations that have not yet been created.

Chapter 8

Teaching for Environmental Awareness

Social studies and science share a common goal of promoting awareness and respect for the environment. One concrete objective for social studies is teaching of cooperative behavior as a balance of competitiveness. One concrete outcome for science, neglected in the education of gifted and talented and other pupils, is education for well being and preparation for parenting. Both content areas build upon discovery, though that is emphasized only in the section on science to avoid repetition.

Both social studies and science studies aim at many objectives in addition to helping students achieve compatibility among themselves and with their environment. Both science and social studies instruction, at all school levels from primary through college, embrace the goals of traditional liberal arts, though employing modern methods to reach those goals. Central to these contemporary methods are inquiry and discovery. These procedures long characterized the approach of historians, scientists, and other scholars, but not of students in grade school, high school, and college. Inquiry and discovery emphasize modes of thinking rather than the accumulation of facts. They encourage thinking for oneself rather than sheer memorizing.

This trail leads to a strong commitment to the intellectual adventure of learning. It also engenders interdisciplinary interests. The result is not extreme specialization, but an understanding of a subject in the broadest sense. Inquiry and discovery appeal to both the budding artist and the physicist. For exceptional pupils and others, this way of learning also becomes a way of life that does not end with graduation.

SOCIAL STUDIES

Accommodations for Able Pupils

Kaplan (1979) refers to the teaching of social studies for gifted and talented pupils as a set of accommodations. One accommodation has the teacher adjusting the nature and structure of the social studies curriculum. Another accommodation adapts to the unique attributes and status of the learner. These accommodations normally are made in every community and in all classes. However, Kaplan highlights their special applicability to the teaching of social studies to highly able learners.

Three approaches to curriculum modification include: (1) replacing the standard curriculum with a new unit, (2) applying process activities (e.g., Structure of Intellect) to the regular curriculum, and (3) modifying learning modes (e.g., from passive to active) to either the new unit or to the standard curriculum. Kaplan calls these approaches only partial solutions. Replacement runs the risk of creating gaps in skills and knowledge. Process emphasis may create the unintentional effect of diluting content. Altering learning modes places undue stress upon the how of learning, ignoring the what.

Kaplan's alternatives incorporate the strengths of previous approaches. She urges substitution, or replacing what is not needed in the social studies curriculum, with what is needed. The open-ended nature of the problems and issues in social studies content provides a multitude of genuine situations to exercise thinking. The open-endedness of social studies also allows students to practice skills of learning how to learn through inquiry, discovery, and in other exciting ways.

Alternatives

One adaptation Kaplan recommends is vertical modification. This is for pupils whose command of content is evident and whose need is for more advanced content plus application of content to problem solving and research and inquiry. A second recommended approach is termed horizontal expansion. This focuses on content and information to expand present learning laterally. The third alternative, supplemental, involves the student in highly personalized studies not usually encountered in the standard curriculum. Examples might be self-appraisal in career education, the pursuit of an avocational interest, or content such as computer science. The teacher's judgment, based on knowledge of the pupil's needs, interests, and capabilities, determines the selection of these options. Kaplan emphasizes the necessity for individualization. She reminds teachers and parents that modifications for a group do not guarantee that the interests of an individual are well served.

While promoting three general approaches—horizontal, vertical, and sup-plemental—Kaplan (1979) is aware that teachers are pressed to select tactics for the day-to-day instruction of pupils. She implies endorsement of the Ren-zulli (1977) model for its: (1) three levels of emphasis, (2) reference to content, and (3) stress upon the investigation of real problems. She also advocates the use of guided independent studies and commends the practice of teacher-pupil negotiations and shared evaluation similar to the constructs of pacing.

Planning Pupil Outcomes

Broad-based topics such as "The Needs of People to Survive" are preferred because the very nature of social studies involves knowledge of the relation-ships of people to institutions, to their geography, and to the origins of their culture. Kaplan reminds teachers to be sensitive to at least three types of pupil outcomes or products. One type is searching. This includes the use of techniques of learning how to learn. An example is the use of journal articles and interviews to gain important information. A second type is assimilating, or the "digesting" of, information. Illustrations include the production of hypothesis and inferences. A third type involves reporting. This means the formal application of what was learned to the production of a written or oral report. It demonstrates to students the validity of inquiry in "real life" prob-lems. These three dimensions also represent forms of pupil aptitude. Kaplan observes that a superior IQ does not guarantee that an individual is equally superior in all three dimensions.

Searching, assimilating, and reporting can be used as an alternative to the structure of the Bloom taxonomy to form a curriculum matrix. The content outline would be the vertical dimension while these three outcomes would be the horizontal. The resulting cells would be filled with teacher-pupil activi-ties.

Integrated Teaching

The teaching of social studies can lend itself at all levels, nursery through university, to the widening of interests as well as the integration and correla-tion of language arts skills. Birch and McWilliams (1955) suggest the follow-ing activities that facilitate these purposes:

1. Develop a favorite toy exhibit.
2. Conduct a survey of how children of our school play games.
3. Attend and cover (in the journalistic sense) local events such as build-ing dedications, county commission meetings, and college commence-ments.

4. Serve as a parliamentarian for class and school meetings.
5. Make a display from advertisements that reflect names from history such as Ford, Westinghouse, Robin Hood, and Revere.
6. Prepare a timeline using postage stamps to depict events or persons.
7. Report on 10 inventions that changed American history.

The Virginia Beach, Virginia, public schools (1975) in their gifted and talented program identified the following as helpful for generating pupil interest:

1. Have students vote on their favorite day in history. Compose a newspaper for that day and attempt to have all the sections of a newpaper represented.
2. Obtain permission from a cemetery to make rubbings from tombstone markers. Prepare charts and graphs to illustrate weathering effects and trends such as life span.
3. Conduct an inquiry as to why tolls are charged on certain bridges, tunnels, and highways and not on others.
4. Compare similar holidays in the U.S. and other countries to trace origins and adaptations.
5. Trace the history of the alphabet and compare present forms with their original forms.

American schools and American daily activities teach competitiveness. That is an integral element in the nation's way of life, so it is not surprising nor inappropriate that American public education reflects it. At the same time, there are many occasions when cooperation is beneficial, too. It is particularly important that those most endowed with competitive potential—the gifted and talented—be prepared to respect and achieve cooperation, too. Pearson (1979) suggests that social studies are replete with opportunities for teaching cooperative behavior.

Pearson advocates teacher-pupil planning and group projects to enable students to experience social relationships and to share excitement at the achievement of common goals. As groups move toward independent activities, teachers need to serve more as consultants (see Unit V) to resolve group dynamics.

As a strategy to foster cooperation, Pearson advances "jigsawing." Four to six pupils work on a social studies lesson or unit on California, Texas, or Maine, for instance, that is divided into five parts: (1) government, (2) topography and climate, (3) history, (4) industry, and (5) people. Each pupil is responsible for one piece, but all students are responsible for all five pieces. Consequently, each student must work with the others in learning. The pupils are tested by the teacher, usually by criterion-referenced procedures. In initial stages, Pearson recommends the use of learning centers so that pupils can concentrate on the teaching and learning. Pearson cites research to the effect that this type of group learning is superior to lectures and that it fosters friendships among the participants, too.

SCIENCE

Science Education and Able Learners

It will be recalled from Chapter 6 that one Key Feature of science is that it can be a personally satisfying way to satisfy curiosity about events in one's world. Exhibit 8-1 exemplifies that avocational potential.

Exhibit 8-1 Hobbyist Discovers a Supernova

Star watching, a district man's "adventure of the mind" for the past 27 years, has enabled him to become only the third man in history to visually discover a supernova in the heavens.

Gustave "Gus" Johnson, 40, a Mt. Lebanon High School graduate who moved to western Maryland in 1961 to better his study of the constellations, made his discovery here last Wednesday evening.

What he saw through his 8-inch reflector telescope was 40 million light years away in the galaxy known as Messier 100.

Recalling yesterday how he noticed that bright little star, Johnson said, "It looked a little odd, tucked in a corner of M-100."

With his pastor, The Rev. David Long, Johnson returned to his residence to check a star chart, which did not list his find. They hurried back for another look, but "the constellation had drifted behind the trees."

After he sent notice of the discovery to the American Association of Variable Star Observers, which in turn alerted observatories, Johnson saw his supernova again the next night. So did Kitt Peak Observatory near Tucson, Arizona, and an Italian observatory.

A supernova has been described as the bright flaring of a star before it burns out. Its brightness up to 24 times greater than that of the sun, a supernova diminishes in intensity over months or years until it becomes identifiable only as a pulse on today's modern astronomical equipment.

Last night, Johnson's supernova was still burning brightly—in fact, it had increased several magnitudes in intensity, indicating it has not yet peaked.

The last time someone searching with a simple telescope spotted a new supernova was in the mid-1920s. The first such discovery was in the 1880s in the Andromeda galaxy, only two million light years away.

"This shows that 19th century astronomy isn't dead," remarked Johnson. He counted his discovery as a victory for the "visual observer" who, without the elaborate technology of the 20th century, still watches the sky and finds it "amazing to contemplate the extent of the universe."

A part-time high school teacher, Johnson began star watching in the seventh grade in Vandergrift, where he was born.

His high school years were "pre-Sputnik" so Johnson is largely self-taught in astronomy, although he has attended three colleges en route to his teaching degree.

He is still active in the Amateur Astronomers Association of Pittsburgh, the country's second largest and oldest group devoted to star gazing.

"It's a wonderful birthday present for our association," said Tom Reiland, president-elect of the local astronomers, who will be celebrating their 50th anniversary in June.

Johnson indicated he may make the trip for the local group's week-long celebration.

But in the meantime, he estimates he has at least an additional two or three weeks of gazing through his telescope at the supernova he was the first in the world to see.

Reprinted from the *Pittsburgh Press*, April 24, 1979, pp. A1, A4, by permission of the publisher, © 1979.

Scientific aptitude, according to J. C. Stanley (1979), consists of reasoning about events, from which one generates inferences and then subjects them to tests for possible verification. To be sure, content *is* essential. A larger objective, however, is to learn and emulate the behavior of scientists.

There are significant parallels between the behaviors of scientists and teachers. Both professions attract problem solvers. This means creating order out of chaos through: (1) specifying events that have prompted a need to make choices, (2) gathering information to confirm perceptions, (3) entertaining new ideas and new data, (4) generating possible solutions, (5) selecting options, (6) carrying out solutions, and (7) evaluating the consequences. In this sense, instruction is scientific, the aptitude/treatment interaction model is scientific, and the Individualized Education Program (IEP) is scientific. Because of how the material is presented, many teachers emerge from required science courses proficient only in content and in the demonstrations of experiments. Their understanding of problem solving remains compartmentalized from their methods courses. They do not acquire the sense of inner pride in confronting the unknown. They learn to be passive receivers and miss the satisfaction of discovery. The overall result reinforces the tradition of the one right answer rather than the ability to think of different pathways to solutions. Science, however, is not divorced from ordinary life.

A stereotype of American scientific education is that it has been mainly a response to scientific advancements in other nations. Science becomes, according to Tannenbaum (1979), a political pawn akin to Kipling's *Tommy Atkins*. A recently produced doomsday weapon glints in the sunshine of public favor only to fade when the nation pulls ahead in another advance toward oblivion. Seen in that light, science falls into disfavor as a captive of the military-industrial complex. Again, public impressions and public policy acquire clarification, for open-minded examination reveals that image to be shallow and false.

Both Gallagher (1976) and Stanley (1979) agree that science curriculum "packages" of good quality abound. They are very useful for personally paced guided individual study. But they are confined, in terms of content, to only biology, physics, chemistry, and perhaps geology. Albino and Davis (1975) identify health education as a neglected orphan. It often falls between the provinces of the science educator and of the physical educator. The Sputnik Syndrome, too, contributed to the orphan status. Yet health education has high science content, facilitates scientific method, possesses career potentials, and provides the gifted and talented student with information of personal relevance.

The Passow (1979) resume contains no chapter specifically directed to science education, although there are chapters devoted to language arts and social studies, mathematics, art, and career education. The subject matter index lists only six citations that deal with public attitudes toward science.

It is to be hoped that a renewed commitment to health education and to science as inquiry and discovery will restore science to the high stature it deserves in the education of gifted and talented and other pupils.

The scientist as citizen concerned about the uses and consequences of technology will assist in the process. Health education offers a fine example of the correlated and interdisciplinary style possible in science education. In addition, this chapter considers science as discovery and inquiry that can have generic application to science as well as to other aspects of curricular content and of extra-school life.

EDUCATION FOR HEALTH AND LIFE ROLES

Health information is most effective when it is believed to be relevant by pupils. Otherwise, health instruction degenerates into moralizing about avoiding "bad habits."

Health education is undertaken by the schools, in large measure, as both instruction and as guidance. For example, Barnes and Nybo (1978) say:

The major goal of health education is to help students permanently improve the quality of their lives. Its aim is to develop positive health behaviors based upon accurate knowledge and sound values. (p. 23).

Hentges (1978), defining health education, says that through it

a person will be aware of what constitutes health; assume greater responsibility for his/her own health; be able to cope with illness; be able to use the health care system appropriately; and enhance the patient-provider relationship. (p. 31).

The components of health education are: (1) informing, (2) personalizing information, and (3) applying information. The first is found in units on nutrition, personal hygiene, or anatomy and physiology. The modern health educator recognizes that education for health also involves internalizing information to one's own body and decisions about its care, protection, and regard. There also is the recognition by health educators that one's information and misinformation are carried into adulthood and continue to influence adult behavior.

The first component—informing—survives for two reasons. First, the study of one's body is of natural interest. Children are interested in their own bodies. Nutrition, as the body's fuel, helps to respond to those curiosities. The onset of puberty creates another occasion for motivation to comprehend a common event with highly personalized meanings. Second, informing stays important because of what teachers, both regular class and health specialists are trained to do.

The second component developed as an outgrowth of the first and as a form of pupil guidance. Personalizing information about health involves decisions about the individual's (1) nutritional habits and weight control, (2) habits of regular exercise, and (3) prudent use of substances. The emphasis accorded all three reflects and is dependent on (1) teacher competencies, (2) community priorities, and (3) school district sanctions.

The third component arose out of both of the others. Applications of health information can have their immediate payoffs as well as deferred outcomes. A pertinent example is the inclusion of parent education, or parenting, as a component of health education.

There are dozens of difficulties in implementing all three components, although most need not be permanent obstacles. One difficulty is the availability of teachers who have accurate information and who are psychologically comfortable about the subject matter. Another is an informed community and informed parents. Controversies are defused when intentions are shared. For example, accurate nutrition information does not have to appear to be an attack on a family's tradition; parenting classes (Rosenberg, 1978) should not be presented as a criticism of the practices of the student's parents or grandparents; and family life instruction should not slur the single-parent family. A further condition is that content should be accurate and realistic. The failure of some substance abuse programs, according to Bard (1975), has been their emphasis upon absolutes and hard sell tactics. In fact, these approaches may cause increased curiosity and abuse. A final condition is that instruction, methods, and materials should be as attractive and educationally sound as those of any other content areas. Too often, according to Bard, programs are initiated in an atmosphere of crisis without sufficient planning and development.

An example of health education that meets the above criteria is illustrated by Albino and Davis (1975). The purposes of their project were to develop good health concepts in an exciting and stimulating way and to help young people learn how to make wise decisions about matters affecting their personal and community health.

One unit for sixth graders was about the heart and circulatory system. A first phase consisted of a learning center that contained a disassembled model of the human body. Working in small groups and directed by a cassette tape, students learned the parts of the body and the circulation system. In a second phase, teachers and the principal donated blood samples. These samples were used to study blood in cells, tissues, and organs in the body. In addition, honors students from an advanced high school biology class assisted the sixth grade students in dissection projects. The sixth graders constructed a floor diagram of the heart by which they demonstrated to the high school students how to pretend to be droplets of blood moving through the heart. In subsequent phases, members of the medical and health community participated in lectures, demonstrations, exhibits, and visitations. Throughout the phases, students investigated comparisons between smokers and nonsmokers. There was no pressure on presumed evils, only the comparisons.

This style of teaching was correlated and integrated with other content subjects through (1) searching dictionaries for the root words of medical terms, (2) writing thank-you notes to resource persons, (3) making graphs to plot diseases, and (4) comparing diseases in other countries. School attendance was at an all-time high and discipline problems were at an all-time low during this period of eight to ten weeks. The level of content achievement among the sixth graders was sufficient to challenge their high school mentors, all of whom had earned college scholarships in the biological sciences. Moreover, the pupils reflected the message of the good news of maintaining good health. Albino and Davis observed that the setting for their project was sixth graders in schools typically considered as serving minority groups and economically disadvantaged neighborhoods.

The difficulties with substance abuse education, according to Bard (1975), can be the overkill atmosphere. This crisis atmosphere with an overload of horror facts can create heightened curiosity to sample what has so exercised adults. He urges that education concentrate on why some people go from use to abuse, what the danger signals of abuse are, and where to get help. He argues for stressing respect for drugs and for the well-being of the human body. Students also need to learn the meaning of risks and that the human body is not like a car whose motor can be readily replaced when something goes wrong. Bard advocates sound individualized education as one of the best remedies for substance abuse. An achieving student is less likely to require escape. Bard also implies that teachers can best assist their students as consultants in the Parent Effectiveness Training (PET) and Values Education sense (see Unit V).

Health education, according to Rosenberg (1978), can prepare pupils for life roles. The Alliance for Health, Physical Education, and Recreation, in cooperation with public schools, health professionals, and the National Congress of Parents and Teachers, has selected parenting as a unifying theme around which to cluster a curriculum. N. L. Johnson (1978) speaks of the purposes to educate parents about:

> (1) ... what behavior to expect at certain ages, (2) ... materials and techniques they can use to enhance the daily interactions with their children, and (3) ... becoming more involved in the institutions affecting their child, e.g., medical care, day care centers, and preschools. (p. 5).

As to education for future parents (including junior and high school students), Gaston (1978) defines instruction on parenting as:

> (1) helping students understand the physical, emotional, intellectual, and social needs of infants; (2) giving students specific skills in child care and child rearing; (3) helping students to learn to meet

their emotional needs and the needs of an infant; and (4) helping students to be realistic in their expectations of themselves and their child. (p. 13).

Gaston urges that students be encouraged to recall and to think about the ways in which they were raised so as to help retain those practices that were most helpful. The overall purpose of teaching parenting is to enable students to acquire sufficient self-confidence to use the techniques and act upon the attitudes they develop. She also insists that parenting not be restricted to future mothers, but that future fathers be included, too.

According to Gaston and Johnson the curriculum content and instructional activities ought to emphasize at least certain basics: essential nutrition, appropriate clothing, physical care of infants (e.g., bathing, diapering), suitable environment and equipment, and the "economics" of parenthood (e.g., prudent purchases). Another unit might center on use of community resources for health care, social services, and educational facilities. A third unit would involve concepts of growth and development and helpful practices of parenting with respect to reasonable expectations and reasonable responses. The unifying concept, according to Walker (1978), is enabling persons to learn nurturance. The theme of nurturance as described by Walker is consistent with earlier resumes of tactics, especially those of Ginott (1972).

Parenting is important for the family of the gifted and talented learner and should be a major program component. As can be seen, the sciences and practices of child development, psychology, nutrition, sociology, physiology, pediatrics, education, and helping relationships all are interwoven into helpful education for one of life's most important roles.

Education for Discovery

The teaching of science (Verbeke & Verbeke, 1972) lends itself to a learning style called discovery.* It has much in common with inquiry, creative thinking, and problem solving. These share a common core of behaviors although the terms vary. They employ the term discovery as the overall, inclusive term. In technical terms, discovery is a generalized process in which the person uses exploration and systematic trial and error to acquire new learning. Inquiry is the individual's structured use of strategies for relating old information to new experiences. Creative thinking refers to flexibility and originality of thought. Problem solving means organized effort directed at the reduction of tension through selection of alternatives. In a general sense, creative thinking, inquiry, and problem solving are aspects of discovery, according to Verbeke and Verbeke.

---

* The discussion of discovery in the next several pages has value for designing education for all children, but in our judgment it is the method of choice for gifted and talented pupils.

Because discovery procedures parallel the scientific method, Verbeke and Verbeke consider discovery tactics especially applicable in teaching science. To a great degree, also, the discovery procedures work well for mathematics and social studies.

Discovery is in some respects pupil aptitude and in some respects treatment. Its most attractive feature, according to Verbeke and Verbeke, is that discovery is a learning style with which children enter school. It seems natural with young children. Preschoolers manipulate objects to form relationships. Children learn to approach, to defer, to try another angle, to deter, and to return again to resolve. They learn to be independent and to take problems to others for consultation. Children learn that some problems and solutions are persistently elusive and then almost suddenly become obvious. This sudden perceiving of the obvious is the theme of discovery. For example, the obvious fact about discovery learning is that it is a "natural" learning style of children. Methods of discovery teaching, consequently, enable adults to readily match educational content to this style that seems so much a part of children's normal behavior.

The antecedents of discovery as a pupil (Verbeke & Verbeke, 1972), are: (1) attitude, (2) accommodation, (3) activation, (4) practice, (5) self-loop, and (6) readiness. They pay tribute to Bruner for his contributions to the concept. Attitude, for example, means the pupils' belief in their ability to solve problems or that problems can be solved. Accommodation expresses the compatibility of new learnings to earlier experiences. In many instances, the pupil will need to be informed of compatibility as in learning the synonyms of terminology. Activating refers to the teacher's use of introduction and context setting and of incentives. Practice is made up of past and present opportunities to experience discovery. Self-looping describes a looking back or a review of one's efforts to evaluate the results of one's efforts. Readiness relates to the prior and current possession of sufficient relevant background content with which to discover relationships or seek solutions.

Attitude and self-looping are critical variables. Because a lesson is labeled as "easy" by the teacher does not mean that it will be so perceived by the pupil. Ginott (1972) observed that labeling tasks as easy is one of the ways students are unintentionally defeated by otherwise well-meaning teachers. If a pupil "fails" an "easy" task, the opinions of inadequacy are reinforced; if the pupil succeeds in an "easy" task, there can be the sense of nonaccomplishment. Labeling as "easy" is no incentive. The best reassurance is active listening and assurance of lending help. Self-looping enables pupils to reflect on their behaviors and accomplishments and to value their efforts from transforming the new into the familiar or obvious.

Another attractive feature is that discovery teaching is applicable from an elaborate minicourse to a discussion of films. Its essence is to enable pupils to move from hunch to intuition to analysis and eventually to a conclusion based upon evidence.

Verbeke and Verbeke (1972) paid tribute to Suchman for the use of discussions for discovery teaching. For example, a film would be shown involving a brass ring and a brass ball. The viewer would see that the ball could be passed through. The ball would then be held over a flame. The ball then could not be passed through. For the learner, this might initially be unexplainable. A helpful pupil-teacher dialogue could ensue:

P: How could this happen?
T: You are puzzled?
P: Yes! First the ball could pass and then it couldn't!
T: There ought to be an answer and you wish I would tell you.
P: Yes! It must be a magic trick. There's some trick!
T: No, there is no trick.
P: Well, if it isn't a trick, what is it?
T: Perhaps you have some other ideas?
P: Were the ball and ring at room temperature to begin with?
T: Yes.
P: After the ball was heated, it didn't go through?
T: Yes.
P: If the ring had been heated instead of the ball, would the results have been the same?
T: No.
P: If they both had been heated would the results have been the same?
T: That all depends.
P: That all depends, what kind of answer is that?
T: You wish I would be specific. You are doing so well. You're feeling that you're losing ground. You're almost going to give up.
P: O.K., if they had been heated to the *same* temperature, would the ball have gone through?
T: Yes.
P: Would the ball be the same size after it was heated?
T: No.
P: Could the same experiment be done if the ball and ring were of different materials?

The episode illustrates how learners use a plan to organize inquiry. First, the pupil is encouraged to identify, verify, and assess conditions. This leads to observation and inferences about changes in conditions that may be related to other changes. Second, the pupil is encouraged to test out the validity of perceptions of relationships. This means that the pupil must assess the relevance of particular conditions to particular events. Third, the pupil can test out concepts (e.g., temperature) as sources of solutions. Yes/no answers by the teacher provide feedback to the pupil regarding the verification or accuracy of perceptions. They are also used to provide feedback for the pupil's hypothesis. As pupils are forming the basis for experimentation (e.g., relationships between conditions and events), the teacher can respond with: That all depends. Can you tell me more? How could you find out for yourself? The purpose of these responses is to maintain pupil initiative, to prevent random guessing about what the teacher is thinking, and to encourage unconsidered possibilities.

This account illustrates also how active listening could be used to diffuse pupil feelings of frustration and to convey support for pupil efforts. Verbeke and Verbeke (1972) recommend the use of review periods to encourage the self-loop process. The tactics of pupil questioning and teacher answering reverses the usual patterns in which teachers dominate 80 percent of conversations and communications.

The same process can be used for demonstrations, pupil experiments, follow-up of visitations, interviewing of resource persons, and the like. Dialogues such as these also are helpful preparation for pupils to experience as a foundation for more complex inquiries and more complex projects of investigation and reporting.

Education As Reporting

Discovery, as recognition, often leads to the reporting and sharing of one's results. Typically, the form is a written report.

With highly able pupils, information about the conventions of reporting provides a helpful context in which to discuss a problem. It helps to comprehend the purposes and goals to be served by investigation.

For secondary level or for graduate level students, a research course too often opens a door only into a maze of footnotes, margins, and statistical methods. Scientific methods of inquiry appropriate to various problems become subordinate. Consequently, the student compartmentalizes research separate from the process of problem solving in general. Our preference is that early introduction to the mission of scientific writing be tied to an actual investigation and its report.

Another weakness in teaching the "how to" of reporting is that the way the parts of a report are presented leads to the belief that one must conduct a study in the same sequence that one writes a report on a study. It can be difficult for students to unlearn these first impressions.

A positive example of constructing a match between inquiry as curiosity and reporting as communication applicable to science can be found in a publication developed under the leadership of Melton (1974). He advances the belief that plain language is the substance of scientific writing and that ideas exist in language, not in footnotes, fixed rules, and conventions of an establishment. The use of footnotes, rules, and conventions should be limited to providing the reader and author with a stable frame of common reference for communication.

In a technical sense, according to Melton, the parts of a scientific report and their sequence in a paper would be the title, author's name and affiliation or sponsor, abstract, introduction, method, results, discussion, references, and appendix. The introduction, method, results, and discussion sections set forth an author's control motivation for reporting.

The function of the introduction is to inform readers about what problem is being considered and what strategy is being employed. Introductions serve to link the problem, the strategy, the theoretical and context base, previous studies of others, and the proposed strategy. Controversies, and options, should be considered. The introduction concludes with a statement of the research question or hypothesis. The purpose of a hypothesis or question is to inform readers of what results are expected and reasons for expecting those results. When the study does not lend itself to hypothesizing, the question to be investigated is stated instead.

The method section communicates to the reader how the study is done. It is usual practice (for reader benefit) to describe subjects, participants, and sample population as a separate subsection. Another subsection covers the materials and apparatus used. The final subsection reports the procedures that inform the reader as to: (1) the use of materials and subjects, (2) the gathering and interpretation of data, (3) the definition of variables, and (4) the means used or thought to influence performance.

The results section summarizes collected data and interprets these data as answering the question or supporting the hypothesis under study. The discussion section is addressed to the consequences of the results as well as implications for practice and for subsequent studies.

Melton advises prospective authors to be guided by journalistic style questions to test out their coverage. Examples of these questions are summarized in Table 8-1. These questions can be understood as a form of self-looping like that advocated by Verbeke and Verbeke (1972). Moreover, these questions may be transformed by a reader to assess personal comprehension of an article. Another transformation for the reader may be as a checklist for the improvement of one's own proposed investigations.

Table 8-1 Pertinent Questions About Reporting An Investigation

Major Components and Subcomponents	*Pertinent Questions*
Introduction	
General	What problem is dealt with? What is the point of the study? What links the study to previous work? What implications can the study have? Why should the study be undertaken?
Hypothesis or Question ..	What results can be expected? Why can they be expected? What variables are necessary for testing?
Method	
Subjects	Who participated? How many participated? How were they selected? What treatment groups were assigned? What were the demographic traits—age, sex, and other variables?
Apparatus	What equipment/materials were used? What links to the experiment are evident? What are the best ways to describe uses?
Procedures	What was done and why was it done?
Results	
Exposition	What is the main idea of results or findings? How do the results or findings fit the data? How sufficient is the detail?
Graphics..............	What purposes of clarity are served? How efficient (e.g., use to summarize) are graphics?
Discussion	
Exposition	What contributions have been made? How has the study helped resolve the original problem? What conclusions and theoretical implications can be drawn from the study?

Adapted from Publications Manual of the American Psychological Association, 2nd ed., 1974.

Able students' investigations often originate with curiosity about an apparatus or about a form of behavior such as a habit. Experimentation (or fooling around, as they irreverently term it) with aspects of method is a productive starting point. Sometimes, the starting point is exposure to attributes of school age learning, and whole vs. part learning. This leads to fooling around with method dimensions. Typically, the student becomes curious about previous efforts/studies and/or the guidance of theory. In this way, students are inducted into a rationale for the introduction. As students express their wish to progress from fooling around to more formal efforts, the procedures necessary for results and discussion become a natural source of guidance. It is instructive to observe that students who seem apathetic in lectures or discussion, and who seem disorganized in library research, can become disciplined investigators. By the same token, students who mumble during recitations often become first-rate orators in sharing their results with their peers.

Students often need to abstract information for their own papers as well as abstract the writings of others. Melton (1974) supplies a helpful format for producing an abstract. Written in 100-175 words, the abstract contains statements about the problem, method, results, and conclusions. Attention is given the sample population (i.e., number, age, sex) and to research design (i.e., pre/post, contract/experimental), test instruments, apparatus, and data gathering procedures. An abstract of a theoretical article would be about 75 to 100 words. Its elements include the topic covered, the central thesis, source used (e.g., opinion, published literature, research studies) and the conclusions drawn.

Integrated Teaching

An irony about teaching science is that gifted students frequently have few opportunities to explore and discover for themselves. Caney (1979) proposes an exploratorium to give pupils just such opportunities for active learning. The concept of the exploratorium applied properly transforms class space into a well-organized display center and museum.

The organization of an exploratorium can center on collections of three types. One is the use of a gifted pupil's already begun collection. A second type is the collective collection, which is a collaborative effort. A third option is the round robin collection in which one pupil contributes the first item, the next student contributes another item that is related in some way, and so the collection builds. The next step is to create sense from (organize) the items. This involves the students in serving as curators to classify items. Student curators make decisions as to the relationships of items to an overall theme.

Patterson, Saino, and Turner (1973) suggest that collections be organized around a journalistic style of inquiry. They cite examples: *what* is an item made of, *where* is it used, *how* is it used, *when* is it used, *who* uses the item. They observe, in passing, that collections can be functional signs or indicators of able students in that such pupils go beyond acquisition. The able student possesses or quickly acquires a degree of organization, a resourceful strategy for collecting, and insists on great detail in descriptions about items.

The final step is deciding upon strategies for display of the collection. For example, an exhibit on "How We Are Alike and Different" could assemble items or it could use equipment to invite viewers to contribute. Viewers could:

(1) have their fingerprints taken, (2) contribute handwriting samples, (3) contribute a strand of hair, (4) trace a hand or foot, (5) draw a hero, (6) share a baby picture, (7) share items of a favorite color or flavor, and (8) share a favorite wish. A display on space could be housed within a model of a spaceship.

Birch and McWilliams (1955) advance ideas that reflect for the gifted and talented the integration of science with other content areas. As examples of individual projects, the student would: (1) conduct experiments in animal breeding, (2) collect, classify, and display collections, (3) serve as a lab assistant to a teacher, (4) build a model to illustrate the structure of plants, animals, or machines, (5) review science fiction for either its technical accuracy and/or its forecasting, (6) keep a file of newspaper clippings and magazine articles on science and analyze their contents as to accuracy or as to the "image" of science, (7) review biographies of famous scientists, (8) review and recommend science texts for the school library, and (9) participate in a science fair.

Examples of group projects also were cited by Birch and McWilliams. The student would: (1) organize and conduct a weather bureau, (2) plant and supervise the landscape of the school, (3) investigate soil erosion and suggest remedies, (4) investigate how the library can help in scientific research, (5) conduct an experiment in habit training of a pet, (6) organize a science-in-the-news for broadcast over the school public address system, and (7) organize and conduct a school science fair.

Key Roles of Teachers

Four special roles fall to the teacher in the context of science instruction for especially able pupils: model, values educator, interest booster, and functional assessment.

As a model of the scientific method, the teacher's flexibility in considering alternatives supplies powerful lessons in demonstrating the value of an open and receptive mind. A teacher's own sense of curiosity, for instance, can be infectious.

Science, like social studies, involves values and beliefs. In this sense, a second role is as a values educator. The schools should have sufficient communication with the community and the home to defuse any controversies before they arise, so values can be openly explored.

A third role is that of motivator or interest booster. Learning centers, the exploratorium, and the like can build upon initial interests and expand them. Within this role, the teacher will encounter opportunities to extend career education, too.

A fourth role is functional assessment. For instance, the way a student behaves about collections was mentioned as an indicator of high aptitude. In a similar way, speed and fullness of pupil comprehension give teachers clues to aptitude. Science, regardless of mode of instruction (e.g., lecture, discussion, learning center) involves comprehension.

According to Spiegel (1979), limited comprehension is not always explained by the pupil's failure to understand a message (e.g., print, verbal). She suggested ten pertinent questions that teachers could use to assess comprehension activities, especially those that might be involved in discussions and in learning centers. These questions and the appropriate steps for teachers are summarized in Table 8-2.

Table 8-2 Pertinent Questions About Comprehension

Pertinent Questions	*Pertinent Steps*
Are the words within appropriate difficulty/decoding levels?	Given confusion about an entire passage, word difficulty should be assessed and appropriate difficulty selections should be introduced.
How specialized is the vocabulary?	Words may be familiar but not in a special context such as cabinet in social studies, product in math, etc. Review of such words prior to task would be helpful.
Did the person follow instructions?	Directions should be practiced prior to attempting them. Directions should be scanned for words that need interpretation such as circle, check, etc. Learners should report direction.
What is the fit between the person's experience and selections/directions?	Reading about cricket can be confusing. Teachers need to review their knowledge of both student and selection and fill in any gaps.
What is/was the student's level of motivation?	Student interest can be heightened if clear purposes are mutually planned in advance.
How appropriate is requested mode of expressing answers to student's preferred mode of response?	Some students write well but are reluctant speakers and vice versa. Ways should be found for the student to demonstrate comprehension through the strength. Improvement can take place elsewhere.

(continues)

Table 8-2 continued

Does the pupil understand
  questions/directions? ..... Students may not be familiar with the task involved. For
                              example, compare and contrast involves similarities
                              between two elements and differences. Pupils may
                              need coaching in the decoding in the language of
                              questions.
Does the pupil remember con-
  tent? .... The pupil should be encouraged to take notes for
                              reference.
Whose answer is "right"?* ... Teachers should be alert to whether either the pupil's
                              answer is right/correct, or both the pupil and teacher
                              answers are correct/valid inferences.
Does the material fit the ques-
  tion/direction?........... Teachers should double check to ensure that there is
                              sufficient content for comprehension.

Adapted from "Ten Ways to Sort Out Comprehension Problems" by D. L. Spiegel, in
Learning, March 1979, *7,* 40-41.
*This is especially significant in the context of respect for divergent thinking. We encourage all teachers, from the earliest grades on, to deliberately elicit pupil responses that illustrate that more than one way of regarding any phenomenon is not only possible but desirable, if the phenomenon is to be fully comprehended.

SUMMARY

The gifted and talented pupil's curriculum is, in the broadest sense, the total environment, animate and inanimate. To reach equilibrium with one's environment is one way of conceptualizing an ideal state of adjustment.

Social studies and science scholars examine and order the environment in ways to make it more comprehensible to themselves and to the rest of humankind. To understand this process, to respect it, and to contribute to it is an essential part of education for all children and youth. It is the last of these activities—the contribution aspect—that constitutes the objective that has special relevance for the education of the gifted and talented. Ways to help attain that objective make up the substance of this chapter.

Chapter 9

Teaching for Career Education

Effective education for a career requires organization on the part of the schools that is as systematic and of as high quality as organization for any other curriculum component. Career education is an emerging priority for gifted and talented pupils. It can be separated into two major divisions: career development and career preparation.

ORGANIZATION CONSIDERATIONS

Guiding Principles

Career education comprises broad principles and policies plus practices tailored to individual pupils. Milne (1979) identifies the following set of principles to guide practice:

1. Meaningful and serious career aspirations emerge at much earlier ages for gifted and talented pupils (e.g., early and later childhood) than for other students. Consequently, formal career education guidance should be timed accordingly.
2. Exceptional pupils tend to be aware of a wider range of career opportunities. They think beyond the known scope of available information and project themselves into careers that do not yet exist. Such speculative careers have, however, a high likelihood of materializing.
3. A gifted student's abilities may or may not appear to lead directly to a career. However, the pupil's abilities should be broadened and directed toward a wide range or combination or careers.
4. Career education for the gifted emphasizes life satisfaction. This is a common attribute for career education; it means a career fulfills physical, emotional, and social needs.

5. Careers undertaken by talented persons often are motivated by a sense of contribution to social purpose. While a career may be complete at any stage in adult life, teachers and mentors should be alerted to possibilities for altering and expanding career choices.

Policies

Milne argues for four policy adaptations specifically for the gifted and talented. These imperatives amplify some items in the above list of five general policies.

1. Early identification is essential. Assessment should include interests and information of relevance to careers.
2. Values education about self and about social contributions is essential. Career education is not confined to a narrow technical preparation.
3. Career information should be made available early and should be directed toward diversity. Careers of gifted and talented persons usually will combine several occupations and content areas.
4. Flexibility in guidance practices, enrollment in school programs, and use of out-of-school experiences should be encouraged. The gifted pupil is likely to be interested in careers that "never were," which may confound standard knowledge about career selection and preparation.

Identification and Guidance

The following generalizations about gifted and talented pupils, derived from data used by Milne, have particular relevance for career identification and guidance. (1) While career interests surface earlier, actual career selection may be deferred longer. (2) Career motivation is more oriented toward the internal/intrinsic than the external/extrinsic. (3) Personal goals and values are important sources of motivation. (4) Gifted and talented pupils learn to resist external coercion in favor of "inner" standards of perfection and service. (5) Life satisfaction and career satisfaction are viewed by the gifted person as inseparable.

Guidance is undertaken to assist, not to dictate. Counselors and teachers should collaborate with the family and the pupil in career selection and in identifying means to pursue and prepare for future work. An essential role of both parents and teachers is to assist exceptional pupils to clarify their interests and to recognize what values are prized, cherished, and acted upon in their daily lives. The avocational and the vocational require a mutual balance. Standard inventories of interests and sources such as the *Dictionary of Occupational Titles* may prove helpful; however, these are supplementary resources, not substitutes for guidance as a helping relation. The greatest need remains for dialogue and mentoring of highly able pupils.

Elements of Programming

A well-thought-out scheme of career education for gifted and talented students provides a concrete example of a school district's commitment to high quality education. It is an overt example of enabling exceptional students to maximize personal qualities and individual abilities and to provide a social contribution of worth and merit.

Components of programming can be sorted into those that primarily involve (1) the person, (2) procedures, and (3) outcomes. These components can be examined in any sequence as long as their interrelationships are recognized.

The personal component covers values, interests, capacities, abilities, and aspirations. This element also involves self-concept as a person, a worker, and a citizen.

Procedures of career education include guidance, instruction, training, and experiences. Guidance takes in monitoring, too. Training has the narrow meaning specific to skills sufficient for job/occupational/vocational accomplishment. Instruction is broader. It involves information, concepts, and projections necessary for choices and options. Experiences, of course, are the hands-on or vicarious activities necessary to fulfill individualized goals and objectives.

Milne (1979) emphasizes and we concur in the necessity to integrate career education within the general curriculum and school experience. Career education is neither to be deferred to high school nor considered a separate "course." It can be most effectively accomplished for gifted pupils when correlated with other content and activities. Emphasis from the primary grades on should bear on the mesh between life and career satisfactions, mastery of developmental tasks, and mobility in one's life and career.

CAREER DEVELOPMENT

General Themes

Decisions made about one's career are among life's vital choices. Consequently, this developmental task deserves emphasis equal to that given to other valued goals of the curriculum. An example of why career development is needed among elementary pupils is presented in Exhibit 9-1.

Exhibit 9-1 God Appointed the Principal, Whose Secretary Is His Boss

Some pupils think the principal was appointed to his position by God and that his secretary is his boss. That's what interviews with 580 K-6 children in Canyon, Texas, show. The interviews were done by W. M. Stoker and a graduate class in education at West Texas State University.

Other pupils believe the principal's authority comes from such sources as the king, the President, two policemen, and even the Chamber of Commerce.

One 5-year-old estimated the principal's age to be 8, while others guessed anywhere from 15 to 80.

When asked how they thought the principal spends his time, different pupils said, "Mostly, talking on the public address system," "Paddling kids with an electric paddle," and "Fixing the smell when a room smells bad."

Pupils were polled for suggestions about what the principal could stop doing. The responses included, "Not paddle so hard," "Not talk all the time on the loudspeaker," "Not smoke," and "Not be so mean."

They also suggested that he could "give more holidays," "turn out school earlier," and "eat lunch with us."

When asked if the elementary school principal should be a man or a woman, the kids generally thought men would be better, because they are "meaner and can paddle harder." A woman, they thought, "would be easier to fool." One youngster said, "A woman can do as much damage as a man."

Stoker says a significant number of children believed a man or a woman should be selected on the basis of ability, not sex.

Students were also asked what their parents had told them about the principal. Many could remember nothing, and the others were evenly divided between, "They told me he/she was a nice person" and "You'd better behave or he/she will paddle you good."

"In summary," Stoker said, "it seems that few pupils realize the principal is a highly trained professional with six years of college, and ex-teacher, and a person who holds both teacher's and administrator's certificates. They have no conception of the fact that he or she is hired by a superintendent and local board of education. Perhaps principals should communicate their roles, background, and responsibilities to the students. They should provide many opportunities for pupils to be 'sent to the office' for doing good work, to be complimented, or to come for a friendly visit. Maybe these practices would help dispel the belief in an ogre wielding the paddle."

Reprinted from *Phi Delta Kappan,* April 1979, by permission of Phi Delta Kappa, Inc., © 1979

The aspect of career education called career development starts strongly in the preschool and early elementary years. The regular teacher and curriculum are the main sources of information and of educational experience.

One theme is awareness and the exposure to information. Another theme is practice in exploration and examination of careers. Students interview, visit, and otherwise consult a variety of sources to facilitate the second theme. A third theme leads pupils to understand the interdependence of all people. This builds respect for all occupations. Each theme is highly valued.

A Question of Format

Teachers should organize career awareness learnings and relate them to pupil interests and community resources. Sandberg and Simon (1975) organized a generic format for initial exploration of careers by elementary pupils. They applied this format to 45 separate occupations under nine career clusters. They selected the clusters from the results of surveys of children who were asked to vote for the occupation of most interest. The materials lend themselves to use in learning centers and to coordination with teachers of a variety of language arts skills. Their question-answer format emphasizes comprehension of Key Ideas and related vocabulary. The constant format facilitates comparison and contrasts.

Hammermeister and Mullins (1977) produced career awareness materials suitable for independent study for all pupils, including those with handicaps. Their format illustrates another alternative for career awareness and development. It emphasizes a place that utilizes varied occupations. For example, their document, *The Hospital,* lets students identify the various places within a hospital and the occupations within each place. Places in this case include receiving visitors, clinics, and the pharmacy. Sample occupations included food service, social service, and nursing.

It is easy to be misled into thinking that gifted and talented pupils, from the outset, should be guided into knowing only about extremely complex and highly responsible callings. More important by far is a broad understanding of vocations, appreciation of their interrelatedness, and inculcation of the value of accomplishment and excellence for their own sake in any work.

Provoking and Maintaining Interest

Able learners usually have little difficulty in expressing interests. The teacher's main task is to challenge and channel in order to maintain subject matter and content relevance. Renzulli's (1977) investigation of real problems certainly conforms to the goals of career education. Visitation and simulation work well, and interviews afford ample opportunities to undercover material discussion.

Career development also involves comparing one's values about life with one's values about the world of careers. The nurture procedures referred to elsewhere are especially significant in this connection for highly able girls and boys.

Torrance and Kaufmann (1977) press for the fusion of content and career education. They advance a variety of ideas to illustrate the application of this principle to the education of the gifted and talented. A sample of their ideas follows:

1. Read an autobiography of an eminent person and analyze his/her motivations to achieve.

2. Brainstorm ways to make a specific, routine job interesting to a creative person.

3. Interview senior citizens with distinguished careers concerning their job histories, career decisions, life style decisions, and motivations.

4. Write a scenario detailing how a gifted and talented person could carry out personal fulfillment and social contributions in a particular career.

5. Invent ten new jobs and write job descriptions that would be in force five to ten years from now.

6. Design an ideal situation of employment for your career.

CAREER PREPARATION

Versatility applies to all sorts of careers. The talented person often can combine several careers, as illustrated in Exhibit 9-2 about a journalist who turned sportscaster and sired the Terrible Towel. One is struck by how the process of brainstorming has its real world applications, and is not just confined to a "creativity" exercise.

Exhibit 9-2 Origins of the Terrible Towel

Miami Dolphin fans wave white hankies. Denver Bronco fans shake orange pompoms. Houston Oiler fans brandish ropes. So when Pittsburgh Steeler supporters found themselves going into the 1975 playoffs empty handed, the forces at WTAE radio and television decided to do something about it. They did what was natural in broadcasting; they held a brainstorming session. As Myron Cope, the gruff voiced, cigar puffing, sports commentator, recalls the fateful meeting, it was Larry Garrett, now a station manager in Erie, who came up with the idea of twirling a towel, but it was Cope who named the creation. Thus was born the Terrible Towel that fired the imagination of Steeler fans, sports media, even the players themselves—and this year made Cope a bigger man than he had ever been before.

Cope and the towel have both been known around town for years but it took this past super football season to make Cope a national figure, and the towel a legend.

With only the slightest of winks, Cope says he thinks the towel now may even have supernatural powers. At the opening of the Super Bowl XIII telecast, during the toss of the coin, something or other cut off the sound from the referee's microphone and instead plugged Cope's steel-shattering radio voice onto national television to the astonishment of perhaps 100 million persons, most of whom had not heard that voice before.

"The Terrible Towel was in a mischievous mood," says Cope.

But he is now wary about carrying its power too far, perhaps even a bit superstitious about it. He is not all that happy when people suggest that perhaps with the baseball season approaching, the Terrible Towel could rouse the Pirate fans to the same peak it whipped up for the Steelers.

"The Terrible Towel has done a lot for us," he says, "but you can't dilute its power by using it willy-nilly. You can't go around using it for any old ball team—not even the Pirates. Besides, I like the Pirates, and want them to fill up the ballpark, but that's up to KDKA."

Reprinted from *Pittsburgh* magazine, 1979, *10*, 12, by M. Pavlik-Walsh by permission of the publisher, © 1979.

Author's Note: According to true believers, Cope may have underestimated the power of his creation. The Pirates subsequently won the World Series and the Steelers Superbowl XIV. The Towel was much in evidence on both occasions.

Career preparation builds on the base of career development. It is not confined or restricted to skill development alone. It flourishes where there are attitudes and values that liberate aptitude and talent. First-rate content preparation plus opportunities to practice and apply learnings are essential, too.

Career preparation calls for a team effort among teachers, career education specialists, guidance specialists, parents, and pupils. The internship represents a concrete example of effective career preparation, as does Stanley's (1979) SMPY project.

A Little Pride Will Go a Long, Long Way

In 1979 it was decided that Junior Achievement Inc.'s, efforts on behalf of young people could be best summarized by the statement: A little pride will go a long, long way. Junior Achievement (JA), though not designed solely for gifted and talented learners, fulfills well Milne's (1979) criteria. Junior Achievement also implements the goals and purposes of career preparation. Exhibit 9-3 recounts one of many examples of a JA program in one community.

Exhibit 9-3 JA Company Solves Adult Business Problems

What is "market research?" Eleven members of IMPACT, a JA company sponsored by Fairhaven Savings Bank of Fairhaven, Mass., found out last year—and became New Bedford's JA Company of the Year while they learned.

First, the idea was presented to the fledgling company by their adult adviser team (Cecilia Ward, assistant marketing director of Fairhaven Savings, was executive adviser, assisted by Patricia Avellar, Jean Hart, Betsy Rego, Carla Grillo, Michaela Champagne and Debbie Lubker.*) Second, their sponsoring firm became their first client, and third, they wrote a sales letter to the business community which began this way:

"Would your company like to know:
—if a new market exists for your product?
—customer reaction to your product or service?
—your current share of the market compared to your competitors?
—the answer to any other questions to help your business?

IMPACT, a Junior Achievement Market Research Company, is willing and able to serve your business firm."

William Pike, president of IMPACT, was eager to talk about the company in an interview with Graduate Achiever Mark Piva of New Bedford.

"At first business doesn't take you seriously," he said, "because market research is such a sophisticated business. Without the bank as our first client we couldn't have made it, and even after that successful survey, our biggest obstacle was 'image'. To help overcome this we developed our own logo and stationery.

"We also found selling our Achiever services to an executive of a corporation or bank more difficult than selling door to door or at a trade fair."

Although Fairhaven Savings Bank's support was essential to IMPACT, they did have a legitimate need for market research. The bank was about to open a new branch, the Dartmouth Banking Center, and was interested in finding out if the area residents were aware of this, if they would patronize it, and what banking services would be most popular.

Members of IMPACT planned and submitted a written questionnaire and demographic neighborhood map to the executives. While waiting for approval, the Achievers and their advisers honed their interview techniques and worked out two-person survey teams. When the go-ahead signal came, the teams were ready to take off.

Statistics piled up as the Achievers worked their way through the selected neighborhood. They did have some close encounters, as is shown by this regulation drawn from the Safety Director's annual report: "Take care to stand at least one foot from the door while requesting assistance with the survey, to avoid the danger of being injured by closing doors."

Survey footwork behind them, IMPACT workers began analyzing their findings for formal submission to the bank. They had learned what percent of those questioned consider a savings account most important and what percent consider checking their first need; the percentage of those familiar with Fairhaven Savings Bank's plans to open a new branch, and how many would bank there.

Having come up with these statistics, the next challenge was to make recommendations based on their findings. In this particular neighborhood surveyors found:

(1) Portuguese is the main language. Recommendation: More advertising is needed in the Portuguese-language media.

(2) Fairhaven Savings is not the best-known bank. Recommendation: Do more advertising stressing the bank's strong points.

Drawing up each survey depended on what the client needed. Usually, representatives from IMPACT talked things through with the client company. In the case of Kalisz Plywood, Inc., another satisfied customer, Mr. Kalisz wanted to know people's decorating preferences; if shoppers were aware of price differences; where they went to buy paint, wallpaper and paneling, and if they were satisfied with store service.

As you can see, activities in a market research company differ widely from those in manufacturing or other service companies. Clients must be secured, service prices set, questionnaires designed and analyzed, surveys carried out, data tabulated and analyzed, a written and verbal report of results presented, and a follow-up made.

In all, IMPACT conducted five surveys during the year; by telephone, by man-on-the-street interviews, and by the door-to-door method. They found out how people felt about a waterfront restoration project and how they felt about a shopping center and a trolley car museum in an historical building in New Bedford. They also conducted a survey for Junior Achievement.

According to adviser Cecilia Ward, "The most important single ingredient of this project was the enthusiasm of the vice president of marketing at Fairhaven Savings, John L. Downey, who introduced the group to the needs, tools and importance of market research."

Another specialist who helped IMPACT get started was Wilfred M. Sheehan, senior partner with Marsh/Sheehan, Inc. Delighted to learn of the company's later success, Mr. Sheehan was heard to exclaim, "These kids are going to put us out of business!"

Although he need have no fear of that, IMPACT has formed again for the 1978-79 program year, again under the sponsorship of Fairhaven Savings, and the company members are presently conducting a follow-up survey on the Dartmouth Banking Center.

Reprinted from *Achiever*, Vol. I, No. 1, by Marcia Livingston, by permission of Junior Achievement Inc., © 1979.
* Debbie Lubker, a student at Southeastern Massachusetts University, was a participant in the JA Applied Management program, whereby an undergraduate or graduate business student earns college credit by serving as an associate adviser with a regular JA company adviser team.

The Bureau of Business Practices (1977) described JA programs as involved in assisting youth to participate in first-hand management experiences. The JA program is not limited to service operations. Production is actively encouraged. The bureau issued a report that outlined the procedures necessary to initiate a JA program and projected a "typical" year. The essence of JA is a form of monitoring and partnership between the community and the schools.

The steps necessary to organize JA in one's community include the following:

First, the national office will extend a franchise to a group at the local area. The franchise gives the local group the sanction of the national program. A local JA board of directors "owns" the franchise. Its membership is composed of executive level management. This board divides itself in any necessary committees.

In the second step the board recruits advisers for JA participants. The advisers come from middle management and represent areas such as production, marketing, and accounting. In some instances a fourth person is recruited for instruction and educational purposes.

The third task is to promote the program in the high schools in the area. One outcome of recruitment is to establish a JA company of 20 to 25 students with three to four advisers. The JA company operates from October through April. The local JA provides orientation during the summer.

Students may reenroll in succeeding years. In some communities, a student who has been through the company experience can participate in a partnership company, and an advanced student can form a single ownership company. One senses that this is JA's form of acceleration.

A year in the life of a JA company is fast paced, with a finely tuned balance of guidance from advisers and freedom for student initiative. The first meeting of the JA company occurs in the first week of October. A company meets once a week for two hours. All company activities are conducted then, except for sales. The next five meetings prepare the students for full management of the company, including incorporation, establishing company objectives, name, bylaws, and other necessities. The students become the board of directors.

At the first meeting, the advisers suggest a starter project or product. This approach is used because product development and research are the most consuming of time and effort. In this period, students engage in the capitalization process by selling stock for about $1 per share to organize capital of $150 to $200. Budgeting is carried out by establishing a cash flow projection of expenses. Each student must purchase at least one share of stock. The JA company will be on schedule if by the end of the fifth week:

1. It has begun production, set compensation rates, and received applications for officer positions (second meeting).
2. It has elected JA company officers, established prices for products or services, and established marketing plans (third to fourth meeting).
3. Its student officers have assumed full control of the company (fifth week); advisers still are involved as consultants.

From October through March, the company is in full swing. Meetings concentrate on management and production. All students, including officers, take turns in production. At least one meeting per month is devoted to educational and instructional conferences. Local business persons are invited to discuss various phases of the American economic system. Conferences vary from lectures and discussions to simulations. During the year, the company may bring out new products with their associated tasks of planning, capitalization, production, and marketing.

During March, the JA company begins the process of disbanding, which should be completed by April. This process includes preparation of the annual report and the steps necessary for liquidation. The latter task involves selling off inventory, preparing the final balance sheet, and returning after-tax profits to shareholders. This liquidation requirement enables students to learn company operations from the ground up and back down.

One cannot help but be attracted to the JA model for its organized structure based upon a national unit's consulting with local units. It provides curriculum crossover for the pupil in a purely academic track (e.g., prelaw career orientation) to experience a real world atmosphere of business and industry. The JA experience is solidly oriented to a leadership training model favored by the U.S. Department of Education definition. Finally, the JA model allows experienced people to provide helpful mentoring to proteges.

SOURCES OF INFORMATION

Teachers and parents rightfully expect to draw on guidance counselors for information about careers. Career preparation resources also may be labeled/termed as vocational/technical education. A career preparation program of good quality reflects coordination of the academic and vocational/technical components (Evans & Herr, 1978). Information obviously lays the foundation for programming. Also, some of the information needs are pupil centered and some are career centered.

Lewis and Kanes (1979) affirmed the use of the Individualized Education Program (IEP) with gifted and talented pupils. They press to include career education as part of the annual statement of goals and objectives. Their analysis of the IEP reaffirms the Evans and Herr emphasis upon pupil-centered information.

Another example that stresses the interlock of career preparation goals and objectives with academic goals and objectives in the IEP for gifted and talented pupils is advanced by Gustofson and Laterte (1978). Their process is of special interest to individuals charged with the responsibility to develop information for the IEP.

Their first step was to locate and review existing definitions of gifted and talented learners available from the professional literature and from school laws and regulations. Their second step was to generate a definition and listing of dimensions (e.g., attributes) to describe gifted and talented persons. Their third step was to generate behavioral descriptors to assist in identification of those learners. Their fourth step was to field test the adequacy of these descriptors with practitioners.

For purposes of career preparation, Gustofson and Laterte (1978) defined a gifted person as

someone with the ability to perform, within his/her own environment, with a high degree of excellence or exceptionality; earlier, quicker, more creatively, and with fewer external sources of information than the general population. (p. 9).

Nine categories of giftedness selected (Gustofson & Laterte, p. 14) were: (1) academic, (2) aesthetic and affective, (3) creative and productive, (4) decision making, (5) leadership, (6) social, (7) physical and emotional, (8) intellectual, and (9) work characteristics. The first eight often are encountered in the literature of identification of gifted and talented persons. The last dimension, work characteristic, would be a "newer" contribution.

Gustofson and Laterte recommend teacher observation of the student's work patterns to pick out indications of actual superior performance as well as signs of potential high ability. These signals demonstrate that the student: (1) shows a long attention span by pursuit of a task of high interest for long periods of time, (2) is truly involved in certain activities, (3) displays powers of concentration, (4) is self-directed, persistent, and resourceful, (5) pursues interests beyond the usual limitations, (6) is easily bored with the routine, (7) needs little external direction in tasks of personal excitement, (8) has the ability to organize a work plan with budget, time, and resources, (9) likes structure but can tolerate ambiguity and disorder, (10) can assess the quality of its own work, and (11) acquires easily preliminary/fundamental/elementary knowledges, processes, and/or skills of instruction for content.

Evans and Herr (1978) point to top priority sources of information germane to career planning. These are the *Dictionary of Occupational Titles,* the *Occupational Outlook Quarterly,* and the *Occupational Outlook Handbook.* These are excellent starting points from which to obtain and organize information about the attributes of an occupation, its specific requirements, and the relationship of courses to occupational alternatives. The *Dictionary of Occupational Titles* lists more than 20,000 titles. It also includes information about personal job attributes, duties, related skills, working conditions, and other realities. The *Occupational Handbook* forecasts the demand for jobs with estimates of decrease and increase. It is revised every two years. The *Occupational Outlook Quarterly* supplies interim estimates.

These U.S. Department of Labor documents project national estimates. State departments of labor have their state and county equivalents. School district divisions of career education have access to these sources. Various trade and professional societies issue documents of guidance for career preparation. The advanced student locates these and government sources with help from teacher, counselors, and librarian in order to develop a career preparation plan.

Gardner and Warren (1978) offer helpful resources for organizing programs for gifted and talented pupils who are handicapped but who have aptitude for advanced preparation. Their recommendations are within the mainstream of career preparation. They include guidance as to use of the resources of vocational education and vocational rehabilitation. Moreover, the reference is solidly grounded within the guidelines of the U.S. Department of Education regarding career education.

TRENDS

Work, according to Evans and Herr (1978), was once the major untaught subject in the schools. With the advent of vocational education, a certain emphasis emerged, as did an unintended separation from general education. The emergence of career education has created a context for the confluence of these unnaturally separated streams, a merger that blends the gifted and talented as well as learners with special needs. (This latter term is used sometimes to encompass handicapped pupils and those who are limited by economic disadvantage.)

To widen and extend opportunities, educators must be alert for chances to demonstrate the necessary cooperation. It has been difficult to arrange career preparation for handicapped students, gifted and talented or not, according to Evans and Herr, because career educators have perceived these pupils as the exclusive responsibility of special education or vocational rehabilitation. One positive trend has been the dismantling of service boundaries.

Increasingly, another trend has been to extend vocational guidance to talented pupils. The most promising trend has been the recognition of high ability among special needs populations. Another trend, less evident, has been to enable pupils who would be eligible for programs for the gifted and talented to pursue both academic and technical curricula. This crossover will require more attention. For example, a person may wish to pursue journalism and might find preparation as a printer helpful in learning the operation of a newspaper. One encounters too many instances of inventors, scholars, writers, actors, artists, physicians, lawyers, and the clergy who must learn the mechanics of budgeting and cash flow, for instance, the hard way.

SUMMARY

In career education, too, the regular teacher has control status for the gifted and talented student. First of all, the teacher is a model of a worker for the pupil to observe. The teacher's response to stress, attitudes toward administrators, relationships with other teachers, and other behaviors expose the pupil to lasting initial impressions. Second, the teacher is in a key position to integrate career development with content. A third role is to integrate inquiry skills with career development. Teachers, in a fourth role, can serve as consultants to parents and students to clarify their ideals and ideas about careers. A fifth role is that of participant in the IEP team with its associated competencies. A sixth role is to encourage exceptional pupils to speculate about the possibilities of careers and the ways in which the extensiveness of abilities may be used.

Chapter 10

Teaching for Talent Education

THE KEY ROLES OF TEACHERS

The nurture of talent challenges the regular teacher in several ways. One is to learn to use consultation from fellow educators with specializations different from one's own, such as dance, dramatics, art, or music. The specialist and the regular teacher together should work out adjustments to allow flexible scheduling for specific pupils.

A challenging second role is to advise parents about sources of assistance and long-range planning. The regular teacher can insist that talent dimensions be incorporated in the pupil's Individualized Education Program (IEP). Such notations alert both the schools and the community to the need for resources.

A third role involves participation in generating community resources for pupils with talent. For example, some communities maintain a Civic Players Association through which amateur talent stages drama and musicals. Some associations use their profits to sponsor a Junior Civic Theater.

A fourth role finds regular teachers and principals helping to locate appropriate outlets and recognition for talent in the school. This can help pupils recognize their own latent abilities as well as enhance opportunities for those already recognized.

A fifth role is career guidance that informs the pupils of the various options available in the talent dimension and in the combination of careers.

The nurture of talent is best achieved as a team effort. The regular teacher often captains or quarterbacks the team.

Certain principles and practices prove helpful. Birch and McWilliams (1955) advise teachers that superior mental ability and superior talent do not necessarily occur together. It is possible to be superior in one dimension and average in another. For example, Sellin (1979) reviewed the literature on instances of genuine artistic and musical abilities among persons otherwise

181

mentally retarded in intellectual functioning and adaptive behavior. It is only recently that these abilities are recognized and nurtured as genuine accomplishments rather than accidents of nature. The central lesson from studies of talent in mentally retarded persons is that extraordinary performance emerges as the result of both the encouragement of a benefactor or mentor and of the retarded person's seeking social recognition. This lesson reinforces the need for nurture for talent and performance in general.

Birch and McWilliams also remind educators that chronological age is not a sufficient index for grouping talented pupils in performance areas. Account must be taken of physical, emotional, and social factors. For example, an artistically talented fourth grader may have the dexterities to participate with junior high school students, but may experience difficulty with aesthetic interpretations. Consequently, the IEP ought to emphasize continued development of skills and to adapt and expand curriculum for aesthetic experiences. The point is, decisions are neither automatic nor based upon narrow criteria.

The characteristics of talent, creativity, and aptitude are not entirely separate, and cognitive behavior is not divorced from these three capabilities. These constructs are perceptions that are centered upon performance as talent, process as creativity, and potential as aptitude. This book has used writing (composition) to illustrate the overlapping nature of the three constructs. Performers in most fields recognize that superior performance is an interaction of skills, motivation, recognition, and nurture.

Regular teachers ought not feel inhibited about sharing their own talents with students. A number of teachers who are highly competent as subject matter specialists also are highly proficient in nonacademic areas. For example, in some communities, one can find a genuine Weavers' Guild. The teachers who belong have moved beyond weaving as arts and crafts to the status of artists and craftspersons. Their products can be faithful reproductions of the tradition as well as combining the traditional and contemporary. As professional educators, they have organized cocurricular clubs/sessions. The study hall and the leftover lunch period have been transformed. These teachers also have transformed social studies content. The social studies outcomes of the craft guild as the origin of unions, the mathematics of geometric designs, the science of fiber strength and of producing colors, and the language of describing the process are but a few examples.

TALENT AS BEHAVIOR

Descriptors of Superior Performance

The essence of talent education, according to Getzels (1979), is instruction that moves the individual from art student to artist and from science student to scientist. The "movement" represents progression from problem solver to problem finder. In everyday language, problem finders are called original. Their products are called novel. Getzels observes that an artist does not manipulate objects and materials per se; the artist manipulates feelings and perceptions. Technical proficiency is application of one's skill and craft to problems whose solutions are available. In contrast, the original person who produces novel work creates problems for solutions. This person is judged by dual criteria: the quality of skill as well as the quality of the discovered problem. Both the solver and the finder are necessary in the range of human endeavor and in social institutions. Education, for example, needs the problem finder such as Binet as well as the problem solver such as Terman. It also needs the problem finder and solver such as Skinner or Piaget. The problem finder is the most likely to create new opportunities for solvers. Problem solvers tend to produce new opportunities for all the rest of mankind.

A 1967 publication edited by Kagan, often cited in the literature of the gifted and talented, affirmed the similarities between persons of original performance regardless of field. As in the Getzels (1979) report, the Kagan material centers on comparisons between artists and scientists. The Kagan volume is an instructive comparison to the Getzels report for understanding common factors of superior performance.

Implications for Education

There is substantial agreement on what needs to be done to improve education for talented persons. There is much variance as to means, however.

One certainty is that identification is a key first step. Kagan promoted identification in the sense of actually locating talented pupils rather than merely predicting which might become such students. He advocated identification also as determining the context and conditions that facilitate the growth of talent, be it scientific or artistic. Kagan and Getzels implied that teachers could be trained and trusted to do that kind of functional identification, namely, actually to pick out gifted pupils and actually to recognize and note the school (and other) conditions that encourage talent.

The Getzels investigation illustrates the potential of teachers and also identifies pertinent behaviors as indicators (not causes) of talent. Art majors in college do not differ from nonart students on tests of intelligence or on tests of perceptual abilities. Demographic variables are not useful predictors, and neither is grade point average. Differences exist only in values (economic security/social services) and temperament (self-confidence, imagination, conformity, and experimental attitudes). Art students have more in common with one another than with nonart students with respect to less worldly concerns and greater independence in temperament. Interestingly, art majors do not differ on measures of aptitude and judgments of technical craftsmanship. Getzels acknowledges that these correlations did little to account for the process/behavior underlying products. The searches for correlation, for him, were better replaced by observation and interview.

Interviews and observations of art students revealed a number of indicators of performance. A sample of 31 students each produced a still life painting. All paintings were submitted to an expert jury of five artists. There was sufficient agreement as to order the paintings. This ordering made it possible to relate product quality (jury ratings) and the behavior/process of the artist.

The rationale for this procedure originated with initial observations of these young artists' behavior in class. The common denominator was that commercial and industrial art majors preferred a structured assignment such as to design an illustration for a box of breakfast cereal. Fine arts majors preferred the blank canvas and to create the problem to work on. The point of the experiment was to identify the means by which an artist selects the problem to be solved.

The setting of the observations was a studio room with two tables. One table contained 27 objects commonly found in art class. The students were asked to compose a still life on the second table using as many, or as few, objects as they preferred. They were requested to produce a drawing of the second table. Only 14 percent reflected constraint about the assignment, 14 percent perceived the task as a classroom assignment, and 72 percent perceived it as a free association activity. Observers identified three distinct behaviors that emerged prior to drawing:

1. There were differences in the number of objects handled from two to 19.
2. There were differences in the amount of exploration of objects. Some objects were picked up and carried to the second table. Some students rolled objects, explored third-dimension attributes, examined texture, and the like.
3. There were differences in the selection of objects.

Frequency counts were taken and students could be ordered as to unusual uses and typical uses. Getzels (1979) compared the problem finders (more objects, more exploration, and more unusual uses) with the artists, who had fewer objects, less exploration, and more conventional subject matter. Thus, the sample of the artists could be ranked from one to 31 on the attributes of problem finding and their paintings could be ranked from one to 31 by the jury. The relationship for originality was found to be .54 and significant and the overall aesthetic quality and problem finding was a significant correlation of .40.

In a follow-up study of these 31 artists, 24 were identified approximately seven years later. Getzels devised success rankings for those 24. Three factors were found to account for the ranking of least successful to most successful. One factor was grades received in studio classes (academic courses predicted failure but not success), teacher ratings of potential (after the first year of art school), and designation (ranking) as a problem finder.

The Getzels report attracts interest for several reasons. First, it is a fascinating example of problem finding. It can be read as a technical report with pertinent findings. It also can be read as an account of the process of problem finding out of which solutions emerge. A second reason is that the Getzels findings about artists parallel those of Kagan (1967) about scientists. Both complement the earlier discussions of talent and creativity. The complementary findings are that producers and problem finders have sufficient self-confidence to tolerate error, to resist ambiguity, and to deal with flexibility of possibilities. A third source of attraction is the verification that educators can identify talented persons. The behaviors of selection, manipulation, and uses are not so mysterious that teachers cannot note them in pupils.

A second implication for educators to derive from Getzels and Kagan is that the processes of problem finding and producing can be taught, for example, tolerance for error and ambiguity and valid pupil aptitudes for selection of teaching tactics. Kagan endorsed teaching by discovery for its combination of freedom and discipline. In general terms, Kagan recommended discovery and inquiry tactics for highly motivated learners who are reflective and who are ready for a colleagueship with adults. As with any other tactics, pupil readiness is a factor. The main point is that the tactics suggested have the attributes of increasing the complexity of pupils' behaviors as well as of helping them gain confidence in their ability to master the new and novel.

The Midwestern Maestro: An Example of Merit

At age 37, John Nelson became the director of the Indianapolis Symphony Orchestra. His commitment to music is part of his larger commitment to his beliefs. The interview in Exhibit 10-1 provides a glimpse into a person whose talents have achieved worldwide recognition. His insights about the nurture of the family reflect insight both for parents and for educators.

Exhibit 10-1 Music for God's Glory

Musicians and theologians seem to have one foot in heaven and the other resting lightly on earth. That must lead to some very interesting experiences.

Anita tells me I'm the only person she knows who has succeeded in running out of gas in the car twice on the same day, if that's what you mean. It is true that a musician that performs the classics leads a very privileged life, always in the presence of greatness. If you take one of the German lieder, for example, you're with Schubert or another great composer. It's like living in an art museum with Michelangelo all around you—it's breathtaking. Ten to 12 hours of my daily life are spent with the greats. And of them all, Bach is to me the very epitome.

You find more rewards in working with his music than with any other composer?

I do. Of course, I wouldn't be happy without a bit of Berlioz, too, to bring me down to earth.

Would you say Bach's music was a unique convergence of Christian and musical streams?

I'm sure it was. Bach's work is so honest, religiously speaking. You feel that Bach understood it and believed it. His intellectual understanding of it and his emotional involvement in it are totally sincere. It's the fusion of Christianity at the highest intellectual level with the highest esthetic. With the works of Bach, you really feel you're on holy territory. When you are performing it there's nothing left to do but go to heaven.

To Bach the most important thing was God's own glory, wasn't it?

That's what he said. He wrote at the end of his pieces, "To the glory of God," and there's no reason to believe he didn't mean it. And on the other hand, when you read about Bach you find he was a very earthy person. He had to provide for his very large family. He had one of the highest posts in Germany, and I'm not too sure he would have been happy in a smaller parish.

I think it's necessary for us to find the right spot—not too high, not too low. For us to be unnecessarily humble about our gifts is not godly. I think we should know exactly what we have, be objective about it, and be where the talent is best used.

When did your musical interest really begin?

I've loved music all my life. My parents were missionaries in Costa Rica, and as I remember we had three records in our house when I was small. One was the Rachmaninoff Piano Concerto No. 2, another was the 1812 Overture, and then the Bach "Jesu Meine Freude" with Robert Shaw as conductor. I just played those things over and over.

You must have recognized then that music was a part of you.

You know how kids are. I was too young to have prejudices when I first listened to Bach. If a kid is brought up on it, he goes in that direction.

How did your interest develop further?

I had that Robert Shaw recording, and I don't think I got further acquainted with Bach until I was at Wheaton College. My piano teacher, Lillian Powers, gave it to me there. That was my first exposure as a performer to Bach, and it was the technical kind of Bach—the preludes, fugues, and partitas. Then my next experience was preparing and conducting the chorales in the St. Matthew Passion for our chorus director, Rolf Espeseth. That was a good experience, but it still didn't win me over. I had not been nurtured in it. It was foreign to my training, to my religious esthetic.

But your appetite for great choral music had been whetted.

Yes, by Rolf Espeseth, who was a Norwegian Lutheran. He's the man who got me into serious conducting. There was a quality about him that I revered, almost worshipped, but didn't understand. He's the one who helped me prepare for my entrance exam at Juilliard. He died of cancer seven years after that. No one meant more to me than that man. He conducted with his eyes. The intensity was extraordinary. Anita and I both sang in the choir; that's where we met.

And after Wheaton?

I went to Juilliard in New York. When I sang in the Bach B minor Mass in my second year, I think that was really my conversion to Bach's music. Then I started performing his work myself, and before I left New York I performed all the major Bach works with my own chorus, and had not only wonderful success, but also deeply satisfying experiences with all the musicians and all the singers.

How do you feel about working in the great American Midwest, with the musicians here? You were mentioning the great talent among your musicians.

(Laughs). Now you've got me on the spot! This is the place where I'm supposed to be. I was in New York for 12 years. Four of those were student years, and eight were performing years. I did a lot of performing before great critics and the great New York audience. The pressure is unbelievable. That was all fine, while I could do ten performances in a year. I really could prepare my scores well. When I did the St. Matthew Passion in Avery Fisher Hall—then it was called Philharmonic Hall—I studied for an entire year, just on that piece. I think that's why it was special—to put in one solid year, I knew every note of that score, I'd read every word that had been written about it, and had my own strong feelings about it, and the results were good! I was doing it as conductor of the Pro Arte Chorale and Orchestra, and with wonderful soloists. I did other performances, had the orchestra in Greenwich, Connecticut, and was doing 10 to 20 performances a year. Then as my career started developing I began guest conducting in many places. Working with a larger repertoire began to be very demanding.

Now I do a hundred concerts a year. I don't think I should be doing those hundred concerts before the New York public. That's one of the main reasons I'm happy here, because I have a wonderful orchestra, an orchestra that I can develop. They can grow along with my growing, and I can do any repertoire I wish to do. It's very satisfying. From a family standpoint, it's lovely, too; great for the children and we have wonderful friends.

When you think back on your childhood, what recommendation do you have for parents who want to cultivate their children's musical tastes?

I would say expose them to all the arts as much as possible, because they all naturally relate to some aspects of all the arts—drawing, or drama, or music. I remember going to the home of Joseph Kalichstein, a young Israeli pianist, and his wife had just given birth to a child, and they were starting out from the very beginning by having a record player in the baby's room, and having records available. No kiddie records—it was Wagner and so on. They let him listen to it from the earliest point. Children love it. The other thing is an instrument. Almost all kids take to an instrument. Both of our kids are taking instruments and orchestra in their schools. Here in elementary school there's a string orchestra, and Kirsten is taking to it like crazy.

How did you take to music training when you were very small?

I don't really recall whether I asked for piano or whether my parents brought it in. That was when I was 6, and I started taking lessons from a Costa Rican lady who lived close by. My parents said to my brother Peter and me, "You take for three years; after that you can keep going if you like." I went to it like a fish to water. Pete decided that his thing was radio and electronics. Our interests kept us happy. We've loved each other—probably if we'd both been musicians, we'd have hated each other!

How do parents discern that a child has musical aptitude or talent, and encourage its development?
The parent has to be sensitive to it. The interest of the parent has to be genuine, and open to the child. If the child doesn't respond to it, I don't feel that he should be disciplined into it needlessly; it just results in wrong tension. I'm talking about gifted areas. My parents put the opportunity in front of me.

The arts are so helpful; they bring out the best in a person. They do for a child the opposite of what TV does. We're really strict with our kids about television. We find they have relatively little frustration, if they have other things to do. Perhaps it's because the arts represent something associated with the establishment, the old fogies. It's also because youngsters are not nurtured to it. The arts should be pleasure for everybody—pleasure in the highest sense. It should give reward to life. When you see people coerced into going to a concert, or frustrated by it, there's some kind of wrong atmosphere being created somewhere along the way. I don't think our educational system is properly geared towards the arts.

Reprinted from the *Christian Herald*, May 1979, *102*, 26-31, by J. Kenyon by permission of the publisher, © 1979.

SUMMARY

The discovery and nurture of talent is not well understood in America and it is even less well organized. It has grown, so far, mainly as a private rather than a public enterprise. Traditionally, elementary and secondary schools—even colleges—gave much more emphasis to developing other aspects of pupils' capabilities. Perhaps that partially explains why none of the 1,528 highly able children identified by Terman in 1922 and 1928, and followed until their senior citizenship years, attained outstanding importance as an artist, composer, or performer, although they did very well otherwise.

Despite past limited attention, however, teachers and principals in public schools have moved to increased awareness that there are ways to find talent and to help it grow. To be sure, teaching to enhance talent still is more art than science. But encouragement and personal support can go a long way.

UNIT ENRICHMENT

Understanding a Common Curriculum Core

1. Consult Table 6-1. Devise a checklist that could be used to select educational materials for gifted and talented learners. You may wish to test it out by having several friends use an available catalogue and your checklist. In this and in all 19 other items below, *share* your material, reactions, opinions, findings, or results.

2. Consult the teacher's manual for a text in any two areas of the common core. Identify its perceptions of pupil outcomes. Identify any modifications advanced for gifted and talented learners. Are there any differences by content areas? Compose a letter to the author(s) recommending two improvements that would benefit exceptional students.

Teaching the Tool Subjects/Basic Skills

3. Review the curriculum content in language arts and mathematics in your school district. What provisions are made for altering the pace of instruction?

4. Prepare a 20- to 30-minute presentation regarding the role of teachers in teaching the tool subjects/basic skills for teachers. Consider the components: (a) What key ideas would you stress? (b) What slides/ tapes would you consider? (c) What reactions would you hope for? (d) What passouts (maximum ten pages) would you consider? How would you vary your proposed presentation for teachers at different levels? How would you amend your proposed curriculum for either parents or administrators?

5. Write a letter to the editor of a state educational journal in support of the Individualized Education Program for the tool subjects/basic skills for the gifted and talented.

Teaching for Information Awareness

6. Construct a jigsaw for any chapter or chapter section in this text. Try out the process with your colleagues. Note your reactions to the group and to those opposed to individual learnings. Do your reactions indicate any insights in your own aptitude for this treatment?

7. Analyze the Summary section for any chapter in this book. Construct an outcomes matrix, use the items as content and searching, assimilating, and reporting. Suggest at least ten activities to complete the cells of the matrix. What insight about adaptation of content did you gain?

8. Consult the science materials in your school district or consult three introductory texts in educational research. Prepare a resume outlining the essentials of the scientific method you uncovered.

9. Examine the health education curriculum in your school district. Prepare a letter to the district's director of curriculum/instruction outlining the adequacy of present effort, or propose a needs assessment for health education. The statement should contain a charge to a committee to identify criteria for evaluation of existing materials. Also include the credentials of 10 to 15 members who should be on the steering committee.

10. Consult the Getzels (1979) report about problem finders and problem solvers. Prepare an abstract according to Melton's (1974) recommendations.

11. Consider how the content of Table 8-2 could be used to conduct discussions and/or to pose directions for learning centers. Prepare a poster to communicate your ideas.

Teaching for Career Development

12. Consult the career education plan for your state and assess its implementation in your district. Make note of inclusions/provisions for gifted and talented learners. Share your findings by preparing a letter to the editor of your local newspaper.

13. Consult the top 20 hit records in your areas that are popular with teenagers. Summarize the main ideas about career education and life satisfaction contained in these selections. What messages should be expanded? What messages would you amend?

14. Have your principal read Exhibit 9-1. Obtain that individual's reactions and ideas for helping pupils to comprehend the role and qualifications.

15. Consider the career of teacher of gifted and talented learners. Write a *Dictionary of Occupational Titles* description.

16. Determine if Junior Achievement exists in your community. Interview its participants and sponsors. Share your findings to enrich the chapter's discussion. Are there other organizations in your community that approximate the JA model?

17. List at least ten ways that a teacher presents a model for pupils regarding the attributes of a worker. Compare your ten items with others. Develop a composite agreement as to the seven most important ways a teacher models working behavior.

192 EDUCATING GIFTED AND TALENTED LEARNERS

18. Develop an IEP format for career education for gifted and talented learners. Consider the IEP format for career education for handicapped students in your school district for inspiration.

Teaching for Talent Education

19. Prepare policies for talent education for your school district, including the use of the IEP. Prepare an outline of your Key Ideas that should be considered for submission to your board of education.

20. Review five biographical sketches of persons considered talented. Describe what in your opinion are the three most salient features in the careers of these persons that account for their achievements. Share your opinions with others and develop a pooled list of five features. From this process derive three implications for education and three implications for parenting.

Using Tactics of Individualized Education

SYNOPSIS

In this unit we focus on ways to adapt schools to the educational needs of gifted and talented pupils. The main reference point turns on adaptation and modification of the standard curriculum. Each teacher has a central place in this process. The Individualized Education Programs (IEPs) delineate priorities for gifted and talented pupil programming to match treatments to student aptitudes.

A continuum of tactics accommodates to the accelerated pace of learning of gifted pupils. Expansion and extension of the standard curriculum is a keystone concept. Teachers balance delicately between initiation of activities and response to the evolving maturity of their exceptional pupils. Authorities on education of the gifted and talented deplore random gimmickry to "jiggle" the intellect. They propose alternatives referenced to content and skills, matched to learning styles of individual pupils.

KEY IDEAS

The principal points of the chapter are summarized as follows:

1. The teacher is the central person in the individualization of education. In fulfilling this role, the teacher serves best as mentor, manager, guide, and consultant to the pupil.
2. Personal attributes influence progress toward completion of projects. These attributes can be managed successfully.
3. Educational alternatives are important only to the extent that they match pupil needs. Alternatives are means to ends, not goals.

4. Curriculum modification opens the way to individualization for gifted and talented pupils, both by pacing and by expanding. The procedure is defined by the goal and the expected product, not by the label of acceleration or of enrichment.

5. Teachers should initiate certain activities. The most common and helpful are discussions, problem solving, visitations, and procedures aimed at developing multiple talents.

6. Productive pupil participation grows through simulations, learning centers, guided independent study, and internships.

7. Individualization works not only in school experiences but also with community resources.

A PROTOTYPE

Using an able child's interest to lead into computer science on the one hand and into computer applications on the other illustrates excellent teaching.

Marie Brings a Friend to School

Yourtowne, N.B., Wire Service Release: The buddy that Marie Williams, 7-year-old second grader, brought to Eisenhower Elementary School sat on a table instead of a chair.

Marie has talked daily with her friend for two years and they now carry on quite complex conversations. The friend, a computer Marie calls "Compie," really resides at the State University branch in Yourtowne. Marie's father introduced the playmates. Marie was sharing her friend with her schoolmates, and particularly those in the basic scholars group which is made up of pupils who are advanced in schooling for their age.

Compie said "Hi!" to everyone. Marie linked Compie to the master computer at the University by twirling a telephone dial to the correct code and dropping the receiver into a cradle on Compie's side. Then, busily tapping letters and numbers on the lighted keyboard, Marie called up on Compie's display panel a running description of the project she and the computer planned to present that day. The basic scholars were enthralled. They asked questions and exchanged remarks that whizzed right over the head of this reporter. But they must have made sense to Compie and Marie, because they flashed back with responses that evoked "Oh's" and "Uh-Huh's" from the second-grader scholars crowded around.

Marie's attraction to the computer started one Thanksgiving when her daddy brought home a computer print picture of a turkey. She asked for and got an explanation of how it was done. Once her interest was piqued, she learned a working knowledge of computer language in about 18 weeks. Now she designs educational games for the computer and battles Compie's programmed brains in weekly chess matches.

Most of Eisenhower's students, regardless of grade, learned something about computers during Compie's visit, for it lasted several days during a midterm break at the University. Several teachers commented that Compie has reading skills, spelling, and arithmetic. The excitement of the technology captivates girls and boys of all ages and holds their interest to their work.

The computer can be scheduled to present problems in a sequence. When a pupil makes an error, it will print an encouraging comment and give the same problem again. After a set number of unsuccessful trys, the computer will print the right answer, show how it was obtained, and then give a similar problem to see if the pupil has mastered the solution.

Arithmetic and higher mathematics can be alternated with language games, puzzles, and grammar exercises. Some youngsters prefer a bout with Compie to outdoor recess.

Eisenhower's principal said that computer-assisted instruction is available in some of Yourtowne's middle and high schools now. She has asked for terminals for Eisenhower. They can, according to the teachers, challenge pupils to go as far as they are able, each pupil paced individually. Marie, for instance, already comprehends and solves square and cube roots. Also, the principal says, there are more and more occupations that call for familiarity with computers.

The basic scholars and their teachers are not surprised that 7-year-olds like Marie have already carried computer technology far past the knowledge of most of today's adults. "After all," as one of Marie's schoolmates commented, "How could grownups know much about computers? They didn't have a chance to learn about them in school when they were kids, like we do!"

Marie's project is not unique. It is a part of Yourtowne Public Schools' way of matching instruction to individual gifted and talented pupil needs and abilities.

Where Might Follow-Up of Questions Such as These Lead?

1. What uses are made of computers in your school system now? Business? Instruction? Athletics? Administration? Personnel? Scheduling? What would it take to adapt existing computer usage to the instruction of gifted and talented pupils?

2. What would a survey of computer usage in your community reveal? What organizations other than banks and airlines would you find employing computers? How might their equipment and staff members help in opening broader educational vistas for exceptional students?

Chapter 11
Understanding Individualized Education

UNDERSTANDING THE CONTEXT

For years teachers and principals have known that no two gifted and talented pupils are exactly alike in *how* they learn, in *what* they learn, in the *quickness* with which they learn, in the degree that they *retain,* and in what *motivates* them. Differences in all of these matters, and more, show themselves plainly to every observant educator as early as in kindergarten and first grade. Those divergencies between and among pupils grow even more apparent in the higher school grades, because education increases individual differences. The farther along pupils go in school the more sharply and widely they become separated in achievements, learning styles, interests, and in selective retention of what they are taught. Pupil variation is large at age 6. It is larger at age 16.

Since educationally relevant individual differences (i.e., rate of learning, style of learning, power of memory) were first noticed, enterprising instructors have hatched schemes calculated to make it possible for one teacher to match education to each of 20 or 30 puzzlingly different pupils. The project system, contracts, individually prescribed instruction, directive teaching—these are but a few of the ingenious ideas proposed to modify standard practice. Every one of those proposed individualization procedures has merit, and so do many others. In fact, the educational art, science, and technology of today come remarkably close to being able to reach the goal of truly personalized instruction for all pupils.

The focus here is on individualized education for gifted and talented pupils. What is known about attaining that has been borrowed from the work of many professionals, most of whom were not necessarily thinking about the gifted and talented as their primary target. For instance, the Individualized Education Program (IEP) required for handicapped pupils under P.L. 94-142 (the Education for All Handicapped Children Act of 1975), certainly did not aim chiefly at gifted and talented pupils, even though many handicapped school children also are exceptional. Yet the IEP concept is so meaningful it already has been adopted for use with highly able pupils in several of the states.

The IEP's widely acknowledged applicability and its great potential combine to make it the method of choice through which to approach personalized instruction for gifted and talented pupils. Through IEPs, it will be seen, teachers, parents, and pupils can move their wishes for individualized education toward realization.

HUMAN ABILITY, CULTURE, LANGUAGE, AND POVERTY

Educators are motivated to "do something" for pupils who come to school with backgrounds that do not match those of the majority. Common expressions attached to such children are: culturally different, economically disadvantaged, children of poverty, bilingual, culturally deprived, low socioeconomic, failure prone, ethnically different, high failure risk, inner city children, minority group, low social class, and similar distinguishing (and usually pejorative) terms. We have concluded that this kind of language should be used with utmost professional discretion, if it is used at all, for it tends to promote and maintain prejudice.

Our first task is to clarify what the educational considerations really are that are embedded in this morass of terminology. Once that is accomplished, we can pick out the components that have special relevance for the teaching of gifted and talented pupils.

It is true that the expressions listed above and similar ones can be accurate descriptions of certain pupils and their families. It is not true, however, that these conditions are synonymous with parental neglect and ignorance. Seldom do these conditions, singly or in combination, actually cause educational problems. What more often causes educational problems is failure or mistakes by educators in accommodating to the varied backgrounds of these "different" pupils.

The practice most likely to mislead teachers and others into mistakes is the tendency to lump cultural, language, economic, ethnic, and racial differences together. To make such a grouping is like putting together trees, tomatoes, and tanks because they all begin with "t." It has a certain arbitrary convenience, but it is otherwise irrational and illogical. The following observations should make that even more relevant:

- Cultures that differ from one another are not necessarily better or worse. To be raised in the culture of suburban Boston instills everyday life patterns quite different from those suited to an Amish or Mennonite community in Pennsylvania.

• Being economically disadvantaged (financially poor) is neither a disgrace nor an evidence of sloth. Many hardworking and highly intelligent people have little or no material wealth. Sometimes it is because of the nation's economic conditions (recession, depression), and sometimes it is because they have not had opportunities for education and vocational advancement (sharecroppers, wetbacks, migrant workers, and others who have suffered legalized repression, such as Spanish-surnamed Americans, blacks, American Indians, and Orientals). Sometimes it is because they elect to work as missionaries or in other occupations that produce little financial reward.

• Immigration often introduces non-English-speaking children into American schools. Some children, born in the United States, grow up in homes where Spanish, French, German, Chinese, or another foreign language is the primary tongue. These children frequently are from families that place high value both on education in general and upon the ideals of American democracy. Yet when such children come to school, the fact that they have at least rudimentary conversational competence in two languages too often is treated as a problem rather than the actual and potential asset that it really is.

• From the standpoint of ability to learn, there are no important differences among Irish, Norwegian, German, Russian, Italian, Turkish, Egyptian, Japanese, Vietnamese, Nigerian, Australian, or other children of different national origins. In learning ability, they are not superior or inferior to American children. These similarities in learning potential among national and ethnic groups hold also for racial groups, be they black, Oriental, Indian, or whatever. It is normal to expect a range of gifted and talented, average, and retarded pupils in all ethnic and racial groups. None has a monopoly on exceptionality or on ordinariness.

• In the midcity life of metropolitan areas there are a great many clean and well-kept homes, loving parents, active and concerned citizens, young and old, and enterprising business people. Civic-minded groups, abetted by church and fraternal ties, work hard to maintain and elevate the recreational and cultural tone of the inner city.

Just as all persons named Smith or Jones are not alike, so all people of a given race or who live in a certain place or who speak in a certain way are not alike. Some are saintlike and some are scoundrels. Some are ambitious, some are driven, some presumptuous, and some are a little of each. But of overriding importance to our objective, some are gifted and talented. Because their backgrounds differ from those of the majority of children, it is necessary to look in different ways to pick up the early signs that they are gifted and talented. For the same reasons that stereotypes about racial minorities, ethnic groups, and others must be combated, so must stereotypes about evidences of being gifted and talented.

In Yourtowne, a task force of educators has responsibility for making sure that the school system adapts to the needs of children whose backgrounds are unusual. This fall, for instance, an American Indian family moved to Yourtowne, and so did a Russian family and a Vietnamese family. All had children who ranged from preschoolers through high school age. The American Indian, skilled in structural steel work, took a position that let him settle down as foreman-instructor for a company that specializes in putting up the girders and other structural metal for buildings and bridges and supplies the crew leaders for such work. He brought his family—a wife and four children, ages 4, 6, 9, and 11—to live in Yourtowne from the reservation where they had lived and gone to school while he worked on jobs that took him all over the world. The Russian couple had been employed in New York City at the United Nations headquarters, she as manager of finances for the Soviet delegation and he as a translator. There they met, married, began a family, and decided to defect to the U.S.A. They elected to settle in Yourtowne, out of the orbit of their previous associates. Their first child was old enough to start kindergarten. The Vietnamese group was an extended family: an elderly aunt, a middle-aged uncle, a husband and wife and their three children, ages 10, 12, and 15, and two cousins' children, ages 3 and 5. The latter's parents died at sea as the group sought sanctuary outside their homeland. A church organization sponsored the settlement of the Vietnamese family in Yourtowne. In their own country the father had been a high school mathematics teacher and the mother worked part time as a salesperson in a bicycle shop.

When the children of these families appeared at various Yourtowne schools for enrollment, they were put in a temporary holding pattern and the task force was alerted. At each school the parents were reassured by the principal's office staff and received immediately a small, clearly phrased booklet that described enrollment procedures. They were told that in a few days, with their permission and cooperation, some assessments would be made of the educational status and learning styles of their youngsters to help arrange the most appropriate school programs for them. The parents were invited to witness the assessments and help provide information.

The task force is chaired by a school psychologist and contains another school psychologist, a school social worker, and the principal or a designated representative from the school in which enrollment is sought. Usually only one school psychologist serves in a given instance. However, two are kept up to date on new developments in assessment procedures particularly designed to overcome language problems and cultural and other unusual background or developmental differences. To accomplish this, the two psychologists are sent annually to workshops on the topic conducted by professional associations. The most recent assessment materials also are purchased and the two psychologists conduct inservice for their associates in Yourtowne. The psychologists and the social worker, among them, have good command of black speech and of Spanish in the Caribbean and Mexican forms. A roster of community members fluent in other languages is kept up to date by a local service club, and these can be called on for assistance as needed.

As the task force nears completion of the assessment of a given child, the teacher most likely to have chief responsibility for the new enrollee is brought in as a partner to give educational substance to the plan being developed. The school social worker and the teacher decide together, then, how best to bring the parents (and perhaps the pupil) into final decision making.

Naturally, the task force's workload varies. Most of the time it is not needed, and the members pursue their ordinary work in the schools. But it always is in a state of readiness to come together and do what is necessary to design and initiate plans for children who need unusual attention.

Incidentally, by midterm three of the children from the new families had moved into basic scholar standing. Which do you think they were? Why? Also, what parts, if any, do you imagine the parents of these children might play as resources for Yourtowne's schools?

Principles

Instructional interactions between pupils and teachers vary. The selection of those interactions, though, should follow and adhere to principles of high quality instruction. Reynolds and Birch (1977) summarize these principles as: (1) the basic tool subjects must be thoroughly emphasized and their mastery must be a high priority for teachers; (2) pupils should be encouraged to proceed through the standard curriculum at their own various paces; (3) teachers should encourage pupils to pursue worthwhile personal interests within and external to the standard curriculum; and (4) curriculum crossover should be encouraged. This crossover principle addresses the fact that schools often are organized into streams in which, for instance, typing, bookkeeping, and shorthand are reserved for senior high, commercial track students. Gifted and talented pupils should have access to these and other subjects at earlier ages and without regard to their curriculum areas.

Processes

Instructional processes for gifted and talented pupils can be matched to instructional competencies of their teachers. According to Reynolds and Birch, these could be summarized as follows:

- The skills of self-directed study that enable a person to analyze and solve problems independently. The related teacher competency would be the ability to conduct guided independent study.

- The skills necessary for a positive and effective conducting of self-study. These skills can be operationally defined as: pro and con analysis, critique, and examination of the validity of sources. (This is the Bloom et al. (1971) dimension of analysis.) As appropriate, pupils should be encouraged to pursue culminating activities of synthesis and evaluation (as per Bloom et al.). This means that pupil activities would emphasize reaching decisions and conclusions, and clear communications of plans, solutions, and status reports.

- The skills of effectiveness in human relationships necessary to execute undertakings within groups. Related teacher competencies, as with the previous point, would be the ability to work with diverse age and diverse cognitive ability groups. Associated with these skills would be the pupils' affective outcome of respect for their own abilities and the abilities of others.

- Skills in building positive expectations about careers and a life as a productive adult. The related teacher competencies would be career education and education about values.

Organizational Aspects

The IEP is a principal rallying point around which to organize services and instruction. The teacher's competence in the standard curriculum and knowledge of materials for that curriculum are significant resources.

The IEP for an able pupil can be no better than the teacher's competence. That is, the base for everything proceeds from the teacher. There are only modest organizational aspects for the selection of curriculum content and materials. According to Reynolds and Birch (1977) the first important aspect is parent involvement. This involvement means more than informing parents as to what is going on. Involvement means prior notice and negotiation so that parent views about the propriety of intended activities can be incorporated into those activities intended by teachers. Second, there is a great body of instructional material that requires careful selection and appraisal for gifted and talented learners. Third, it is assumed that curriculum planning and development for the district has been accompanied by detailed listing and documentation of available resources. Fourth, access to resources and materials for both pupils and teachers must be arranged. For example, library privileges can be an obstacle. Younger children may be inappropriately denied books and references in the "Adult" section without helpful intervention.

The Key Role of Teachers

The teacher is the key figure in individualization of instruction and in the selection of teaching tactics. How can teachers be sure that they do those things in ways most helpful to able students? Passow (1978) pointed to research about what gifted and talented learners recall regarding their experiences with helpful adults, in and out of school. A most significant element was the response to and treatment of student ideas by adults. Effective adults (1) encourage the ideas of children and youth, (2) encourage the examination of ideas on their merits rather than respond with an automatic rejection, (3) encourage the interrelatedness of knowledge rather than its separateness, and (4) integrate school learning with events in the student's world. These are the behaviors of the helpful adult. Passow encourages teachers to be sources of help to enable competent children to become competent adults. It is Passow's belief that teachers can perform this role more appropriately than most other adults gifted and talented pupils encounter.

Leaders such as Renzulli (1978) and Passow (1978) deplore programming for precocious learners that degenerates into little more than a random bag of tricks to tickle the fancy and play at the edges of development. Without a sound rationale, the procedure becomes the program. Teachers, lacking confidence and self-direction, may place more value in packages than in their own knowledge of pupil aptitudes.

Teachers do well to use the recollections of gifted adults about their early schooling to reinforce perceptions of the educator's central role. The well-designed IEP suggests the proper combinations of tactics needed to fulfill goals of merit.

UNDERSTANDING THE CORRELATES BETWEEN
PERSONALITY AND EDUCATIONAL ACCOMPLISHMENTS

Relevant Processes

Teachers who accommodate gifted and talented pupils often advise and instruct them in projects, investigations, and independent studies. From their own earlier experiences as students, teachers appreciate that the pursuit of complex inquiry involves various skills, not just a "research" skill. Teachers recall that preparing term papers has emotional overtones, too. For some, the term paper is an opportunity for mastery, for others an opportunity to explore a personal interest, and for still others an opportunity to achieve recognition. For some, the idea of a term project still evokes a sense of dread. Sensitive teachers recognize that the feelings they remember may be welling up now in their students. Such awareness on the part of teachers helps lay a foundation for empathy.

Gallagher (1976) advises teachers to consider all the demands on them and on pupils involved in the selection, execution, and completion of projects. He points particularly to four processes always present in critical thinking or problem solving: preparation, incubation, illumination, and verification.

When a pupil, a teacher, or anyone else confronts the unknown and is committed to moving to the known, these four processes come into play. Preparation involves investigation of sources, understanding of background and current knowledge, identifying a plan for completion, and allied activities related to familiarization. Incubation resembles assimilation and accommodation. It calls for reorganization of one's previous ideas to adjust to the new information acquired by preparation. Illumination is the Aha! experience. It arises from the formulation and reformulation of relationships, leading to solutions or plans that are mentally tested and discarded until one emerges that seems feasible. Finally, there is verification—the validation or confirmation, in a real life trial, of the results of illumination.

Expectations

The execution of projects (Gallagher) gives another opportunity for the application of the Aptitude/Treatment Interaction Model. In the context of projects and independent study, pupils will reveal different styles of learning and various approaches to preparation, incubation, illumination, and verification activities.

For example, Griggs and Price (1980) found that the learning styles used by gifted junior high students were different from those of the rest of their classmates. The gifted students proved less teacher-motivated and more self-motivated. They persisted more. They chose some sound over complete quiet while concentrating or studying. They also elected to study alone rather than with classmates or grown-ups. When engaged in learning they opted for tactile, visual, and kinesthetic means over auditory means. Griggs and Price determined, too, that teachers could pick out gifted children three out of five times by looking for these five characteristic learning styles.

Attention to cognitive styles and other relevant personality attributes will pay dividends when the teacher is considering ways to help pupils to complete a product that will give personal satisfaction and be of high quality. Gallagher's conception is summarized in Table 11-1.

Teachers may view the dimensions suggested in Table 11-1 as an inventory to apply to individual pupils as a basis for expectations and guidance. For example, pupils will vary as to willingness to assume risk. Allowing sufficient time is supportive of students in the illumination phase. Students also vary in their attention to the details involved in the sometimes mundane aspects of verification. This variance among pupils can suggest areas of special emphasis for teachers.

Table 11-1 Summation of Gallagher's Views of Pupil Aptitudes

Processes of Critical Thinking/Problem Solving	*Intellectual-Cognitive*	*Relevant Personality Attributes*	*Product Form*
Preparation	Memory Cognition	Sustained attention and studiousness	Orderly search and clarity of problem statement
Incubation and illumination	Divergent thinking	Intellectual freedom	Sloppy
		Risk taking	Confusion about results
		Tolerance for failure and ambiguity	Incoherent
Verification	Convergent thinking	Discipline Logic Sequence	Neat and orderly Well organized Clearly reasoned conclusions Pride and satisfaction Self-criticism of product

Adapted from *Teaching the Gifted Child* (2nd edition) by J.J. Gallagher, Allyn and Bacon, 1976.

Differences such as those probably are due to time dimensions rather than aptitude dimensions. For example, the superior paper typically is done by a person who had allowed sufficient time to progress through all four processes, especially illumination. Moreover, such productive persons also possess an inner sense of standards, plus motivation to persist. Less adequate papers are submitted while the student still is in the stage of either incubation or illumination. Prematurity rather than lack of ability often results in submission of an incomplete product.

Educators may share the insights of Table 11-1 with their gifted and talented students as anticipatory guidance. Moreover, students will vary as to their present ability to cope with this "independence" aspect of independent study projects. Consequently, rather than receiving an assignment with a projected due date, some exceptional pupils are aided if a series of subelement completion dates can be established. The teacher then will monitor continuing progress. Obviously, the need for this type of guidance can be faded as the student internalizes a sense of responsibility.

Helpful Tactics

Creative thinking and problem solving are developmental, like many other human qualities. They do not appear suddenly, in full flower. They are learned behaviors and can be influenced by teaching.

When pupils spend years nurtured in an atmosphere of mainly convergent education, they may seem shocked, reluctant, and even confused by more independent approaches. They may require step-by-step experiences designed to encourage self-confidence about their own potentials for using divergent thinking styles. Kirk and Gallagher (1979) agree that Wilson's (1958) pioneering work in brainstorming can help fill that need for increased self-assurance while stimulating the incubation phases of productive thought.

Brainstorming means unrestrained and spontaneous participation in discussion under a "no criticism" caveat ensuring psychological safety. Emphasis is on process rather than "right" answers. Brainstorming encourages able pupils to generate ideas, posit relationships, and formulate speculations. There is sharing without evaluation of the generated ideas. As a group activity, it builds both confidence and trust among participants. Wilson lists four associated tactics: (1) sensitivity, (2) ideation, (3) originality, and (4) redefinition.

Sensitivity refers to predicting social and psychological consequences of an event. For example: What would happen if all the rivers, lakes, and oceans dried up? A more content-oriented question might be: What were the consequences to Europeans that followed the invention of the compass? The difficulty can be that the content-loaded question requires a significant amount of prior information. That can paralyze the uninformed person, no matter how gifted and talented. The ocean question, less content-based, moves directly to the process of speculation. There is every reason to believe pupils can be guided to more content-oriented questions as confidence and proficiency are gained in the process of sensitivity, and as their knowledge of content warrants.

Ideation parallels divergent thinking. For example: How many ways could a toothbrush be improved to make people comfortable? Closely related is *originality.* For example: How could a hammer be used in different ways? Content-oriented questions might be: How many words beginning with *re* can you produce? How did Edison improve Bell's telephone? In what ways has the transistor been improved? Security with the process is necessary before it is introduced into complex content areas.

Redefinition is finding new uses for familiar things. For example: If you went to a picnic without a frying pan, how would you cook eggs? The emphasis is upon solutions. The intent is to move pupils toward generation of their own abilities to cope. The content parallel would be the discussion section, or the summary and conclusions section, of a research paper.

Wilson's (1958) ideas can help teachers structure time and activities to foster the processes of critical thinking and problem solving. In this way, daily activities are not pulled randomly from a bag of tricks but are orderly and based on principles. The overall goal is to promote in pupils increasing complexity of problem solving behavior. Guilford prepared activities matched to these processes as well as related to certain intellectual operations. Without the overall structure of problem-solving references to content, activities lost direction and purpose.

Some educators and psychologists are so committed to process-oriented activities as to credit them with "improvement" of faculties of the mind. It is more conservative and reasonable to believe that activities in the tradition of Wilson provide (1) a sense of psychological safety while learning the processes of preparation, incubation, illumination, and verification, and (2) a context of structure for acquiring skills.

It is neither feasible nor desirable, though, to plot each gifted and talented pupil's school day in terms of minute-by-minute teacher-made plans. One teacher tried to do that when he was first employed as a teacher in Yourtowne. He was shocked and his carefully laid plans were in disarray when what he had anticipated was an hour of work for two able pupils was completed (and done very well) in 20 minutes. He quickly learned to plan ahead with the students themselves, respecting and using their ideas plus his own to maintain direction, purpose, continuity, and interest.

UNDERSTANDING A CONTINUUM OF EDUCATIONAL ALTERNATIVES

Options remain available to teachers as to how they proceed to fulfill goals and objectives. Even if they select general strategies of adjusting the pace of curriculum (e.g., acceleration) or of modification and expansion of the curriculum (e.g., enrichment), there still is the need to implement these alternatives. Strictly speaking, these strategic alternatives give permission only to modify and adapt; these options do not prescribe fully the selection of tactics.

A Rationale for Selection

Figure 11-1 summarizes strategies of curriculum adaptation. Even this partial listing covers 19 different methods clustered around seven categories. The figure represents an application of Piagetian influences that undergird a rationale for selection of methods. No one cluster is superior to any other cluster. The key idea is that the clusters illustrate treatments to be applied to learner

Figure 11-1 Examples of a Continuum of Educational Experiences

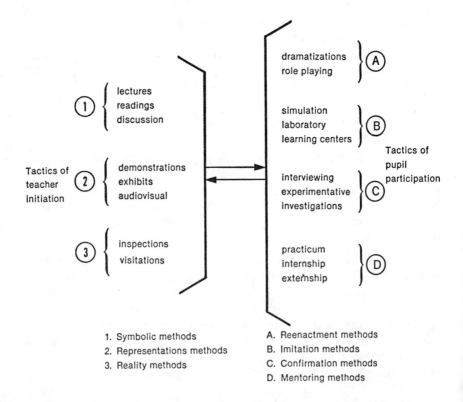

1. Symbolic methods
2. Representations methods
3. Reality methods

A. Reenactment methods
B. Imitation methods
C. Confirmation methods
D. Mentoring methods

aptitudes. The figure calls attention to educational options that require high teacher initiative and activities that call for high pupil participation.

Teacher-initiated activities reflect the influences of accommodation and pupil participation. These are related to assimilation of new experiences. Prior experiences and motivation of pupils influence readiness for independent activity. Initial learnings require feedback to prevent inaccuracies from becoming stabilized.

The selection of tactics thus approximates the Piagetian dialogue between assimilation and accommodation that increases the complexity of the person's behavior. In general terms, the pupil's own readiness, motivation, and prior experience dictate instructional content and method. In the Piagetian sense, experience refers to prior achievement and familiarity with a given topic. Psychologically, this equates with meaningfulness. No task is intrinsically any more meaningful than any other task. Meaningfulness is individually referenced by the pupil's own background and its congruence with the existing environment.

For the gifted and talented pupil, there is the likelihood of greater self-stimulation and exploration. Environments that nurture and mentor are likely to encourage these attributes.

In very general terms, teacher-initiated activities serve as highly useful treatments in certain cases. Lectures, readings, and discussions can arouse interest and focus purpose. This class of activities provides security for the pupil who is uncertain of expectations. These tactics also are helpful in reviewing or in summarizing familiar material. Demonstrations, exhibits, and audiovisual aids provide concrete (e.g., sensory) examples to illustrate verbal statements. These heighten familiarity with material; they add sensory/perceptual representations to verbal/symbolic material. Visits and inspections organized and guided by teachers serve to provide firsthand, actual realities. That brings able pupils into direct and guided confrontation with prescribed learnings. These tactics in particular can build meaningfulness, especially when cognitive grasp has outrun the pupil's life experience, as often can be the case with students who are gifted and talented enough to read about G-forces or deep shaft mining without having enough direct or vicarious experience with either to understand them adequately in any realistic way.

Pupil participation activities, on the other hand, are best designed to foster practice and refinement of learnings and to encourage persistence and pursuit of interests. Gifted and talented pupils are more ready at earlier ages for direct involvement in their own instruction. Dramatization and role playing enhance comprehension and activities of application in the Bloom et al. (1971) sense. They help to internalize learning by way of motoric modes.

Imitation enables pupils to approximate the behaviors of persons engaged in certain subject matter, as a laboratory experiment approximates the behavior of a chemist, or as interviewing to assemble facts about a past event simulates the work of an investigative reporter. Confirmation continues an imitation mode, except that the pupil pursues a hypothesis whose outcome awaits data. Long-range weather forecasting is an example. Often this involves independent study that is guided and supervised. Mentoring methods require an alliance with an appropriate role model. That, of course, has an implied vocational/career outcome, so more than one objective is served.

In the implementation of an IEP, these example tactics all may be used in the course of an academic year in various combinations. There will be crossover between teacher-initiated and pupil participation activities. The strategy can be acceleration if: (1) their products serve to waive standard requirements, (2) the student is awarded advanced standing, (3) the pupil is allowed enrollment with older students, (4) the product is viewed as fulfillment of prescribed competencies, or (5) the pupil can complete requirements at a more rapid rate. The same tactics can be called enrichment if their pursuit enhances learning and interests that are complementary to the standard curriculum.

SUMMARY

This chapter summarized tactics of individualized education. The tactics selected for highlighting meet criteria that they: (1) are relevant to gifted and talented pupils, (2) are applicable in the mainstream of the regular class, (3) constitute priority tactics for the teacher but may be absent in preservice preparation, (4) are consistent with mentoring, (5) are likely to be an outgrowth of an IEP, (6) are content referenced, (7) facilitate team planning, and (8) encourage community participation. These criteria may be used for educators to consider in IEP development for a specific learner.

Chapter 12

Adjustments for Learning Rate

A RATIONALE

Advocates of curriculum acceleration and age-grade acceleration for able learners find that J. S. Stanley (1976) makes a persuasive case for both. His advocacy rests on his own and earlier work from many sources, well documented by Reynolds and Birch (1977). Stanley's central thesis is that acceleration is vastly preferable to most usual types of provisions. He identifies four main types of provisions, ranging from completely unsatisfactory (busywork) through highly appropriate (talent relevant).

1. *Busywork:* This option implies an increase in quantity of work but no increase in variety or in difficulty level.
2. *Talent irrelevant:* This refers to setting up a special class for all gifted learners, either part-time or full-time. Such grouping may enrich the lives of some pupils, but it does little to adjust curriculum to special aptitude. For example, the algebra course for special class students is the same content or pace for both the able/talented in math as for the able/talented in language.
3. *Cultural enrichment:* This supposedly introduces a wider span of experiences to the pupil, usually before such experiences would be available to most students. For example, a special class may receive foreign language, creative arts, and the like to enrich existing curriculum.
4. *Talent relevant:* This is instruction linked to the pupil's special areas of talent so as to be relevant to enhancement of ability. It may mean instruction at an early age. It could mean that a pupil could satisfy high school math credits while in elementary grades as well as completion of college credit while in high school so as to receive advanced standing upon entering college. Stanley was emphatic that continuity has to be

present. Otherwise, adaptations present at one age level, but not at another age level, generate deferred boredom and frustration.

Operationally, talent-relevant enrichment is a parallel to acceleration of curriculum. However, the actual acceleration is talked about as enrichment—a horizontal modification of the curriculum—because it is: (1) tied to a particular grade, (2) couched in an age range, and (3) does not affect the in-grade status of the student. Thus, enrichment for the most part is disguised curriculum acceleration.

Acceleration seems to mean, for Stanley, a vertical modification of curriculum. It literally is nothing more nor less than either moving the pupil into a higher grade than others of the same chronological age or into curricular content and skills sooner than chronological age peers. Those options also are correctly termed acceleration of subject matter, or grade acceleration. A seventh grader who takes ninth grade algebra on an individualized basis in the seventh grade mathematics class illustrates the subject matter approach. A seventh grader who joins a ninth grade algebra class for mathematics illustrates the age-grade acceleration approach. There are many variations and combinations of both approaches that can be matched to pupil aptitudes. A combination might be age-grade acceleration for some subjects while earning advanced credit in a field of specialty through individual study and remaining with an age-peer report room.

Stanley and others enumerate these advantages for acceleration and there is unanimity on most of them—that acceleration:

1. is less expensive to the school district in terms of time and money
2. reduces (but does not eliminate) the need for separate specialists trained as teachers of the gifted and talented at each school level (e.g., elementary, secondary)
3. reduces the effects of the inequities of school curriculum
4. benefits the most able and most motivated student in dimensions of both mastery and challenge
5. applies equally to boys and girls
6. is readily applicable in skill areas such as spelling, reading, mathematics, several forms of athletics (i.e., swimming, figure skating, gymnastics), and the performing arts (i.e., instrumental music, acting)
7. benefits the able pupil in personal/social adjustment
8. minimizes subjectivity of identification and maximizes the proved potential of objective criteria

AN EXAMPLE OF ADJUSTING LEARNING RATE

Seth, at age 14, illustrates the positives of acceleration coupled with talent relevant enrichment. The highlights of Seth's odyssey are as follows (Stanley, 1976):

In fifth grade his teachers noted his ability in math and counseled enrollment in a summer program sponsored by the state academy of science. It featured an institute in computer science. At the same time Seth came to the attention of Stanley's special project (see Chapter 2). Seth completed the institute but it was noted that he did not have much math knowledge (e.g., the rule for dividing one common fraction by another was unknown to him). However, his superior reasoning ability enabled him to learn the rule (e.g., invert the second fraction and multiply) and its proof, to use Stanley's phrase, with the speed of summer lightning.

At sixth grade, Seth enrolled in Stanley's project, a Saturday morning class. In 60 Saturdays (each morning consisted of a two-hour session), Seth completed four and a half years of math equivalent to Algebra II, Algebra III, plane geometry, trigonometry, and analytic geometry. He accelerated through seventh grade, and in eighth grade his math was in Stanley's Saturday sessions. During the second semester he received an A for a University computer science course.

At age 13, Seth became an 11th grader. During this year he (a) took calculus with 12th graders, (b) won a letter on the wrestling team, (c) led the school's gun team, (d) in eight months tutored a brilliant 12-year-old through two and a half years of algebra and one year of plane geometry, (e) learned to play golf, (f) completed college courses in set theory, economics, and political science, (g) managed the successful campaign of a friend to be elected student council president, and (h) prepared for advanced placement tests in calculus and physics. He earned the equivalent of 14 college credits from those exams.

At the end of the 11th grade, Seth completed a year of chemistry at the University during the summer, earning an A grade. In the fall he enrolled in the University with 34 credits, or sophomore status. He took advanced calculus and number theory (As) and sophomore physics and American government (Bs). He became involved in campus politics and was socially accepted by other students. Stanley noted that Seth's mother was employed at the University, so Seth could live at home and commute. (At 14, Seth could not be licensed to drive.)

Other instances of learners similar to Seth are cited (Stanley, 1976). It was noted that Seth's progress began with talent-relevant enrichment subsequently expanded into radical curriculum acceleration (e.g., telescoping content) and grade skipping. The use of early admission represents another option for acceleration.

LESSONS LEARNED

Stanley's report contains both guiding principles for acceleration and observations about its implementation. The principles and observations reveal lessons learned about acceleration regarding student-centered concerns, school-centered concerns, and talent nurture concerns.

Student-centered lessons include the finding that acceleration is workable when there is both ability and eagerness to be engaged in a speedup. The motivation for acceleration must be internal, not based upon an incentive to escape parent or adult demands. Stanley recognizes the usual question about supposed social and emotional development of accelerated students. His countering response is addressed to the intellectual development, emotional esteem, and future success of students who are denied acceleration when they want it. It is Stanley's contention that the concept of peer is relevant. He cites personality data to suggest that his students have as much or more in common with able students who are older than with their chronological age mates. In essence, Stanley finds that social and emotional development are fostered, not penalized, by acceleration. This is confirmed by Pressey (1955) through interviews with students in college and in the adult years, with the added benefit of earlier career entry and success.

School-centered concerns focus on a number of practical factors. One is costs to the school district. Stanley and others note that acceleration can save money since students are not confined to 12 years of school. It is costly in dollars to require a student to endure 180 days of 50-minute sessions if the student knows the material on the first day of class, to say nothing of the emotional wear and tear on both pupil and teacher.

Schools do not need large appropriations to: (1) encourage age-grade acceleration, (2) encourage early high school graduation, (3) arrange enrollment in nearby colleges, (4) make available independent study, (5) promote advanced placement exams, (6) organize fast pace courses, and (7) identify and guide students through elementary and intermediate schooling at a faster than usual rate.

Nurture of talent through separated special classes is expensive and awkward because of the focus on special teachers, gifted and talented pupil identification, enrollment, and, often, transportation. Preparing specialized teachers of the gifted and talented for special classes simply to enrich curriculum is far too costly and of too narrow scope to be of effective help to such pupils. We believe with Stanley that such teachers should be prepared in the tactics of acceleration, guided independent study, use of community resources, and in counseling and consultation with regular teachers and parents in the use of all appropriate tactics, individualized to student needs.

Educators know that mathematics and reading are two of the most universally applicable subject matter domains in the array of human knowledge. They open doors to other forms of learning and they enhance understanding in general, making all the rest of life more meaningful. Thus, precocity in mathematics, like precocity in reading, allows and encourages advancement on all cognitive and affective fronts. It is Stanley's contention—and ours, too—that acceleration is especially valuable for those who want to specialize in a subject they truly enjoy and know best. Further, populations with latent talent (i.e., undereducated minorities, socially or physically handicapped children) should continue to receive the attention of educational specialists to ready them for special programs. Sound programs, like Yourtowne's, draw participants from a varied demographic background.

Stanley (1976) is noteworthy for his contemporary advocacy position on acceleration. Experience demonstrates, for him, that acceleration can be selective in that a pupil need not be accelerated in all curricular areas, and acceleration can be done in heterogeneous groups. It does not require special classes per se. It becomes clear, too, from the work of Stanley and many others, that the procedures of acceleration require thoughtful consideration and development by educators, as well as attention to nurture for those accelerated.

CIRCUMSTANCES OF PRESCRIPTION

Acceleration should be undertaken on an individual-by-individual basis. Acceleration can be focused on a particular part of a subject matter area or can be as comprehensive as the curriculum of an entire grade or grades. Acceleration can mean moving the learner ahead of chronological age peers and into advanced learning situations with students older but more compatible socially and educationally, or it can mean presenting content and skills sooner to a learner than is usual but still in the company of age peers. All acceleration options have in common enabling the learner to telescope the usual length of time to complete the usual scope and sequence of schooling.

As schools undertake this adaptation, it should be considered as a prescription for individualized education. This prescription can be referenced to the learner and the environment.

Considerations of learner variables to help decide to arrange this option would include situations when:

1. the learner is motivated internally to pursue an accelerated pace rather than motivated by external pressures to please others;
2. the subject matter and skills attainment, per se, are not necessarily dependent upon life experience but are associated with superior intellectual operations;
3. the pupil's demonstrated mastery of subject matter and skills is substantially beyond the attainments of age peers;
4. there is evidence that the learner can master schooling at a faster rate than age peers;
5. the learner's rate of mastery is so advanced and accelerated as to be beyond a reasonable expectation of the grade-appropriate educator to manage; and
6. there is recognition that this option is in the best educational, intrapersonal, interpersonal, and career interests of the learner.

Environmental factors, in actual practice, make up either a support system or a deterrent system. Effective acceleration approaches (e.g., in the best interests of the person) are characterized by a support system that:

1. has established valid criteria to assess mastery levels to allow for advanced placement testing to bypass needless courses;
2. has established policies to take advantage of acceleration throughout the entire school—for example, it is of maximum value to start to accelerate at the earliest elementary level and to follow through at later levels;
3. has alerted teachers to any necessary provisions for a younger pupil who will be placed as to subject matter and skill appropriateness;
4. has initiated ties to a local institution of higher education such as a community college or a four-year degree facility to advise and counsel, arrange for, and chart progress for early admission students as appropriate;
5. has initiated ties to early childhood programs to be alert for possibilities for early admission to kindergarten or first grade;
6. has enlisted competent volunteers to serve as either tutors, consultants, or mentors;
7. has a commitment to counseling the family and the learner as to sources of financial help—in appropriate instances, counseling may mean more than referral, it may mean active assistance to locate sources and to help students qualify for help;
8. has access to a team or committee structure to fulfill functions of identification, utilization of resources, and continuing evaluation;
9. has commitment to involve the family and the pupil as valid team members; and

10. has provisions for inservice training of teachers to recognize evidence of learner appropriateness for acceleration and to implement curriculum for accelerated pupils.

We believe these factors could provide useful guidance of Individualized Educational Programs. These proved factors should be taken into account as tactics of acceleration are used.

SUMMARY

Adjustment for learning rate must be considered very high on the priority list of educational accommodations for gifted and talented pupils. Probably no other educational adjustment for able learners has such a long history of use and so much favorable research to support its continued employment. Like any other procedure, it can be abused. But when rational guidelines are used, such as those detailed in this chapter, acceleration can offer an adaptation that is time tested, relatively inexpensive, applicable across the whole age range of schooling, beneficial educationally and in personal and social adjustment, and valuable for career development.

Chapter 13

Adjustments for Expanding and Extending Learning

A VALID PRECEDENT

Teachers know that adjustment of content and of skill expectations for different learners is a normal activity. Adaptations and adjustments on behalf of gifted and talented pupils may need to be more frequent and more extensive, but they are the same in principle as the adaptations teachers are experienced in making.

Adjustments take place in a variety of settings. In junior and senior high schools, the emergence of elective courses and cocurricular activities has been a form of curriculum adjustment. A school that sponsors a photography club is engaging in enrichment of the curriculum. A school band is another example. Some schools may organize study projects on regional history for which pupils spend part of their school time in specialized study. These, too, would be adjustments of an enriching nature.

Various forms of organization for instruction such as open classrooms, ungraded primary grades, individualized education, learning centers, and similar movements illustrate ways to adjust the standard curriculum at primary and intermediate levels. These options concentrate on the individual rate of progress of the learner rather than on a grade-by-grade progression of a group. These movements, whatever they are called, share a common recognition of the inherent difficulties in expecting all pupils to learn the same things in the same way at the same time for the same motives. It is this recognition that makes expanding and extending curriculum an attractive, logical, and valid option for gifted and talented pupils and for other exceptional children and youth, too.

A MODEL FOR CURRICULUM ADJUSTMENTS

The research of Renzulli (1977) offers the educator every confidence that previous training and present curriculum are suitable bases for instructing gifted and talented learners. Renzulli's observations provide helpful guidance as to: (1) a definition and rationale of enrichment, (2) anticipatory questions about implementation, (3) alternatives; and (4) management considerations.

A Rationale

Renzulli noted that enrichment, however defined, usually encounters two perplexing questions that hamper its implementation: (1) Is not enrichment and its activities good for all learners? and (2) How are the activities prescribed for the gifted and talented really individualized?

Renzulli's experiences as an evaluator of programs for exceptional pupils led him to identify those two and the following additional questions and concerns:

- Practices of instruction were observed to be little more than a random collection of kits, games, puzzles, and artsy-craftsy projects that could be described as either (a) a cosmetic redressing of sound practices for all children and youth, or (b) a means to entertain gifted and talented learners rather than an adaptation to their attributes.

- Feedback from students enrolled in special projects for the gifted and talented was disquieting. Renzulli declared that the comments of gifted persons universally were superlative but reflected an attitude that a special project was a kind of educational recess. For example, children would be observed walking into a special projects room and selecting a game. The child played the game until the end of the period and returned it to the shelf. The teachers' response was that such games are challenging and fun.

- Observations of project-oriented sessions led Renzulli to another misgiving about practices that pass for enrichment. Evidence of freedom of choice and flexibility for pursuit of topic selection were admirable features. The disappointment was at the level and quality of inquiry.

Renzulli's interview questions, were of the following types:

- What was the most interesting project you have done this year in your special program?

- What ways did you pursue the goals for your project?
- What type of resource and references did you use?
- What did you learn from your project?
- What was the purpose of your study?
- If you were doing this project in your regular classroom, how would you do it differently?

He noted that the common responses of the students tended to be: (a) a style of inquiry composed of stilted footnotes, (b) use of the same encyclopedias, reference works, and library books available to all students, (c) learnings couched in facts, and (d) recitation of the usual conclusions. He did commend freedom of topic, absence of pressure, and release from grading. His main concern was that the special projects were neither quantitatively nor qualitatively different.

Another source of distress that increased as a result of observation and interview in special programs was the preoccupation with mental processes as such and a persistent neglect of the structure, methodology, and content of organized fields of human knowledge. To Renzulli (and to us) the work of Guilford is best understood as a psychological contribution. Similarly, the work of Bloom et al. (1971) is best understood as a measurement contribution. Renzulli expressed doubt as to their direct educational applications as curriculum content, and we agree that the doubt is justified on several grounds. The difficulty with Guilford's mental operations and Bloom's taxonomy is that they were meant for purposes other than curriculum substance. They are and can be used for understanding the processes of learning and of measurement of learning. The persisting difficulty is that teachers have been led astray about these processes. The processes may be a path toward learning, not the goals of learning per se. Moreover, even as paths (processes) they have not been validated. Paradigms of intellectual processes certainly are useful models of structure of intellectual anatomy if used as intended, namely, to stimulate organized investigation of human thought processes. To press them into use as the substance of curriculum for gifted and talented pupils has little justification, in our view.

The Turned-On Scholar

Renzulli (1977) shared several examples of interviews with scholars of various disciplines. He noted that he had tried to "sell" mental processes. He met rather polite resistance from these scholars. They resisted because the processes did not match the reality of a discipline's way of inquiry. It became apparent, though, that the enthusiasm and excitement of the scholar in pursuit of inquiry could be an inspiring model for enrichment for both gifted and talented learners and the vast majority of all children and youth. The model involves pupils in investigations that approximate the work of persons actually engaged in professional and creative roles. Seldom are scholars engaged in "training exercises" of games, puzzles, showcases, or stunts. The investigative activity of scholars and professionals caused Renzulli to press for the "turned-on scholar" model.

Inquiry, as we view the concept, is engagement in solving real problems. Methods of inquiry are methods of doing something. Inquiry, per se, is an activist mode. The practicality of inquiry is that after information is outmoded, inquiry methods remain; they are enduring. Another practical consideration identified with inquiry is that of the real impossibility of fully keeping pace with the expansion of knowledge. Accordingly, the prudent person maintains awareness of methods of inquiry.

Principles of Inquiry

Six general principles for teachers in undertaking enrichment as inquiry are stated below in brief (Renzulli, 1977):

1. Students should be allowed to pursue their own interests to whatever depth and breadth of attainment personal incentive dictates. A little knowledge may be a dangerous thing, but one cannot learn too much.
2. Pursuit of interests should be consistent with the learner's style of learning.
3. The teacher's role is to provide assistance to the learner, including removing impediments and limitations that might deny access to the material and equipment the learner needs.
4. Assistance should be directed to enabling the student to identify interests and structuring realistic and solvable problems.
5. Assistance will involve the student's gaining investigative skills and access to resources.
6. Assistance also will involve finding appropriate outlets and recognition for student products.

Understanding a Triad

There is reason to think of enrichment as three interrelated elements, not as one master process. The three elements supply a rationale for enrichment for all learners, plus differentiations for gifted and talented pupils. In a technical sense the elements really are prototypes of enrichment. The three are called:

(1) General Exploratory Activities, (2) Group Training Activities, and (3) Investigations of Real Problems. Renzulli refers to them as Types I, II, and III of enrichment.

Use of the regular curriculum as a base has several advantages for gifted and talented learners. One is that the curriculum will specify essential competencies, especially literacy standards. Second, the curriculum allows for pursuit of the student's current interests and learning style as a foundation for expansion of both dimensions. Third, use of the regular curriculum does not bind enrichment to a place such as a regular classroom, a resource room, or a special class. Enrichment, as inquiry, can serve one student and at the same time can serve several gifted and talented learners interacting with other pupils anywhere in the school and community.

Enrichment as a General Exploratory Activity

General Exploratory Activities (GEA) are meant for all students and were defined by Renzulli (1977) as:

> those experiences and activities that are designed to bring the learner into touch with the kinds of topics or areas of study in which he or she may have a sincere interest. ... They should involve very little structure, but at the same time ... should ... have very purposeful objectives. (p. 17).

To apply GEA, teachers must recognize that freedom of choice based on pupil interest is an essential, and there also is the need to allow sufficient time for exploration. Interest centers are advocated. They should feature ways of knowing as well as knowledge objectives. Contact with resource speakers, field trips, and browsing are encouraged. Students can be expected to weigh a variety of interests. Teachers may have to learn patience and resist the temptation to rush a student into a premature commitment to an interest.

Teacher-initiated questions enable educators to help students clarify their interests. These questions also can serve as selection criteria for choices about interest centers, resource persons, and field trips. Such questions may be applied to content areas. For example, they could be used to guide a high school pupil interested in psychology, as follows:

1. Why do people study psychology?
2. What does the study of psychology contribute to people's lives?
3. What kinds of questions does a person interested in psychology ask, and whom?

4. Where can information or evidence about psychology be found and used?
5. What are some of the great discoveries of psychology?
6. What are the different types of psychology and how is information and practice categorized?
7. What qualifies as a bona fide source of evidence in psychology?
8. How does a person in psychology move from facts to either conclusions or generalizations?
9. What are the kinds of problems psychologists attempt to solve?
10. How does a psychologist know when problems are solved?
11. What are the attributes and qualifications of persons in psychology?
12. What would be a good first step to begin an investigation of psychology?

For typical pupils who express interest in psychology this list probably would be too long; it might better be given in shortened form or a third at a time. That might be best for young gifted and talented children (preschool and primary age), too. But older able pupils are fully capable of a simultaneous many-sided examination of a topic, and that should be encouraged.

This style of initial probe can be adapted to individual or group use. It also is adjustable to almost any domain of knowledge. Questions can be added or deleted or amended to suit the topic being investigated, from a biogenesis to zymurgy.

Enrichment as Group Training Activities

Renzulli (1977) defined Group Training Activities (GTA) as

> methods, materials, and instructional techniques that are mainly concerned with the development of thinking and feeling processes. . . . The objective will enable a student to deal more effectively with content. . . . The thinking and feeling processes can include critical thinking, productive thinking, problem solving, values clarification, and brainstorming. (pp. 24-25).

This form of enrichment is an outgrowth of General Exploratory Activities. Here, the work of Bloom et al. (1971) and of Guilford (1977) can be of substantial guidance to the teacher. However, we join Renzulli in urging the use of these sources as pathways, if they are used at all, not as goals in themselves.

Students should be grouped, if there are enough of them, according to their interests and around common content areas. These two dimensions—interest and curriculum—can then become vehicles for skill and process building. For example, a thinking exercise could be "Let's Write a Slogan." This exercise excites the student's commitment to pursue advertising in greater depth and sophistication. This Type II enrichment becomes a foundation for subsequent expansion into Type III enrichment, which is discussed next.

Enrichment as Investigation of Real Problems

Renzulli (1977) defined Type III enrichment as

> activities in which the youngster becomes an actual investigator of a real problem or topic by using appropriate methods of inquiry.... An investigator is one who is actively engaged in the process of adding new knowledge, ideas, or products to his or her field of study. (p. 29).

Highly able pupils require this type of enrichment. Pupils and teachers both need to understand the differences among three levels of development: an initial beginning, a substantial mastery, and exploration at the frontiers of knowledge. Renzulli cites evidence that students learn more and attain greater commitment to a field of inquiry if allowed to act and feel like a professional or artist rather than being presented abstract, detached exercises.

This type of enrichment best matches the three distinctive attributes of these learners: high mental ability, creativity, and task commitment. The underlying skills teachers need for this type of enrichment involve adapting to student interests, providing assistance, and finding suitable outlets and recognition for student products.

INVESTIGATIONS OF REAL PROBLEMS

A Case in Point

An example of Type III enrichment is presented here in adapted form to show the match between teacher competencies and the procedures.

Student Interests. A group of students in a middle school became involved in heated arguments over candidates for election to city government posts as a part of a civics class dealing with that topic. The issue was construction of an oil refinery that would have impact on both the ecology and on employment.

The teacher watched the discussion and noted student interests. Certain pupils, in the teacher's judgment, seemed interested in assessing voter attitudes about the impact of the refinery. These students and the teacher agreed that a questionnaire form of survey could supply information on that matter.

Assistance. The teacher enlisted help from the librarian. Pupils were able to obtain books on issues and techniques in public opinion sampling. They also were able to obtain journals that reported examples of surveys. Although the material was of college level, these youngsters were able to manage it with a minimum of assistance. Their interest level was heightened by journal articles.

Following suggestions found in the books and journals, the students conducted a pilot study of their questionnaire on parents and relatives. The results of the pilot were used to polish it into finished form. The teacher and the librarian provided information about procedures to select a random, but representative, sample. The students then conducted their survey.

The students became aware that the results needed to be put into a final form. Again, assistance was found from available texts and journals about how to analyze and interpret data from a questionnaire. The students published a final report that included statistical, graphic, and narrative descriptions of their data.

Finding Outlets. Students were able to share their reports before the school assembly and as a presentation before a PTA meeting. A version of the report was featured in the school newspaper and in the school news section of the local newspaper. This kind of activity and the form of reporting fits well into the Yourtowne scheme for gifted and talented children and youth.

Management Considerations

One sign of a teacher's mastery of the Individualized Education Program approach is evidence that the educator can identify and involve resource persons. Other indications are success at identifying pupil interests, finding outlets for student products, and arranging a suitable environment. Key roles of teachers could include:

Sources. It is customary to think of sources as textbooks and encyclopedias. For gifted and talented pupils, an expanded list includes yearbooks, atlases, record books, catalogues, periodicals, concordances, digests, and almanacs. There also are sources beyond print media, such as microfilms, records, tapes, films, models, and kits.

Management Plan. Renzulli (1977) detailed the content of an IEP contract (an agreement between learner and teacher). In school systems where IEPs are required, the contract can be the essence of the program, thus requiring no duplication of planning documentation. Elements include a description of the problem to be undertaken, identifying what sorts of persons would be interested in this problem and its solutions, intended products and outlets, methodological resources, and kinds of information required to achieve the project's goals. This agreement is a checkpoint for specification of teacher assistance, learner commitment, and involvement of school and non-school resources.

The Interest-A-Lyzer. This survey form uncovers both overt and covert interests. It examines 12 sources of interest, including pretend activities, identification of collections, what the pupil would like to write about, preference for activities, and making priority decisions.

Community Resources Survey. This document helps find in-school and out-of-school resources. It covers eight content areas: trips and travel, academic training, intercultural experience (e.g., living in another culture), hobbies, collections, compositions, community service interests, and professional and vocational interests. There is a final checklist of topics, labeled a scavenger hunt.

Evaluation occurs on two levels. One focus is on student performance, the other is on the school's performance to provide identification of interest, methodological assistance, and product outlets. The conceptual framework of the evaluation model rests on inputs, process, and outcomes of the IEP approach. The model is portrayed in Figure 13-1.

Evaluation is to be undertaken for professional growth and development. The intent of evaluation is to improve educational practice, not for simplistic fault finding.

The IEP is quite useful as a basis for designing assessment and evaluation. Pupil accomplishments, of course, should be made a part of the student's record and carried forward in subsequent revisions.

CIRCUMSTANCES OF PRESCRIPTION

Certain indicators should alert educators as to the appropriateness of enrichment by means of Investigation of Real Problems. These indicators sometimes are individual and sometimes environmental.

Individual Indicators

Is there evidence that the learner is:

1. ready, or inclining, toward a product orientation?
2. prepared to assume the role of investigator-producer?
3. committed to pursue an inquiry of lengthy duration and of sufficient complexity beyond that usually expected of age grade peers?
4. of sufficient maturity to pursue a contract agreement system?

Figure 13-1 Elements of Evaluation in the Investigation of Real
Problems Approach

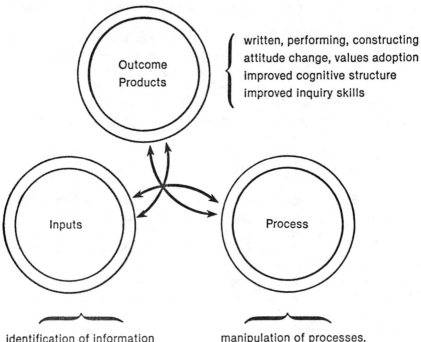

written, performing, constructing
attitude change, values adoption
improved cognitive structure
improved inquiry skills

identification of information
sources

acquisition of information

use of empirical (e.g., ob-
serving, experimenting,
interviewing, and survey)
sources

use of authoritative and
vicarious sources

use of aesthetic resources

use of print and nonprint
media

use of community sources
and the environment

manipulation of processes,
i.e., verifying, comparing
classifying, discovery

creative processes of
inquiry, i.e., designing,
constructing, planning,
inferring, estimating,
establishing credibility

Adapted from *The Enrichment Triad Model* by J. S. Renzulli, Creative Learning Press,
1977.

5. genuinely and sufficiently interested enough to fulfill task commitment?
6. sufficiently skilled to conduct investigations of this type?

Environmental Indicators

Is there evidence that the educational system:

1. is sufficiently explicit in its regular curriculum as to expectations for attitudes, understandings, and skills?
2. has inventoried its resources in the community, sources for methodological assistance, and inquiry resources?
3. has located genuine and meaningful sources for the outlet of students' products?
4. acknowledges that learners can be producers, regardless of the their ages?
5. is accustomed to providing exploration and training as a foundation for investigation?
6. shows the flexible scheduling needed to manage investigative enrichment?
7. provides inservice preparation to enable faculty and staff to have the resources to implement investigation?

We believe these factors should be considered in the IEP. We further commend this list as an inventory to be considered in implementation of an IEP.

Examples

Illustrations of IEP activities for use with gifted and talented pupils can be kept in a resource notebook by teachers and added to as ideas develop. These are after Renzulli's (1977) suggestions.

- A group of 6- and 8-year-olds developed a white paper for 110 state legislators describing the aesthetic and ecological values of the dragonfly. They engaged in a media campaign of petitions, T-shirts, bumper stickers, and TV coverage that resulted in legislation designating the dragonfly as the state's official insect.

- A 12-year-old student was commissioned to lecture on Ancient Egypt at the community museum. This student also translates original Egyptian documents into English.

- A proposed highway was shown by a small group of 13-year-olds to be of potential ecological harm to a nearby reservoir. Their findings contradicted a state panel of experts who favored construction. The results of the student survey resulted in blocking construction.

- A 12-year-old persevered in four years of research and public relations to persuade a state to mark the actual birthplace of a U.S. president.

- Ten-year-olds used a stopwatch and diagram to research the frequency of failure to halt at a stop sign. Their report was used to persuade the authorities to install a stoplight.

- Students studied old newspapers, property transfer records, and town maps to identify historical homes. They constructed a model of their town in colonial times, with a narrative tape. The exhibit was featured in a shopping center.

- Students identified the number of napkins taken in the cafeteria but not used. Their report enabled school officials to eliminate waste.

- A group of 8- to 9-year-olds initiated a school newspaper that was not confined to school news. Two of the paper's reporters scooped the wire services as to Vice Presidential nominees by persistent interviewing.

One common denominator among these examples is that none of the teachers had any particular or special training in either the topics or the tactics of the inquiries. It was their skillful management of the investigative process, enlistment of resources, and commitment to production that made possible the pupils' accomplishments.

SUMMARY

Certainly some forms of enrichment can be helpful to any pupil. But virtually all of the schooling for mentally advanced students must extend and expand the basic curriculum if it is to be effective. To think of curricular modifications for able students solely in terms of higher level processes drawn from the structure of intellect work of Guilford and the taxonomic constructs of Bloom, et al. is to risk shortchanging gifted and talented pupils in the content domain. Exploration, group training, and real problem investigation, with painstaking evaluation of the thoroughness and match of each, offer challenging opportunities for teachers and pupils alike.

Chapter 14

Using Tactics of Teacher Initiation

This chapter shows how well-known teaching tools such as discussion and problem-solving activities are especially useful with gifted and talented pupils. The use of field trips (e.g., inspections and visitations) is included to renew interest in this and other uses of community resources. The material about multiple talents also illustrates how seemingly ordinary procedures can have extraordinary applications.

DISCUSSIONS

Description and Outcomes

Discussions require sustained two-way (or more) communication. Discussion differs from recitation where the exchange is very one-sided and essentially stimulus-response oriented. The recitation, of course, is appropriate and necessary where the requirement is for feedback as to accuracy. But it falls short of being discussion.

Discussion also puts demands on the skill of passive listening in the Carkhuff (1977) and Gordon (1970) sense. The tactics of active listening described in Unit V certainly are applicable to stimulate pupils and as a basis for serving as a consultant, whether to parents, other teachers, or, as in this case, to gifted and talented pupils.

McKeachie (1978) pointed out eight possible instructional outcomes of discussion: (1) use of the resources of the group, (2) opportunities for student applications, (3) provision of prompt feedback, (4) practice in thinking, (5) evaluation of one's own logic or one's position about issues, (6) awareness of problems and issues, (7) awareness of information to refute folklore, and (8) development of motivation for further learning. The difficulties of the method can be: (1) gaining participation, (2) informing students of progress

231

toward objectives (e.g., the discussion is having a point, leading somewhere), and (3) handling the emotional reactions of students. Worthwhile discussion takes skill on the part of both teacher and student.

Problem Centeredness

The problem-centered discussion provides focus. Students sometimes become "lost" because they are unsure of the intended outcomes. To avoid that, discussions can be prestructured for clarification into: (1) formulating a problem, (2) suggesting questions or hypotheses, (3) generating relevant data, and (4) evaluating alternatives. The leader is responsible for informing the group about progress through the sequence of components.

Starting a discussion can be the most difficult, awkward, and frightening part of the process. McKeachie suggested the following ways to ease into a discussion:

Asking Questions. Generally a factual "what" question is less effective than a "how" question that presses for relationships and application. For example: "What is the U.S. Department of Education definition of gifted and talented?" would inhibit pupils while, "How does a definition influence practice?" would be more likely to stimulate ideas.

Using Surprise. This tactic is effective if the teacher prefaces the outset of the discussion with, "Suppose I take the position that _____." If the teacher takes a covert devil's advocate position and later reveals this was a false premise, students often will feel distrust.

Coping with Nonparticipation. Teachers will need to tolerate silence. Many students are used to being passive receivers. Seating in a circle can be helpful. Calling students by name is helpful, as is becoming acquainted with pupils' interests. This allows for using their expertise in the discussions that will follow. It also has the advantages of (1) demonstrating student centeredness and (2) reducing fear about participation.

For nonparticipants, the teacher may contrive assignments tailored to their interests. For some students, a large group can be intimidating. One helpful device is to use "buzz" groups of two to six people to counteract this dread. Another procedure is the inner circle. This involves seating a portion of the class in a circle surrounded by an outer ring of observer students. This inner circle can be composed of recorders from buzz groups who discuss their results with the teacher.

Two dynamics that inhibit discussions are monopolizing and argumentation. The former can be handled by out-of-class counseling. Assigning observers to chart contributions can be of help to objectively confirm instances and degree of domination.

Arguments can become so heated as to thwart problem solving. Leading the group in the direction of stating a problem and formulating hypotheses tends to reduce heat. The generation of relevant data and the facing of alternatives also keeps conflict within bounds. The two-column tactic suggests dividing a chalkboard in "For A" and "For B." Students state their positions for either "A" or "B" without attacking the other. Evaluation is deferred until later.

Evaluation of discussion helps students learn how to learn from discussion. McKeachie (1978) sees student-centered outcomes:

1. Learning to clarify, to escape from confusion. Students can learn to create for themselves and request from others that diverse material be structured into manageable problems.
2. Learning to share one's own ideas and to listen to and entertain the ideas of others.
3. Learning to manage time for effective planning.
4. Learning to build on the ideas of others and to elaborate ideas into solutions.
5. Learning sensitivity for the feelings of others in the exchange of ideas. Here, the teacher needs to be alert to both the feelings and the content of discussions and serve as referee rather than judge.
6. Learning evaluation skills. This may take the form of reports that inform students about their progress and about their growing ability to lead, participate in, and evaluate discussions.

Discussions as Leadership

Discussions can foster leadership development, a very desirable outcome. Students can be encouraged to call a group to order; introduce the topic, problem, or resolution; clarify goals; maintain the group on task; summarize points discussed, and mediate differences. Evaluation of the group by the group should be encouraged. Time should be set aside to record progress and establish an agenda for the next steps.

With students conditioned to be passive receivers and to guess the teacher's "right" answer, discussion skills may be limited or absent. For them, the teacher can stimulate and initiate discussions on topics that have no "right" answers. The Values Clarification Approach offers clues about how to do that. Discussion of topics with no right answers will encourage students to prize their contributions as well as value their ability to make contributions to others.

TEACHING TACTICS FOR PROBLEM SOLVING

Organizing Generalizations

Feldhusen and Treffinger (1977) analyzed the experiences of teachers in the initiation of project-type experiences. They extracted six generalizations (in the Bloom sense) generated from examination of practices that teachers found exciting and rewarding. Neglecting any of these guidelines invites disappointment and frustration. The six guidelines call upon the teacher's ability to:

1. define the pupil's intended (or goal) behavior in either ability or process terms
2. describe objectively the skills, content, and procedures to be used by students
3. try out proposed tactics (teaching techniques or procedures) before introduction to pupils
4. describe the environment (i.e., space, materials, equipment) necessary for achieving the intended behavior by pupils
5. use teaching and learning procedures that encourage varied activities and pupil products
6. plan revisions based upon pupil learnings and upon student progress toward goals (principle of feedback and revise)

Overcoming Aggravation

Even the best of anticipatory planning can be sidetracked. Feldhusen and Treffinger warned about ten temptations. Those temptations and some alternatives are:

1. The teacher must not quit with a first attempt; with practice, success will be easier to attain.
2. Any innovation can become a routine; retain variety in methodology.
3. "I don't know" *is* an appropriate answer to pupil questions (and gifted and talented pupils can ask tough questions!). Security is shown by willingness to admit one's lack of immediate information.
4. Confidence in one's own ability to manage varied and diverse student investigations can be acquired. There may be initial feelings of uncer-tainty in keeping track, but initial chaos will subside.
5. Locating resources can be difficult, even defeating. As one gains experi-ence and as others become aware of the program, locating resources and routing pupils to resources becomes more efficient.

6. Overcoming previous beliefs about pupil ability can be difficult. For example, thinking and performance are learned as a result of opportunity, and opportunity is what teachers can offer best. Talents are not genetic traits for a fortunate few, nor are gifts of intellect. Teachers are at their best when they are alert to potentials in a variety of pupils.

7. It may be difficult to put aside previous patterns of teaching temporarily. For example, brainstorming requires deferred evaluation, or judgment, of the pupil by the teacher. It is difficult to resist correcting spelling errors, sentence structure, and validity of ideas in the earlier stages of proposals.

8. It may be difficult for both teacher and pupils to resist sex stereotyping. For example, art, poetry, and dance may be, consciously or unconsciously, reserved to girls. It is essential to be aware and alert to the danger that certain performance areas are restricted to a particular sex.

9. Project teaching is demanding, especially in time and preparation. If there is belief in the process and in its outcomes, these demands will be accepted as associated responsibilities. Project teaching is not a "bag of tricks."

10. A final observation termed *the principle of pupil readiness:* As one shifts from teacher-dominated instruction to pupil-teacher planning, there can be a temporary psychological discomfort for students. There may be the perception of the teacher as *the* authority and source of all knowledge, even by gifted and talented pupils. They can distrust their own abilities to be either an authority or a valid source. Pupils such as these will need reassurance to help build confidence in their own abilities.

It will take time and patience to assist pupils as they shift from passive receivers to active participants.

A Case in Point

In Yourtowne, Lucy Boone, a first-year teacher, was eager to test the Feldhusen and Treffinger (1977) process. She was committed both to its rationale and to its validity.

Responsible for a group of sixth graders of varying abilities, Boone knew that the Yourtowne school district's sixth grade curriculum conveyed mixed messages. For example, the curriculum guide specified what topics were to be covered by what dates of the school year. Yet the guide declared that the interests of pupils were to be valued-centered activities. Moreover, the district's policy was that films and materials must be ordered three months in advance, even though spontaneous activities were to be encouraged.

So here it is, Thursday, the day after a rousing inservice session regarding the use of project-centered methods. Despite the mixed messages, Boone thinks this tactic holds real promise.

The morning recess is nearly over. Pupils are assembling to return for the stretch between recess and lunch. Standing by the south door, Boone sees that the pupils are beginning to cluster around her. A quick count shows that all are present except Philip, Mike, Martha, John, and Elizabeth. With a sigh, she gets ready to organize a search party. If project methods seem especially necessary to challenge bright pupils, those five would be it. However, she hadn't planned to start with a simulation of the Bureau of Missing Persons.

Boone found in the first week that they were known as the Flying Five in the teacher's lounge. Their questioning always went beyond the obvious. One had to admit, though, that their humor was lively and captured the essence of the topic.

Just before the search party is officially sworn in, the Flying Five are discovered by the west fence. Five forms huddle around a burly workman. It resembles a press conference. The workman is fielding their questions with respect. The water tower between the school and the firehouse is being painted.

Drawing closer, the rest of the class becomes engaged as well. As the details of ropes and pulleys, scaffolds, and the like wind down, the unanswered questions remain: What does a water tower do? Why are water towers constructed? How does a water tower figure in the school's drinking water? Who operates and maintains the tower? Where does the water come from? When are water towers used? The members of the work party are responsive; however, they were contracted to paint it, not to understand it. It is time for both work party and pupils to return to their respective roles.

Walking back through the south door, the Flying Five, all basic scholars, talk animatedly about the interview. They seem more purposeful than ever before. However, the task is to "Value and Understand Our Democratic Form of Government" after lunch in the social studies period and to "Comprehend Our Wonderful Balance of Nature" after that, during science.

Suddenly, the operational meaning of convergence becomes clear. The situation's irony also comes into bold relief. Studying democratic relationships through imposed topics appears inconsistent. Planning for immediate interests six months in advance chafes. It is incongruous.

The contrast between the lively interest around the fence and anticipation of the afternoon becomes overpowering. A sense of opportunity grows. Besides, what does a water tower do? Disregarding the straight and narrow path, Boone's resolve grows deeper. What a wondrous marvel the human mind is, she reflects. All these thoughts while completing 100 steps from the south door to the sixth grade area. In a few minutes the teaching space is going to look very much like the city room of a newspaper. The analogy is pleasing for its clarity and sense of adventure.

Later that evening, Boone reflects that it was worthwhile to become a teacher. The follow-up discussion with the pupils was inspiring. At first, some were puzzled by their teacher's lack of information about water towers. However, they recovered fast. Their questions, at least, were clarified. It was a good start indeed. The building principal was super. She remarked wistfully that the sixth grade was the only group to be seriously pursuing this very natural encounter. She also is "hooked" as to what a water tower does. Besides, she turned out to be an experienced project-centered educator. The next challenge is to execute those six generalizations, and the principal already has volunteered to help.

Defining the Intended Outcome

The expressed interests of pupils are excellent starting points from which to select the content to use in reaching instructional objectives. Boone did that with the water tower incident. She found and used a way to start where the children were and to lead them to the objective about both democratic government and nature's balance.

In situations of high motivation for pupils, an especially exciting process is problem-solving. It is almost universally applicable and very adaptable to content (even to the study of water towers). While definitions may vary, the problem-solving process can be organized into five stages:

1. Fact finding involves the location of data and their sources.
2. Problem statement means refining and organizing information until it can be framed into a statement. A good statement is often in the journalistic style of who, what, when, where, how, and why. Statements also can be in hypothesis form.
3. Idea finding is the search for new information that bears on the stated problem. Students may need to be made to feel it is safe to risk suggestions and to volunteer. Suggestions become like a resource file or a data bank.
4. Solution finding is the selection from among the alternatives proposed during idea finding. In this stage, judgment is appropriate. Of the many ideas presented, pupils select those that have the greatest potential for satisfaction or solution of the problem.
5. Acceptance finding is the active decision making about solutions. It also involves drawing conclusions and indicating how certain one is of their validity.

Feldhusen and Treffinger (1977) in listing five steps such as those above acknowledged their indebtedness to Guilford's constructs of divergent thinking and to Torrance's expansion of this construct. Divergent thinking implies fluency (e.g., recall of many ideas, facts), flexibility (e.g., variety and switching from one train of thought to another), originality (e.g., unique, infrequent), and elaboration. This last refers to filling out an idea, adding interesting details, deriving conclusions, and stating relationships.

Problem solving by way of the five stages and the behaviors associated with divergent thinking do appear to be in harmony.

Student Outcomes

Here the spotlight is on what the individual gifted and talented pupil is expected to learn as a consequence of special instruction. Put another way, what new skill, concept, or ability will the exceptional pupils have because of what the teacher does? Performance objectives ought to enable educators to monitor student learning of prescribed content or functions. The Individual Education Program (IEP) is a fine source for process (e.g., problem-solving) objectives. Books and other print materials can be equally fine sources of content.

The interest in water towers triggered by the Flying Five remains a fruitful opportunity. Science content possibilities in terms of water treatment and relief of pressure abound; water is certainly a fundamental natural resource. A wealth of material about government suggests itself, for water towers are maintained by tax funds and each one is part of a larger system. Reference skills will be needed. Interviewing and allied communication skills can be employed. Decision-making skills can be applied to questions such as:

1. How can water towers be improved?
2. How could the environment be changed in order to eliminate water towers?
3. What would happen if there were no water towers?
4. How would one write a newspaper story to support taxes for a water tower?
5. What additional use could a water tower serve?
6. What other problems can be seen from the top of a water tower, in case you are tiring of water towers?

Tryouts

It appears that the students are ready. The principal has joined with the school librarian and raided the district instructional materials center. The sparkle of the Flying Five infects the other pupils. Philip, of the fine mind, generates information and sources. He seems to soak up information. Mike, the inventor, will constantly offer improvements, each from a unique perspective. Martha and John will stay with the project to the end. Their joy in knowing is akin to owning an ice cream factory. They are executive types, making maximum use of Phil's memory and Mike's inventiveness.

Elizabeth is the organizer. She likes to keep tabs. She also is capable of the positive comment and of the tactful reminder to remain on task. Philip also is helpful as "the judge." He relates diverse ideas and suggestions to practical outcomes. The meaning of critical mass, a cadre, or a core group becomes clear when one sees these gifted and talented pupils in action. While the Flying Five can be a trial, they are considerate of one another and of their other classmates. They will be the first to share, the first to include others, and they do their part of the work and more.

There already is demonstrated evidence that the class has group identity and can organize itself to work in independent groups. The pupils are committed. Consultative help is available. It would be nice to have a "trial run;" however, the opportunity seems too promising to defer.

Considering the Environment of Learning

This may well be the acid test. This dimension (Feldhusen & Treffinger, 1977) focuses on the environment as the physical material as well as on the teacher. An inventory can be helpful. For example, physical space for small groups can be helpful. Space for interest centers, if appropriate, can be helpful. Storage space may be helpful. Supplies for construction of charts and models may be required. Tolerance can be important. Tolerance for noise and physical movement is important. Helping pupils to be tolerant of the ideas of others will be considered. Tolerance for keeping track of activities and of logistics needs to be considered. Facilitation is another area.

The ability to defer judgment is to be fostered. This is a balance between the freedom to risk ideas without premature criticism and the need for feedback. Pupils will be responsive and appreciative of teacher intentions. Sometimes a comment by the teacher to another pupil is viewed as a squelch when intended only as a suggestion. If that appears to happen, an honest apology will produce an honest response.

Selecting and Using Tactics of Problem Solving

Both teachers and gifted and talented pupils are more effective if they know how to proceed in several different ways to solve problems. Feldhusen and Treffinger (1977) spelled out an inventory of problem-solving tactics particularly applicable to content areas. The user might be either the pupil or the teacher. It is especially important that students feel safe in venturing an idea, particularly one aimed at solving a complex, difficult problem. There should be minimum risk to anyone who volunteers ideas.

Psychological safety for pupils depends heavily on sensitive practices of the teacher. Examples of good practices include: (1) reinforcing and supporting unusual ideas of pupils, (2) viewing failure (of oneself or of students) as a learning experience to progress toward attainment, (3) allowing for choices, (4) listening to students, (5) allowing sufficient time for development of ideas, (6) supporting the involvement of all pupils in projects, (7) demonstrating respect for each student's participation, (8) showing awareness of the facets of problem solving beyond information, (9) recognizing that the use of information is significant, and (10) maintaining a sense of humor, not ridicule.

Some problem-solving activities are best used as "warm-up" or "readiness" for pupils who have neither experienced, nor possess, high trust in their own abilities. Others are more appropriate for pupils who are prepared to move directly to apply information to content.

Feldhusen and Treffinger propose four types of tactics: (1) brainstorming, (2) facilitation, (3) attribution, and (4) relationships.

Brainstorming was introduced in Chapter 9 as a means for curriculum adaptation and is mentioned earlier in this chapter. It is particularly suitable for creating a sense of trust between adult and learners for open-ended inquiry. It also can serve well as a warm-up and icebreaker.

Facilitation includes three interdependent tactics: (1) inquiry/discovery, (2) critical thinking, and (3) synthesis. These parallel problem awareness, adequacy of solutions, and implementation. Table 14-1 offers a concise overview under the headings: attributes (or description of behaviors), outcomes of benefit to the pupil, stages of development, teacher role, and evaluator criteria.

Attribution procedures are helpful when pupils tend to be passive. They familiarize pupils with two ways to carry out observation and inference. One is attribute listing and the other is morphological relationships. Table 14-2 outlines them.

Table 14-1 Tactics of Facilitation for Problem Solving

Inquiry/Discovery

Attributes: Recognition of obstacles, or inabilities to act. Requires identifying solutions. Also involves evaluating and acting out the solution to test out validity.

Outcomes: Most likely to sustain pupil interest and commitment. Also likely to be highly motivating and meaningful to students.

Stages/Sequence: First, pupils realize that a problem exists or are aware of an obstacle to some personal goal. Possible solutions, sources, and strategies are explored. Second, there is the testing out of strategies involved in the searching phase consistent with awareness.

Teacher's Role:

- Use of student interests to generate problems for solving, or use of media or learning centers to generate interests.
- Provision of guidance, reassurance, and encouragement to students.
- Assistance in locating resources and sources.
- Use of open-ended question; use of questions to check out solutions and to clarify focus.
- Issuance of rewards for efforts and accomplishments.

Evaluative: Observation of pupil ability to link behavior to consequences and to derive solutions to obstacles.

Questioning

Attributes: Use of divergent, open-ended tactics to supplement traditional convergent questions.

Outcomes: Questions provide pupils with opportunities to think and reflect. Questions also provide opportunities for teachers to: assess pupil preparation, review previous experiences, summarize, provoke further questions, and evaluate goals and objectives.

Stages: Questions can be appraised as to their higher order of difficulty by reference to sources such as Bloom, et al. (1971).

Teacher's Role:

- Preparation of questions in advance to provide some structure; they may be discarded when appropriate.
- Rewards for all the efforts of all the pupils.
- Movement from simple to complex.
- Inclusion of varied types of questions, especially: how, just suppose, comparison, and improvement formats.
- Allowance of sufficient time for responding.

Evaluative: Observation of pupil fluency, flexibility, originality, and elaboration. Observation of one's own performance as to use of divergent techniques.

(continues)

Table 14-1 continued

Critical Thinking

Attributes: Elaboration of problem-solving that describes the ability to assimilate and accommodate to information. Its product is the formation of hypotheses. It can be thought of as the implementation of the discovery method.

Outcomes: Similar to discovery/inquiry tactics but has the additional advantage of moving beyond location of obstacles. Critical thinking is the comprehensive consideration of what will work and under what circumstances.

Stages: Similar to discovery/inquiry with components of: recognition of a problem, forming hypotheses, gathering pertinent data, testing and evaluating, and drawing conclusions.

Teacher's Role:
  Partnership with students to be critical (e.g., evaluate sources) about solutions as to:
  • Authority and credentials of sources; distinguishing between assumption vs. fact, the reliability of observations; distinguishing among fact, generalization, and theory.
  • Specificity of definition of a problem, appropriateness of solution to fit problem.
  • Encouragement of pupil to pursue the quest.

Evaluative: Similar to inquiry/discovery plus the evidence that the pupil will persist.

Synthesis

Attributes: Parallel to Bloom et al. (1971) synthesis trait. It is beyond speculation. It has the somewhat formal nature of a plan. Its testing out has the somewhat formal nature of scientific verification, or verification appropriate to a particular field and performance.

Outcomes: Pupil can apply tactics of synthesis to performance, to problems of social worth, and to personal problems.

Stages: Pupil performance involves, in part, the ability to respond to analogies of three types such as fantasy, direct, and personal.

Teacher's Role:
  • Fantasy analogies—posing of solutions to a fantasized problem (i.e., a 16-ton block of foam rubber on the playground). The problem might be either to improve it or remove it. Any solution is tolerated, with the option of moving toward practical solutions.
  • Direct analogies—posing of real-life problems that parallel pupil experience or directly affect them. For example, moving school furniture would apply.
  • Personal analogies—posing a person in the context of a problem. For example, if I were a bookcase, how would I want to be moved?

Evaluative: Evidence of responding to analogies; evidence of generating plans.

Adapted from "The Role of Instructional Materials in Teaching Creative Thinking" by J.F. Feldhusen and D.J. Treffinger in *Gifted Child Quarterly*, 1977.

Table 14-2 Tactics of Teaching for Attribution*

Attribute Listing

Attributes: Examination of qualities, attributes, characteristics, traits of a problem or object. Emphasis is on modification.
Outcomes: Clear definition of a problem as to its components and exploration of possibilities for change modification.
Stages: No particular stages except move from simple comparisons to more complex comparisons.
Teacher's Role:
   • Use restricted to three components such as: problem component, characteristic/attribute of the problem, and ideas.
   • Teacher will conduct discussions with attention that all contributions are recorded and that there is respect for participation.
Evaluative: Attention to increasing willingness of pupils to participate.

Morphological Analysis

Attributes: Similar to attribute listing except emphasis is on combination of attributes.
Outcomes: Gaining of practice in bringing ideas or attributes together. This tactic is a foundation for inquiry/discovery procedure.
Stages: Same as above except emphasis is on combination of components rather than on modification of individual components.
Teacher's Role:
   • Use of a matrix technique to array two diverse components. Similar tactics of encouragement apply.
Evaluative: Similar to above except emphasis is on combination of attributes.

Adapted from "The Role of Instructional Materials in Teaching Creative Thinking" by J.F. Feldhusen and D.J. Treffinger in *Gifted Child Quarterly*, 1977.
   * See discussion for examples of teacher role.

244 EDUCATING GIFTED AND TALENTED LEARNERS

Reflection on attribute listing will be helpful for the water tower project. For example, certain observable components of the water tower might be its location, its appearance, and its surroundings. They could make up one side of a grid. Across the top of the grid could be listed water tower characteristics and ways of improvement. Thus one would have six cells: (1) location x characteristics x improvement, (2) appearance x characteristics x improvement, and (3) surroundings x characteristics x improvement. Examples of outcomes might be: Location is highly appropriate for protection. Its appearance of slate gray metal could be improved by repainting it white with a smile face. The surroundings of bare ground could be improved by flowers.

Morphological analysis would use another type of grid. In this instance it might be best to change to a problem directed toward "Improving the School Gym by Using Common Materials and Available Equipment." A grid would be constructed of the common materials and equipment along one side and the components of the gym on the other. For example, components could include: (1) walls, (2) floors, (3) ceiling, (4) bleachers, (5) drinking fountains, and (6) doorways. Materials could include: (1) paper, (2) cardboard, (3) plastic, (4) paint, (5) cloth, and (6) glass. There would be no compulsion to complete each cell. It is the movement in vertical and horizontal rows and columns that creates the opportunity to combine and recreate ideas and to transform the old and familiar into novel ways so necessary for problem-solving.

Relationships enable pupils to move more directly into critical thinking and toward synthesis. This sphere of problem solving involves the combining of common elements, facts, qualities in generalizations, and speculations. Table 14-3 identifies suitable tactics.

Evaluation—A Continuing Process

The class is still glowing three weeks later about the water tower. The Flying Five will lead testimony before the Mainstream County Commissioners regarding policy for appropriate use of river resources. Other learners, too, have emerged as competent. Some want to become basic scholars. The project is a source of pride for the school board and for Yourtowne. It is a model for their continued support. It will make future innovation more welcome.

Table 14-3 Examples of Tactics of Relationships

Tactic	Materials	Outcomes
Listing	Common objects of varied types without logical relationships contained in box	Child pulls object from box and makes statements regarding its application to problem. Free association is the medium.
Catalogue	Available catalogues from supply houses.	Same procedure except that pages are opened at random. Items on page are to be related to the page.
Focused relationships	Ideas or items of a presumed relationship to problem. Can be written on slips of paper.	Ideas are drawn at random from a fish bowl. Free association of relationship is encouraged.
Arbitrary relationships	Similar to listing or catalogue technique	Either objects or items written on paper are drawn at random, two at a time. Pupil is to describe a common relationship, use, etc., that is free association. There is no application to a problem.

Adapted from "The Role of Instructional Materials in Teaching Creative Thinking" by J.F. Feldhusen and D.J. Treffinger in *Gifted Child Quarterly*, 1977.

VISITATIONS

Description and Outcomes

Field trips have long been used to give pupils first-hand acquaintance with waterfalls, factories, ships, mines, skeletons of prehistorical animals, art collections, legislatures, and a myriad of other natural and man-made phenomena that are difficult, if not impossible, to comprehend from within the walls of a school alone. The educational outcomes enable pupils to become aware of and to understand the facilities, occupations, and other components of their community. The outcomes could be considered affective if they help pupils to develop pride, ambition, and other feelings. If field trips emphasize observation, data gathering, and analysis of information gained, they have more cognitive intentions.

Cox (1979) recommended that visitations be viewed as the planned use of community resources. She believes that their use enriches the lives of gifted and talented pupils and serves to expand and extend school learnings rather than to replace the school program. She emphasizes the need for cooperation between schools and community facilities to maximize the potential benefits to pupils. With respect to outcomes, consider the reaction of Matthew preserved by Heaton (1979) and presented in Exhibit 14-1.

Exhibit 14-1 Thanks a Million

December 15, 1978

Dear Mrs. Frankel,

I think Carnegie museum is the best museum cause of you and other docents. It's the truth! Thanks a million for the tour. The best pictures I thoght was Venus, Life is a passing shadow, The reck, 1,001 nights, The rabbit hanging on the door, St. George, The flamingoes and Homer St. Gaudens. I think you can learn at the museum. I've been to the library too. Do you give tours there too? Well anyway I'm happy because there is such a thing as Carnegie museum. How do you get those membership cards? When we went to the tour it was December 13, 1978. I'm part of the third grade. The 2nd grade went with us. If I was rich I would spend all my money on going in the musuem and library one time after another. I think going to the museum and library is a lot of fun. You know it's so much fun I love going. I'll tell you one thing you're not wasting your money, now that's the truth!

By

Matthew

Reprinted from *Carnegie Magazine* by William B. Heaton by permission of Carnegie Institute, ©1979.

Cox (1979) is not opposed to visitations oriented toward cultural facilities such as museums, libraries, theaters, to historical points of interest, and the like. However, she presses, and we agree, for more visits to hospitals, business firms, industries, airports, and other workplaces to arouse and extend vocationally oriented learnings.

Organizational Aspects

B. B. Weiner (1979) analyzed organizational aspects of visitations to public facilities. She highlighted considerations for enabling both handicapped and nonhandicapped pupils to participate fully with one another. The organizational aspects itemized were: (1) orienting facility personnel as to objectives of the class, (2) arranging for dates and time required, (3) developing an itinerary, (4) orienting volunteers, (5) informing pupils of expectations, (6) obtaining parent permission, (7) arranging for transportation and lunches, (8) obtaining endorsements from other teachers if class time is missed, and (9) developing procedures for evaluation and follow-up.

B. B. Weiner also proposed activities that could be helpful in follow-up and evaluation of visitations. One was "Where Were We?" The intent is to help label the trip for pupils and to recall the sequence of events. Example questions could be: Were we in an airport? How do you know? Did you need a ticket? Do you have it now? Why? Did you see paintings? Why not? Did you walk a lot? Did you ride in anything? Did you come back to school in a truck? "Facing Feelings" can be used with cartoons or pictures of the common emotions. Pupils can select the one or ones that describe their reactions. "Ballot Box" allows students to vote on their favorite aspects of the trip. "Detective" has the teacher giving clues to interesting features about the trip. Students are encouraged to guess. Students also could make up their own clues to share. In "Now and Then" students decide if illustrations are from the present or past. "Visit Alphabet" requires a poster board containing each letter of the alphabet. Students recall items encountered that complete the alphabet. For example, a museum alphabet may include armor, bed, chariot, dragon, earrings, fur, gallery, and so on. The alphabet also could be transformed into a directory of the facility.

Teaching Values

Visits, according to Tanner (1977), can teach values. He recommends prepackaged case study materials along with visitations to give personal meanings to terms such as democracy, truth, and courage.

He chose the context of ecology as a vehicle to teach pupils to relate technical sources of information and media coverage (commercial and news) to the environment of their community. Democracy in one sense is seen operationally as the citizen involved in the processes of influencing policy beyond voting every two years. Truth is linked to the ability to recognize and resist propaganda that uses euphemisms to soften and thus distort realities. Courage becomes willingness to get at the truth. Pupils, too, need to understand that courage does not guarantee life's rewards. Persons who resist vested interests sometimes are fined, demoted, blackballed, and otherwise harassed. Not all persons experience the public acclaim of a Dixie Lee Ray (a scientist who chaired the Atomic Energy Commission and later became Governor of the State of Washington). Students can be encouraged, in the ways illustrated, to visit, interview, and otherwise engage in real world problems.

Source of Help

Visitations have their challenges both in funding and in technical aspects. Cox (1979) thinks of the university or college as a community resource. She specified how private foundations also help. Kimche (1979) delineated the role of the U.S. Department of Health, Education, and Welfare (now the Department of Education) in funding and stimulating financing for facilities that wish to engage in educational activities. The Institute for Museum Services assists community resources. The discussion of simulations identified the U.S. Park Services, also, as a helpful resource. Cox insists that schools reach out to each other. Pooling scarce resources can maximize and enrich opportunities for pupils.

DEVELOPING MULTIPLE TALENTS

Using Pupil Strengths

Excellent teachers try to develop the learner's strengths as well as concentrate on areas of weakness. Maker (1979) notes that weakness sometimes looms so large that strengths are ignored.

Maker cites the example of a youngster who began producing three-dimensional drawings with perspective at age 4. In his early school years, he produced reams of pictures of trains, telephones running into the distance, and realistic representations of airplanes in various positions. Another youngster, of junior high level, was absorbed by living things, reflected in collecting, classifying, and learning about the life cycles of butterflies. He also became interested in plants and learned to identify the plants of his neighborhood by their scientific names. Both boys, according to Maker, met common educational fates: (1) their abilities were dismissed as educationally irrelevant by parents and teachers, (2) both were considered disabled readers, (3) both were in a phonic remedial reading program, and (4) their products and interests were consigned to "free time."

What might have happened with these pupils in Yourtowne? What interventions did they really need? What should their IEPs include?

Helpful Outcomes

An avenue for adopting a talent-oriented approach begins with the teacher's commitment to using the learner's talents. Maker pays tribute to Taylor's (1963, 1964) work on talent development. His ideas, in turn, pushed for using strengths and interests to compensate for and to help remediate spots that needed improvement. In general education, this approach is fostered by the correlated curriculum, or Core Curriculum. Skill and content learning is important in itself and also as a means to develop and refine career interests, develop satisfying hobbies, and promote self-esteem.

An Example: Using Book Reports

Maker's (1979) imagination lifts ordinary activities into creative methods for the multiple talent approach. Her own application of divergent thinking transforms ordinary activities.

Consider the typical and useful book report. Usually, the student is directed to prepare an oral or written report that identifies bibliographic references, author's purpose, resume of content, estimate of author's ability to fulfill purpose, personal reaction to the book's strengths and weaknesses, and recommendations to appropriate audiences. This format usually is followed for both fiction and nonfiction works. The divergent question might be: How many ways can a book report be related to multiple talent development? Table 14-4 presents some of Maker's ideas. She divided them into related activities that can be classified as curriculum related and those of process that cross over curriculum content.

SUMMARY

"How do I teach basic scholars at the middle school level? Well," said a Yourtowne teacher of several years' experience, "I start things going and then I just stand back!"

While everyone knows that is an oversimplification, there is an important truth in it, too. Getting instruction off to a good start stands high on any priority list of characteristics of effective teaching. This chapter put emphasis on a problem-centered approach. Ways to lead discussion and to stimulate participation were presented. Culminating activities of merit were described.

Table 14-4 Book Reports and Multiple Talent Development

Curriculum Dimensions and Related Activities

Dramatics: present a play based on your book ● dramatize an episode from your book ● share your book with the class as one of the characters might tell it ● read your book to younger children ● devise a puppet show about your book.

Arts: draw pictures to present the sequence of events ● design a dust jacket for the book ● make your book into a comic strip ● make a poster to advertise your book.

Music: develop or adapt a song about your book ● if the book's characters could sing to one another, what current songs would they sing ● compose a musical theme for your book ● find a song or tune that expresses how you feel about the book.

Communication: make up a new ending for the book ● write a different character into the book ● describe your feelings about your favorite character ● write a report on any of the following topics: the life of the author, the geography of the book, the time period of the book ● write a thank you-letter to the author.

Process Dimensions and Related Activities

Planning: (e.g., describing the strategies without having to execute) ● plan a play, a bulletin board ● plan a party to introduce the book to your friends ● plan an advertising campaign to promote your book ● describe how the characters in your book solved problems.

Forecasting: find cause and effect relationships in the book ● predict what might happen in the next chapter ● predict what a chapter in your book might say about the book ● predict what some historical character might say about this book ● predict what you might say about this book ten years from now when you read it.

Decision Making: list things that would make your book better ● list ten words that describe your book and select the one that most describes your book ● describe the attributes of your favorite character using five adjectives.

Adapted from "Developing Multiple Talents in Exceptional Children" in *Teaching Exceptional Children* by C. J. Maker, 1979.

Chapter 15

Using Tactics of Pupil Participation

This chapter reviews four categories of instruction: simulations, learning centers, guided independent study, and internships. These tactics allow gifted and talented pupils to experience active participation within the mainstream of education.

SIMULATIONS

Definition and Structure

Simulations are activities contrived to model real life. Used in teaching, they stimulate the active participation of students. The simulation planner specifies objectives for the miniplay and builds in activities to feature and highlight these objectives.

The structure of planning for a simulation (McKeachie, 1978) resembles that of a lesson plan. The elements include: (1) title, (2) curriculum goal addressed and course in which to be used, (3) enrollment, (4) time required, (5) preparation required, (6) educational objectives, (7) structure and directions for use, and (8) evaluation techniques.

Types

Case studies and histories are good raw material for simulations. A purpose or goal is essential, of course. Then the true-life situation or the imaginary plot and characters can be developed to stimulate students to attain the desired end.

The major use of simulation is to furnish practice in problem solving. In the process, pupils would be expected to use knowledge, concepts, and skills encountered in instruction. The process encourages students to integrate lectures, readings, discussions, and other resources. At more advanced levels, material can be purposely overloaded with details. This requires students to display their skills in selecting essential points.

Simulations add reality, personalization, and zip to topic initiation and to topic culmination. With guidance, there is every reason to believe that a teacher and even primary age gifted and talented pupils can devise simulations from their own local case materials. Naturally, with more mature gifted pupils the plots and actions can be more complex and can deal with more advanced themes.

Expanding Class Learnings

Suppose a teacher wanted to enliven a phase of history. Pupils can simulate what it was like to live in a different day and age. Thompson (1979), for instance, told about a cooperative program between a school district and the U.S. Park Service. Fourth through sixth graders, as a result, learned what it was like to pull guard duty in the Civil War, or swab the deck of a three-masted ship. The program took planning and participation by teachers, Park Service, pupils, and parents. Together they combined the essentials of simulation, field trip, even mentoring, in that nonschool persons and teachers shared their interests with pupils. Consider Exhibit 15-1 for an example of an overnight experience. This kind of program is not restricted to exceptional pupils; it is applicable for all learners, including the gifted and talented.

Exhibit 15-1 With the Fort Park Regulars

Fort Point: December 5 and 6 with Cindy Silva's fifth grade from the Forestville Union School

Weather, even when it's balmy for the rest of San Francisco, is chilly at Fort Point where a bone-penetrating wind sweeps down the channel from the outer bay. "You recognize us," says a member of the Park Service staff at this National Historic Site, "by the perpetual wetness at the end of the nose, known as the Fort Point drip." At 4 p.m., when the bus had deposited Cindy Silva's fifth grade from Forestville, which lies in the apple country north of the city, the wind was fierce and piercing. It howled through the fort's open parade ground as the youngsters drilled. It whisked artillery hats off heads and whipped the flag into a loudly snapping frenzy. What with the racket of Old Glory, the rumble of Golden Gate Bridge traffic almost directly overhead, the crashing of waves against the sea wall, and the clatter of booted feet against stone paving, it took close attention to hear the commands of Mike Bell, the slender fifth-grader who, as first sergeant, was leading the troops. Drill as a result was ragged. And the 30 youngsters and seven adults looked a scraggly company indeed, all but lost in the gathering darkness of so vast a brick and stone fortress designed to house 600 men and to mount 126 cannon in its open, arched casemates.

Events moved briskly, though, on a known schedule. Bedsacks were unrolled in the dark of the second-tier sleeping quarters, illuminated only by the children's homemade tin candlelanterns. And the mess squad soon fanned hot coals into a blaze and considerable smoke in the east bastion where, stamping their feet against the cold, they toiled over oil-drum stoves to provide johnnycakes and stew.

Other squads, meanwhile, moved through a series of 20-minute chores. One was the polishing of a pile of boots, arduous work and boring, but rewarding for its good leather and polish smells. Then there was sentry duty—on the roof, or barbette tier, and at the sally port (entrance hall). A tour of duty at the port post was enlivened by challenges ("Who goes there?" "Friend!" "Advance, friend, and be recognized") and by passwords ("Petrified") and counterwords ("Powder"), and by the appearance from time to time of a spy who had to be captured and tossed into jail.

Still another activity, requiring fancy footwork, was the mock firing of a muzzleloading 12-pounder cannon—a drill practiced earlier in school using chairs and brooms for props and much practice here, too, to achieve the historically correct every-30-seconds explosions. On commands Load! Ready! Fire! Number one of the gun crew sponged, Two took the round from Five (who had run it from Four at the ammunition wagon) and put it in the gun, One rammed it home, Three placed a left thumb over the vent and Six in the end pulled the lanyard. The POW! itself was provided vocally, in chorus.

Only one activity took place indoors and that was in the medic's office, a drafty ground-level room almost as cold as the courtyard. There First Lieutenant Elisha Weirich, surgeon, a pert young girl, demonstrated period medical practice—splinting shins, knotting up slings, "cupping" to raise blisters on the chest of a "pneumonia" victim, discussing shock, burns, the uses of chloroform, opium, liquor, showing off the saws and syringes of her trade in the fort's museum cases. From time to time this medic treated patients who came to her on receipt of activity cards that described their misadventure. "You have fallen down the spiral stairs," or "You have dropped a cannonball on your foot." For victim one: splints, securely bandaged ("Here, corporal, tear this bandage for me with your teeth. Now, out you go on these crutches"—made to specification in the classroom). To victim two: "Aha, you're lucky! Just a bruise." As it turned out, though, power went somewhat to this medic's head. She began whacking patients with splints, snapping bandages at inattentive listeners. Her squad appeared ready to tiptoe beyond her range when mess call mercifully sounded. Welcome hot food and coffee (decaffeinated) were doled out for the troops into tin plates and cups (no plastic)—followed by a circulation-enhancing night march.

The march was led by the Park Service's Richard Drezner, impeccably outfitted for the Union Army: skyblue pants, frock coat, square-toe bootees, collar button made of bone. He was a lowly private, he explained, though his uniform sported considerable brass—on buttons, on eagle plate, on shoulder scales. His black felt hat, turned up on the left side to indicate artillery, was trimmed with crossed cannons and one ostrich feather (an officer, he pointed out, would have had three).

Drezner's march took the company out through the small door in the sally port to an exploration of the fort's immediate environment—to the high knoll level with the roof, a prime viewing spot across the bay toward the Marin headlands, Angel Island, Alcatraz, and the concentrated twinkles of San Francisco. A Spanish fort first stood at this elevation. It was the Americans who later cut away the 90-foot cliff to bring their cannon to sea level as a protection against any hostile ships in the Golden Gate.

The youngsters count the beams of four lighthouses. Tide is out, the wind still strong, and the moon is but a thin crescent. With each viewing of the fort from a new angle, the night casts a spell. The marchers, eschewing flashlights, feel their way over tree roots, down steep gullies, up steps. They note the whiff of roses from General De Russey's long-ago gardens, the spicy smell of eucalyptus along with pods and strips of bark underfoot, characteristic of the Australian trees planted by the army as a windbreak. There's a strange, disoriented sensation from standing together silently in the total darkness of a powder magazine tunneled into the hill.

Later in the mess hall, clusters of soldiers play cards and checkers (games they made at school) and they write in their journals— first impressions, notes, to be refined in the classroom. Lefthanded Corporal Kitsy Jordan, a slight figure, well muffled, her artillery hat riding atop a knit cap, moves the pencil without pause across the page. "I long to go home, but I have to stay in the army. This army life is long and hard but I serve the Union. In mess I have to churn the butter. That is the funniest thing I do. I have to peel the potatoes, too." At dismissal to quarters the guard is set. One squad after another patrols the windswept barbette tier, walking the four sides of the roof till morning. Its members, climbing onto cannon blocks to peer over the parapet, scrutinize movements by land and by water.

General Silva pulls 12:40 to 1:30 guard duty. Waked by Private Cindy Sawyer, Silva pulls on boots and great coat (bought at surplus), buckles on her black belt ("I can use it again with my Santa suit"), shoulders her musket. This general keeps a steady pace—around the four sides enclosing the courtyard. Half the way she walks in deep shadow, half in a bath of yellow light from the bridge. On the night march she had been greeted with warming hugs. Here she is addressed formally. "Cargo ship passing safely, sir. I'll enter it in the log." "Permission to use latrine, sir." "Suspicious lights, sir, possibly a submarine." The general's advice is to get a good look at the lights from a different angle to see if they might be attached to the bridge pier.

As the teacher-general walks, she talks with a visitor in a hushed voice about using a part of the past for learning history. The daughter of teachers, married to a teacher, six years a teacher herself (her major interest, history), Silva considers the Environmental Living Program [ELP] a lot of work—"the kind of work that makes it exciting to come to school mornings. We began in September," she says, "reading up on Clara Barton, Mathew Brady, Harriet Tubman, Lincoln, researching the roots of the war, military terms, weaponry, uniforms, provisions, interviewing local resource persons on Civil War songs, medical care, bugle calls, drilling and marching.

"In class we roll bandages, design playing cards, sew on chevrons and stripes. We ask ourselves: How could we prepare for the cold and, beyond that, for the bleakness, the loneliness and boredom? How was it on soldiers to take orders from their peers and how would we like it? What could it have been like as Union soldiers to guard this fort where no shot was ever fired at an enemy, where no enemy ship ever appeared, where so many people sickened with respiratory diseases? Our California children are so remote from the Civil War." Silva goes on to say, "On our return from the fort we will write a newspaper reporting the events which occurred while we were here. Then we'll look at the war from the viewpoint of the South. How did the South justify slavery? I dress up as U. S. Grant and visit the other fifth grades. Another teacher comes to ours as General Lee."

Silva finds that the ELP experience varies in its effect on classes. This year's class—her second to come to the fort—is cooperative, enthusiastic but somewhat insecure. Most of its leaders were moved last fall into another section. She is counting on the fort experience to bolster confidence and spirit. The high winds, she says, have helped build a sense of drama. "I don't think rain would have done the job," she adds.

Parents are eager to join in the program. A father who gave up two days' work said it did him good to see the lively interest on the part of children whom he knew to be reluctant participants in class. Another father, a Civil War buff, authentically garbed even to period whiskers, was clearly pleased to play at his hobby and share it.

By 0530 the mess crew was lighting fires, then serving hash. A mother and daughter came down together from the last tour of guard duty on the barbette. Spirits were high and remained that way through fatigue duty, a euphemism for "Let's clean up the place." Sergeant Bell had abandoned his mother's black boots for better-fitting sneakers. There were no fine points of military procedure here. But laughs, horseplay, snatches of "Glory, Glory, Hallelujah" as brooms sent the dust down spiral stairs and as dishwater was dumped through a screen into the drain. A nature walk, which began with an introduction to topographic maps, repeated by daylight the ground covered on the night march. It included looks at moss and seaweed by the granite sea wall, identification of the cliff rock as serpentine, scrutiny of the red toyon berries from which the Indians made cider, and coastal scrub that once covered the land on which San Francisco now sits. By 0830, Sergeant Bell has assembled his company in a final formation, and Drezner was handing out cannoneer certificates in recognition of service well performed, exchanging salutes with each participant, and—General Silva smiling on with pride—releasing the boys and girls back to civilian life and the 20th century.

Source: Reprinted from "A Step or Two Back in Time" by P. Thompson in *American Education,* 1979.

LEARNING CENTERS

A Proven Tactic

Learning centers prove especially helpful for gifted and talented pupils, though they work well for all pupils, too. A center supplies one means of sharing appropriate education for highly able pupils with all pupils. It also is a means to fulfill Type I enrichment described earlier in Chapter 13.

Understanding a Rationale for Learning Centers

There are many initial questions teachers might raise about the use of learning centers. One obvious question might be: Why use this procedure? Others might be: How are learning centers used? What kinds of learning centers are there? Moreover, there are important questions about the who, when, and where of learning centers. Answers should equip teachers with a sound professional rationale for centers and with the confidence to plan, implement, and evaluate the procedure.

Learning centers serve pupils in a variety of ways. Joyce (1975) as cited by Turnbull and Schultz (1979), listed potential outcomes as: (1) achieving a wide range of educational objectives, (2) acquiring an expanded range of learning strategies, (3) encountering materials appropriate to one's learning style, and (4) encouraging and motivating for learning. Teachers report that the use of centers fulfills their needs to: (1) provide variety and novelty in teaching, (2) exercise their own creativity and originality in materials development, (3) help pupils of widely different learning styles, (4) master new instructional strategies, (5) implement Aptitude Treatment Interactions, and (6) further individualization of assessment and pupil evaluation.

The Variance of Learning Centers

The learning center concept can be put into action in so many different ways and under such a variety of physical plant conditions that the answer to: What is a learning center? results in a bewildering array of illustrations. According to Thomas (1975),

> learning centers may range from a center as simple as, Make a Muscle Center where pupils observe contraction of muscles by crushing newspapers, to a center as sophisticated as a Space Center in which pupils build rockets. The possibilities are restricted only to the input of you and pupils. (p. 56).

Commenting on the variety of uses and purposes of learning centers, Turnbull and Schultz (1979) observed that they

> may be added to emphasize materials that support basic skills programs or relate to a unit of study or as an enriching element in the classroom. ... Learning centers may be used to provide activities

for independent study, follow-up for teacher taught concepts, activities in place of regular assignments. (p. 112).

Turnbull and Schultz suggest the use of learning center activities as rewards for completion of teacher-assigned tasks. They cite Piechowiak and Cook (1976) to the effect that this procedure fosters pupil confidence in self-selected and self-paced activities.

One common attribute of the learning center is that students and teachers can participate in their design and construction. A second attribute is that a single center may serve multiple purposes such as skill development, motivation, enrichment, and accelerating the pace of content. Learning centers can be used by a single pupil, too, without mediation, by a student proctor to tutor other pupils, or by a group of five or six pupils. Gifted and talented pupils can tutor, peer model, and share their products and projects at interest centers.

Skill building in arithmetic and language arts as well as content studies in science, literature, and social studies can be based on commercially available "packages" for diagnostics, prescriptions, and instruction. Teacher-prepared learning centers complement the curriculum, appeal to the interests of pupils, and foster generic capabilities such as problem solving and inquiry.

Steps in Development

How does a corner of a room or a section of a library or hall become a learning center? Kaplan, Kaplan, Madson, and Taylor (1973) outline the evolution. Thomas's (1975) recommendations are in essential agreement with their recommendations.

Any learning center ought to grow out of teacher assessment of pupils. (Thomas provided examples of interest and learning style inventories.) Accordingly, the learning center is an ingredient in the prescription to fulfill pupil goals.

The first step, consequently, is to decide upon goals, content, and skills to be emphasized or acquired. The second step moves to the preparation of manipulation activities and activities of observation and experimentation. Examples of the former would include cutting or matching, and the latter would include charting or keeping a log.

The third step takes in activities of application. These might be: (1) filling in, (2) arranging an order, (3) taking apart, (4) matching, (5) labeling, (6) locating, (7) listing, and (8) classifying.

The fourth step goes to activities of extending. One example is divergent thinking such as unusual uses or product improvement. Other extending procedures might call for problem solving and inquiry, for instance.

The teacher may build steps two through four, or may set up only one or two, depending on the purposes to be fulfilled. The final operational step would be as critical as the first—that is, placing all the games, worksheets, charts, or other essential material together in one area for use by the learners. It would be assumed that pupil ideas and products would be included. Parents, school volunteers, and student teachers can be additional, helpful sources for ideas and materials.

A learning center is enhanced by the inclusion of pupil-developed ideas and exercises. A competently designed and maintained learning center can be used to improve education for all pupils and, as the next example shows, it can be especially stimulating for advanced pupils.

An Example

Seven basic scholars at the middle school level congregated at the center: Dee, Martha Jane, Elizabeth, Philip, Mike, John, and Andrew. Their teacher has given each a Learning Passport allowing them to gather in an area sectioned off by low bookcases. A rug on the floor gives warmth and the windows admit winter sunlight.

When the group gathers, Elizabeth reviews the directions accompanying the passport, which state the expectations of "on task" performance and an agreement to complete at least two activities and to report to the class on findings. The directions further instruct the group to select the Map Suitcase (actually a carton appropriately decorated). The carton contains activity packets, worksheets, appropriate materials, and contract forms. Dee logs in the other members on the time sheet. Mike reads the descriptor cards on each of the packets and the group self-selects to organize itself for purposeful activity. The common denominator in each packet is a map of Michigan prepared and widely distributed by the secretary of state's office.

The eight packets are labeled: Dramatics, Art, Music, Measurement, Communicating, Predicting, Decisions, and Planning. Each has its own materials, directions, and worksheets.

Martha Jane unfolds the Dramatics packet. She finds four activity cards. She soon becomes absorbed in outlining her plans. She elects to pretend that she is a map of Michigan and she outlines what she will tell the class about the state if she were a talking map. John and Philip have consulted the Music packet. They are fascinated by the map symbols. They select the activity card that directs them to make up sounds for symbols. They decide to embellish the idea by presenting a "Guess What I Am" to the class. They decide upon sounds for: a state park, an airport, a town, a city, an interstate highway, a river, and a county line. Mike is so pleased to discover his ideas have been used in the Art packet that he convinces Andrew to cooperate. They decide to combine two activities into one project and begin to redesign the state map to create one that will be both more beautiful and more useful. They decide to invent symbols for road construction, toy stores, movies, all-night gasoline stations, and their favorite hamburger haven. They progress so well that they have time to pursue other packets in the time remaining.

Elizabeth and Philip are drawn to the Communicating packet. They hit upon a way to combine several activities into one. The first requires that they tell a blind person how to get from Kalamazoo to Lansing and a deaf person from Flint to Lansing. They temporarily interrupt John and Andrew to field test their directions. Meanwhile Mike, joined by Dee and Martha Jane, has solved more than the required number of Measurement activities. He has found his home town, another town 20 miles to the north and one 20 miles south. He has computed the number of gallons of gasoline it would take from Iron Mountain to Detroit if his car averaged (a) 15 miles or (b) 35 miles per gallon. John and Andrew are completing their Predicting packet by making a list of all the things a mapmaker would have to know in order to make a map.

John encourages his friends to come together to do one more thing. All by now have done more than required and the rules entitle them to free time. John is persistent and speaks glowingly of the merits of both the Decision and Planning packets, both of which he helped develop with his teacher. The Decisions activity was narrowed down to this problem: Suppose your family were to move from Kalamazoo to South Haven. List all the reasons for and against the move. The Planning activities were narrowed down to this: Suppose you have an aunt and uncle in Milford, a grandparent in Alpena, and friends in Traverse City, and you live in Freeport. Plan a two-week vacation. Trace your route to show how you would spend equal time at each place, identify points of interest, and what kinds of things should be brought along. The group settled on the first of the two choices—Decisions. However, it was decided to terminate for the day and to begin the next time they were together. Andrew logged the group out. Mike was delegated to report to the teacher on completed assignments. He and the teacher agreed on a schedule to share the completed projects during the next Friday afternoon Funshine Period.

The amount of work that can be completed varies in proportion to the time available. The range and diversity of activities, however, is typical. The level of self-direction and cooperative behavior also is typical of gifted and talented learners oriented to the process. The ability of the teacher to keep track of assignments is especially important. Pupils can help with that, too.

In some schools, the physical space of the ordinary room may not be sufficient or appropriate. Sometimes parts of the library can be divided into designated learning centers available and scheduled for students. In some schools, a vacant room can be transformed into a learning center. This allows for expanded use of audiovisual aids, slide-tape exhibits, models, and a wider range of materials. Community volunteers, parents, higher education personnel, and mature student assistants can staff these centers. The building principal and librarian can be helpful resources in organization of these centers. The goals and objectives of the IEP can generate ideas for the focal content and skills of learning centers.

Evaluation

Thomas's (1975) rating scales give criteria with which to evaluate learning centers. His forms allow for pupil feedback about activities and for pupil progress. He also provides forms for teachers to use to assess their own mastery of the procedure.

Musgrove and Estroff (1977) provide a scale to measure the reactions of gifted pupils toward educational activities. It has 20 times clustered around these themes: (1) thinking about a career, (2) using one's abilities, (3) considering the value of further education, (4) considering the worth of time and effort, and (5) considering duplication of learnings.

Magnetizing Learning Centers

Learning centers need not be confined to a class or to a portion of a school. The magnet school demonstrates an enlargement of the learning center concept designed to fulfill a number of valid educational objectives. Strictly speaking, magnet schools are not undertaken for gifted and talented pupils per se.

A magnet school serves pupils from all parts of the school district. The curriculum approximates the district's standard curriculum. However, the magnet school also sponsors programs not available in every school in the district.

According to Brandstetter and Foster (1976), magnet schools may be of four types. The *Add On* option means a special program is added to each school in the district. This means that every school has some unique feature besides its regular program. The *School Within a School* describes a pullout option in which selected pupils meet for individualized projects and courses of study. *Separate and Unique Schools* describes separate facilities that cater to particular student needs. These needs can be for a Fundamental Skills School that emphasizes literacy skills, or the emphasis can be upon Talents Unlimited to nurture the performing arts. The *Career Cluster* concentrates on attractive options for vocational preparation. Magnet schools are further characterized by reduced pupil-teacher ratios, flexibility in scheduling, specially prepared staff, motivated students, and ample supplies, materials, and equipment, as well as individualized educational planning.

Brandstetter and Foster cite these examples of elementary magnets: bilingual, music academy, literary academy, fine arts academy, physical academy, physical development academy, science and math centers, and fundamental skills. Elementary clusters also have included international trade, children's literature, career orientation, and outdoor education. Secondary levels have highlighted aerodynamics, engineering, foreign language, business administration, petrochemicals, contemporary learnings, and fundamental skills.

An account by Pfiel (1978) is typical. It starts with a 111-year-old elementary school located in the central city. The school attracts pupils from all district attendance areas plus three suburban school districts. Its identification guidelines for gifted and talented learners employ multiple criteria and follow recommended patterns, though teacher nomination and parent referral are given somewhat more weight than test measurement criteria. Pupils already enrolled in the school also serve on the selection committee. As is typical of magnets, parents and pupils volunteer to attend and transportation is provided. The school was remodeled and teachers were oriented to the education of the gifted and talented. This school also maximizes its city location by using its proximity to such community resources as gourmet restaurants, the performing arts center, the central library, the museum, city hall, and the art center. These facilities provide a ready and willing pool of resource persons.

The school follows the general guidelines of the school district but the faculty has the freedom to expand and extend clusters within the curriculum such as the Lunch Bunch (clustered around expanded learnings), the Mac's Pack (math, arts, crafts, science), the Round Table (interviews and dialogue), For Pete's Sake (an infant care class), the Classic Club (literature), and the Student Senate. This is only a minimum listing. The intent of the clusters is to ensure a well-rounded education for responsible and responsive persons.

Yourtowne's magnet scheme, started six years ago in a small way, now finds expression in every school in the system. It complements the basic scholars and related programs, especially in high schools. The public announcement in all the local media for a recent year featured three points:

1. Types of Offerings:
    —Elementary Options: Full-Day Kindergarten, Traditional Academy, Open Space School, Bilingual Instruction
    —Middle School Options: Creative and Performing Arts, Traditional Academy, Classical Academy

—High School Options: Army Junior ROTC, Computer Science, Health Careers, Traditional Academy, Math-Science, Law and Public Service, Journalism and Publishing, Engineering-Architecture, Business and Management, Creative and Performing Arts
2. Attention to Basics:
—Strong, basic courses plus exciting new options
3. Willingness to Serve All Pupils:
—The Options in Education Programs are open to students in private, parochial, and suburban schools.

The specializations in particular high schools attract interested pupils to them. In addition, though, each high school in Yourtowne has access to the Advanced Placement Program of the College Entrance Examination Board. That allows every high school to increase the attraction of its own magnet by offering a selection of 13 subject areas created and monitored by school and college experts nationwide.

Like the rest of Yourtowne's attention to gifted and talented pupils, these opportunities stem from and extend or expand the regular education curriculum. They are open to all pupils willing and able to do the necessary work to meet the requirements.

Imagine you are the parent of a gifted or talented youngster aged: (a) 4, (b) 7, (c) 10, (d) 13, or (e) 16. What questions would you have about magnet schools for your child at each of these ages? Why would you have those questions?

Suppose Yourtowne employed you as a consultant to advise about how the magnet school concept might be improved over the next two years? What questions would you raise? What directions do you think might be best to consider first? Why?

As might be expected, magnet schools do not succeed automatically (Levine & Moore, 1976). Success can be attributed to attention to certain action steps.

The selection of principals and internal planning probably should come first. A community task force should endorse the concept and the central administration should establish the actual plan. Principals must be included for their knowledge about the district. Released time must be granted.

Another early step is to obtain the active, demonstrated support of middle management. Some administrators, at building levels, could subvert recruitment of pupils if they were unwilling to lose pupils. Support is required to reflect benefits to pupils and the system.

It is essential to offer incentives for participating schools in the form of enhancement of resources that can spill over freely into the regular program. Resources are necessary, too, for planning in the form of space, time, secretarial support, and consultation. This support also must include sponsorship of a competent and comprehensive needs assessment. It is equally important to take actions designed to orient teachers, advise parents, and eliminate red tape for purchasing and remodeling. Recruitment of pupils and arranging transportation is necessary in an orderly way and with the absolute minimum of difficulty.

Outcomes of magnet schools (Levine & Moore) benefit families, the community, and the district. In a technical sense, the benefit to the district really is a spinoff of the first two.

One outcome is upward mobility for pupils and families. Since the program is voluntary, it attracts middle income pupils and lower income families seeking the perceived advantages of the operation. Since actual performance, interest, and motivation serve as major criteria, families easily understand magnet schools and often are eager to escape the conventional and pursue a desired purpose. As talented pupils are drawn into magnet programs, a new wave of student responsibility emerges. The program also offers a form of upward mobility for teachers to develop courses, experiences, and activities that they previously had not had sufficient opportunity to do.

A second outcome is development. Faced with declining enrollments and neighborhoods, the magnet school is credited with providing stability for both the district and, to a degree, for the city also. This latter outcome results from cooperation and joint planning by the schools and governmental agencies.

GUIDED INDEPENDENT STUDY

Key Features

For sound application with gifted and talented students, guided independent study needs to be a rigorous form of monitored individualized work in which the pupil takes the lead. Teachers, as college students, may have experienced independent study as more of a casual procedure than as a genuine instructional mode. As the expression "guided independent study" is used in this chapter, it is a direct outgrowth of the Individualized Education Program. *Individualized* means the structure, content, and objective are tailored to a given pupil. *Guided* means a teacher or mentor provides activist, technical, and substantive consultation. Pupils are not allowed to grope or flounder to the point of becoming seriously discouraged. Moreover, there are standards and agreements so the product represents the student's best efforts within available time limits. *Independent* means that the student takes the initiative and the chief role in planning, implementation, and evaluation.

McKeachie (1978) grouped independent study and the project method together. Each assumes that the student has entered into a quasi-contract. The purpose of each is to afford a concrete experience for the student to engage in continuing learning. Motivation, work habits, and information background are important student aptitudes for both.

Either individual or group enterprises can operate as independent study. In the latter, there still are opportunities for individual leadership. The critical treatment variable is clarity of outcomes mutually negotiated by participants. Motivation and work habits are crucial pupil aptitudes.

Personal guidance in independent study can be especially helpful in extending knowledge. If grading is a problem, a "contract" or agreement can be negotiated in which teacher and participants identify criteria. A helpful approach is to agree to assign some arbitrary number of points to be ascribed to each element of the final outcome. The grade can be associated with a percentage of points earned.

A Continuum

Independent study need not be "all or none." McKeachie (1978) observed that this option can vary as to proportion of teacher and pupil independence. Initial projects may arise out of assigned topics very closely related to the standard curriculum. The teacher may provide quite close initial guidance, with the pupils having perhaps only 25 percent of the leadership. With increased mastery by the student, this proportion can reverse itself so the study is 75 percent or more independent.

The structure, substance, and complexity of the project, itself, will be a function of the goals of the experience, the nature of the subject matter, the curriculum area, the age and maturity of the pupil, the available resources, and the priorities of the participants. For example, not all independent learnings need to culminate in a formal, written document. Culmination can take the forms of an oral report or a demonstration to the class, a letter to the editor of a newspaper, testimony before policy makers, or organization of a campaign or of a series of activities. Other forms can be sharing reactions in an interview with the teacher, preparing lists for fellow students, background information for tutoring other pupils or leading discussions, or transforming information into alternate forms such as displays, exhibits, short stories, interpretive dance, or plays. Culmination can be the record of an experiment in the natural or behavioral sciences. This last option often is attractive because the criteria appear more explicit than those for transforming activities. Regardless of the tactic, however, evaluation would be referenced to the declared goals and to the product. Also regardless of tactic, evaluation should be participatory between teacher and pupil and plainly related to what was intended and what was the result.

Contracting and Pacing

Thomas (1975) details a process for reaching and completing a contract between teacher and pupils. He suggests a sequence that starts when the pupil initiates interest, moves to a teacher and pupil conference on what is needed to execute the interest, and culminates in the signing of a contract. The teacher then directs the pupil to appropriate sources from which the student may select. The pupil next searches out sources and organizes material, starts to carry out the plan, and comes back as necessary to seek help. The teacher or mentor then teaches the skills necessary. The pupil continues the project with teacher help as necessary. When the student completes the plan, an evaluation is conducted according to the terms of the contract.

Thomas offers a number of possible formats for a contract from primary grades to more complex levels. The salient contract features are: (1) the topic, (2) the time to be spent, (3) the activities to be completed, (4) the teacher's responsibilities, (5) the pupil's responsibilities, and (6) spaces for signatures of teacher, pupil(s), and parent(s). Contracts also can specify evaluation criteria as well as the circumstances for contract revisions.

To illustrate pacing, Pohl's (1976) levels of independent study suggest a range. These levels are summarized in Exhibit 15-2.

Exhibit 15-2 Example of Pacing in Independent Study

School District #145 in Freeport, Illinois, has been developing various models of independent study during the past 14 years. Our initial work in this area enabled us to establish a program we called "Special Projects." Students at the 5th and 6th grade levels were identified and released to a special teacher one full day per week, where independent projects were begun, completed, and evaluated by the individual student. These projects for the most part were extensions of regular classroom work. During these years of developmental work, we have established four maturational levels of independent study, which the center is now attempting to carry out.

Levels of Independent Study

I. Independent study projects: Teacher-supervised, groupwide, in the teaching areas for the most part. Projects are related to an academic area.

II. Independent study projects: Partially teacher-supervised, originating from academic work. Some research freedom permitted on an individual basis.

III. Independent interest projects: Originates from individual interests. Teacher guidance where needed. Does not have to be related to a specific academic area. Student given as much research time outside of class as possible.

IV. Independent study: Completely independent in all areas. Has an advisor for guidance, determines own needs and areas of the curriculum where they feel they need to work. These students submit a contract for each individual pursuit to the team for any suggestions or questions which the team might have. These students have complete freedom in the center at all times.

Independent studiers report to large groups or small groups of students when they feel the desire or need to share information they have gathered during their project.

The evaluation criteria (sic) is set up by the student. We give no letter grades, but report to parents via a three-way conference—student-parent-teacher.

The use of the independent study contract has led us to the following observations:

1. Student awareness of the ability to communicate through the medium of writing.
2. Fosters the organization of ideas in a realistic and meaningful fashion.
3. Causes the student to set a guideline; an educational road map.
4. Permits them to contruct their own evaluative criteria.
5. Brings them into close working relationships with many adults. Through the use of a contract they are individualizing their own learning situations.

Independent studiers meet weekly or bi-weekly to discuss common problems, share their findings, and seek advice from their peers about projects which they are pursuing.

Some of our students have reached the IVth level of independent study. These students have complete freedom to set up their own learning schedules. They report to their large group when their own schedule calls (sic) for the mastery of certain skills.

Adapted from "Independent Study" by R. Pohl in *Gifted and Talented Education,* 1976.

If one preferred a more structural format, consider Table 15-1. It is modeled after investigative reporting.

This approach, it will be noted, has two dimensions. One is the structure for guiding the content of the project. It follows the model of the investigative journalist. The second describes phases of independent study: (1) assignments (negotiations and refining purpose), (2) investigation (implementing assignments), and (3) presentation (culminating and sharing). This format allows participants to complete each cell and maintain an informative record.

INTERNSHIPS

Orientation

Educators are familiar with the use of practicum to enable the future teacher to observe practice and to take preliminary steps toward engaging in teaching under highly supervised conditions. This experience enables teachers to appraise their own interests and competencies against the realities of a vocation. The intern (sometimes labeled student teacher) usually is a full-time, unpaid apprentice to a master teacher. During the course of the experience, the apprentice more and more assumes the role of the practitioner.

Table 15-1 A Model for Investigative Reporting

Structural Elements	Assignment A	Phases Investigating B	Presentation C
Why (1) rationale and goals/objectives.............			
What (2) format and form product			
Who (3) responsible persons as sources			
How (4) process and procedure			
When (5) estimated time and due dates, criteria for completion...........................			
Where (6) settings and locations			

A. Describes location of project, negotiation, and refinement of goals. Culminates with plan for completion.
B. Describes activities to complete the elements of Phase A and culminates in project product completion.
C. Describes project sharing and project recognition.

The practicum and the internship concepts are quite applicable in educating gifted and talented pupils. In this case, though, it is really the exploration, testing, and familiarization phases that have highest priority. Though referred to as an internship, the arrangement for a gifted student to work with and be supervised by an adult is chiefly to make available a role model in real life. Of importance, too, is the chance for the exceptional student to gain realistic, first-hand experience in the work environment of whoever serves as the role model.

A Sense of Urgency

Certain children placed in states of high risk have been able to resist environmental shocks. A report by H. Wexler (1979) provides additional insight into sources of resistance. She reported on the education careers of 135 persons over a 14-year period. As pupils, all were characterized by failure on reading readiness tests upon entering school. Her report summarized their accomplishments and compared the achievers and nonachievers. Wexler found that 50 percent of the sample was college bound. Two already were enrolled, one in economics and the other in prelaw.

Four factors were found to account for the "successful" achievers: (1) presence of a strong role model, (2) encouragement of curiosity, (3) perseverance in pursuing desired ends, and (4) "pressure" to do well in school. Pressure was described as encouragement, persuasion, and discipline without negativism. These conclusions are highly consistent with the findings about SuperKids (see Chapter 16 under *The Significance of Environment*). That is to say, the presence of a mentor, a role model, is significant.

The urgency about role models was emphasized by Wexler (1979) with the thought that schools

> would be well advised to ... give ... children a chance to spend time with role models of their choice, carpenters, bakers, florists, firefighters ... (and) ... incorporate a child's interests into the school experience. It is important for teachers to reward perseverance as well as educational achievement. (p. 48).

The internship for gifted and talented pupils is undertaken for just such sound educational purposes. They are the same purposes as those behind matching pupils with helpful mentors for nurture.

Status

Although the idea of the mentor is as old as recorded history, only recently has it been incorporated as a standard feature of educational programs for gifted and talented pupils (Gold, 1979). The internship, a form of mentoring, is based on an agreement between the school district and an individual to work with an exceptional student interested in the same field. The contract is intended to provide sufficient structure to give the student and the mentor a mutually satisfying and helpful experience. (The nature of the contract would be similar to that described in the Independent Study section.) The potential mentor is a person of proved competence.

Administrative awkwardness and inconvenience are the major reasons for failure to implement the practice more widely, although it has a sound educational base. Internships can provide the context for experimental learnings, can develop and further vocational and service commitments, and can provide freedom and flexibility for learning and for the orderly use of community resources. As with other aspects of gifted and talented educational programming, internships require planning to match the protege and the mentor as well as continuing evaluation. Cox (1979) paid tribute to the use of internships as expanding school resources into the community. There is at least one example cited by both Cox and by Gold that provides an illustration of practice. This example was Hirsch's (1976) description of an executive internship for gifted and talented high school students.

An Example: An Executive Model

The Executive High School Internships of America (EHSIA) was described by Hirsch as establishing a national base for consultation to local schools from its New York City headquarters. It sponsors a week-long Coordinators Training Academy to prepare local school district personnel. It provides technical assistance to participating school districts through conferences, program materials, newsletters, and intern insurance. Conditions of participation include the district's willingness to fund a full-time coordinator, to release students for an academic semester for full-time internship, to release students from having to make up "regular" academic work, and to grant full academic credit for the internship. The EHSIA receives funding from both public and private sources. The program is not restricted to identified gifted and talented pupils, but does attract highly able students.*

---

* In some states, the program is funded under state provisions for the gifted and talented.

The role of the coordinator, according to Hirsch, involves responsibilities of: identifying potential sponsors/mentors, defining the role of the student, briefing school staff, and recruiting students. The coordinator is expected to arrange student and sponsor interviews, schedule appointments, and make final placements based on the mutual consent of student and mentor. To carry out these responsibilities and expectations, the coordinator engages in speaking to student groups, distributing application forms and literature, and providing follow-up to students. Since students are expected to maintain extensive records of their daily activities, the coordinator devotes time to their review.

The placements and outcomes for students are varied and comprehensive, according to Hirsch. The student spends a full semester as an intern to an executive. Placements have included working with business managers, government commissioners, administrators, newspaper editors, television producers and directors, judges and attorneys, directors of social service agencies and civic associations, and hospital administrators. One advertising intern found herself interviewing clients, designing storyboards, appearing in commercials, editing commercials, performing accounting, and carrying out other aspects of production. An intern to a county planning commission produced research findings for a comprehensive economic development plan. Another intern wrote news reports and commercials, and presented sports reports for his sponsoring radio station.

Students usually spend Mondays through Thursdays in full-time placement. Fridays are given over to seminars that ordinarily focus on topics related to management, administration, and decision making. The outcome is to enable students to function as consultants and analysts of organizational problems. The method involves case studies developed by the coordinator for the first weeks, after which students are expected to present their own case studies. Independent Study also is used to supplement the seminars for specific student interests.

An Example of Flight Makes Right

Conway (1976) has shared a detailed example of mentoring and the internship process that illustrates the applicability of these tactics to disadvantaged youth. His report also illustrates how identification of able pupils is conducted in the context of instruction. Conway wrote from the perspective of an external evaluator rather than a participant with a vested interest. This example has merit for its illustration of how gifted and talented pupils can emerge in response to challenge and opportunity.

A group of 25 eighth grade boys was selected for intervention. All were characterized by reading retardation, skipping school, and suspension from time to time for discipline infractions. Conway was not specific about the criteria by which these pupils were selected, but did report that they were typical of their elementary and junior high schools.

The program consisted of four units. Unit I was in-school classes centered on "aerospace." Unit II consisted of field trips to airports and related facilities. Unit III concentrated on matters linked to flying, such as navigation, mathematics, and related computations. Unit IV involved instruction in a light, single-engine, 150 horsepower airplane. The project was funded by a private foundation to cover the costs of flight time and instruction by non-school pilots. The ratio was one instructor or tutor to four students. The units were rooted in vocational-technical spheres rather than in the academic-technical spheres.

Commenting on the relationship between flight instructor and pupil in responding to curiosity, Conway (1976) quoted one instructor as follows:

No matter how stupid the question might be, I get them to ask it. As they get more confidence in me, they are increasingly unafraid to ask questions. So they ask, What's this? and I say, Now that's a good question. This results in their increasing their questions. (p. 571).

The outcomes of the project were evaluated by comparing before and after performances of the students as well as using a contrast sample. Conway also reported longitudinal results. After one year, the Flight Group (FG) members had averaged three days absent compared to 14 days for the contrast sample. No FG member was suspended while 48 percent of the contrast sample (CS) were. Prior to intervention 60 percent of those who became the FG had been suspended. In academic areas, the FG made significant progress. For example, 13 percent were A students, 35 percent were B students, 37 percent were C students, and the remainder were D students, with no failures. By comparison, the CS had distributions of 0 percent for A and B averages, 59 percent for C, 23 percent for D, and the remaining 18 percent failing.

In 1975, the FG youth were found enrolled in higher education and armed forces training schools. The college group was earning averages of 3.0 to 3.5. Their college interests included biochemistry, economics, business administration, education, special education, construction engineering, pharmacology, dentistry, and coaching. Self-esteem data and mastery data reflected significant gains. The FG exceeded their CS and national norms for higher education study and employment. The program also was characterized by parental involvement. Parents were pleased to participate in orientation and to be respected for their support for their children.

Conway (1976) concluded that:

> Their flight instructor's non-critical, non-judgmental, non-threatening evaluation of their abilities gave them a sense of specialness which overcame the judgments, negative attitudes to which they had grown accustomed. Our evaluational data appear to prove that moral and imaginative capacity, and not measured achievement or IQ, are the real defining characteristics of human beings ... Activities which feature risk, sensory stimulation, speed spatial imagery, and the opportunity to master high status, technically complex enterprises could include mountain climbing and ballet. But clearly for disadvantaged youth, flight completely captures and captivates. It is generally a power trip. (p. 574).

One can speculate about the "what if" of the careers of these 25 fortunate youth. The imaginative use of mentoring and internship had its origins in the competence of school and nonschool persons. The main point was that these youngsters experienced much the same kind of special educational processes that are widely recommended for gifted and talented children and youth. The project resulted in persons whose careers and performance are sharply advanced over equivalent controls who did not receive mentoring of this kind. The Conway report is powerful as a source of practical guidance.

SUMMARY

There is little question but that high intelligence can operate as a potent "enabling factor" in childhood and throughout life. That is, if other factors are equal and one person has significantly higher intelligence than another, the one with higher intelligence very likely will fare better by accepted standards of success in educational, personal, social, career, family, and financial matters. It is our view that educators can and should play major roles in influencing those "other factors" as well as fostering intellectual growth as such. Zeal for work is teachable. So are goal orientation, self-understanding, self-confidence, joy in living, good health habits, and pleasure in serving others. These teachable personal and social behaviors are the very ones that made the difference between full and partial realization of early promise in the gifted population that Terman and his associates followed from childhood through retirement age. Those follow-up study reports furnish much of the foundation for the process and content curriculum concepts presented in this chapter.

UNIT ENRICHMENT
Understanding Individualized Education

1. Consider your own experiences as a producer of term projects. How does Table 11-1 help you understand your own performance? Are there aspects, or processes, of production you prefer more than others? What steps have you taken to take advantage of your preferences? How could you use Table 11-1 in a helping interview with a student? Note: In this and all other points in this section, share your examples, opinions, insights, results, findings, products.

2. Consider your own aptitudes as an educator with reference to Figure 11-1. Of the alternatives, which three do you consider your strengths, which three would be needed areas of improvement, which four represent comfort to you, and which four represent some distress? Can you account for the variety in ratings? Is there any relationship between your learning style and your teaching style? What steps could you take to widen your array of educational alternatives?

3. Consult journals such as *Exceptional Children, Journal of Education of the Gifted and Talented, Gifted Child Quarterly,* and the *Journal of Creative Behavior.* Select two to three issues. Given the items in Figure 11-1, make a list of the alternatives described in these issues. What appears to be the most frequently used? What contributes to popularity? What impressions of American education do you perceive?

Adjustments for Learning Rate

4. Review the Reynolds and Birch (1977) discussion regarding principles, practices, and organizational aspects at the beginning of Chapter 12. Does your school encourage the use of accelerating curriculum for pupils? Can you locate documents that describe its principles, practices, and organization?

5. Consider the Unit IV prototype. Which one or combinations of adapting curriculum does the special friend represent? Defend your position.

6. Consider the circumstances of prescription. What data would be necessary to incorporate these into an Individualized Education Program (IEP)? What role do you assign teachers?

7. Acceleration would be the tactic of first choice. Describe in your own words a rationale for this view. Outline a plan that would support this view.

8. Interview two to three persons (a friend, a relative, a parent, etc.) who have experienced this practice. Summarize their experiences—educational, personal, and social. What do you learn to support this procedure? What improvements did your sample advocate? Interview teachers

who have engaged in this tactic with learners. Summarize and interpret their reflections. What three to four priorities did you identify?

Adjustments for Expanding and Extending Learning

9. Consider a formal debate between Stanley (1976) and Renzulli (1977). Draft a letter of invitation to each to participate. What points would you wish each of them to make? Design procedures to publicize the debate. What points would you make to attract parents, teachers, school board members, administrative staff, and community persons? How would you tailor your points for each audience?

10. Consider the Reynolds and Birch (1977) principles, practices, and organizational aspects. What applications would Renzulli's recommendations have in your school district? How difficult would it be to implement your perceptions?

11. Consider the development of an IEP. Develop a rationale for including the school librarian as a member of the IEP. Cite three specific reasons.

12. Consider your own professional situation in light of Renzulli's (1977) advocacy of the investigation of real problems. What circumstances would, in your judgment, be necessary to implement this procedure in your own situation? Write a letter in support to your director of curriculum. Devise a poster.

Using Tactics of Teacher Initiation

13. Observe a discussion. Plot out its ebb and flow. Could the tactics of problem centeredness prove helpful?

14. Organize a discussion on the topic of discussion. How would you organize such a project to maximize the values of this procedure. What tactics would you employ? What would be the irony of a lecture about discussions? Evaluate your role as a discussion leader.

15. If possible obtain both the Renzulli (1977) and Feldhusen and Treffinger (1977) texts. Prepare two different collages depicting salient features of each text. Share your project and explain your points of similarity and contrast.

16. Prepare an inventory of community points of interest. Suggest points of interest for educational, cultural, scientific, vocational/career, etc., purposes. Share your listing and expand it.

17. Review the policies of your school district regarding visitations. How are these arranged and funded?

18. Prepare an inventory of resources within a mile of your school. How could a dry cleaner, a fast food place, and a gasoline station be relevant for gifted and talented learners?

19. Review the Feldhusen and Treffinger (1977) or the Renzulli (1977) text using the suggestion in Table 14-4.

Using Tactics of Pupil Participation

20. Review Exhibit 15-1, the Fort Park Regulars. Simulate the role of an external program evaluation for the U.S. General Accounting Office. Prepare a one-page report that will be the basis for further permission for the U.S. Park Service to participate.

21. What might a learning center about learning centers look like? Draw up a plan of specifications in outline form describing the components. If possible, expand and cooperate with others. Share your learning center with parents and staff.

22. Draft a letter to the director of personnel for your school district. State your views as to whether teachers should or should not receive incentives for sponsoring guided independent studies for pupils. Could independent study as conducted in institutions of higher education be applicable to public schools?

23. Prepare an outline of a publication for your district titled "A School's Guide for Mentors." What differences would your proposed document have with respect to independent study and internships.

24. Consider the music popular with you or with others. What music (songs, instrumental) would describe the mentor, the protege, and the sponsoring teacher? Select three choices for each category. Share your nominations and select one for each category.

Understanding Tactics of Confluent Education

SYNOPSIS

Education is the systematic cultivation of the whole person. Under the best of circumstances, high quality education takes place in the planned and ordered setting of the school and, at other times, informally in the home and community.

Confluent education includes instruction, especially closely individualized instruction, that is directed by and dependent upon normal home life and personal association with teachers in and out of school. Nurture has special relevance to moral and ethical qualities, but it does not overlook the intellectual.

This unit addresses nurturance, a significant characteristic very important in the education of gifted and talented students. There is a large body of case studies and anecdotal information that justifies particular attention to nurturance by educators and parents. Certainly all children need nurture. It may well be, however, that extraordinary human ability requires extraordinary emotional support and competent guidance to flourish.

These chapters highlight the natural collaboration between the home and the school to achieve helpful communication. Special emphasis is given to affective outcomes to round out content and skill outcomes.

Educators and parents share a common role as teachers. Both assist children and youth in forming a value system for life's vital choices. The chapters review what is known and understood about well-founded procedures for personal and for group guidance in the clarification of choices.

KEY IDEAS

1. Parents and teachers share common goals of fostering positive self-esteem and establishing a responsible philosophy of life.

2. Education of gifted and talented persons is confluent in that affective and cognitive outcomes come together in a balanced way in all curricular offerings.

3. Affective outcomes can be as specific and measurable as cognitive outcomes.

4. The laws of human development (e.g., increasing complexity, readiness, and invariant sequence) apply to affective development.

5. People acquire self-esteem and responsible ideals through the mediation of reflection and examination of life experiences. Strategies of practical guidance do exist that acknowledge this reality and that serve to assist concerned adults in helping relationships.

6. Strategies of helping that build self-esteem and social relationships are as diagnostically based as strategies for content areas.

Unit V presents known resources to build a helping relationship. In an educational context, this unit describes the procedures of personal guidance attributed to a role of mentor. The primary medium of the helping relationship is language. It is recognized that reading about helping relationships has its limits. However, it is anticipated that this introduction will encourage seeking out additional information and opportunities for practice.

This unit also is addressed to group aspects of education. It is addressed to the U.S. Department of Education priority for leadership development. It also is addressed to competencies of class management and discipline. A major thrust is to identify tactics and resources for arranging an educational environment that rewards performance and fosters positive beliefs about interpersonal relationships. While the skills of one-to-one relationships are applicable to group settings, there are practices specific to group processes, especially with respect to values education.

A PROTOTYPE

Highly able adults in communities all over the world face the question of how to generate and maintain environments that keep them alert and developing rather than stagnating. That helps account for study groups, hobby clubs, theater groups, and many other intellectual and artistic organizations that meet for enlivening recreation.

This story from the Yourtowne News illustrates how some highly able adults band together to provide a source of nurture for each other.

Yourtowne, N.B. (ATIDISPATCH)—Carl Jenkins's IQ is one of the highest in North Boltucky, but he claims no interest in worldly success.

"I'd like to keep a steady flow of sufficient dollars coming in each week and to be easygoing and relaxed, too, with a minimum of work to do." The words fitted his lay-back posture in the recliner in his modest living room. His wife, Ida, grinned assent as she paused in her housework.

Carl, a 40-year-old father of two, belongs to Mensa. That is an organization of gifted persons, an international group that requires an IQ in the top 2 percent of the general population as a minimum standard for membership. He also runs an agency that does indoor and outdoor house maintenance service on a contract basis.

Mensa is Latin for "table." The round table symbolizes equality of place among members. The organization gives its members contact with other good minds. Also, it works with schools and research agencies to improve education for bright pupils.

Jenkins is no snob, and neither, he says, are very many of the other 28,000 members in the U.S. and the rest of the world. He became a member in 1965 and likes to be in the same IQ group with members Buckminster Fuller, Isaac Asimov, and Theodore Bikel. Nobody, he says, wears forehead stickers proclaiming "Mine is higher than yours!" He adds, "This is not an 'elite' in any negative sense. We just don't act high and mighty about anything."

Jenkins's weekly lunch meeting with a group of male friends stiffened a little when the local paper carried the story of his election as Mensa's state president. They hadn't known of the group, much less his membership. "That didn't make any long-run difference, though," volunteered Jenkins. "We're (he and his wife) too much like everybody else for Mensa membership to matter among friends."

About 70 percent that take Mensa's qualifying test pass it. Once in, it is a lot like other clubs. The annual dues are $20 and there are monthly meetings with speakers, interspersed with special lunches, parties, singles nights, and weekend brunches.

Jenkins tells of dismal early schooling in one of the New England states. "It was boredom every day. My grades were not good. The whole thing was pitched to the slowest students. I'm glad they got something, but sorry it had to be at my expense."

After sliding uneventfully through high school, Jenkins found work in a foundry. He quickly became a skilled worker, earning good money. Using savings, he went into business for himself, first part time, then full time. He likes to work with people.

Mrs. Jenkins goes to Mensa meetings with her husband, but she hasn't applied for membership. "I don't have to prove I'm smart," she says, "I already know it. I'm not concerned about failing the test. It's just a test. I'm passing life's tests every day, and that's what matters to me."

Chapter 16

Understanding the Confluence of Education

Nurture is an essential ingredient in high quality education of all pupils and particularly of the gifted and talented.

For the educator there is recognition that nurture is a responsibility, but there may be questions of what to nurture and how, when, and where to nurture. There also may be the need to understand the why of nurture.

Phillips (1976) proposes that the nurture of highly able students can be assured through a teacher-preparation program called *Confluent Education*. His views evolved in part out of personal experience, including recollections as a student in an honors program during his school years, and as an observer of the school experiences of his bright 7-year-old son. Professionally, he is a teacher educator.

Phillips defined confluent education as:

> A flowing together—of thoughts, feelings, and action; . . . and of the intrapersonal, interpersonal, and extrapersonal. The program emphasizes a holistic approach to human development and assumes that such confluence is necessary for individuals to live fulfilling lives and take creative and responsible positions in society. (p. 239).

THE NURTURE OF HUMAN ABILITIES

Favorable Environmental Influences

A 1955 essay by Pressey has endured because of its continuing validity regarding nature and nurture. Pressey observed that the incidence of gifted and talented persons had varied across time and regions. These observations led him to examine the careers of precocious persons so as to identify nurturing environmental influences. He found that exceptional persons of recognized competence had experienced one or more of the following:

1. Excellent and early opportunity for abilities to emerge and to be encouraged by families and friends.
2. Access to early and continuing individual guidance and instruction.
3. Opportunities for regular and sustained practice as well as the opportunity to progress at an individualized pace.
4. Participation in close association with other performers (not necessarily of equal ability) that formed the basis of a continuing stimulating acquaintance.
5. Stimulation by frequent and increasingly strong success opportunities.

Origins of Ability

Pressey advanced the provocative observation that the range of human attributes of height, strength, quickness, and mental abilities might be less extreme than was supposed. It was his view that a purely genetic view about intelligence and ability resulted in a passive social stance with respect to the location of superior students and their education. Furthermore, he contended that to assume that superior students made up a fixed percentage of the population reinforced the image of superior ability as an oddity of nature that was independent of influence through intervention.

It was Pressey's conviction that high human ability resulted from the interaction of good, original, innate capacity that flourished under a favorable set of circumstances. Thus, inherent ability of high order, augmented by excellent nurture, results in superior performance. He hypothesized, therefore, that fostering favorable circumstances could increase the absolute numbers of superior persons and enhance the capabilities of each individual. Pressey's position has been reinforced over the years since 1955 by similar conclusions on the part of many other scholars including Lyons (1974). Thus, the Pressey hypothesis is one of the major justifications for special education for gifted and talented pupils.

Tactics for Arranging Favorable Circumstances

Pressey offered two major suggestions for action by educators for the nurture of favorable circumstances in the lives of gifted and talented pupils. The suggestions were advanced to help assure for such pupils five positive influences: (1) early opportunity, (2) continuing individual guidance, (3) sustained practice, (4) association with competent persons, and (5) recognition. His suggestions were:

1. A school system or college should create a position with responsibility for special programs. This position would involve a number of role assignments. One task would be the monitoring of school records for evidence of superior potential. A related task would be to establish a network among faculty to nominate students. An especially critical role would be to establish personal contact with each student. In addition, this position would facilitate association and companionship among students. The role also would include soliciting the support of faculty. Moreover, this special staff member could identify sources of financial student aid, or sources of aid for projects, materials, and other resources for education of the gifted and talented.

2. Adaptation of the standard curriculum should be the prevailing policy. There is not so much need for a special curriculum as there is for allowances in pace of learning, especially speedier rates of completion. This means completing experiences faster, early enrollments, schedule telescoping, and other forms of acceleration.

Recasting the Meaning of Giftedness

From the discussion of Pressey's views it should be clear that genetic and statistical concepts, by themselves, are insufficient explanations for giftedness and talent. Able persons have not simply been singled out for a golden passport to status and success in life. Pressey's resume presents a more realistic slant. Consider his composite of the careers of able persons. They were provided: (1) early mentoring by an able and nurturing adult, (2) the opportunity and freedom for individualized attention, and (3) the experience of early and encouraging recognition. These are not chance "gifts;" rather, they are deliberate consequences of a nurturing environment. Pressey's account creates a sense of urgency to design and arrange these circumstances for all highly able persons.

School tasks, even the most humble ones, have their affective, their emotional, overtones. If one can recognize the approach and avoidance aspects of learning, one has the properties commonly described as empathy, or the ability to view a situation from the perspective of another person. This involves the suspension of one's own perspective while attending primarily to the person. Empathy is: (1) the result of practice, (2) attainable by parents and teachers, and (3) a central quality in positive human relationships. As a skill, having empathy means engaging in active listening. This skill is discussed more fully in Chapter 18 of this unit.

DEVELOPMENTAL BENCHMARKS

A Framework

Suppose one were a judge. There are four separate but related cases to be heard. In one way or another, these cases parallel Hersey's (1960) *The Child Buyer.* Hersey's central character is Barry, a gifted sixth grader who has been "sold" to an aerospace firm in Houston. His fate is to recycle scientific knowledge through computer interactions. The computer will instruct Barry in its knowledge, comprehension, and applications of aerospace. In turn Barry will assimilate and accommodate these data and transform them into analysis, synthesis, and evaluation. The computer will transform Barry's insights into gathering new data. In turn, Barry will act upon these data and so the cycle proceeds. Barry's life companion will be the computer and the controlled environment for both of them.

Barry's situation has been brought to the attention of the court through the advocacy of a state legislator who pleads for criminal charges against the Child Buyer who "purchased" Barry.

The Child Buyer defends his practice since there is no specific law against impounding national resources for the national defense. He cites the spectre of death rays that have been developed by and placed in outer space pointed at U.S. cities. There is a desperate need to catch up swiftly. He dismisses Barry's barren life with the claim that eggheads are needed now, and besides the state director of programs for the gifted endorsed the sale.

The state director disclaims responsibility. She contends that her role is only to identify superior children and channel their talents into constructive efforts. As a government person, she contends her obligation is to follow policy, not to make policy. As the Child Buyer's firm has a federal contract, she believes him to be a legitimate person. Therefore, she can't be blamed. Besides, the principal advised the parents to sign the consent agreement that transferred guardianship of Barry to the firm.

Barry's principal did admit to advising the boy's parents to make the sale. She claimed that state and local policies prevented her from assisting Barry. Besides, she said, the boy was so bright and his family was so financially disadvantaged. This would be such a wonderful opportunity for him to receive advanced training. Moreover, the project wouldn't go on forever. After it was completed, he could pursue his own interests.

Barry's parents were defensive. They were concerned about him. However, the "authorities" had said it would be all right. Anyway, the $25,000 would be a helpful source of income for their two other children.

Barry, himself, was confused. He also was resigned. The judge found all four parties guilty. The possible sentences totaled to 100 years. Question:

Should each receive 25 years apiece? Should the sentences be assigned differently? Should some of the parties be absolved?

This story, and its unanswered questions, can be used as a simulation exercise, especially to gain insight into how values play their part in decision making. One pupil can be assigned to act the judge. Others, under teacher guidance, can prepare to interview the judge after decisions on sentencing are handed down.

The interviewer's purpose would be to identify the "judge's" reasons for assigning "guilt." It is the reasons that provide insight into the content of belief. This interview approach has proved appropriate with teenagers and adults to assess the "rules" (or reasons) that regulate their behaviors. The study of the rules by which young people regulate their personal and social relationships can be founded on the use of such simplified interviews and observation.

For example, suppose one is interested in simulation for very able children (see Unit IV). Further, suppose one wants to devise a "strategy" game that does not depend on chance and is not as complex as chess. More specifically, the object would be to design a game that feels right to the child and also gives practice in higher order abilities, especially predicting and planning.

Kohl (1974) tells about his solution to this situation. He related how he observed his 6-year-old daughter and her friends. The children were playing with a checkerboard and plastic animals. At first, there were no apparent rules. After a bit, an unspoken agreement emerged that the owl would chase the snake, the snake would chase the mouse, and the mouse would chase the elephant. The children then devised rules for a different type of move for each animal. In that context, the children reached agreements that would regulate their own behavior. Out of that observation, plus questioning, Kohl developed his own simulation.

Combinations of interviews and of observation of the sort just noted have revealed much of what is known and understood about how people regulate their personal and social behavior. In more technical terms, the human values aspect of affective development is termed moral development. The term has its communication hazards. Moral, as the word is used here, is not to be equated with straitlaced. Moral development does not mean acquiring some set of "right" values. It does mean the internalization of universal principles for the conduct of human relationships.

Kohlberg (1971) finds that there are three levels of moral development, each of which has two stages. His work relates to Piaget's in that, together, they: (1) produce stable and orderly knowledge, (2) demonstrate interrelationships between affective and cognitive development, and (3) suggest strategies for education.

Developmental Attributes

Kohlberg's three levels are: preconventional, conventional, and postconventional.

The preconventional level includes behavior regulated by pleasure-pain consequences. Good vs. Bad and Right vs. Wrong are defined by the person in terms of rewards and punishments and by the power of others to administer these consequences. In Stage 1, Punishment-Obedience Orientation, a person's behavior is conditioned by avoidance of punishment and deference to authority because of its power. Stage 2, Instrumental-Relative, operates on the principle of reciprocity. Values of good or right are attached to actions that satisfy personal needs and, incidentally, the needs of others. The "scratch my back" view dominates. Personal comfort is the key.

The conventional level considers loyalty to order as good in its own right. This level reflects a shift from the purely personal to social conformity. Stage 3, Interpersonal Concordance, describes behavior regulated by social approval. The good boy-nice girl ideal is prized. Stage 4, Law and Order, is conformity to a fixed set of rules, the maintenance of order. Right and Good are equal to respect for authority. Order and rules are endorsed for the sake of their security. "Fairness" is demanded from others.

The postconventional level includes the most complex stages. This level is characterized by examination of conduct apart from: (1) the authority of the persons or groups who endorse the conduct, (2) influence on one's own peers, and (3) the majority culture. Its outcome is to produce a philosophy of life that provides inner controls for behavior. Stage 5, Social Contract behavior, recognizes one's own right to opinions as well as the rights of others. The Right and the Good derive from a conscious examination of values that have been democratically agreed upon. Order for the protection of individual and group behavior is grounded in codes and laws. However, there is the recognition that new knowledge and events may alter the conventional. Kohlberg (1971) identified this stage as the fundamental principle of the United States. That is to say, the U.S. Constitution is respected and preserved; however, it also is perceived a "living" document. The Constitution is viewed as subject to amendment as there is a perceived and collective need. Stage 6, Universal-Ethical behavior, has role reversal as a central theme. This means treating another in a manner consistent with how one would wish to be treated if roles were reversed. This stage depends heavily upon empathy. Persons who function by this principle are not motivated by either preconventional or conventional levels. Rather, they are committed to ideals of justice, equality, human rights, and respect. It is viewed as the essence of the Golden Rule.

Correspondence

In general terms, the preconventional level of knowledge encompasses the sensorimotor and preoperational stages of development described by Piaget. The conventional level corresponds to the concrete operations period. Formal operations and postconventional periods overlap one another. The generalizations about affective development and cognitive development apply. However, there is a notable possible exception. A person in the stage of formal operations does not automatically possess postconventional principles. Historical figures of infamy may have been intelligent but their moral behavior was the self centeredness of the preconventional.

One outcome and implication of Kohlberg's (1971) moral levels concept is its use in suggesting a structure for curriculum. Affective education can attend to the individual and social order, so far as moral development is concerned, in an orderly way based on upward mobility in the levels and stages.

THE SIGNIFICANCE OF ENVIRONMENT

The acquisition of moral principles derives from what the person learns from environmental interactions descriptive of Piaget's notion of adaptation. The family, the community, and the schools provide the experience. It is not the experience per se, though, that affects the person. It is what the individual learns from the experience that is significant. This distinction has helped to identify the construct of SuperKids.

SuperKids

A SuperKid is described accurately as an invulnerable child. Pines (1979, p. 53) says they "... sail through the most horrendous difficulties without obvious damage."

The study of SuperKids has proceeded on a reverse track. Previous studies have stressed pathology more than wellness. Research had identified vulnerable persons and examined their careers retrospectively. Such studies usually yield an unbroken series of damaging events that seem to cause difficulty.

The study of SuperKids has stressed wellness, and longitudinal study shows that potentially harmful events seem to be weathered without distress.

According to Pines, SuperKids are characterized by the following:

1. They seem at ease with themselves and possess the ability to put others at ease. They seem to form friendships easily.

2. They know how to attract and use the support of adults. Adults have played a key role of encouragement. The adult may be an intact parent, a babysitter, or a teacher.
3. They have a sense of inner power. They also are very willing to help others.
4. They think for themselves and have high degrees of autonomy of belief and moral principles.
5. They possess interests and hobbies. They tend to do well in school and their out-of-school interests seem to serve as a compensation. They are able to make much of very little.

One 11-year-old boy was cited as an example. After school, he and his best friend would retreat to his attic to get away from his seriously disturbed mother. The children had created in the attic a model city out of cast-off fabric and bits of sewing materials. They had a variety of houses, a railroad, two airports, and hundreds of airplanes. They knew the history and strengths of each plane. When 12, the boy taught a course on war games at his school, where he has an A average.

The source of the SuperKids' strength is still unknown. Genetic endowment, favorable birth history, and learning from life experiences appear to be promising avenues for research.

From the limited amount known about invulnerable children, the following points can be made about how to foster that quality in the early years:

1. Help the child build a solid relationship of emotional warmth with at least one good adult.
2. Provide challenges to the child's abilities and reward achievement.
3. Arrange outlets for stress build-up. Identified stress in studies of Super-Kids has included: (a) severe marital discord, (b) extreme poverty, (c) sexual abuse, (d) physical neglect, (e) criminal father, (f) seriously disturbed mother, (g) overcrowding in the home, and (h) admission to foster care/institutions. Research cited by Pines suggests that the presence of one of these risk factors does not alter development significantly when compared to a child who had none. However, two such risk factors may have a four-fold effect when compared to a child with none. Elimination of just one stress factor may help a child to cope with other demands.
4. Interventions are indeed helpful and effective. Engaging in ordinary activities of recreation or tutoring are examples. Informing the child that the parent's difficulties are not the child's fault is another way to supply emotional release.

The Roles of Teachers

Confluent education is a mediation process. The teacher serves as mediator by which the learner is inducted into curricular skills and content as such and into the career implications of skills and content. As a mediator, according to McKeachie (1978), the teacher fosters self-confidence in the student. McKeachie describes the mediation function as composed of the following roles: (1) expert, (2) formal authority, (3) socializing agent, (4) facilitator, and (5) role model. His discussion was advanced in the context of educating able students who may not possess high motivation for the teacher's subject or skill area.

The teacher as expert serves to transmit the knowledge and perspectives of curricular skill or content. As a result, the student would be expected to increase in knowledge and perspective. The pupil also would be expected to become more curious and motivated about the field. The student is expected to listen and raise clarifying questions. The teacher is expected to be organized about presentation(s) and prepared in the skill or content field.

The teacher as formal authority represents the educational agency to students. Secondarily, the teacher is seen by gifted and talented pupils as a career representative of persons engaged in the skill or content. The teacher's main role in authority is to clarify goals, expectations, and evaluation criteria. The student is expected to comprehend the teacher's standards. It is assumed that the teacher is motivated to be clear and that the pupil is motivated to respond to expectations.

The teacher as a socializing agent can induct highly able students into the career expectations of the field. The teacher is expected to clarify the demands and rewards of: (1) the career itself and (2) formal study within the educational institution. Students are expected to clarify their own interests and "calling" to demands and rewards.

The teacher as facilitator removes obstacles to learning (runs interference) and promotes growth within the student. The teacher is expected to be insightful and solution oriented to assist students to move toward goals and avoid obstacles.

The teacher as role model is a living example of the excitement and value of intellectual inquiry in a given field. This role fulfills gifted and talented students' needs for personal examples to illustrate their own ideals. The teacher is expected to develop a trust relationship that encourages the student to overcome the fear of formal authority. Both teacher and pupil achieve an identity beyond the task at hand. (The rudiments of mentoring often appear as part of this role, though it is not the same.)

A Leadership Perspective

In 1977, the National Institute of Education issued a report on the relation of fundamental research in education to the day-to-day process of education in public schools. The report, edited by Keisler and Turner (1977), affirms the precept of educational nurture in general and of educational nurture for able pupils in particular.

The Keisler and Turner report identified eight priorities for education that are summarized in Table 16-1.

Their report did not rank order priorities. Those priorities reflect and illustrate the wide range of educational nurture.

Table 16-1 Examples of Priority Considerations for Educational Nurture

Examples of Educational Goals	Examples of Relevant Educational Goals and/or Pupil Outcomes	Examples of Implications and/or Program Emphasis
Understand the Brain and Neural Process	To increase learning To increase the capacity for learning	To understand how environmental stimulation/deprivation alters cerebral chemistry To understand how pharmacology improves/alters cognition, attention, etc.
Understanding Cognitive Development	To produce people who can critically evaluate new information To produce people who can recognize when their own information is incomplete To produce people who can think on their own	To determine the ways in which the work of Piaget applies to understanding environmental interaction To assist teachers, measurement personnel, and administrators to translate findings into curriculum and teaching tactics

Table 16-1 continued

Examples of Educational Goals	Examples of Relevant Educational Goals and/or Pupil Outcomes	Examples of Implications and/or Program Emphasis
Reading	To develop skill in reading to be informed about government affairs, parenting skills, and consumer competencies To develop skill in reading sufficient to manage the demands of employment, family protection, and leisure	To apply cognitive research to acquisition of reading skills To more fully understand and emphasize reading comprehension
Educating Children for Pluralistic and Multilingual Society	To educate children in the dominant language sufficiently to permit participation in national life To educate children to respect and prize differences within society To develop responsiveness to families and communities of origin	To identify appropriate educational accommodations To assess the advantages and disadvantages of learning two more languages To understand the timing and extent of intervention efforts
School Environments	To assure that schools are safe, productive environments To develop pupil conduct that is self-fulfilling and respectful of others	To understand and implement procedures to reduce crime, vandalism, and disorder in the schools To emphasize prevention of conflict as well as treatment To manage the effects of community conflicts that intrude upon the schools
Innovation and Change in the Schools	To predict the consequences of change To evaluate the effects of change	To understand the basis (e.g., educational, economic, political, etc.) of decisions for change and/or to resist change

Table 16-1 continued

Examples of Educational Goals	Examples of Relevant Educational Goals and/or Pupil Outcomes	Examples of Implications and/or Program Emphasis
	To understand that to change is not automatically "good"	To understand how schools organize efforts to pursue and manage goals, objectives, and resources
Education Outside the Schools	To enable children and adults to use media of all types To encourage adults to broaden, upgrade, and increase their technical and humanistic skills and understanding	To enable consumers of media (especially TV) to be intelligent users of their presentations as to accuracy To understand that adult learning is lifelong and adult development has educational implications
Opportunities for Pupil Education	To offer higher education to all qualified citizens To understand the personal and economic effects of higher education	To maintain resources for opportunity To develop and use systems of accountability To emphasize variety in post-secondary education

Adapted from *Fundamental Research and the Process of Education*. Keisler and Turner eds., published by the National Institute of Education (1977).

UNDERSTANDING CONFLUENCE

How Schools Make A Difference

Public confidence in education influences school systems to initiate special programming for highly able learners. The literature of education (mass media and professional) sometimes encourages pessimism about the value of schooling.

Walberg and Pinzur-Rasher (1977) reviewed the available literature regarding the outcomes of schooling for the individual person. They concluded that (1) schooling does make a difference, (2) differences can be ascribed to practices, and (3) there is reason for confidence that schooling has positive outcomes.

Walberg and Pinzur-Rasher advanced four conclusions about the outcomes of education for the person. First, the longer one attends school, the better chance there will be significant achievement differences among elementary, secondary, and college students. Second, the opportunity for schooling (e.g., free and appropriate) is essential to produce significant achievement gains. Third, the "psychological" environment of the schools influences achievement. Factors such as pursuit of declared goals, teacher/pupil planning, and individualized education produce positive differences on measures of cognitive and affective outcomes. Fourth, gross indicators of community resources and educational costs are only remotely related to achievement. It is how resources are allocated rather than the amount of resources spent per pupil that is most important, once basic personnel and facilities are made available.

Research regarding educational outcomes has found many variables. Allowing for the exercise of statistical controls and demographic adjustments, only two of these variables are related to school achievement, according to Walberg and Pinzur-Rasher: (1) percentage of public school enrollment to nonpublic school enrollments and (2) teacher/pupil ratio.

Walberg and Pinzur-Rasher (1977) believe that teacher/pupil ratio is the most significant as an index. Their data reflect, for example, that reducing one pupil per teacher reduces school failure by 7.9%. They further observe that increments in individualized education produce increments in achievement.

Left Brain—Right Brain

If education is effective and if nurture has positive consequences, the *what* of nurture is significant. A resume of educational practice for highly able students by Lyons (1974) offers guidance. His essay also is supportive of the Pressey (1955) point of view reviewed earlier. Lyons observed that personalized education for the gifted and talented too often has meant one-dimensional education. According to Lyons (1974):

> Gifted pupils are likely to be forced down the purely cognitive track ... We need to encourage the development of a gifted child's capacity for love, empathy, awareness, and communication with fellow human beings. (p. 66).

A balance in educational emphasis also is supported by advances in neurological understanding of learning processes. Rennels (1976) summarized the educational implications of recent information about brain functions. The essence of the implications lies in the notion of cerebral symmetry. The human brain is not a two-part computer with one side dominant and the other nondominant. In general, one side of the brain is responsible for certain kinds of cognitive functions while the other side has different responsibilities.

Education and educators, according to Rennels, have been oriented to the left brain, or dominant cerebral hemisphere. There has been good reason since the dominant brain hemisphere is credited with responsibilities for verbal, numerical, rational, logical, and linear relationship skills. It is acknowledged that these abilities have made possible the evolution and refinement of human accomplishments. It also is being recognized, though, that nondominant hemisphere responsibilities enable human beings to exist as humane, sensitive, and effective persons. This right side of the brain appears responsible for a person's visual/spatial perceptions, intuitive thought, imagination, fantasy, and imagery attributes. Certainly today's educational procedures should prize both. Knowledge of neurological findings provides support for the nurture of both cognitive and affective dimensions.

Confluent Teachers

It is not sufficient to demand that teachers of gifted and talented pupils should be confluent, according to Phillips (1976). There is the need for consultation with teachers of preservice and inservice levels. One topic would be to enable teachers to examine the hidden curriculum of norms, teacher behavior, and pupil interactions. For example, it is unlikely that investigative techniques can be taught through lectures exclusively. A second topic would be to encourage teachers to formulate their own definitions of giftedness. This activity should enable educators to become aware of their own abilities and talents. In turn, this awareness should enable teachers to enhance, within themselves, the very abilities they will attempt to foster within children and youth. A third consideration would be that teacher preparation should reflect cerebral symmetry. The tactics described in the next two chapters are illustrative of nurture as balanced emphasis. They are oriented toward translating self-knowledge into competence and contribution.

APPLICABILITY OF APTITUDE TREATMENT INTERACTIONS

The Aptitude Treatment Interaction (ATI) model does apply to affective aspects of instruction, according to Gage and Berlmer (1979). The process of knowing pupil aptitudes and of scanning various possible complementary treatments, and then matching to the maximum interaction, applies to affective dimensions as well as to cognitive goals. For example, they cite a study in which the aptitude was anxiety (low vs. high) and the treatment was discussion vs. lecture. The objective was mastery of facts, terminology, and procedures necessary for scientific understanding of human behavior. In very general terms, as might be expected, low anxious students perform better on conditions of discussion than they perform under conditions of lecture. By contrast, high anxious students perform better under conditions of lecture then under conditions of discussion. Gage and Berlmer observed that the usual research tactic of comparing Method A to Method B is appropriate. However it is more accurate when amended by the phrase: "for some students under certain conditions a given method is more appropriate."

The ATI model was applied by Kindsratter (1978) to class management, discipline, and classroom control. Misbehavior, from the pupil's view, may be the only feasible response in a given situation. Kindsratter formulated a diagnostic model to prevent conflict, to make misbehavior unlikely, and to guide pupil decorum constructively. The purpose was to deemphasize the mystique of discipline.

Kindsratter uncovered three types of student aptitude and several varied treatments to deal with the three. The focal concept is that one single method is not sufficient, but rather that a matching is required.

One case was that of the pupil whose misbehavior was a temporary lapse or straying from a usual cooperative norm. The response of the teacher here would be to use tactics of reminder, mild restraint, and withholding approval. The teacher would need to be certain that expectations about pupil behavior had been clearly communicated and comprehended.

A second aptitude situation—and a quite different one—would be the pupil whose behavior arose out of dislike for either the current school work, fellow students, or the instructor. Responses by the teacher would aim at defusing the affective sources. The teacher might need to restructure instruction to ensure success. There might be a need to separate students for a time. Or the right move might be to put the pupil temporarily in the charge of an aide or another teacher. There also would be the continuing need to foster group cohesiveness.

The third aptitude type might be a pupil whose difficulties arose out of extreme and generalized adjustment problems. Here the preferred treatment would require, first, explicit communication of expectations. Kindsratter advocated specific pupil guidance as to acceptable alternative behaviors, too. He also observed that teachers in any such cases should not fear or hesitate to call for consultation. It would be a sign of professional strength and competence to know when consultation was needed and to seek it.

The ATI model also can be applied to helping relationships. Welter (1978), for example, defined five levels of encounters and corresponding responses of helping. The levels were listed as problem, predicament, crisis, panic, and shock. His levels and responses can enable teachers to be responsive to their able pupils in times of crisis. His discussion identifies dimensions of mentoring.

Shock and panic, according to Welter, are relatively rare events. Shock is characterized by inability to take action. Helpers may need to act in place of the person. Panic is the state of fear or anxiety in which the individual is unable to select more than one solution. There is dread of the future. The helper would respond to the person's need for understanding. Active listening without critical judgment of emotionality would be most helpful.

Crisis and predicament may be encountered more frequently. Predicament is the state of feeling trapped because there is no feasible and satisfactory solution. Information or advice is not altogether helpful. The "block" usually is a belief that requires examination. The helper reflects empathic understanding and confidence in the person's ability to succeed. Crisis is an escalation of predicament. There is such urgency that thoughtless reaction displaces examination and confrontation. The helper needs to be close by and in touch, to convince the person that attention and caring are present.

Examples of Welter's continuum take place in very ordinary situations. For example, consider the parent who wants to know about the school success of an able son or daughter in first grade. At this problem level, supplying the names of school officials and appropriate readings might be sufficient. Suppose, though, that in a week the parent reports that the school official has suggested that testing is advisable to be more precise about the child's status. The parent may believe such procedures are inappropriate. Events have reached a predicament. Attentive listening uncovers the parent's sense of distrust of "objective" measurement, but also the parent's perception that the school staff probably will not act without it. Crisis results later when the parent contends that there is an impasse. The parent wants to know the child's status, but won't agree to testing. There is resentment and discord. Events could balloon into complete panic if the parent withdrew the child from school. As the child's teacher and "consultant" to parents, the role of helper would be to assess available information and structure a satisfactory resolution.

Welter and Kindsratter both acknowledged that matching aptitude to treatment posed the pitfall of too literal interpretations and rigid applications of their ideas. They emphasized that the principles of a helping relationship should guide practice. The key idea of relevance for gifted education would be to enable pupils to define and act upon their own values. Action, in turn, would focus on development of feelings of self-worth as well as commitment to goals of social contribution.

SUMMARY

The central message of this chapter is to revitalize an old phrase—to educate the *whole* gifted and talented person. There is a press for balance and for deliberate affective, motoric, and cognitive education to form that balance. Psychophysiological evidence and new knowledge about moral development join to support the advisability of confluent education. The regular teacher is seen as the chief agent to both devise and deliver confluent education to gifted and talented pupils.

Chapter 17

Preparing Affective Outcomes

OBSTACLES TO PREPARATION

In general terms, the affective domain of gifted education has been couched in concepts such as attitude, values, beliefs, and feelings. The language of educational goals for able pupils within this domain has included such terms as appreciation, valuing, prizing, selecting, feeling, and the like.

Specific obstacles to the inclusion of affective objectives have been identified by Bloom, Hastings, and Madaus (1971). They point to reservations regarding statements about affective outcomes. For example, fear of indoctrination is a principal obstacle. There is understandable concern about the creation of an Orwellian *1984* system. The vision of a single value orientation is truly repugnant and foreign to citizens and teachers alike.

A second reservation is "grading." Some argue that if affect is an intended outcome, then students should be given letter grades.

The third source of hesitation involves how to measure affective development. Anything difficult to measure is also hard to evaluate. For example, consider the following objectives that typically are encountered in curriculum guides for gifted and talented pupils. The objectives seek:

1. to develop a spirit of inquiry
2. to value compliance with the law
3. to abide willingly by school rules
4. to acquire the ability to appreciate the structure of the real number system
5. to listen with pleasure to good music
6. to display an increased appetite for good literature
7. to acquire a sense of obligation to become a responsible scientist

School attendance produces affective outcomes. For example, the educator who engages in genuine teacher-pupil planning is providing powerful lessons in democratic relationships. Increasingly, world history provides examples of persons who are technically well prepared but who apply their knowledge and skills to brutalize human beings.

Acquisition of cognitive data does produce affective responses. For example, the learning of a fact, concept, or principle (Bloom et al., 1971), is objectively verifiable, but educators lack a reliable procedure by which to state affective outcomes in quantifiable terms. Concurrently, there is the puzzle of how to make use of the subjective data that often is being gathered in the name of affective outcomes.

A DOMAIN OF AFFECTIVE OUTCOMES

Attitude, or affective influences, refer to one's feelings, emotions, and inclinations. Krathwohl, Bloom, and Masida (1964) achieved a breakthrough that does help educators of the gifted and talented to identify, describe, and demonstrate a feasible system for the preparation of affective outcomes. The system allows the classification of objectives without ambiguity.

The assumption underlying affective measurement is that abstractions such as interests, values, appreciation, and the like can be described operationally. Krathwohl et al. viewed affect as *approach behavior.* Affect is the person's expressed inclination to pursue, agree, etc. Responses can range through nonawareness, indifference, hostility, tolerance, acceptance, and adoption, to avowed endorsement.

Krathwohl's group identified five dimensions of affect appropriate for measurement (see table 17-1). This table also provides examples of measurement adapted from the Bloom et al. handbook.

Krathwohl et al. (1964) illustrate that affective outcomes can be ordered or sequenced. Moreover, the sequence of outcomes can be stated with enough precision to justify the effort. Affective program objectives also can be independent—that is, not tied to limited cognitive objectives.

For example, there are indeed attitudes toward the gifted and talented. Initially, certain teachers, patrons, board members, or administrators might range from hostile to indifferent to a district's gifted and talented program

Preparing Affective Outcomes   301

Table 17-1 Dimensions of Affective Outcomes

Descriptor	Dimensions and Related Components	Example Item of Measurement
Receiving	Awareness, willingness to receive, selective attention	Student will develop a tolerance for a variety of music forms
Responding	Compliance, obedience to attend; voluntary responding-attending; satisfaction in response	Student voluntarily will read newspapers of different editorial opinions.
Valuing	Personal endorsements acceptance; preference for a belief(s) system; commitment-conviction	Student will write letters to legislators about topics of personal interest.
Organization	Conceptual-acquiring abstractions to describe values-beliefs; ordering of related ideas into a harmonious whole	Student forms judgments as to policy directions of the U.S. Chamber of Commerce.
Characterization	Generalized set so stable and consistent that a person is described as an advocate; characterization—a consistent philosophy of life	Student develops a consistent philosophy regarding vital life choices.

Adapted from *Handbook on Formative and Summative Evaluation of Student Learning* by B. S. Bloom, J. T. Hastings, and G. F. Madaus, McGraw-Hill, 1971; and from *The Classification of Educational Objectives. Handbook 2. The Affective Domain* by D. R. Krathwohl, B. S. Bloom, and B. B. Masida, McKay, 1964.

---

aspirations. Perhaps a TV program arouses interest that causes a suspension of past feelings. This event has provoked a willingness for *receiving* information. There is at least a passive awareness that information exists. Suppose one then conducts an after-school presentation about gifted and talented pupils' needs. Attendance may be viewed as evidence of *responding*. At this level, the initially hostile or indifferent persons have expended some effort to be engaged further. There may even be willingness to read materials and share helpful suggestions. *Valuing* is a transition from passivity to active participation. At this level, persons will speak in favor of programs, will try to influence others, and will display other overt acts of endorsement. An outgrowth of valuing can be the *organization* of beliefs about gifted and talented persons and beliefs about all learners. For example, educators have beliefs about individual differences as well as tactics for managing them. The attribute of organization describes the conscious effort to achieve a consistent integration of beliefs. *Characterization* describes the achievement of harmony between belief and behavior. The observation—do as I say, not as I do—is an example of nonharmony. The observation—practice what you preach—is an example of a press toward harmony.

The Krathwohl et al. outline can be applied to content areas as well. For example, one could set both cognitive and affective outcomes regarding the metric systems. Affectively, pupils could be characterized by states of passivity (e.g., receiving and responding); by a state of organized effort (e.g., valuing); and by states of activism (e.g., organized and characteristic behavior). For example, persons who can demonstrate high achievement and mastery of the metric system may also use the English system of measurement in everyday life. There can be converts who cast their favorite recipes into metric equivalents. One convert was so committed to metrics as to observe that, "Give that person 2.54 centimeters and he'll take 1.609 kilometers."

GENERAL APPROACHES TO MEASUREMENT

Bloom et al. (1971) paid tribute to the work of Krathwohl, Bloom, and Masida (1964) as one source of help in preparation of affective outcome. Their own text is a resource in the application of the Krathwohl et al. procedures. These two sources are encountered frequently in the literature on education of the gifted and talented to guide practice in the preparation and evaluation of pupils' responses, written or in the form of interviews. Both have had major impacts on the design and evaluation of educational programs for gifted and talented pupils.

While the Bloom et al. and the Krathwohl et al. procedures enjoy a continuing status among educators, a nonverbal response approach has gained acceptance as well. This approach denotes affect, or attitude, as the person's behavior, or expressed willingness to behave. It recognizes that what persons declare may be different from their actual actions. For example, the acid test of an appreciation of historical evolution would be registering and completing an advanced course. Appreciation for good literature could be assessed by reference to books checked out of the school library. Commitment to social awareness of the needs of others could be inferred realistically by a volunteer experience as a citizen advocate for a developmentally disabled protege. The work of Webb, Campbell, Schwarta, and Sechrest (1966) popularized this approach among educators. Mager (1970) also demonstrated that valid inferences could be drawn from sources other than interviews or questionnaires.

Technically, this type of evaluation is termed nonreactive in that the pupil is neither questioned nor required to respond in pencil-paper fashion.

Reactive Approaches

Affective responses of gifted and talented pupils can be assessed by reactive measures such as interviews and questionnaires. The Krathwohl et al. dimension can be applied to evaluate the items selected for use. Moreover, congruence between intent and results can be obtained.

The Bloom et al. handbook suggests a variety of tactics for each dimension. The general types include: (1) personal interview, (2) open-ended questions, (3) closed-item questionnaires, (4) semantic differential techniques, and (5) projective techniques.

Interviews with able pupils can be both structured and unstructured. In the former, a fixed set of questions proceeds in a fixed sequence with little latitude for flexibility. By contrast, according to Bloom et al., the unstructured interview allows for more freedom to follow the leads provided by the questioning. In addition, this type of interview allows for real-life examples to emerge. For example, suppose one wanted feedback as to an inservice workshop concerning the need for individualized education for the gifted and talented. Sample questions might be: How much did you like the experience? Why? What did other persons think? What did you learn? Response can be left open ended or choices can be entered that reflect opinions.

The open-ended format consists of a series of statements to be completed in a free-association manner. For example, attitudes toward gifted and talented education could be assessed by questions such as: (1) If I had $100 I would _____, (2) If I had my way I _____, (3) My advice to teachers would _____, and (4) I would like to know _____. This approach, according to Bloom et al. has the advantages of both the structured interview and identifying common areas of concern and reaction.

The closed-item questionnaire is similar to the structured interview. Commercially available interest inventories are common examples. Respondents usually are asked to state preferences, choose from among alternatives, and select explanations for choices. Persons can respond in modes of true-false, rank order preferences, or agree-disagree. This approach has the advantage of obtaining numerical counts and quantitive scores. It does not tap the person's spontaneous contributions.

The semantic differential technique, as described by Bloom et al. (1971), is a series of paired adjectives that are equally spaced (usually five to seven pairs). For example, the person might be asked to rate characteristics of the gifted and talented as: good_ _ _ _ _bad, puny_ _ _ _ _strong, or sane_ _ _ _ _insane. Scores can be assigned to allow five points for the most positive trait checked to one point for the least positive trait marked. This procedure has the advantage of easy quantification. Reactions to courses or other activities can be assessed in a similar manner. For example, this course was: interesting-boring, organized-disorganized, or comprehensive-narrow.

The projective technique is the least understood. Its educational use serves to gain information relevant to educational matters.

The most frequent form of projective method, according to Bloom et al., is the story completion technique. A picture, perhaps on the order of those produced by the late Norman Rockwell, might be the stimulus. Sample questions might be: Who are the people? What has been happening? What will happen next? How will these problems be solved? Completing the ending of a story may be another common tactic. Responses such as: In my opinion, I'd . . ., I'm for . . ., and similar expressions are indications of attitude. The advantage of this approach is that a content activity such as theme writing can serve a dual purpose of cognitive and affective measurement.

In actual practice, Bloom et al. observed, the measurement of attitude will reflect a blend of tactics. The information needed will dictate the mix. In general terms, the newer the program, the more the open-ended, unstructured tactics will be favored. With experience, increased structure would be appropriate.

Nonreactive Approaches

As noted earlier, nonreactive assessment is the gathering of data through observation. This approach is indirect in that it does not involve direct questioning of individuals. But it can be as precise as reactive techniques.

Mager (1970) advocates the assessment of affective dimensions in order to identify sources of behavior. It is his thesis that affect influences cognitive achievement. In this context, the measurement of attitude acquires an operational urgency for program improvement.

In instances of nonperformance or indifference, Mager identified three explanations or situations that require observation of the pupil: (1) performance as punishing, (2) performance as of no consequence, and (3) nonperformance as rewarding. For example, completion of drill assignments may be followed by the allocation of similar tasks. Volunteering may be followed by the allotment of more tasks. In other instances, student products may be unrecognized. Papers may be uncorrected. Conversations may be one-sided monologues. Performance then becomes viewed by the child as having no meaning or value. Studies of creativity cited in other chapters certainly confirm this concept. Finally, gifted and talented pupils may learn that conflict, filibusters, debate, and other evasion is the most satisfying response pattern to adopt for themselves. In this sense, nonperformance becomes a reward; it allows them to escape.

Mager identified several little-noted sources in school environments that do affect pupil and teacher attitudes. These include instructional materials, space, school policies, and peers. For example, peers can provide social reinforcement and encouragement for efforts. A peer culture that is opposed to learning can be difficult to overcome.

Policies can be an influence. There may be no policy-based incentives for individualized curriculum. Lockstep mandates for the same learning by a predictable schedule can certainly be discouraging.

Materials may be restricted. They may be unsuitable for age groupings. They may be present but not accessible. Physical space may be cramped and with static furniture. Teacher or administrator behavior may be of the type that discourages pupil initiative. The Mager book illustrates additional sources that can affect attitudes toward learning. All invite solutions, especially for gifted and talented pupils.

The Webb et al. (1966) handbook affirms the Mager position. The system depends on the use of unobtrusive measures. The unobtrusive data are available already. Acknowledging similarity to the tactics of Sherlock Holmes, they cited examples from a mystery novel to illustrate the process and used examples from the evaluation literature to illustrate applications. For example, Dr. Watson was perplexed as to which building to buy for his medical practice. Upon the advice of Holmes, Watson did indeed make the best choice. It was elementary, of course, in that Holmes had noted which steps were worn the most. In another instance, the telltale clue was a walking stick left at the scene of the crime. Holmes identified the owner as left-handed, a former resident of India, and a person of wealth. The wood of the stick, the design of the handle, the worn grooves on the handhold, and the inlays all pointed to one person who had motive, opportunity, and means.

The use of unobtrusive measures, according to Webb et al. (1966), requires attention to two main types of data—erosion and accretion. These are forms of physical evidence that result from behavior. Erosion means the result of wear and tear, while accretion means accumulation. Erosion measures, for instance, can be wear and tear on vinyl floors in front of exhibits, or the wear on library books. Accretion measures could be drawn from sudden increases in sales or frequencies of modes of behavior, such as drinking or eating. They can be as humble as noseprints on a glass exhibit, or as complex as frequency of questions and inquiries. Respect, or valuing, of a minority group could be inferred by evidence of bilingual signs, ethnic foods in cafeterias, bilingual editorials in the school newspaper, and use of both languages. The content and targets of jokes can be another index toward valuing.

Webb et al. noted that observations could be cross-checked against one another and against records. For example, wear and tear on library books can be validated against frequencies of books checked out or of books requiring reshelving after in-library use.

SUMMARY

The sources cited in this section reflect four areas of common agreement as to the assessment of affective outcomes applicable to the gifted and talented:

1. Each of these systems is neutral as to values, attitudes, and beliefs. Decisions as to specific affective outcomes rest with program sponsors.
2. Measurements of attitude must respect confidentiality of information. Those tactics should not be used for entrapment. Honest responses should not be used against individuals. Unsigned responses can be employed to preserve anonymity.
3. Affective assessment is undertaken for program improvement. Otherwise, invasion of privacy could be possible. There should be a provable need to know behind every question.
4. Affective factors are not necessarily separate from cognitive outcomes.
5. Tactics should be used in conjunction for purposes of cross-validation.

It is reasonable to expect that almost every gifted and talented pupil's Individualized Education Program (IEP) would contain some goals or objectives that include affective outcomes. Bloom (1977) lists four categories of affective outcomes that could appear in IEPs for gifted and talented pupils. The first is labeled Subject-Related Affect. This alludes to the pupil's reaction to a particular school subject. The second category is School-Related Affect. In any given school year, the average student will study five to six subjects and encounter about 150 different tasks. Pupil experiences become generalized from particular attitudes toward the school, per se. Academic Self-Concept is the third category. This is an index of one's worth as a person and as a learner. The fourth category is Mental Health. It refers to a person's tolerance for stress and frustration; it is an internalized view of one's competence in dealing with the ups and downs of life.

We do not advocate either making schooling "easy" by the creation of artificial success or making it "tough" by building unrealistic and irrelevant hurdles. We favor tactics akin to the aptitude/treatment interaction and emphasis upon cocurricular activities. In large measure, we advocate challenge matched to ability to build symmetry between cognitive and affective outcomes.

Chapter 18

The Acts of Helping

Suppose you were a coach at Yourtowne High. Pat, a senior, has an outstanding record as a basic scholar and is an all-state first team basketball player. Pat calls you aside and says,

> Coach, I'm really knotted up. I don't know what to do. My parents have been pushing the full scholarship at State U. I thought I wanted that too. Now, Rose College has said they want me. It's a good college and I can prepare myself there for the ministry. My dad wants me to go for the pros. I'm in Dump City! Nobody seems to help.

What might be the exact words one could say to this student? What words might be a source of comfort for feelings and suggest resolution? Adults might respond with any one of the following statements. Each represents one of five clear-cut options open to the adult.

1. "Making choices is really tough, especially for a jock."
2. "You're saying you don't know what to do, and nobody knows what to do."
3. "You're feeling mixed up. You want one thing; your parents want another. Worst of all, nobody's helping you sort things out."
4. "You're feeling swamped and angry with yourself because you feel you should be able to sort things out. You really want to make the right decision."
5. "You're feeling angry with yourself because you feel you should be able to make the right decision. A good first step might be for us to list your career goals and how your choices might affect them. Then we can see how your decisions stack up against your values."

Twenty years of research is available to assist you in sorting out which of these responses is potentially the most helpful to the person.

Helping responses are not confined to any one counseling or guidance method. Research cited by Hansen, Stevic, and Warner (1977) shows that three attributes or skills characterize the helpful adult. This research is based on studies of persons who sought professional help.

By the 1960s it was observed that most persons were no better off, worse off, or improved after professional intervention. The 1960s, according to Hansen et al., were characterized by intensive study of the behavior of helpers whose clients improved as compared with those whose clients did not. It was found that no one school of helping was superior to another. Effectiveness, rather, was linked to three actions on the part of the helper:

1. Convincing the client that the person was important and worthy.
2. Showing that the client was understood by the helper.
3. Assisting the client to devise a plan to resolve difficult choices and alternatives.

It was found that helpers might have different scientific and professional knowledge about human personality but that these differences were not relevant so long as these three actions were accomplished. Now, review the five responses stated earlier and evaluate them according to presence of all three elements? How would you talk with Pat?

The 1970s were characterized by research and demonstration projects to design and test strategies to impart improved counseling skills to teachers and others in professional practice. Preferred procedures have factors in common: (1) their emphasis is on acts of helping, (2) they are supported by ample validation, and (3) they are designed for parents and teachers.

THE ART OF HELPING

The work of Carkhuff (1977) is an example of bringing precision into the practice of counseling. His associates use a four-part model to enable potential helpers or mentors to become skilled at actions of helping. These model parts are known as attending, responding, personalizing, and initiating. A mentor's attending and responding convinces the protege of their personal worth. The protege shows willingness to trust because of the perception of nonpossessive and nonjudgmental caring. Responding and personalizing serve, in turn, to convince clients that they are indeed understood by the counselor. This is an expression of empathy. Initiation is the devising of a plan of action for the protege that is natural because of trust and empathy.

That often may be done jointly by the protege (pupil or parent) and mentor (teacher of gifted and talented pupils or other educator). We share in the belief of the Carkhuff Institute staff that the skills of helping should be distributed widely rather than restricted and confined. Teachers of gifted and talented pupils especially need to employ those skills in their daily work.

The attending component enables the helper to focus attention on the client. Eye contact and client-oriented posture are significant indicators to persons being counseled that they are important. A teacher's sloppy and slouching demeanor may convey the opposite. Practice helps in verbatim recounting of a person's conversation. Then the helper "graduates" to the paraphrase of what a person says. Accuracy is the best single index of attending. Consequently, if we return to the coach's answers to Pat, responses one and two would be examples of attending, although the first is not really helpful. Response two is a paraphrase. It is helpful to the extent that the person is aware that the helper's attention is being given.

The responding component reaches toward the feeling behind the content of the message. Prospective helpers can pair off to practice this. One partner makes a statement. The other responds with a statement to the effect that, "You are feeling _____." For example, "I try to get my desk drawer stocked with clips. My children take them without asking." An appropriate response might be, "You are feeling frustrated."

Participants engage in activities to generate synonyms to increase their affective inventory. This is the essence of empathy. People will provide very direct feedback as to accuracy of interpretation. In this sense, response three was an example of responding to the person's feelings.

The personalizing component is addressed to the client's stated content, apparent feelings, and the real, current situation. For example, one partner in training might say, "I was accepted for a Summer Institute on Critical Thinking, but the principal of the school where I work says that all teachers must report early for school orientation. I don't think I can do that." The partner responds with a message that follows a "script" of "You're feeling (supply feeling) because (supply situation). You are in a bind and pulled two ways at once. It is difficult to choose between the demands of the job and your interest in helping students. You wish the principal were more helpful." It is not necessary to say "because" so long as the situation is addressed. In this light, response four is an example of personalizing. It is further evidence to the client that the person is being attended to, experiencing empathy, and can identify the source, or situation, of difficulty.

Initiation is the fourth and final component. It offers direction toward a way out. Response five is an example. Its script, or components, are, "You're feeling (emotion) because of (situation) and a first step might be (define action)." Response five has all these elements. Subsequent conversations would be directed toward initiation.

The most common difficulties in helping are (a) how to use past experience to help another and (b) readiness. According to Carkhuff and the other sources in this chapter, the most deadly response can be, "I know exactly how you feel; the same thing happened to me when I was your age." The message usually is decoded by the person as, "I'm not important. Just my luck; everybody has this problem. It didn't get them down; I'm a failure." The helper can scan personal experience to retrieve the feeling to match the person's content. This is the most appropriate use of experience. Readiness describes the person's receptivity to initiation. Carkhuff's extensive research demonstrates that when initiation is offered prior to personalizing, advice will be rejected. Pupils and parents are accused of playing games. This may mean advice was advanced without consideration of the feelings provoked by a situation.

THE TACTICS OF EFFECTIVENESS

In the course of human relationships, there will be blocks to initiation (Carkhuff, 1977). These blocks are the frustration or nonfulfillment of needs. Education, for able pupils, will involve initiation.

The extensive research and demonstration projects of Gordon (1970) can provide helpful guidance. His models, called Parent Effectiveness Training (PET) and Teacher Effectiveness Training (TET) are illustrated in what follows.

Active listening and personalization are components of both PET and TET. If one were to become a participant (usually a course of eight to ten weeks of two- to three-hour sessions), a teacher would experience a curriculum of: methods of influence and relating; the concept of needs, skills in active listening (e.g., similar to responding and personalizing), problem ownership, and tactics of effectiveness in dealing with problem ownership.

There are four different tactics of influence and of relationships, according to Gordon. One is I Win/You Lose. This pattern preserves the physical health and safety of a person, but it also is the tactic of power, dominance, and authoritarianism. One person in the relationship experiences fulfillment of needs and the other must subordinate needs.

The I Lose/You Win pattern, on the other hand, is one of permissiveness (in the destructive sense), overprotection, and indulgence. Need fulfillment is reversed from the I Win pattern.

A third pattern is the I Lose/You Lose. This actually is the typical outcome of either of the first two patterns.

The pattern of greatest effectiveness is I Win/You Win. Gordon and his followers termed this the No Lose Method (NLM). The limits of each of these tactics would be explored in a course in terms of building trust and helpfulness in relationships. Only a short overview is feasible here.

The discussion of needs parallels Maslow's (1962) framework: (1) physical comfort, safety, and security; (2) social caring; (3) educational skills and knowledges; (4) achievement recognition; and (5) self-actualization. The first need provides the physical strength and psychological security for subsequent development. It is the kind of protection appropriate for the early years of life. Social caring grows as the basic needs of security and comfort are met.

Skills and knowledges, in turn, occur in the context of caring. Recognition and achievement are the outcomes of caring as well as arising from both internal and external sources. The outcome can be self-actualization. This attribute (frequently encountered in the literature on gifted and talented persons as both a goal and as an attribute of the population) describes an individual who is confident about control of the environment and about personal potency. Potency in this context is the absence of fear and the possession of self-esteem.

The period of later childhood and adolescence sees the fading need for external permissions and the acquisition of internal potency. (For gifted learners, the fading will be sooner and conflict may come earlier due to the adult's unwillingness to respond to the learner's precocious potency.) At this juncture, the linkage between potency, self-actualization, and the No Lose Method would be established.

Subsequent sessions would center upon active listening and its practice. Participants need experience under guidance to gain confidence. Difficulties are treated with empathy by the group facilitator.

The remaining sessions would be devoted to problem ownership and tactics of effectiveness. Active listening reveals three possible types of problems in a relationship. (Teaching is viewed as a relationship just as marriage or raising children are considered relationships.) The three problem types are: *I* (parent or teacher) own the problem, *You* (pupil, child) own the problem, and *the relationship* owns the problem. Problems in a relationship arise when needs are not fulfilled.

The *I own the problem,* according to Gordon (1970), occurs when the teacher's or parent's needs are not being fulfilled but the other person's needs are fulfilled. For example, noise may be fine for the child and distracting to the adult. Smoking by another person in a crowded room is another example.

After reaching an understanding of how problems have their origins, the course would move on to an analysis of the tactics of working with problems. The I-message would be introduced. The I-message has the intent of sending my perceptions without a personal attack. For example, "You are late for class, *again.* Don't you have any respect for the rest of the class?" is a You-message, opposite to an I-message. You-messages label the recipient and are viewed defensively. The I-message has three parts: (1) a nonjudgmental, nonblaming description of unacceptable behavior; (2) a demonstration of the tangible effects on me, and (3) a statement of personal feelings. For example, "When a student comes to class after the bell, I am interrupted in starting assignments. It makes me upset to have to repeat directions all over again." The student can understand a rational basis for expectations. There is guidance. This use of I-messages can trigger thought about a preventative plan.

The *you-own-the-problem* pattern derives from nonfulfillment of the other's needs. The parent or teacher may not have direct control, or the means, to redress the situation that causes discomfort. For example, homework, classroom assignments, lack of friends, and age requirements for driving are beyond direct remediation. (This situation can be especially applicable when communication among the parent, the regular class teacher, and the educational consultant have broken down. Assignments can really pile up.)

Such a situation calls for the use of active listening. The situation of Pat and the basketball coach illustrates problem ownership. It was the young person's problem. The coach was helpful in active listening.

Concluding sessions would be devoted to the topic of *problem ownership,* a matter that usually concerns unmet needs of both participants. Common examples are managing time, completing assignments, and privileges. I-messages and active listening are necessary for eventual initiation.

Gordon (1970) observed that there are helpful attitudes that facilitate reduction of needs conflict. These attitudes would be pertinent to teachers of gifted and talented pupils.

The most helpful attitude is commitment to I-messages and active listening. Belief in and respect for the other person's potency is essential. There also needs to be the belief that solutions can be found and that the ideas of others can be of genuine value. Doubts and hesitancy must be acknowledged openly. Finally, there should be overt recognition that all solutions are not final and can be renegotiated.

Gordon detailed a six-step procedure for problem solving. These steps need to be rehearsed.

1. Locate unmet needs; the outcome, through sending and receiving of I-messages, is to identify the needs of all persons involved and their tangible effects.
2. Brainstorm possible solutions, no matter how foolish and remote.
3. Weigh alternatives and determine if they account for all needs.
4. Agree upon solutions.
5. Manage or implement the solutions.

6. Provide a thoughtful evaluation of the plan and the possibility for revision.

Consider, as a teacher in Yourtowne Middle School, not being able to locate your felt markers of various colors and hues. You recall that they were loaned to Elizabeth, a basic scholar, so a science project could be completed. An hour later you find Elizabeth in the library cheerfully reading a novel. In the display case nearby you see a "blue ribbon," multicolored, scientific exhibit, obviously prepared with the help of your felt markers. There is a feeling of happiness for Elizabeth, but also the irritation about the pens.

It may be time to pass, yet the pens are needed. Elizabeth's needs are met; the project has been completed. Your needs are not met. The relationship is impaired because the process of sharing was not rewarding.

A helping conversation between the teacher and Elizabeth could approximate the following:

T. I can't find my pens and I need them for my work. That really irritates me because I want them right now.

E. I left them in the science lab. I was going to return them but then I remembered that I had to read this book before I recorded it for Don. (Don is a visually impaired student.)

T. Having a lot of things to do can be tough. Sometimes things get lost in the shuffle.

E. That's right. You really understand. I'm really sorry. I hope it won't happen again.

T. I still have a problem in that when I lend things, I am pleased when they're returned.

E. What can I do? I said I was sorry!

T. You're feeling accused and I seem to be blaming you. I believe we can find some answers so we'll both be satisfied.

E. So what do I have to sign?

T. That would be one idea. You're feeling locked into a fixed solution. We can negotiate anything. I'm willing to listen.

E. Well, O.K.! People don't often ask for my ideas. Now, let's see
. . .

This account was intended to illustrate the tactics of the I-message and active listening as the prelude to initiation. It can end in a variety of ways of mutual benefit. The willingness of the teacher to solve the problem, however, will be the most important affective lesson for the pupil, a lesson that can generalize beyond the immediate situation.

CONGRUENT COMMUNICATIONS

The principles and practices of Ginott (1972) offer practical guidance that complements Carkhuff (1977) and Gordon (1970). These tactics also complement the aims and goals of confluent education for able students. Ginott's writings have been influential because the style is clear and the situations common to teachers, parents, and pupils.

Ginott called his system of principles and practices Congruent Communications, which means harmony among one's ideals, words, and deeds. For example, if one's goal is confluent education, then the words and deeds of PET are congruent.

Congruent communications as a system works best when the relationship is free of resentments and when channels of understanding (e.g., empathy) are open. Ginott's work complements Carkhuff and Gordon in its emphasis upon active listening and upon the distinction between the destructive You-message and the helpful I-message. His writing is filled with varied examples of I-messages as well as examples of active listening to "decode" the messages of children and adolescents.

Congruent communications should be understood as preventive in nature. Unlike the two other systems, which assume training under supervision, congruent communications was advanced as a book to be read and applied without mediation. However, the text is sufficiently clear that one could organize a helpful training session based on it. Its content for confluent education could be structured around sessions or topics devoted to: (1) Teachers at Their Best and Worst, (2) Congruent Communications, (3) Discipline and Praise, (4) Homework and Motivation, (5) Defusing Clashes, and (6) Touching Life in the Classroom. The first three sessions might parallel Carkhuff's responding and personality.

Ginott's notion was that praise had perils. He advocated the use of words directed toward effort and accomplishment rather than labels. For example, "You're a strong boy" is better than no comment but even better yet is, "The desk was large. You moved it across the room. I am so pleased." The child will internalize the message "good and strong."

The I-message was endorsed for conflict situations. Ginott advocated, for conflict situations, expressions that instructed as to the what and what. For example, "Don't scribble on the wall," only informs the child what not to do. Consider the alternative of: "Crayons are for paper, crayons are not for walls. Here is paper. Color on the paper."

Homework can be touchy. Ginott viewed homework as a joint problem for the teacher and pupil. the parental role is to respond with sympathetic active listening and to arrange for "suitable time and place for homework." Teachers may perceive homework as the student's problem (and hence the parent's problem) rather than the school's problem. Ginott was specific in his attitude that teachers should view completion of homework as an educational responsibility and one that is primarily the shared property of teacher and pupil.

Motivation, according to Ginott, is the development of inner responsibility and self-esteem. For example, there may be many helpful ways of saying yes. To say yes, is information. However, to say, "You can decide that for yourself. That's your choice," conveys potency. It is assumed that the request is within the child's potential and approved by the adult.

Reassurance has its limits as a builder of motivation and self-esteem. To tell a person that a test is easy may be meant to comfort. However, if the test is failed, the internal message can be, "I flunked an easy task. I'm dumb!" If the test is passed, the message is that there is no genuine accomplishment.

Defusing clashes and developing constructive solutions centers upon channeling (not suppressing) emotional reactions. Touching life in the class offers models of behavior for teachers gleaned from the recollections of students and from studies of effective educators. The thrust of this latter dimension is to offer positive examples of congruence between one's actions and one's intentions. For example, learning to respond calmly to anger teaches lessons to pupils about self-control. The literature on modeling (Bandura, 1971) is closely allied, so far as examples are concerned, to the procedures recommended by Ginott. In that sense congruent communications is a system for preventing and correcting conflict at the same time that it is a set of principles and practices appropriate for adoption as a communication style for all purposes and seasons.

ACQUIRING SKILLS

Reactions by teachers and other educators to any of the three systems (e.g., Art of Helping, Effectiveness Training, and Congruent Communications) will certainly vary. Persons do not reject these systems as much as they resist receiving, according to Carkhuff (1977), Ginott (1972), and Gordon (1970).

One obvious factor is that an adult may have a mentoring or helping relationship that developed bit by bit over time, rather than one that resulted from systematic preparation. Also, it may work quite well. In this instance, change would not be warranted.

In other cases a person may wish to change but want to select from alternative approaches akin to the Aptitude Treatment Interaction model. Such a person probably would not attain a level of characterization. This person's approach would be characterized as eclectic.

According to Hansen et al. (1977), an eclectic orientation is characterized by a purposeful examination of various theories, systems, and beliefs from which valid and tenable ideas and procedures are extracted. The result is the formation of a unified, personalized, and validated approach. The eclectic person is a distinct contrast to the syncretic person who simply "borrows" ideas from various sources without regard to either their origins or evaluating their validity. Most teachers as helpers and mentors would be eclectic in orientation unless they had specific training in and had adopted a particular counseling system.

Resistance also can arise out of lack of readiness in both pupil and adult. Pupils, especially gifted and talented ones, may experience an initial shock in having their views respected. Adults may not trust their own abilities to use helping skills. Expectations may be too high. Everything will not be beautiful all the time for all parties. There are acceptable ranges and rates of using the I-message, active listening, and problem ownership. Initial trials should be viewed as just that—initial trials, not as perfection.

The initial difficulties tend to be in the areas of I-messages or active listening skills. Practice and feedback are helpful. Competent facilitators will provide psychologically safe opportunities. Practice followed by feedback will enable the participants to recognize their levels of effectiveness.

The most distressing course of resistance in our opinion arises over the zeal of inservice sponsors. In their enthusiasm for a helping system, they attempt to dominate and indoctrinate participants. The discrepancy between the ideals of the system and these tactics of force, in themselves, teach lessons. The tactics of needs assessment and of collaborative innovation would be more appropriate as a context for introduction.

A common reservation centers on a reluctance to be either the only one or the first one to espouse a helping role. The collective experience of Carkhuff (1977), Ginott (1972), and Gordon (1970) can be reassuring.

SUMMARY

The theme of this chapter is that *helping is something you do;* it is not a passive state of mind or simply positive empathy. Gifted and talented pupils, because of discrepancies in their own development, because of variances of development with their age peers, and because of the many opportunities and choices they face, have their share and more of difficult decisions to make and problems of self-understanding to resolve. Several established approaches to forming helping relationships are available to teachers. Any can be adapted readily to the needs of very able students.

Chapter 19

Values Education

UNDERSTANDING THE CONTEXT OF VALUES EDUCATION

Commentaries about the decorum of pupils abound. Williams (1979) cited two examples. The first:

> The children now love luxury; they show disrespect for their elders, and love chatter in place of exercise. Children are now tyrants, not the servants, of their households. They no longer rise when their elders enter the room. They contradict their parents, chatter before company, gobble up dainties at the table, cross their legs, and tyranize their teachers.

and the second:

> The lamentable extent of dishonesty, fraud, and other wickedness among our boys and girls shocks the nation.

Williams (1979, p. 387) attributed the first to Socrates circa 400 B.C. and the second to a Massachusetts newspaper circa 1830. He also noted that while discipline problems were not new, increasing years had not lessened their significance. Personal and social responsibility are appropriate outcomes to expect from sound education. Should gifted and talented pupils be expected to achieve higher personally and socially responsibility levels than others is a pertinent question.

Thomas and Richards (1979) reviewed the literature on values education. They concluded that: (1) most institutions of society have retreated from the teaching of choices about conduct, (2) education about values emphasizes social norms and neglects individual responsibility, (3) documents such as the Mayflower Compact, the Declaration of Independence, and the U.S. Constitution are resources for the content of individual choice, and (4) a pluralistic society can prize a common set of values.

They proposed a set of common values about respect, rights, and responsibilities: (1) an individual's right to dignity and worth, (2) respect for property and rights, (3) the right to learn and to achievement, (4) the right to personal liberties, (5) responsibility for one's own actions, (6) democratic societies based on laws, (7) problems solved through reason and orderly processes, (8) tolerance for beliefs of others, (9) respect for each individual's beliefs, and (10) individual rights to pursue an occupation and personal satisfaction based on personal effort. These common values can be understood as concrete outcomes for highly able pupils as well.

Thomas and Richards consider parent and teacher involvement as critical. Initial negotiations, in our judgment, begin quite a little earlier with able children. Parental questions center upon:

(1) Who shares the responsibilities for teaching values?
(2) Who shares the responsibilities for the behavior of students?
(3) What relationships should exist between values and behavior?
(4) What are appropriate and inappropriate strategies for teaching values and for altering behavior?
(5) What teaching competencies are necessary?
(6) How can levels of moral development be related to curriculum?
(7) How can conflicting values be handled within the schools?
(8) What process can be used to obtain community endorsement of values education?

The design of values education for gifted and talented pupils flows from decisions and choices regarding its goals, content, and method. Education for values is highly regarded and is prized as an outcome for exceptional pupils. The challenge is to implement a process of values education that respects the individual's freedom of belief as well as fosters respect for positive social processes.

GOALS OF VALUES EDUCATION

Kohlberg (1975) cites the theme of justice as the universal subject for American education. He identified in part ten commonly held universal moral values: (1) punishment, (2) property, (3) affection, (4) authority, (5) law, (6) life, (7) liberty, (8) justice, (9) truth, and (10) sex. It will be recalled from earlier units that justice is a pertinent concern of able adolescents.

A person behaves in accordance with the *what* one finds valuable and with the *why* of one's belief. Kohlberg isolated justice as the universal theme for values. First, there may be relative rather than absolute choices regarding these ten issues, with the exception of justice. Second, it is not clear that schools have the mandate to engage in instruction in all ten areas with the exception of justice. Third, schools do have a mandate to teach, inform, and create awareness of the individual rights and social responsibilities protected by the Constitution and the Bill of Rights. Fourth, there is sufficient understanding about the developmental aspects of justice that (a) balances individual rights and responsibilities, (b) balances majority rule and protection of minorities, and (c) postulates the possibility of change to provide a framework from which to regulate one's own behavior.

Values education for all gifted and talented pupils is not inconsistent with the pursuit of the ideals and ideas of social justice. Simon and deSherbinin (1975) found that values education produces the following outcomes:

1. People become more purposeful when they know what they want. With the knowledge of what goals are valued, they don't fritter away time.
2. People become more productive. An outcome of values education enables one to devise a plan of action and to implement one's plan. The results produce personal, material, and social contributions.
3. People learn to use thinking skills fully. People are found to be less vulnerable to fads and peer group pressures. They are more likely to know the values of substance.
4. People experience better relationships with others. People who know what they want and follow up on commitments are valued by others. They are sought after to resolve conflicts because they are willing to give of themselves to others.

THE CONTENT OF VALUES EDUCATION

Values education typically is lodged within curricular subject matter and is made operational in the school's "rules" of discipline (Christenson, 1977). Subject matter content is the formal source of values education, particularly for personal guidance. The content exalts self-understanding, knowing the kind of person one wants to become, and understanding one's own and others' behavior. Desirable personal values couched in curriculum content include: (1) applying self-discipline, (2) doing one's work well, (3) using honorable means to achieve ends, (4) having the ability to admit mistakes, (5) treating another as one would want to be treated, and (6) assuring that the guarantees of the Bill of Rights are applied to those in agreement with us as well as to those with whom we disagree.

Christenson presses for content to include recognition of inconspicuous, unsung people who show admirable qualities and live worthwhile lives. He cites these examples:

- The handicapped person who, despite the temptation to find excuses for not doing this or that, struggles against heavy odds and does something anyway.

- Parents who sacrifice their time and energy to provide their children with encouragement and training to make the most of life.

- Adults who sacrifice some personal dreams to welcome an infirmed parent in their own home.

- Persons in comfortable occupations, in comfortable surroundings, and near their friends who depart these securities to join VISTA, the Peace Corps, ACTION, and similar ventures of service to others.

- The single parent living in extreme poverty who raises several responsible, honest, and compassionate children.

Simon and deSherbinin (1975) observed that values education need not be confined to any one content area. Examples applicable to gifted and talented pupils could include: (1) time set aside within a content course, (2) an elective course titled Clarifying Personal Choices, (3) career education and drug education as information and as choices, (4) family relationships, and (5) religious education.

Too often, Hodgkinson (1976) observed, teachers are expected to discharge values education roles without either the opportunity to examine their own values or to acquire helpful preparation. The outcome can be that teachers think they are expected to be either instruments of indoctrination or paragons of absolute values neutrality. It seemed reasonable that values education for teachers should precede their values education of pupils.

Hodgkinson suggests a way to prepare teachers to conduct values education. There is every reason to support the practice of informing able learners about these components. The first component examines the concept of value. A value may be viewed as "good" or "right" or both. A "good" value ordinarily has strong affective (emotional) loadings. A "right" value has legalistic or ethical reference points. Honoring one's parents illustrates the former. Respecting property is an example of the latter. Taking care of family belongings obviously is both "good" and "right."

The second component looks into the factual values aspects of educational issues of interest to prospective teachers. The outcome of this component is that prospective teachers understand: (1) the factual and valuation base for their positions, (2) how to distinguish the course of their beliefs as good vs. right or some combination, and (3) their level of commitment.

The third component is an interdisciplinary reading program drawn from psychology, sociology, anthropology, and philosophy. The final component is review and practice in a variety of tactics of values education.

TACTICS OF VALUES EDUCATION

A variety of options are open to teachers. An obvious one is to take a neutral hands-off posture. This escape hatch declares all values relative to time, place, and situation. Consequently, no person has the right to consider any values.

A second option is to imprint various forms of indoctrination or inculcation. The adult assertively pursues a declared set of the "right" values. Pupils are expected to comprehend the *what* of beliefs, and the *why* is bypassed.

A third tactic is modeling. The adult image is a living, daily ideal. The difficulty of this otherwise helpful approach is that many situations confronted by students cannot be modeled.

Values education of lasting influence involves conscious investigation by gifted students. These are the appropriate tactics of confluent education. Two program alternatives that have their advocates plus research validation and wide endorsement will be presented next. One is the Cognitive Development Approach (CDA) and the other is the Values Clarification Approach (VCA). Their common roots are in the work of the American philosopher and psychologist John Dewey. Both emphasize the process of valuing as much as content of values. Each offers several alternatives, so far as instructional tactics are concerned.

The Cognitive Development Approach

The Cognitive Development Approach builds on the work of Kohlberg (1975). It is rooted in the six stages of moral development.

The teacher is the instrument of the process. The teacher's thrust is to assist pupils in their reasoning about situations in which they must make choices. The intended outcome is the reasoning of the postconventional level (e.g., stages five and six will be internalized). We cannot quote research on the point, but it is our impression that gifted and talented pupils are capable of earlier attainment of this level and of more consistency in maintaining it.

Research is persuasive that judgment influences moral behavior. The CDA emphasizes reasoning as to the *why* of belief. For example, at preconventional levels, life is valued as personal power or possession and for its self-satisfaction of needs. At conventional levels, life is valued for relationships with others and their esteem as well as in terms of laws. At the postconventional level, life is valued for its inherent worth aside from other considerations.

The teacher's role, according to Kohlberg, is: (1) to promote change in the way the gifted and talented pupil is reasoning, not necessarily in the content of belief; (2) to foster movement of students to their own next stage, not the convergence on a common pattern; (3) to bear in mind that the teacher's opinion is one of many authorities, not the sole authority, and (4) to convey that some judgments (e.g., reasoning) are more adequate than others. This means the students formulate opinions that are most adequate for their positions and evaluate the positions of others.

The content of belief as cited previously would be the theme of reasoning for postconventional levels of justice. However, the teacher's tactics, according to Kohlberg, should expose students to situations posing problems and contradictions at their present stages, to the next higher stage, and to dialogue and comparison of conflicting views. The particular relevance for this with gifted and talented pupils must be self-evident.

In one study (Kohlberg, 1975), gifted students at junior and senior high school levels were randomly assigned to CDA and non-CDA treatments. These students were found to be operating at three different stages. In the course of discussions the pupils used different reasoning to justify their positions. The teacher always supported the highest stage, for instance, stage three rather than stage two. As a student moved to stage three, stage four views would be supported. After one semester the experimental group showed significant gains while the contrast sample showed no improvement.

A project in a prison using a stage five social contract process between guards and inmates was cited. Rules were developed and administered jointly. This work has been extended to mutual negotiation among teachers, pupils, and administrators. The discussion was in the spirit of the helping relationship of nonjudgmental reflecting of content and feelings. Gifted and talented pupils can understand Kohlberg's findings (if teachers explain them) and often can test themselves as to how their behavior matches levels.

The CDA approach also prizes commitment. For example, it was reported in one project that as an outgrowth of discussions, students investigated pricing in low and middle income neighborhoods. They found a significant economic disadvantage to low income families. They prepared a buyer's guide, filed complaints with the legal assistance office, and wrote letters of complaint.

Values Clarification Approach

The Values Clarification Approach (VCA) is ascribed to Simon and his associates. Its advocates, Kirschanbaum, Harmin, Howe, and Simon (1977) and Simon, Howe, and Kirschanbaum (1972) describe it as a three-component system.

The VCA starts (1) with the premise that valuing is a process of understanding what goals or ideals one prizes, and (2) advocates choosing from alternatives to fulfill one's goals and ideals, and (3) calls for action upon one's selections. According to Kirschanbaum et al., these components involve thinking as referenced to the cognitive behaviors of Bloom (1977), divergent thinking as per Guilford (1977), and the moral reasoning of Kohlberg (1971). They acknowledge the work of Gordon (1970) regarding skills of empathetic, active listening. They emphasize that three components—prizing, choosing, and action—are necessary for a complete VCA procedure.

The VCA involves seven steps to complete the cycle. The steps are applicable to most choices in one's life. Prizing covers two activities that enable pupils to (1) identify their goals and ideals and (2) to publicly affirm these. Choosing involves three activities that enable students to (1) consider alternatives to implement their prized beliefs, (2) assess the consequences of alternatives, and (3) select alternatives freely and without pressure. Acting requires two activities that enable the exceptional pupil to (1) design a personal action agenda and (2) carry out a plan.

Simon et al. (1972) list 79 different activities cued to these seven steps. In addition to activities categorized as prizing, choosing, or acting, there are two other forms of activity. One is used to identify gifted students' interests and learning style preferences. The second is used by pupils to evaluate their learnings.

The VCA is carried out by discussions that center on semistructured activities. The teacher serves as a consultant to the group in the *PET* (Parent Effectiveness Training) sense. To assess the student interests, the "I Wonder" style of open-ended questions is employed, such as "I wonder about," "I wonder why," and "I wonder when."

Pupils identify topics and share them with the group. (Students are allowed to pass up commenting and never are publicly shamed for nonparticipation.) Contributions can be the basis for guided independent study or for group projects. Prizing activities might include the coat of arms. This activity encourages the person to divide a sheet of paper into four to six parts. Each part would be descriptive of the pupil. Discussion of these attributes enables the student to identify goals and attributes. Sharing with the group allows for public affirmation. Choosing could be stimulated by New Year's resolutions.

This activity allows pupils to identify resolutions appropriate for their own goals.

A format for the transformation of resolutions would include: (1) stating the topic (e.g., choosing an occupation), (2) stating goals (be successful, help others, have a family, make money), (3) stating alternatives (training, preparation), (4) considering consequences (expenses, pursuit of goals, personal aptitudes), and (5) choosing from alternatives in light of one's goals. Action could include the telegram, in which the pupil formulates a communication to inform others of specific plans. The action grid is another tactic that arrays steps and strength of interest (e.g., I would, I might, I wouldn't). Checking the cells orients pupils to think in priorities. Finally, the "I learned" statements (see Enrichment at end of this chapter) enable pupils to consider outcomes. This activity can be in the form of a progress journal.

The VCA is criticized by some for being either neutral or wishy-washy about values. Kirschanbaum et al. (1977) believe that this charge is unfair, based on an inaccurate perception. They cited the following as the belief and affective base of the VCA as valuing: (1) thinking critically is better than thinking impulsively, (2) considering consequences is better than acting thoughtlessly, and (3) choosing freely is better than a passive yielding to peer pressure. Furthermore, they declare that VCA's (1) no-lose methods (in the PET sense) are better than domination, (2) divergent thinking is better than imposed dogma or packaged solutions, (3) personal autonomy is better than imposition, and (4) reasoning encourages the sense of justice.

The VCA approach distresses some thoughtful persons because it appears neutral in its guidance. For example, a pupil with an IQ of 145 might select a career in automobile mechanics. Some persons might feel that guidance should be directive, moving such gifted persons toward college. Another objection is that the VCA has no fixed position about substance abuse, and about sexuality. Some believe that there should be firm direction on these matters.

The research and evaluation literature is clear. Persons who know what they want out of life and have defined their goals and strategies will not engage in distractions. Moralizing heightens curiosity to experiment.

The VCA, like any other educational program, does succeed best when parents and gifted pupils have been informed and involved and consent freely. To impose it is to violate its spirit.

SUMMARY

There are many tactics to influence the values and beliefs and related behaviors of the young. Most center on indoctrination of the conventional.

There is increasing recognition and sensitivity, though, to the ineffectiveness of indoctrination, especially with gifted and talented children and youth. Rather, there is the need for human beings to understand the why as well as the what about advocacy of principles and rules for conducting personal and social relationships. Values education serves to supply the why as well as the what.

Values education, like other educational practices, suffers from stereotypes. It often is misunderstood as being without values and is perceived as a permissive endorsement of "anything goes since all values are relative." Values education, by contrast, prizes postconventional standards. Its research shows, too, that such standards resist simplistic indoctrination. Moreover, it recognizes that such standards are not acquired full blown. There is the realization that these standards evolve and develop in a manner similar to cognitive behavior.

One approach to values education is through cognitive development. Its emphasis is upon the reasoning (preconventional, conventional, postconventional) for behaviors/choices. It also prizes the tactic of social contracting as a method for human relationships.

Another approach is known as values clarification. It prizes activities of understanding one's own goals and values, of selecting appropriate and honorable means and actions. It is characterized by targeting pupil attention to each of these dimensions. Its outcome is toward action to fulfill one's goals.

The chapter has highlighted alternatives for consideration by teachers and parents in establishing relationships of nurture, helping, and mentoring for values development among highly able pupils. This chapter was written in the belief that the tactics are essentially complementary and represent resources for communication and interactions appropriate for the nurture of able students.

UNIT ENRICHMENT
Understanding the Confluence of Education

1. Prepare a poster that depicts the educational intentions of confluence. Make use of the idea of two rivers joining/flowing into one. What elements have you placed in each stream? What is in the newly formed stream? In this as in all other points in this section, share with others your results, opinions, findings, etc.

2. Prepare a musical review to illustrate confluence. Select six recordings from your preferred music. Make a tape that would inform persons about confluent education. Given the idea of two streams producing a third stream, what have you selected for each of the three streams?

Preparing and Using Affective Outcomes

3. Cast a quiz show. Write role descriptions for receiving, responding, valuing, organizing, and characterizing. Describe their voices, their physical attributes, their dress, their manner of speech. Suppose you were to devise a variation of "What's My Line." Write a script that would give clues to the individuals' identities.

4. Consider your reactions to the topic of SuperKids. (If possible, locate the original article in the January 1979 issue of Psychology Today.) List your reactions as to the continuum of receiving through characterization with respect to learning more about the topic. Attempt to identify the frequencies of responses and to account for reasons.

5. Consider some topic of personal interest. Devise a 15-item survey to assess evidence of interest ranging from receiving through characterization. Try out your survey.

The Acts of Helping

6. Consider the tactic of a learning center. Prepare a list of specifications for three learning centers to inform parents about the Art of Helping, Parent Effectiveness Training, and Congruent Communications. How would you stock your proposed centers? What points would you emphasize? How would you evaluate the outcomes of your centers?

7. Find a partner. Find an issue about which you both have some disagreement. First, carry on a usual conversation. Second, carry out passive listening of repeating your partner's exact words before you reply. Your partner must do the same. Third, attempt active listening. Do you and your partner notice any differences under the three conditions?

8. Develop a feelings inventory. Consider these words: love, angry, sadness, helpless, satisfied, pleased, depressed, and happy. Within 15 minutes, generate as many synonyms as you can for each word. Which words have the most synonyms? Which words were the most difficult? The least difficult? What conclusions do you draw from these differences? What steps could you take? How could your listing be helpful in active listening?

Values Education

9. Simon et al. (1972, p. 163) recommended "I learned" statements as a means of evaluation. Considering this unit as a whole, complete the following activity. As a result of reading a unit about Confluent Education:

    a. I learned that I:
    b. I realized that I:
    c. I relearned that I:

d. I noticed that I:

e. I discovered that I:

f. I'm surprised that I:

g. I was pleased that I:

h. I was amazed that I:

i. I was displeased that I:

j. I would like to add that I:

10. As you read over your responses, isolate one common theme. In 25 words describe the Key Idea that summarizes your responses.

11. Identify three concrete steps you take to implement your Key Ideas.

Epilogue

An epilogue, technically, is an appendage to a completed play or other literary work. It often is spoken by one of the actors who, in the process, may step somewhat out of character to convey thoughts the author wishes to leave with the audience or readers.

This epilogue has some qualities of a reverse Preface. It is intended as a communication between the reader and the authors, who wish to more than simply summarize the highlights of the book. We felt strongly that we should reaffirm our position that the nation's teachers have the primary role if the basic principles of American citizenship are to meaningfully touch the lives of gifted learners. Finally, we thought it would be helpful to identify promising avenues for continued efforts.

We hope that the use of Prototypes, Exhibits, and Enrichment Activities proves helpful. We welcome the sharing of ideas and examples from our readers.

What Has Been Accomplished

- We believe we have accomplished our main purposes, which were to provide educationally relevant information and guidance and to create bridges between and among educators, parents, exceptional students, and concerned citizens.

- The chapters provide documentation and examples to confirm and encourage the central role of the teacher. The book affords a concrete and helpful blueprint for the process and practices of mentoring.

- We call upon a wide and varied array of background material. We use pertinent guidance and information from the popular media and the technical journals; we draw from sources internal and external to the

329

field of education of gifted and talented learners. Our willingness to do this, we hope, will encourage readers to be alert to unexpected sources regardless of their labels or packages. We believe that this practice further encourages the widest possible sharing and collaboration.

• We have not been unalterably committed to any specific approach. The reader is offered alternatives. There are different ways to achieve goals of worth and merit. The presentation of alternatives represents and reflects our confidence in the abilities of teachers to select for themselves. We have attempted, throughout, to affirm the teacher's right to exercise professional competence on behalf of individual learners. We believe that constraints based upon distrust of teacher sensitivity and skill do not fit the realities of today.

• While we prize the central role of teachers, the book is intended to promote collaboration. There is sufficient rationale and there are enough examples to document the positive advantages for gifted pupils of a shared partnership among the home, the school, and the community.

• No book ever is complete when the subject matter involves human beings. However, we believe that the content we selected demonstrates that there is sufficient information to launch and maintain instruction of high quality. We hope, too, that the material will generate a sense of excitement and purpose to help motivate readers to pursue lifelong learning as committed mentors of gifted and talented learners. If some readers do that, then our work has indeed been effective.

• As a culminating activity, how would you write this section if you were in our position? What key ideas would you select for emphasis? What would be your recommendations for improving the text as to purposes, content, and presentation modes? List your recommendations in the form of a memorandum. Then send your memo to us.

IMMEDIATE PRIORITIES

We hope this text has generated a sense of confidence that will encourage educators to act upon its information and suggestions. We suggest certain priorities for immediate consideration by teachers, building principals, parents, and other allies. We believe that there are generic considerations and that thoughtful people will find solutions appropriate for the circumstances of implementation.

- We recommend a needs assessment at all levels in the school system. It has been our experience that most school districts either have informal arrangements for able students or have practical provisions that have not yet been perceived as applicable to gifted and talented learners. We also recommend an inventory of community resources, including institutions of higher education as well as resources in the public and private sector to augment instructional resources.

- We recommend comprehensive efforts to identify and plan for gifted and talented persons from earliest childhood through secondary and college levels. Such efforts should be in concert with needs assessment efforts. We also advocate liaison with nonpublic schools. Attention of a special kind should be given to economically disadvantaged and handicapped pupils in both needs assessment and identification.

- We recommend the genuine involvement of teachers and building principals in planning, implementation, and evaluation. Since identification and individualized education are prime indicators of quality instruction, we have serious reservations about continuation of programs if these key persons have not been involved meaningfully.

- We recommend the thorough involvement of parents in programming. Experience has demonstrated the validity both of parent education and of encouragement of parent/citizen associations.

- We urge the continuing examination of curriculum at all levels to identify opportunities for altering the pace of schooling and the expansion of curriculum. We advocate opportunities for teachers at varying age levels to communicate their expectations and experiences. We recommend that teachers assume major responsibility for the content and structure of inservice experience.

- We believe it is helpful to review school policies and practices with a view toward encouraging flexibility for students to advance and expand their learnings. We also recommend examination of policies regarding teacher assignments/recognition/encouragement for mentoring activities and independent studies.

- We encourage educators to seek ways to involve gifted and talented pupils in activities that allow them to make contributions to others. We recommend schools give serious attention to taking advantage of the out-of-school interests and activities of able pupils.

- We believe the educational community should be a major source of advocacy on behalf of gifted and talented learners. This influence should be brought to bear upon teacher preparation institutions as well as upon policy makers. We recommend that individual teachers seek personal and professional memberships in associations that aim to improve the quality of education for able students.

PROMISING PROSPECTS

One continuing theme of this book is that there is now more than sufficient knowledge and example upon which to base and deliver sound and comprehensive instruction for gifted and talented pupils. We are impressed by the vast extent of available sources of information. We also are impressed by the willingness of educators, parents, and able students to share their experiences as guidance for anyone who asks. We also encountered many sources of information and guidance that merit further attention for inquiry to be added to what also is known and understood.

- We are attracted to the studies of SuperKids, those who resisted life's adversities. We believe it would be helpful to understand the circumstances that enable the human spirit to endure, especially the positive influence of educators.

- We believe that definition of gifted and talented pupils is a critical issue. We have been impressed by the outcomes achieved by organizations working with other exceptional children when they concentrate on the definitional problem. We believe that Renzulli (1978) has added an important dimension of task commitment. We urge serious consideration to finding a definition that could unify advocates of gifted and talented learners.

- We have been content to employ the terminology "gifted and talented." We acknowledge both the wide use of this descriptor, and its troublesome aspects. If we had our preference, we would advance the construct of *developmentally advanced* for its scientific accuracy. It *is* the person's performance at an early age that is the significant aspect for education. We believe this term could defuse or minimize the elitism of giftedness and direct attention to educationally relevant considerations.

- We recognize that the education of exceptional learners will involve investigation of a variety of potentially sensitive issues. We believe advanced planning and consultation does much to prevent potential conflict. We believe that there should be continued interest in the study of academic freedom and the schools.

- We recommend investigations directed toward the needs of educators in implementing individualized education and in managing the continuity of education for all learners.

- In preparing this text, we were not surprised to encounter examples of quality education evident in urban/rural and advantaged/disadvantaged settings. We believe the experiences and strategies in all locations merit further attention.

- We initiated this book with the firm conviction that *mentoring* would be a key construct. The availability of sources was *not* disappointing. We encourage continued attention to the effective utilization of persons and to the outcomes of the relationship between mentor and protege.

References

Abrahams, W. Parent Talk. In B. Johnson, 1977.

Adler, R.P. A Parents' TV Guide. *Learning*. December 1978, *7*, 54-62.

Albino, J., & Davis, R. A Health Education Program That Works. *Phi Delta Kappan*, 1975, *57*, 256-259.

Anderson, R.E. Institutional Attractiveness to Bright, Perspective Students. *Research in Higher Education*, 1976, *4*, 361-371.

Baker, S. Pi Is a Piece of Cake. *Pittsburgh Press* (UPI), March 25, 1978, p. J7.

Bandura, A. *Psychological Modeling*. Chicago: Aldine/Atherton, 1971.

Bard, B. The Failure of Our School Drug Abuse Programs. *Phi Delta Kappan*, 1975, *57*, 251-255.

Barnes, R.C., & Nybo, V.E. Health Classes Can Change Health Behavior. In Rosenberg, 1978.

Barry, M.M. *Education for Einstein's World*. New York: Council for American Unity, 1976.

Bartlett, S. Protocol Analysis. *Journal of Creative Behavior*, 1978, *12*, 181-192.

Berkovitz, I.H. A Psychiatrist Views Underachievers Among Gifted Children. In B. Johnson, 1977.

Berne, E. *Games People Play*. New York: Ballantine Books, 1964.

Birch, J.W., & McWilliams, E.M. *Challenging Gifted Children*. Indianapolis: Bobbs-Merrill, 1955.

Bloom, B.S. Affective Outcomes of School Learning. *Phi Delta Kappan*, 1977, *59*, 193-198.

Bloom, B.S., Hastings, J.T., & Madaus, G.F. *Handbook on Formative and Summative Evaluation of Student Learning*. New York: McGraw-Hill, 1971.

Boston, B.O. *The Sorcerer's Apprentice*. Reston, Va.: Council for Exceptional Children, 1976.

Brandstetter, J., & Foster, C.R. Quality Integrated Education in Houston's Magnet Schools. *Phi Delta Kappan*, 1976, *57*, 502-506.

Briggs, D.C. *Your Child's Self Esteem*. Garden City, N.Y.: Doubleday, 1970.

Brophy, J.E., & Everton, L.M. *Learning From Teaching: A Developmental Perspective*. Boston: Allyn and Bacon, 1976.

Bruce-Mitchell, P., & Erickson, D. The Education of Gifted and Talented Children: A Status Report. *Exceptional Children*, 1978, *45*, 12-16.

Bureau of Business Practices. *Employee Relations Bulletin Junior Achievement, Special Report*. Waterford, Conn.: Junior Achievement, Inc., 1977.

Caney, S. How Kids Can Create a Classroom Exploratorium. *Learning,* March 1979, *7,* 42-45.

Carkhuff, R.R. *The Art of Helping.* Amherst, Mass.: Human Resources Development Press, 1977.

Christenson, R.M. McGuffy's Ghost and Moral Education Today. *Phi Delta Kappan,* 1977, *58,* 737-742.

Conway, L. Classroom in the Sky: A Power Trip for Disadvantaged Youth. *Phi Delta Kappan,* 1976, *57,* 570-574.

Cornish, R.L. Parents', Teachers' and Pupils' Perception of the Gifted Child's Ability. *Gifted Child Quarterly,* 1968, *34,* 14.

Cox, J. Community Based Programs. In Passow, A.H., 1979.

Dawkins, B.J. Do Gifted Junior High School Students Need Reading Instruction? *Journal for the Gifted and Talented,* 1979, *2,* 3-8.

Diehl, I.W. Attracting the Talented Student. *Agricultural Education,* 1976, *49,* 28, 42.

Drew, C.J. *Introduction to Designing Research and Evaluation.* St. Louis: C.V. Mosby, 1976.

Eason, B.L., Smith, T.L., & Fagot-Smith, M. Perceptual Motor Programs. *Journal for the Education of the Gifted,* 1979, *2,* 10-21.

Eberle, R. Scamper: *Games for Imagination Development.* Buffalo, N.Y.: D.O.K. Publishers, 1971.

Elam, S.M. Are Role Models Better Living or Dead? *Phi Delta Kappan,* 1978, *60,* 58-59.

Ellington, J. Is the Living Bible Accurate? *The Lutheran,* January 17, 1979, *17,* 10-12.

Evans, R.N., & Herr, E.L. *Foundations of Vocational Education* (second edition). Columbus, Ohio: Charles Merrill, 1978.

Feldhusen, J.F., & Treffinger, D.J. The Role of Instructional Materials in Teaching Creative Thinking. *Gifted Child Quarterly,* 1977, *21,* 450-458.

Fern, L. Individual Development. *Journal of Creative Behavior,* 1976, *10,* 56-66.

First Monday, Republican National Committee, February 1979, 9, 11.

Frasier, M.M. Rethinking the Issues Regarding the Culturally Disadvantaged Gifted. *Exceptional Children,* 1977, *45,* 538-542.

_____. The Third Dimension. *The Gifted Child Quarterly,* 1977, *21,* 207-213.

Furths, H.G., & Wachs, H. *Thinking Goes to School: Piaget's Theory Goes to School.* New York: Oxford University Press, 1974.

Gage, N.L., & Berlmer, D.C. *Educational Psychology* (Second Edition). Chicago: Rand McNally, 1979.

Gallagher, J.J. *Teaching the Gifted Child* (Second Edition). Boston: Allyn and Bacon, 1976.

Gardner, D.C., & Warren, S.A. *Careers and Disabilities: A Career Education Approach.* Stamford, Conn.: Greylock Publishers, 1978.

Gaston, C. Parent Education at New Futures School. In Rosenberg, 1978.

Getzels, J.W. From Art Student to Fine Artist: Potential, Problem Finding, and Performance. In Passow, A.H., 1979.

Ginott, H.G. *Between Parent and Teenager.* New York: Avon, 1971.

_____. *Teacher and Child.* New York: Avon, 1972.

Ginsberg, C., & Harrison, C.H. *How to Help Your Gifted Child: A Handbook for Parents and Teachers.* New York: Monarch Press (Simon and Schuster), 1977.

Gold, M.J. Teachers and Mentors. In Passow, A.H., 1979.

Gordon, T. *Parent Effectiveness Training.* New York: Peter H. Wyden, 1970.

Gowan, J.C. Background and History of the Gifted Child Movement. In *The Gifted and Creative*, Stanley, J.C., George, W.C., & Solano, C.H. (Eds.). Baltimore: The Johns Hopkins University Press, 1977.

Griggs, S.A., & Price, G.E. Learning styles of gifted vs. average junior high students. *Phi Delta Kappan*, V. G1, M.5, January 1980, p. 361.

Guilford, J.P. Way Beyond the I.Q. Buffalo, New York: Creative Foundation Press, 1977.

Gustofson, R.A., & Laterte, O. *Identification of the Gifted and Talented in the Secondary and Vocational Schools of Vermont.* Montpelier, Vt.: Vermont Department of Education, Division of Vocational-Technical Education, 1978.

Hallahan, D.P., & Kauffman, J.M. *Exceptional Children.* Englewood Cliffs, N.J.: Prentice-Hall, 1978.

Hammermeister, K., & Mullins, J. *The Hospital.* Pittsburgh: Division of Library Services, Western Pennsylvania School for the Deaf, 1977.

Hansen, J.C., Stevic, R.R., & Warner, R.W. Jr. *Counseling Theory and Practice.* Boston: Allyn and Bacon, 1977.

Heaton, B. Thanks a Million. Carnegie Magazine, March 1979, 43.

Hentges, K. Health Activism. In Rosenberg, 1978.

Hersey, J. *The Child Buyer.* New York. Alfred Knopf, 1960.

Hirsch, S.P. Executive High School Internships: A Boon for the Gifted and Talented. *Teaching Exceptional Children*, Fall 1976, *9*, 22-23.

Hodgkinson, C. Values Education. *Phi Delta Kappan*, 1976, *58*, 269-271.

Institute for Social Research. Young People Look at Changing Sex Roles. Ann Arbor, Mich.: ISR Newsletter, 1979 *7*, 3, 5.

Jacobs, J.C. Teacher Attitude Toward Gifted Children. *Gifted Child Quarterly*, 1972, *16*, 23-26.

Jahsmann, A. *1979 A Year for the Child.* Philadelphia: Division for Parish Services, Lutheran Church in America, 1979.

Jarvis, O.T. and Rice, M.J. *An Introduction to Teaching in the Elementary School.* Dubuque, Iowa: Wm. C. Brown, 1972.

Johnson, B. (Publications Editor) *Gifts, Talents, and the Very Young: Early Childhood Education for Gifted/Talented.* Los Angeles: National/State Leadership Training Institute on the Gifted and Talented, 1977.

Johnson, C. Secondary Schools and Student Responsibility. *Phi Delta Kappan*, 1978, *59*, 338-341.

Johnson, N.L. Vocational Home and Family Life Education. In Rosenberg, 1978.

Johnson, R.L. Teachers and Student Perception of Student Creativity. *Gifted Child Quarterly*, 1976, *20*, 164-167.

Jordan, T.E. *American Education: An Introduction to Education.* Chicago: Rand McNally, 1973.

Kagan, J.E. *Creativity and Learning.* Boston: Houghton-Mifflin Company, 1967.

Kaplan, S.N., Kaplan, J.A.B., Madson, S.K., & Taylor, B.K. *Change for Children*, Pacific Palisades, Calif.: Goodyear, 1973.

Kaplan, S.N. Language Arts and Social Studies Curriculum in the Elementary School. In Passow, A.H., 1979.

Karmes, F.A., & Collins, E. State Definitions on the Gifted and Talented. *Journal for the Education of the Gifted*, 1978, *1*, 44-62.

——————————. Teacher Certification in Gifted Education. *Gifted Child Quarterly*, 1977, *21*, 206-207.

Kaufmann, F. *Your Gifted Child and You.* Reston, Va.: Council for Exceptional Children, 1976.

Keating, D.P. Secondary School Programs. In Passow, A.H., 1979.

Keisler, S.B., & Turner, C.F. (eds.) *Fundamental Research and the Process of Education.* Washington, D.C.: National Institute of Education, 1977.

Kennedy, B.T., & Newman, M.A. An Exploratory Study of the Effects of Games. *Gifted Child Quarterly,* 1976, *20,* 297-299.

Kenyon, J. Music for God's Glory. *Christian Herald,* May 1979, *102,* 26-31.

Kimche, L. Introducing the Institute of Museum Services. *American Education,* March 1979, *15,* 36-40.

Kindsratter, R.A. New View of Discipline. *Phi Delta Kappan,* 1978, *59,* 322-325.

Kirschanbaum, H., Harmin, M., Howe, L., & Simon, S. In Defense of Values Clarification. *Phi Delta Kappan,* 1977, *58,* 743-746.

Kirk, S.A., & Gallagher, J.J. *Educating Exceptional Children* (Third Edition). Boston: Houghton Mifflin, 1979.

Kohl, H. Teachers and Kids: Partners in Game Making. *Learning,* 1974, *2,* 22-25.

Kohlberg, L. The Adolescent as Philosopher. Cambridge, Mass.: American Academy of Arts and Sciences, 1971.

——————. The Cognitive-Developmental Approach to Moral Education. *Phi Delta Kappan,* 1975, *56,* 670-677.

Krathwohl, D.R., Bloom, B.S., & Masida, B.B. *The Classification of Educational Objectives. Handbook 2. The Affective Domain.* New York: McKay, 1964.

Laycock, M., & Watson, G. *The Fabric of Mathematics.* Hayward, Calif.: Activity Resources, 1971.

Lee, J.S. Teaching Talented Students in Vocational Agriculture. *Agricultural Education,* 1976, *49,* 29-30.

Levine, D.U., & Moore, C.C. Magnet Schools in a Big City Desegregation Plan. *Phi Delta Kappan,* 1976, *57,* 507-509.

Lewis, C.L., & Kanes, L.G. Gifted IEP's. *Journal of Education of the Gifted and Talented,* 1979, *2,* 61-69.

Lyons, H.A. Jr. The Other Minority. *Learning,* 1974, *2,* 64-66.

Mager, R. *Analyzing Performance Objectives.* Belmont, Calif.: Fearon, 1970.

——————. *Analyzing Performance Problems.* Belmont, Calif.: Fearon Publishing, 1970.

——————. *Goal Analysis.* Belmont, Calif.: Fearon, 1972.

Maker, C.J. Developing Multiple Talents in Exceptional Children. *Teaching Exceptional Children,* 1979, *11,* 120-124.

Mantz, R. Schools: Where Does the Gifted Child Fit In? *Better Homes and Gardens,* May 1979, *57,* 19-26.

Marcus, C. Just Call Them Mathematically Precocious. *Pittsburgh Press,* May 13, 1979, J1.

Maslow, A.H. *The Farther Reaches of Human Nature.* New York: Viking Press, 1962.

Mauer, R.A. Young Children's Responses to a Physically Disabled Storybook Hero. *Exceptional Children,* 1979, *45,* 326-330.

McCurdy, J.K. *Career Education in Michigan.* Lansing, Mich.: Michigan Department of Education, 1975.

McKeachie, W.J. *Teaching Tips.* Lexington, Mass.: D.C. Heath, 1978.

McRoberts, D. What's in a Name. *Lutheran Brotherhood Bond,* March 1979, *55,* 10.

Melton, A.W., Chairperson, The Publications and Communications Board. *Publications Manual of the American Psychological Association* (Second Edition). Washington, D.C.: American Psychological Association, 1974.

Milne, B.G. *Career Education.* In Passow, A.H., 1979.

_____. Vocational Education: A Challenging Alternative for the Gifted and Talented. Vermillion, S.D.: Educational Research and Service Center, University of South Dakota, 1976.

Musgrove, W.J., & Estroff, E.H. Scale to Measure Attitudes of Intellectually Gifted Toward an Enrichment Program. *Exceptional Children,* 1977, *43,* 375-377.

Nathan, C.N. Parent Involvement. In Passow, A.H., 1979.

Newland, T.E. *The Gifted in Socio-Educational Perspectives.* Englewood Cliffs, N.J.: Prentice-Hall, 1976.

Olivas, M.A. *A Statistical Portrait of Honors Programs in Two Year Colleges.* American Association of Community and Junior Colleges, Washington D.C.: National Collegiate Honors Council, 1975.

Parker, M. Are We Delinquent in the Area of Giftedness? *Phi Delta Kappan,* 1976, *58,* 240.

Passow, A.H. Enrichment Triad (a book review) *Exceptional Children,* 1978, *45,* 217-218.

Passow, A.H. (Ed.) *The Gifted and the Talented: Their Education and Development. The Seventy-Eighth Yearbook of the National Society for the Study of Education. Part I.* Chicago: University of Chicago Press, 1979.

Patterson, J., Saino, J., & Turner, J.R. *Why Doesn't an Igloo Melt?* Memphis, Tenn.: Memphis Public Schools, 1973.

Pavlik-Walsh, Cope, Myron M.: The Man Behind the Terrible Towel. *Pittsburgh,* 1979, *10,* 27.

Pearson, C. Cooperating Learning. *Learning,* March 1979, *7,* 34-37.

Pfiel, M.P. Fourth Street School's New Claim to Fame. *American Education,* March 1978, *14,* 10-14.

Phi Delta Kappan, God Appointed the Principal. 1977, *60,* 582.

Phillips, M. Confluent Education. *Phi Delta Kappan,* 1976, *58,* 238-240.

Piechowiak, A.B., & Cook, M.B. *Complete Guide to the Elementary Learning Center.* West Nyack, N.Y.: Parker, 1976.

Pines, M. SuperKids. *Psychology Today,* January 1979, *12,* 53-63.

Pittsburgh Post-Gazette. The Genius Gap. October 21, 1978, p. 4.

Pittsburgh Press. Hobbyist Discovers a Super Nova, April 24, 1979, A1, A4.

Pittsburgh Press. The Oldest Known Professor, March 24, 1979, p. B1.

Plowman, P.D. Futuristic Views of Education. *The Journal of Creative Behavior,* 1978, *12,* 90-97.

Pohl, R. Independent Study. *Gifted and Talented Education,* 1976, *1,* 4-5.

Pressey, S.L. Concerning the Nature and Nurture of Genius. *Scientific Monthly,* 1955, *81,* 123-129.

Radcliffe, S.A. and Hatch, W.R. *Advanced Standing.* Washington, D.C.: U.S. Office of Education, 1961. Report Number OE-5414.

Rennels, M.R. Cerebral Symmetry. *Phi Delta Kappan,* 1976, *57,* 471-472.

Renzulli, J.S., *The Enrichment Triad Model.* Waterford, Conn.: Creative Learning Press, 1977.

_____. What Makes Giftedness? *Phi Delta Kappan,* 1978, *60,* 180-184-261.

_____ & Callahan, C.M. Developing Creativity Training Activities. *The Gifted Child*

Quarterly, 1977, *19,* 38-45.

———————— & Smith, L.H. Issues and Procedures in Evaluating Programs. In Passow, A.H., 1979.

Reynolds, M., & Birch, J.W. Giftedness and Talent: High Rate of Cognitive Development. In *Teaching Exceptional Children in All America's Schools.* Reston, Va.: Council for Exceptional Children, 1977.

Robert Sterling Clark Foundation. *On Being Gifted.* Student Perceptions, New York, 1977.

Robinson, H.B. Current Myths Concerning Gifted Children. In Johnson, B. (1977).

Robinson, H.B., Roedell, W.C. & Jackson, N.E. Early Identification and Intervention. In Passow, A.H., 1979.

Robinson, N.M., Robinson, H.B., Darling, M.A. & Holm, C. *A World of Children.* Monterey, Calif.: Brooks/Cole, 1979.

Rockman, M. Teenagers Preparing for the Future. *Pittsburgh Press,* April 4, 1979, C-3.

Rosenberg, N. (Ed.) Parenting Education. *Health Education,* July-August 1978, 9-17.

Sandberg, J., & Simon, K. *How to Be a Bartender.* Midland, Mich.: Pendall Publishing Co., 1975.

Schauer, G.H. Emotional Disturbance and Giftedness. *The Gifted Child Quarterly,* 1976, *20,* 470-476.

Scott, R. Translating Intra Child Achievement, *School Psychologist,* February 1975.

Sellin, D.F. *Mental Retardation: Nature, Needs, and Advocacy.* Boston: Allyn and Bacon, 1979.

Sheehy, G. *Passages.* New York: Bantam Books, 1976.

Simon S.B., & deSherbinin, P. Values Clarification. *Phi Delta Kappan,* 1975, *56,* 679-683.

Simon, S.B., Howe, L.W., & Kirschenbaum, H. *Values Clarification.* New York: Hart, 1972.

Smidchens, U., & Sellin, D.F. Attitudes Toward Mentally Gifted Learners. *Gifted Child Quarterly,* 1976, *20,* 109-113.

Soverly, R., Soverly, A., Giannini, A., & Matusik, W. The Newspaper as a Tool for Teaching Kids to Read. *Phi Delta Kappan,* 1975, *57,* 200-261.

Solano, C.H. Precocity and Adult Failure: Shattering the Myth. Paper presented at the Annual Convention of the National Association for Gifted Children, Kansas City, Mo., October 14, 1976.

Spiegel, D.L. Ten Ways to Sort Out Comprehension Problems. Learning, March 1979, *7,* 40-41.

Spring, M.B. *Step-Up.* Pittsburgh: Office of External Studies, University of Pittsburgh, 1979.

Stafford, Senator R.T. Testimony in Support of PL 95-561. Congressional Record, Senate, April 5, 1978, p. S 4185.

Stanley, J.C. The Study and Facilitation of Math Talent. In Passow, A.H., 1979.

Stanley, J.S. Identifying and Nurturing the Intellectually Gifted. *Phi Delta Kappan,* 1976, *58,* 234-237.

Tannenbaum, A.J. *Adolescent Attitudes Toward Academic Brilliance.* New York: Teachers College University Press, Columbia University, 1962.

————————. Pre-Sputnik to Post Watergate Concern About the Gifted. In Passow, A.H., 1979.

Tanner, T. A Far Out Mind Stretcher. *Phi Delta Kappan,* 1977, *58,* 603-605.

Taylor, C.W. Multiple Talent Approach. *The Instructor,* 1963, *27,* 142, 144-146.

Taylor, C.W. (Ed.). *Widening Horizons of Creativity.* New York: John Wiley and Sons, 1964.

Terman, L.M., cited in Gowan, 1977.

Thomas, D., & Richards, M. Ethics Education is Possible. *Phi Delta Kappan,* 1979, *60,* 579-582.

Thomas, J.L. *Learning Centers,* Boston: Holbrook Press, 1975.

Thompson, P. A Step or Two Back in Time. *American Education,* March 1979, *15,* 27-30.

Time. Was the Kid Too Smart To Learn? April 29, 1979, *113,* 85.

Torrance, E.P., & Kaufmann, F. Teacher Education for Teachers of the Gifted and Talented. *Gifted Child Quarterly,* 1977, *21,* 176-185.

Treffinger, D.J. Guidelines for Developing Independence and Self Direction Among Gifted Students. *Journal of Creative Behavior,* 1978, *12,* 14-20.

Tschudin, R. What Makes an A Plus Teacher? *Phi Delta Kappan,* 1978, *60,* 267.

Turnbull, A.P., & Schultz, J.B. *Mainstreaming Handicapped Students.* Boston: Allyn and Bacon, 1979.

Verbeke, M.C., & Verbeke, K.A. *Discovery and Inquiry: Their Relevance as Approaches for the Gifted.* Pitman, N.J.: Educational Improvement Center, 1972.

Virginia Beach Public Schools, Va.: Gifted and Talented Programs, 1975.

Walberg, H.J., & Pinzur-Rasher, S. The Ways Schooling Makes a Difference. *Phi Delta Kappan,* 1977, *58,* 703-707.

Walker, Y.E. Everyone Needs a Parent. In Rosenberg, 1978.

Ward, V.S. *The Gifted Student.* A Report of the Southern Regional Project for Education of the Gifted, 1962.

Webb, E.J., Campbell, D.T., Schwarta, R.D., & Sechrest, L. *Unabtrusive Measures: Non-reactive Research in the Social Sciences.* Chicago: Rand McNally, 1966.

Weiner, B.B. Evaluation in *Reaching Out to a Neglected Audience.* Distributed by the Metropolitan Museum of Art, New York: 1979.

Weiner, J. Attitudes of Psychologists and Psychometricians Toward Gifted Children and Their Education. *Exceptional Children,* 1968, *34,* 354.

Weiner, J.L. and O'Shea, H.E. Attitudes of University Faculty, Administrators, Teachers, Supervisors, and University Students Toward the Gifted. *Exceptional Children,* 1963, *29,* 163-165.

Welter, P. Helping Yourself By Helping Others. *Christian Herald,* September 1978, *101,* 15-18.

Wexler, H. Cultivating Late Bloomers. *American Education.* March 1979, *15,* 48.

Wexler, M. Behavioral Sciences in Medical Education. *American Psychologist,* 1976, *31,* 275-283.

Whimbey, A. Teaching Sequential Thought: The Cognitive Skills Approach. *Phi Delta Kappan,* 1977, *59,* 255-259.

White, B.L. *The First Three Years of Life.* New York: Avon, 1975.

White, J.F. Honors Programs in North Central Association Community Colleges. Paper presented at the Annual Meeting of the American Association of Community and Junior Colleges, Seattle, April 13-16, 1975.

Wilde, J.W., & Sommers, P. Teaching Disruptive Adolescents: A Battle Worth Winning. *Phi Delta Kappan,* 1978, *59,* 342-343.

Wilhelm, J.L. A Singular Man. *Quest,* 1979, *3,* 33-36, 39-40.

Williams, J.H. Discipline in the Public Schools, *Phi Delta Kappan,* 1979, *60,* 385-387.

Wilson, R. Education for the Gifted. *57th Yearbook of the National Society for the Study of Education* Part II. Chicago: University of Chicago Press, 1958.

Wolf, J.S. Effect of Modeling on Reading Selections of Gifted and Non-Gifted Students. (Ph. D. Dissertation, Ohio State University.) Microfilm Number 76-24-712, 1976.

Wooster, J. Teaching Students the Art of Self-Evaluation. *Learning,* February 1979, *7,* 88.

Wyne, M.D., & O'Connor, P.D. *Exceptional Children: A Developmental View.*.Lexington, Mass.: D.C. Heath, 1977.

Index

learning
 centers, 257
 opportunities, 71, 72
mentor
 protege relationship, 107, 108
 qualities, 105, 106
Triad, 222, 223
values education, 317
United Nations Declaration of
 Childrens' Rights, 36

V

Values
 visitations, 247
Values Clarification Approach
 values education, 323, 324
Values Education
 cognitive development approach,
  321, 322
 content, 319-321
 goals, 318, 319
 tactics, 321
 teachers, 154
 understanding, 317
 See also Education
Variance
 educational priorities, 52
 learning centers, 257, 258
VCA. *See* Values Clarification
 Approach
Violence
 television, 79, 80
Vista. *See* Government Agencies

Visitations
 aid sources, 248
 description, 245-247
 organization, 247
 values, 247
Vocational Prospects. *See* Career
 Prospects

W

Widening
 prospects, 90
Writing
 teaching, 134, 135
 See also Language Arts

Y

Yourtowne
 adolescence, 86
 Basic Scholars Program, 86
 early childhood, 44-47
 education
  confluent, 278
  programs, 4-8
 individualized education, 200
  program, 31
 learning center, 262
 making history, 118
 parents, 58
 philosophy builders, 111, 112
 prototype, 4
 teacher initiation, 235
Youth-Arc. *See* Mentoring